ALAN WHICKER

Whicker's New World

America Through the Eyes and Lives of Resident Brits

Weidenfeld and Nicolson   London

For Valerie, without whom ...

Published in Great Britain by
George Weidenfeld & Nicolson Limited
91 Clapham High Street
London SW4 7TA

ISBN 0 297 78691 1

Made and printed in Great Britain by
Butler & Tanner Ltd
Frome and London

CONTENTS

CONTENTS

US – AND US!

If you could leave home tomorrow and go to live *anywhere* in the world
... where would you choose?

Probably the United States – that familiar land where more than a quarter
of the population already claims a British background – for most of us
suspect the rainbow ends somewhere on the real estate of Uncle Sam. Our
wealthy relative may be basking in good fortune or writhing in anxiety, but
at worst, life over there is going to be better than most places; at best –
unimaginable!

The scenery, the plenty, the ease and luxury, the outgoing people, the
excitement of living where things *begin*.... We're drawn to the enviable
image we know so well, for America offers the world a poolswinner's pros-
pect: what fortunate achiever enjoying the best of British luck would not
wish to experience life in a wide white penthouse above Central Park, high
in the night sky among the lights of Manhattan, its terrace an excitement
of models and writers and tomorrow's people.... When not at her house on
Long Island a friend of mine lives just like that – and she was a typist from
a council flat in Hackney Wick.

Like millions of pioneers during the last hundred and fifty years, Brits by
the thousand still gamble upon finding a better life somewhere else. Escaping
in one mighty bound from our climate, inflation, unemployment, strikes,
vandalism and all frightful things to come, many of them head across the
Atlantic into their dreams, into a land moulded and created by migration.

Its flavour seems as familiar as our own for it is on display every night in
the world's living-rooms. We grow up with a mirror-image of Americana,
yet despite its well-known majesty and menace it is a foreign land. To
discover how reality compares with images and hopes I have just travelled
through all the States, joining in the lives of some of those who are today
recolonizing America....

I went to hear about this Redcoats' Return in the Eighties, to explore
today's America through the eyes of the least visible, most integrated immigrants: the enterprising Yankee Doodle Brits. You may have seen excerpts
from some of these meetings in *Whicker's World* on BBC-1 – the sort of
casual conversations-with-point I've been having on television during the
past twenty-eight years, as we eavesdropped upon the attitudes of a cross-
section of great British exports and learned what it's like to be on the inside,
looking out.

I

In this book it seemed wise to let them speak for themselves – as I do in my programmes – rather than write *my* impression of what *they* think. A mega-millionaire on Park Avenue, a football star in Atlanta, a black social worker in Palo Alto, a professional poker player in Vegas, a cowboy in the Rockies ... these are Brits who've made up their minds. Their bets are down. Now, from the land in which they've chosen to live, they have their say about the way it *is* ...

The invisible invasion began in 1607 when the suitably-named Captain John Smith founded the first British colony at Jamestown, Virginia. Between 1820 and 1981, 4,804,520 Britons crossed the Atlantic to drop anchor in America, mingling with another forty-five million from other lands. That was a high proportion of the total population of the first defecting British colony; to the north, Canada is populated entirely by immigrants as, bar a few aborigines, is Australia.

Today, whatever the Statue of Liberty may say, the *last* people the US Immigration want are the tired, the poor, the huddled masses; they have quite enough of their own. They are prepared to receive a few of the vigorous and the accomplished – though not too many of them either; the house is almost full.

The 1980 census showed some 670,000 British-born among the 226 million Americans; 134,000 were living in California, 84,000 in New York, 51,000 in Florida. In the previous twenty years 175,000 of them took American citizenship, and now about 8,000 are naturalized every year. Green Cards – permits to reside and work – seem limited to an annual 15,000, though Whitehall records that in the first six months of 1981, 29,000 left to live in the US. The overflow are the British wetbacks, those untold thousands surviving illegally without the benefit of the priceless Green Card.

Many of that original forty-five million had reached the New World and Ellis Island after some traumatic escape from Hitler or Communism, Castro or the Viet Cong, Stroessner or starvation ... Only the Brits seem to have arrived by choice.

Emigration is like marriage; it should be undertaken with the assumption, at least, that it will last forever – yet even the word has connotations of escape. This is unfair: we all have the right to leave Britain whenever we wish. The majority, defeated by conditions at home, leave for the most innocent of reasons, merely hoping to be better off elsewhere, to find for their families a fuller life. Some wish to make their fortune, some to keep it.

All go to trouble, expense and occasionally heartbreak uprooting themselves and starting a new life in an untried environment where they must strive harder than the natives merely to keep afloat. Not everyone Exits Laughing.

Adaptability is imperative: the quick acceptance of new behaviour, new climates, new neighbours, new vocabularies, new values. Not all of them – and especially not the wives, who do not have their husbands' structured lives – are resilient enough to absorb this break with family ties and familiar social patterns. It takes a while for the roots to go down, and sometimes they never do; some immigrants feel like visitors until the end of their days, and Expatriate Stress is now a recognized mental condition.

Younger arrivals, untroubled by change, head for the apex of the American myth: Manhattan, a teeming island of disunited nationals, a city of strangers. Today they must number between 100,000 and 200,000 in New York alone, making up a large proportion of the migratory body known as Eurotrash. Some indeed did come to drop out, to join the growing druggy fringe; some to enlist in the metropolitan sponge-fleet of educated freeloaders who live on one pinstripe suit, a supply of small talk and the generosity of Americans. Others, determined to succeed, have joined the Yumpies – the young upwardly mobile professionals – and today row faster than anyone else in the boat.

Whatever their ambitions they are patently *not* huddled masses yearning to breathe free, arriving with their possessions in bundles – but singles with their hopes in little black books of telephone numbers. Most of the girls drift into vague jobs in public relations and art galleries where they look decorative and answer the telephone, or become chicretaries hired for style and speech. They seek only a good time, and with rare tolerance New Yorkers look upon them as exotic toys with funny voices, refreshingly different from the traditional hard-driving success-obsessed women who battle before them for space, position and men.

Such English girls may get taken-up, but don't expect to stay for too long – Mummy wouldn't *stand* for it. They soon discover it can be hard to sustain an American relationship because if the man sees them more than twice a week he fears it could be some kind of commitment. . . .

Certainly girls expecting to find the streets paved with Redfords, Geres and macho models suffer withdrawal shock and deprivation; those tanned all-American boys with splendid dentistry can be more interested in making-up than making-out, and at parties tend to flirt with each other. The once-boring nice *ordinary* guys seem almost extinct around town, so the girls – fagged out – must fall back on the over-forties, the Cholesterol Set.

On the social scene in New York women rarely speak to each other, not wishing to waste valuable party time in feminine conversation when offered the chance to talking to an available man. However a British girl may have the edge, should there be one, as a status symbol: to the American Anglophile any English accent means aristocracy and a castle in Kent – forget about that bedsit in South Ken. For men, appearance and personal appeal has little relation to pulling-power; even I was in demand.

Man-shortage may be observed in most cities. Kelly, the Texan wife of our Dallas Maître d' David Cotterill, is a pleasant maternal woman who loves dogs and wears black nailpolish. She was in some bar with her daughter when she first saw Dave's comfortably unromantic figure: 'I said, *That* one's for me! From then on I never let him out of my sight. . . .'

In a land where persistence is understood and success admired, Brits who decide to strive, to play the Corporate Game, are prospering. They find they have escaped the malevolence and jealousy, disparagement and suspicion with which the British Left regard such wealth-creators. It's the difference between looking with yearning at a Rolls and resolving to own one, one fine day . . . or savaging it with a brick on the way to a football match.

They have been welcomed into a society with an excessive work ethic where everything is a commodity to be mined for dollars, where you *are* what you achieve, where everyone expects to be rich tomorrow. Or, even better – famous. It is unimportant what you are famous *for*; being a Celebrity, however briefly, is quite enough.

Some Brits find the restless ever-changing population of Manhattan disorientating, for they work alongside people who were disenchanted with Poland or Jamaica or Israel, so there is no one against whom they can measure themselves. When the men at the next desks come from Taiwan and Bombay, there is no index to consult.

They soon discover it is un-American to be poor. The big thing is to be well-liked, so it's wise to avoid negative attitudes like anger or exasperation and assume instead the sincere smile and eager handshake. In this harsh economy they need to go out and sell themselves. Not too many Brits are comfortable doing that.

Few countries market such determined but automatic *niceness*. Have-a-nice-day is mandatory, enthusiasm a duty; companies teach *bonhomie* as once they taught book-keeping. Shop assistants click into the obligatory instant-smile, waitresses tell you to Enjoy your hamburger, telephone operators Thank you for using AT & T, stewardesses are taught to suppress irritation by thinking of passengers as children.

The y'awl-come-back syndrome does not seep through to every level. In New York there remains a high degree of snarl – I can't *imagine* how cabbies are taught to regard passengers. . . . They spend their lives making a public impression and, struggling to be generous, one could say they are in the main aggressive, venal, hostile and seriously horrible. Least objectionable are the newer arrivals – the Haitians, Russians, Dominicans, Mexicans. . . . However the price you pay for their relative amiability is a lack of communication and a total ignorance of the city: many have yet to discover the whereabouts of the Waldorf Astoria and Grand Central Station. This does not make for a relaxed ride.

I have long believed the true Hell must be to sit for eternity in the back of one of those battered yellow cabs in the steamheat of a New York summer, crouching on the torn oilcloth among the detritus with the driver's defensive partition a few inches from your face while the cab crashes furiously through potholes along nightmare streets stretching to the horizon where odious underground steam belches from the awful depths below pitted tarmac, the meter ticks implacably and the driver snarls his hatred at passengers, pedestrians, passing cars. . . .

Having said all that, every now and then you can step into a clean cab with its radio on and find a polite driver listening, enraptured, to a concert. . . . But don't bank on it.

Such aggressions fall away, happily, as soon as you leave the metropolis and move into the countryside. The flight from the cities – usually black and brown and bankrupt – continues. In two generations white America became a suburban society, and today Small Town America is ever more appealing. Even the phrase evokes a sense of community, a leafy serenity free from sinister strangers who menace the cold canyons downtown where urban struggle exposes any frailty, the old and the sick are always at risk, and concern about safety and survival is very real.

Economically life can be just as stern and unforgiving; many workers need two, sometimes three jobs to keep up with their repayments. They are constantly badgered from all sides to buy and to borrow – but the impending repossession can be merciless.

Such an approach to the phrase 'labour-intensive' comes as a shock to newly-resident Brits accustomed to workers' rights, union rules, short hours and long holidays – and unused to a 6 a.m. rush-hour to work. On Veterans' Day, a public holiday dedicated to the US Armed Forces, I was in Los Angeles where it was of course business-as-usual; the only place that had taken the day off and was firmly closed . . . was the British Consulate.

Most policemen, for example, moonlight as security-guards in department stores, office blocks, homes. Arriving in the LAPD fresh from the Kensington Police Station our Cop Peter Vanson also took on security work but stopped when – unlike his colleagues – he found himself unable to turn a blind eye to crime merely because he was off-duty. Around him people would be selling drugs and breaking the law conspicuously in various ways while he was expected to let them get away with offences for which he had just spent his eight-hour tour arresting others. Deciding whether to 'cuff his employers was equally unsettling.

On the other hand, I found his quiet acceptance of guns and death and violence surprising. After Notting Hill, where a hooligan's boot or a stroppy motorist would be something to talk about back in the Station canteen, he was patrolling a Precinct which regarded the nightly murders, shootings and stabbings as merely non-events.

Carrying a shotgun, a .38 Special, a back-up gun and an electronic tazer to still the deadly frenzy of angel-dust spasms with a 50,000-volt jolt, he had without any change in his cool affability moved from the world of the truncheon to one where killing was unremarkable and commonplace. In 1980 handguns killed 8 people in Britain, 24 in Switzerland, 18 in Sweden, 77 in Japan, 23 in Israel, 4 in Australia – but 11,522 in the United States. . . .

Britain's class system drove others into migration: Ken Crutchlow, a cheeky-chappie from Bethnal Green, believed his accent caused his rejection by a Thames rowing club. Reaching America, he hardly noticed its complicated and under-cover class distinctions though did observe the pervasive influence of money – which will get anyone *everywhere*.

The Federal Government must believe in equality for all – yet divides employees into eighteen grades, from Messenger up to High-level Administrator. Since there are no hereditary ranks or titles, no honours to confer, no good regiments or truly smart clubs, Americans depend for snobbery upon their college and university hierarchy – and even that Ivy League has lowered its standards. So class-conscious Americans fall back upon Britain as their model, and the Upper and Middle can be impressed by regimental ties, Savile Row, green wellies and suitable tartans.

The British who operate within tolerant America are observed to be amused by trends without feeling the need to make money out of everything, and some of their habits are seeping into everyday life: keeping drinks in the living-room on a tray instead of behind that ugly wet-bar; not going to the drycleaners quite so often; tea in the late afternoon instead of dry martinis, and long lunches with a roast on Sunday afternoons. This civilizing influence can do nothing but good, yet with few ways to receive official public approval, without Royals or aristocracy, the new tea-sipping elegantly-scruffy upwardly-mobile find themselves hard-put to invent status, to promote social leaders.

In Palm Beach the Duchess of Windsor, who was impossibly regal and gave everybody an awfully hard time, might charge $4,000 to attend a party. She would only allow twelve other guests and insisted on selecting the menu – but after dinner you did get your picture taken with her to keep in a silver frame on your piano for ever. The American Duchess is now sorely missed, for no replacement has emerged haughty enough to provide a summit for the ambitiously ascending ranks.

Agnes Ash, Publisher of the Palm Beach *Daily News*, told me 'Our Queen must set the standard – after all, if the social ladder is an escalator, there's no fun in climbing it. And once you get into Society you never really know if you're *there* – you always fear there might be some other tight little circle which is better. That's one reason they follow the Queens. They think: If I'm in her entourage, she won't go wrong. It's like following the platoon leader in combat.'

So the old-money in Palm Beach or the Hamptons on Long Island, at Haddam in Connecticut, Bar Harbor in Maine, Newport on Rhode Island ... scorns workaday America – and particularly the class-inferiority of their capital, despite all those Embassy parties. Its main paper, the *Washington Post* – a sort of even greyer *Daily Telegraph* – typically provides its bureaucratic prole readers with plot summaries of TV soap operas and advice about behaviour from agony aunts. Even President Reagan's Sun Belt style has been designated Los Angeles WASP-chutzpah: if you truly believe you're as good as those educated and civilized Eastern dudes, then by golly – you *are*. . . .

In Reagan's America, a week in hospital can cost as much as a year in College. Everyone has a horror story about aspirins at $5 each or an account for $250,000 thrust at the grieving widow as her husband's body is lifted from his bed in the ward. In turn, Americans point a warning finger at medicine in Britain: 'Half the patients with chronic kidney failure are left untreated – and die as a result,' says the *Washington Post*, reminding readers how in Britain we 'Cut costs by choosing who lives, who dies. . . .'

The report does not touch upon one accepted practice of their profit-making hospitals: critically ill patients who are unable to pay their fees or have no insurance will be pitilessly transported on stretchers to the nearest State-aided hospital – and dumped.

However it does underline one thought hard to resist: that at the end of the day, at the end of the illness, it is better to overpay than to go without, fatally: 'British doctors order only half as many X-rays *per capita* as their American counterparts. They do only one-tenth of our coronary by-pass surgery. British hospitals have only one-sixth of CAT scanners and less than one-fifth as many Intensive Care Unit beds.' I must admit one doctor now practising in Louisiana recalled his last English District General Hospital: 'Intensive Care was the bed nearest Sister's desk. . . .'

Our psychiatrists must also be relatively thin on the ground. . . . In an attractive wooden house among the foothills of the Rockies outside Denver there's an English Nanny who adores America and intends to stay for ever. For two years Jackie Huskell has been looking after the precocious six-year-old daughter of a standard *angst*-filled guilt-ridden modern American couple: Father is away much of the time, Mother has been in analysis for years.

One day, to sort things out once and for all, the whole group – Nanny included – went to a family therapy session and spent an hour and $75 tackling a long list of their more acute problems. The first was: *who* should fill the dishwasher?

After earnest debate with proper professional guidance they came to a conclusion: paper plates! They never reached Problem 2.

Today their guests drink out of crystal but, following medical advice, eat off paper plates dealt from the kitchen pile of a thousand and use plastic knives and forks. The dishwasher stands quiet.

It may be hard to conceive, but some Americans are so desperately active they cannot even find time to visit their psychiatrist. . . . There's busy-ness for you! For such seriously deprived, two enterprising New York doctors have set up Shrink-Link, or counselling-by-telephone. From ten 'til ten Monday through Friday, seven psychologists and psychiatrists discuss callers' marital problems, phobias and stress management, in twelve-hour shifts. Each consultation averages ten minutes and $15 – after which, hopefully, everyone feels better.

Many high-profile people across the land – and all Californians – think *not* going to a psychiatrist almost as bad as not using a deodorant. 'The

British believe they don't need shrinks or showers', said one cryptic New York woman. 'They are wrong on both counts.'

This was brought home to me while dining with Anthony Thompson and a friend in Beverly Hills, when it emerged I spurned deodorants. She was visibly shocked. As she edged away down the booth I mentioned in mitigation that I did bathe every day – sometimes twice, for heaven's *sake* – and also changed quite frequently. This was unacceptable. She had me down as a twelfth-century savage, and kept a suitable distance. I left the restaurant feeling I should be clanging a warning bell.

Such is the power of advertising. People can be programmed to need almost anything – indeed after watching daytime television you have to concede the first step towards proper self-esteem must be the purchase of a wig, and feel downright odd if you're not constipated: I say, I'm awfully sorry but I'm afraid I *don't* have jock-itch. . . .

Brits reluctant to go along with the game can irritate those who have decided to blend: the Professor of American Studies at the George Washington University, Prof. Marcus Cunliffe, retains his distinct Anglo-Saxon style but complains 'After a few months here Englishmen begin to strike me as affected and absurd. Their voices, their mannerisms and what seems to be their tedious gamesmanship offends me. . . .' The Professor's sense of 'having gone native' has been heightened by having married three Americans.

As one of the Absurd, I relish the American language which – like Australian – is fertile and colourful, but confess to mild irritation at the inescapable Case of the Disappearing T: Winner has become the opposite of Summer, and it's possible to be inner-rested in an inner-view about innernational annie-semitism. This has nothing to do with education; it's at all levels – on television they just think it's softer. Or possibly, soffer.

National breath may be drawn in when Dick Van Dyke tries to talk Cockney or some English actor plays a Hollywood heavy; we remain separated by enunciation – and by the occasional misplaced noun. On television Dan Rather introduces a news item from London – an event in itself: 'Spy scandals are as common in today's Britain as the umbrella and the boater . . .' The *boater*? The last time I saw a boater in the street I dropped my schoolbooks.

OK, so we are all funny to the people next door. I watched an American programme about the silly commercials other nations show, and the audience fell about when they saw the Japanese had a bottled drink with an English name: Sweat. In the next break the first actual commercial was for an American soft drink: Gatorade – which must sound to Japanese as though it came out of a swamp.

Similar adjustment is of course required in restaurants: salads, steaks, ice-creams remain superb – but step into some large restaurant on a Washington avenue and you may pay $20 for two plates of tepid mush, proffered under many another name. Hamburgers in Dallas – where you expect to eat high on the steer – prove inedible. A resort hotel on a lake outside Atlanta, where there was nothing to do but enjoy the scenery and eat, offered warmed-over platefuls of glutinous yuk prepared by malevolent dwarfs in some underground laboratory beneath the Rockies and served by bemused college girls who didn't know what it was either, and could not bring themselves to care.

If the food is different, so is the style of consumption: in a Chicago club atop a lakeside block I neglected the stunning view when transfixed by a tableful eating eggs benedict – traditional breakfast dish of ham on a sort of crumpet topped by a poached egg covered in hollandaise. The approach was: first *stab* your egg with a fork as though it's still alive. Hold it still and then, when safely immobile, saw your way through it. . . .

I have always found in America it's easier to get a back-axle changed than a button sewn on, but on this visit there was an innovation: Executive Floors topping hotels across America, charging an extra $20 a night but offering a light breakfast, an honour-bar, toiletries in the bathroom and – imagine – your own helpful Concierge! To discover the Crossed-keys operating in America seemed too good to be true: someone to mark your card in a strange city, a local expert to *do* things for you and ease the way. . . .

It was of course not like that at all. They had copied the name, but not the *raison d'être*. The Concierge girls on duty were merely programmed to smile and nod at standard questions. Anything as outlandish as 'Could you airmail this script to England?' was met by an uncomprehending stare as the robot eyes switched off: 'I'm sorry, sir, that is not part of our schedule of duties.'

Jim Dale, late of *Barnum* on Broadway and all those *Carry-Ons*, asked the Concierge in his stately Park Avenue block to arrange for a ten-foot refectory table to be sent up to his apartment. The service elevator could only handle things up to eight-feet, so to carry it up they asked $30 a floor. Since he lived on the 23rd floor it seemed economic to saw it in half . . .

On his leafy terrace New York seemed fine, if noisy. The city has constantly fluctuated from some dazzling dream at the end of the rainbow the whole world yearned to reach . . . to a dirty dangerous nightmare one could not escape fast enough: 'Just give me a ticket to *anywhere*!'

Today it seems half-way up that roller-coaster once again as the sense of tingling excitement over-compensates for the night-and-day tension that churns the adrenalin. Constantly reinventing itself, New York has become the world's capital: it was Rome in the Forties, Paris in the Fifties, London in the Sixties. Now Manhattan is the place to be – if you can stand living poised for fight or flight.

The reactions of resident Brits to their new homeland also fluctuate dramatically. When filming a *Whicker's World* series in California in 1979 I spent a morning with Christopher Lee, just freed from much Transylvanian horror. On a leisurely 18-holes around the Bel Air Country Club he sat in his golf cart gazing across smooth sunlit greens and reflected 'Nothing is Utopia – but this comes pretty close.' Now, as you will read, he's had quite enough of wonderland and wants Out.

Roderick Mann, show business columnist for the *Los Angeles Times*, was then not at all enchanted by Hollywood: 'I think Albania's more fun. When I lived in Great Portland Street I fantasized about Beverly Hills – now I'm in Beverly Hills fantasizing Great Portland Street. London seems absolutely wonderful and I'm still outside the cheese shop in Jermyn Street. I haven't walked along the beach with Raquel Welch – not yet, anyway. I haven't got a white Cadillac convertible – they've stopped making them. It rained a lot last winter. The air is like poison gas most of the time, it truly is. For a non-smoker living here's like being a two-pack-a-day man anywhere else.'

I wondered why someone who had been writing about California all his professional life, and visiting often, should be so unprepared for its impact when he emigrated. 'I think everybody is, because what you're prepared for doesn't exist. I mean, London never disappears for me when I'm here, but as soon as I leave Hollywood this place vanishes. It doesn't exist any more, except in a fantasy. I don't understand why that is, but I do know that all these people feel cheated. They've made their pile and come here and it *isn't* as good as they hoped it would be – so they resent it.

'One of the things I've found is that it's easy to feel underprivileged because I don't know *anybody* who hasn't got a million dollars. There's just me and my maid – and my maid'll make it before I do, the way I'm paying her. . . .'

Since then Roddy had bought a house, got married – and suddenly Beverly Hills is a *far* better place! Pretty close, you might say, to Utopia.

America has always been a target, often a forbidden one: soon after the United States became independent there was a migration of skill across the Atlantic, though until 1825 it was illegal for artisans to leave Britain. The first group of Mormons left Liverpool in 1840 and during the next half-a-century some 50,000 'saints' followed, to the relief of those left behind: the unions saw emigration as thinning-out labour ranks and benefiting stay-at-homes.

Our skills thus became a key factor in the rise of US industry and from the early 1800s Britons were teaching Americans new techniques in the textile mills of New England, Pennsylvania and New York. They found it easy to get started, but were not always pleased with their new jobs: many discovered wages were higher but hours longer, accidents more frequent and conditions less healthy.

Leaving their fifty-four-hour week in South Wales, miners found upon arrival in Pennsylvania in 1872 that American miners worked between sixty and a hundred hours a week – though since there was no accepted industrial working-class they at least enjoyed greater social equality, if that mattered. Already they were upwardly-mobile wage-earners!

At the end of the century mechanization and a flood of cheap unskilled labour from southern and eastern Europe began to displace skilled British labour; emigration declined and by the start of the 1914 War, it had ended.

Most of those early migrants treated the US as a place to earn money, and saw no reason to become citizens. The homesick who returned to Britain found it hard to fit in again; like many of those who down the years followed them across the Atlantic, they were suspended between two ways of life while belonging wholly to neither.

The Brits now colonizing America must, like all migrants, be out of the ordinary: GI-brides, the brain-drain, the flight from the pound or from tax, the flood of Hollywood people and rock musicians, the opportunity-hunters and risk-takers ... whatever their reasons they needed more than average get-up-and-go, for it requires enterprise or ambition or desperation to pull up your roots, cut off the past and start a new life somewhere else.

Many soon discover, as did those mill-workers and miners a century ago, that in America it may be easy to succeed but it is also far easier to fail; and there are no safety nets. Descent is not cushioned. Once on the floor, you are on your own; there is little Welfare to make it better....

They also find it disconcerting to live where no interest at *all* is shown in their homeland. As three English jazzmen settled contentedly in Louisiana told me, nothing that happens fifty miles outside New Orleans matters – let alone what goes on in Europe, wherever that is.

This must in part be caused by the absence of a national Press – so all news is local, all attitudes parochial. The only truly national newspaper of any consequence concerns itself, surprise surprise, with money: the excellent *Wall Street Journal*.

In seeming contradiction there is a compulsive internal churning of population: once the national instinct was to stay home – now it is to take-off, to be somewhere else. From the sky this mobile, rootless society looks like some furious ant-heap. The eight-lane freeways are solid night and day, and in airports like bus stations it is as easy to pick-up a 2,500-mile transcontinental flight as a candy bar; computerized machines digest credit cards and chatter-out tickets while wide-bodies leave for everywhere, on the Hour. Each day there are 24,365 internal commercial flights.

During five months on this pilgrimage around America, for ever flying-on at any hour, I never once saw a concourse that was not congested nor an aircraft that was not full. On some ordinary inter-city flight, one of a dozen services a day, airline men would tempt boarded passengers with free travel later if only they would surrender their seats to those in the overbooked queue outside. So where is everybody going – and why?

Few preconceptions survive among the contradictions of the United States. Despite my thirty-year record of regular attendance, almost everyone had some revelation that overturned a conviction. I had always believed, for example, that we were poor cousins – yet it seems today the impecunious United Kingdom is buying-back America. Since the end of Exchange Control in 1979 British big-business has been in love with America's free enterprise and capital invested directly has risen by billions despite, or because of, the sensitivity of sterling. Sir James Goldsmith has been one of the most successful of the corporate raiders.

Direct British investment is almost $70 billion; three years ago it was $14 billion. Even those figures underestimate the value of American firms under British control for there is no record of deals involving local borrowing, as used by the smart operators: the wily Sir Gordon White, arriving ten years ago with $3,000, now controls an empire worth $1 billion – bought with *their* money.

In 1982 Britain's earnings from America were 60 per cent up on the year before: £1,800 million – the dividend of so-called Funk Money, returning home to help.

British property men are developing more than seven million square feet of office building in Manhattan alone, where they already own twenty skyscrapers. Union pension funds, the Coal Board, ICI, Banks, County Councils are all in the extraordinary real estate boom which followed New York's near-bankruptcy in 1975.

They find the underlying philosophy of City officials quite different from that of their counterparts in England who will delay a building for years if they think the developer might make too much profit; in the US they *want* him to make money.

In turn, their real-estate men were surprised by the care Brits lavish upon buildings, right down to the lavatories. Americans, for their own good reasons, create narrow tin shelters around their loos with partitions ending a foot above the ground. A Washington architect hired by British developers buying a massive block on 19th Street recalls 'They asked if we could enlarge the bathrooms. I told them they were up to Code but they said "We'd like them bigger, with better fixtures, more stalls and none of these metal partitions." They wanted *real* doors on the stalls, right down to the floor – they thought it was undignified for people to see their feet while they were sitting in there!'

Whether sitting comfortably or not, Britons and Americans have always shown distinctive attitudes towards change. In 1875 a Post Office official named Priest reported to a Parliamentary committee at Westminster about a new American invention: the telephone. He informed the committee that such new-fangled apparatus was quite unnecessary in Britain 'for we have a plentiful supply of messenger boys'.

Years later when, despite Mr Priest, the telephone had crossed the Atlantic, he assured another Parliamentary committee that to install the new American automatic telephone-exchange was equally unnecessary: 'We have an ample supply of female telephonists.'

The not very prescient Mr Priest died in 1912 and in his obituary was described as 'The Father of the British telephone system'.

As with Mr Priest's wrong numbers and crossed lines, we may not always be right but we make it *seem* right, for though the United States came into being by rebelling against us, we remain the parent country who has given them a language, polite behaviour, real theatre, men's clubs and dignity. Though we may envy Americans their affluence they remain nervous of us, uneasily recalling that we conquered the world while appearing only to worry about the roses on the south wall.

Those who long to age their new money in a gentlemanly way may admire our understatement, assurance and disdain, but have so far only achieved the business style of the robber-baron. Mrs Trollope reviled Americans as brutes, Kipling and D.H. Lawrence admired their primitive vigour, Victorians felt threatened by a society in which people conferred value upon themselves, Dickens believed an Englishman might save his life by emigrating, but lose his character – for in a land lacking social amenity and historical depth everything was temporary and makeshift, with no past to validate it.

Not too much has changed, except that today the nation they were patronizing has wealth so abundant and so easily acquired that its people can afford to be dismissive about it. For Europeans with a history of earnest and stealthy acquisition, such indifference is confusing, and seen as flashy.

California is America, only more so, and was feared by Christopher Isherwood because its hedonism weakened the will and persuaded you 'to sign that seven-year contract, buy that house you don't really want, marry that girl you secretly despise....' Discontent has always been a product of affluence.

Brits who have dropped anchor in this fortunate and welcoming country know that by emigrating they have merely exchanged national problems. Some were pursuing to its source the Horatio Alger myth: that with dedication and hard work even the poorest of the poor can make it. Millions have proved the truth of this, but many others have not.

Like all western societies, the giant US economy has proved incapable of producing stable non-inflationary growth. Serious internal conflicts threaten: the rapid growth of a permanent under-class – the black and Hispanic uneducated under-skilled inhabitants of inner-city ghettos. The accelerating regional split between Sun Belt and Frost Belt which will leave northerners permanently in the cold. Long-term unemployment, as automation spreads and traditional manufacturing sectors contract. Social tension following the ever-growing illegal immigration, especially from Mexico: Hispanics have nearly double the fertility rate of whites. On the periphery of such future-shock comes the decline of education, reading and the written Press, and the dominance of television in the political dialogue.

But today, rough or smooth, there is an America for each newcomer, whether Sloane Ranger or deep country Vietnamese. The reality is selective, optional. Upon arrival each migrant can re-imagine himself....

And finally, a few American flavours. . . .

Few Americans decorate their own houses or organize their own parties, if they can afford not to; they just hand their lives and homes over to a Professional – and then fight about the bill. Having received power of decision, successful Organizers become social arbiters and wield considerable authority. The vast Church of Heavenly Rest on New York's 5th Avenue is a splendid setting for a marriage, yet its stained-glass and dramatic lighting failed to win over the Floral Decorator employed to co-ordinate one big Society wedding. He absorbed the scene petulantly and after much creative thought turned to the patient Rev. Hugh Hildesley: 'I love it – but that cross has *got* to go. . . .'

═══

The Rev. Hugh, a gentle rugger-playing giant, recalled his visits of comfort to a parishioner, a doctor dying of cancer at the age of fifty-nine: 'He had consulted himself and predicted his death in exactly three weeks. In fact he lived four days longer – and got rather cross about being wrong. . . .'

═══

Outside West Palm Beach, a large and reassuring sign: English Pub. Then below it: Topless Barmaids. . . .

═══

At a Gay Parade in Dallas 20,000 homosexuals congregated along Cedar Springs in stifling heat to watch their flamboyant floats. It seemed curious that their community which had opted to be different, to be out of step . . . had instantly reassembled as clones. Along the sidewalk fringeing the parade every Gay wore Levi's 501 jeans and a white T-shirt. They looked like the massed and regimented Chinese workers I saw at a football match in Qingdao. . . .

═══

Among guests at the Mountbatten Ball in Houston, organized by the formidable Daughters of the British Empire, I met an Englishman who had originally come to America to sell Aston-Martin cars. One day Michael Ashley drove his latest deep-throated James Bond model to a San Francisco mansion where he hoped to make a sale. The prospective client finally decided, after much reflection, that for such a hefty price he ought to have a Rolls-Royce instead. However, his *butler* bought the Aston-Martin. . . .

═══

THE COP

*Brutalitywise we could kill a lot more people
than we do . . .*

For five years Peter Vanson was a policeman at Kensington and
Notting Hill stations. He took a year's unpaid leave in 1978, arrived
in America – and stayed, selling encyclopedias in Harlem, working
on a ranch, as a tour guide in Florida, an ambulanceman on the
Mexican border. . . .

Then he and another Briton, David Jones, entered the Los Angeles
Police Academy. As polite ex-bobbies who'd never carried guns –
unthinkable innocence in California – they were much ribbed by the
other probationers, so after graduating both applied for the toughest
assignment in the LAPD: the South West Division, which includes
Watts – the black suburb which on 11 August 1965 suffered America's first race riots.

Now a senior policeman instructing the division's newcomers,
cheerful and confident, he lives in West Covina with his American
second wife, a hairdresser. In a black-and-white we toured his patch,
and the hostile streets of Watts. His daily routine is not at all the way
it was back in the Earls Court Road: last year he earned £650 a week
– but Los Angeles saw 2,300 murders. . . .

━━

As a policeman in England I had my truncheon – and I'd forget that most
of the time – but here I have my shotgun, my .38 Special and a tazer gun,
this electronic gun we use because we have a lot of trouble with a drug
called PCP.

This is angel dust?

This is angel dust, yeah. Anyone who takes it gets the strength of ten or
fifteen people, so fighting them's a no-win situation. What we do is point
this gun at them, the light comes on and when I push the button electronic
darts fly out and hit them with fifty thousand volts. Normally that does the
trick – puts them on their back. In this station we sometimes use this five,
six times a night.

Angel dust is a cattle tranquillizer?

That was the original use of it, then it came on the market in the Sixties in San Francisco and now it's become a lethal drug in the United States. It's cheap to make. People OD on it – even children. I was in a hospital the other day, we had a baby OD'd on PCP. In fact it stays in the system for seventy-four years – the most dangerous drug in the world.

A guy broke my back three months ago. He was five foot three and he picked up my partner, who's a very muscle-bound individual, and threw him. The next thing he picked me up and threw me over a car. It took about ten of us to get him in the end. You can have someone four foot six wreck a house and take on ten police officers and nearly win.

But we taze them, what we call *zap* them. You hear 'I need a zapper' and you get there and hope it'll be raining because they light up and it's really neat. Some of them of course it won't effect. I've had guys we've tazed three or four times and they're standing there laughing at you.

We got them in 1979 and they have a maximum range of about fifteen feet – the ideal range's eight to ten feet. It shoots out two wires and on the end of them is like a fish-hook barb, and it sticks on the clothes. It completes an electrical circuit – it's a pulsating charge of about fifty thousand volts and it interrupts the body's central nervous system and the nerve impulses. You have, like, a seizure, an epileptic fit, and the person's unable to control their body movements and they fall down.

How long does this giant strength last?

It depends on the individual, it depends on how many times they've taken it before. It could go away and come back. During the effects of the drugs they'll have periods of lucidity. I remember once before we had tazers dealing with a PCP, rolling around in the street down at Figueroa. Each of us had a limb, and a fifth officer was sitting on the guy's torso. He was out of his head, screaming he was God. Then suddenly he turned and his eyes were clear and he looked at me and said, 'What's the problem?' And I said, 'Sir, you've been taking drugs, so put your hands behind your back, slowly.' He started to do it, and then his eyes clouded over again and he started screaming he was God.

We're having a problem now in hospitals. Babies are having seizures – their mothers have been on PCP. I was at the hospital about a week ago and they were asking the woman if she took PCP and she said, 'Yes.' The baby was seizing when it came out.

It tastes similar to marijuana, but the temperature in your body goes up, you lose control of your eyes, they start boggling and your whole body becomes like a piece of metal. When you touch them you feel you're touching a piece of steel. They'll kill you. If you let them get their hands on you, you're dead. That's why we use this thing.

The effect PCP has on a human is just totally different than it was on the bull. When I first joined here we didn't know what it was, and I got thrown through a window by a tiny woman. It was embarrassing because I'm six foot two and a woman picks me up and throws me through a window. I won't even take on a female if I know she's under that condition. She'll kill me. So I point this, a light will shine on them and two darts come flying out. It's a civilized way of handling the situation. If we have to fight them, it's probably going to need ten of us and we may have to kill them to control them. With this I can handcuff them, and that's the end of the problem.

We have a place called Shome Alley. It's like driving into a supermarket. You go in and get your cigarettes and you dip them in PCP and make your buy that way.

The trouble is – angel dust is so cheap, compared to other drugs?

The overheads for a PCP dealer on the street are very, very low, and the profit margin is tremendous. For a hundred dollar's worth of chemicals to make the PCP you can look at a profit margin of at least several hundred per cent. It goes a long long way. We have officers in plain clothes in schools here just *trying* to control it. We have schools in this neighbourhood where we have armed guards in the classrooms. It's quite tragic. This thing stays in the system up to seventy-four years so you can actually go two years without being on it and suddenly, boom!

Do you get officers here saying, 'I'm tired of PCP, I'd rather go up to the Station in Bel Air among the rich folk . . .'?

Oh yes, all the time, but some officers stay here in the South End all their careers.

Just natural-born masochists?

Yes, it's more socially acceptable than beating ourselves with knotted ropes – people don't stare quite so much!

What made you decide to leave the Metropolitan Police where you were leading a good clean life, and come out here and face the angel dust?

When I left England I had no idea I'd end up in Los Angeles. I took off in a van to drive round the world – it was the done thing in the Seventies. I came to America and did a variety of jobs. For an Englishman to be in the Los Angeles police then just wasn't heard of. I did it five years ago and I'm still enjoying it.

What about this other Brit?

David Jones? Very very good policeman. David was walking his beat in Leeds one day and there was snow on the ground and he said, 'To hell with this!' He'd just watched *Hill Street Blues*, so he wrote to Los Angeles. He had to keep it pretty secret because they think you're nuts in Yorkshire if you do something like that. He got a letter back saying, 'We'd like to see you'. He couldn't believe it, so he flew over here and they said, 'You know you've got to be a citizen,' and somehow he got himself a Green Card, and he was on.

I thought that was *one* thing a foreigner couldn't do when coming here: you can't vote and you can't join the police?

You can join but I think within two years you have to achieve your citizenship. I was married and then divorced, so I got my citizenship last year. I still consider myself English. David hasn't got his yet. He's been married three times, to two English girls and one American girl.

I didn't just walk into this job, I sold encyclopedias in Harlem, I worked in Disney World ... I did a lot of different things before. And when I joined this Department the training was far more rigorous physically than London. It was like a Marine boot camp. Shooting's an important part of the training, whereas in England you hardly learned. When I was in London they'd offer you all sorts of things to fire guns, and policemen would refuse. They'd offer us a week's vacation free, our Chief Superintendent would *plead* with us.

Why were they refusing?

Well most of the armed jobs those days were guarding embassies and you knew if you did your gun course you had to guard an embassy. Plus it was a tradition. Even today a lot of my friends over there who're lieutenants – inspectors – most of them don't like the idea of carrying guns. In Leatherhead where my mother lives they think I'm nuts anyway, but when I left it was a big event for me to become a London policeman. Now I'm a Los Angeles policeman most people can't relate to that at *all*.

I was guarding the Thatcher residence when four of us were planning this round-the-world trip in a van. I was on duty outside on Christmas Eve in 1976 and Denis invited me in for a drink. I was telling him this plan and said, 'I'm worried about my career.' He said, 'Go for it.' I think we *did* have a gun in those days and my inspector turned up because he couldn't find me outside. He came in and I was all over the place and he said, 'Pete, what are you *doing?*' Denis said, 'You've got two choices, you either get drunk with this young policeman or if you report him I'll report *you* and get you demoted.' The next thing I knew my inspector and me were both smashed. It was actually Denis who convinced me to go ahead and travel.

Maggie Thatcher's a great lady. She's marvellous – and so different in private. In fact we met the Queen here in LA and she's also totally different. In London I'd been many times on royal traffic control but when she came here David and I got a chance to meet her – in fact she asked to meet us. We were with all these dignitaries, like Elizabeth Taylor. She spent about ten minutes with us – I could see everyone getting a little upset. She was asking us exactly how was it over here and she was really interested. I said, 'Most of the time I get asked, "Have you met the Queen?" At least I can tell them I *have*, now!'

Do they look upon a British bobby here as an ornament?

They do. I'm still treated as an ornament by the public and by my fellow officers. In America everyone categorizes each other – you're either black, white or Mexican. I'm English so they put me in a separate category, and I like that because I can solve a lot of problems just by being English. You see English are *liked* in this state, and in America. It helps in family disputes, which are horrendous. If we arrested them we'd have no policemen out on the street. A family feud to us is a minor call, although it can turn into a major call. We don't get to burglaries sometimes till two days later.

Some nights I'll have six shootings to deal with, one after the other. I was at one the other day – there was a fight between two women. They were hitting each other over the head with cans and one bit the other one's nose off. It was a helluva mess. It looked like a stabbing when I first got there. I took the nose to hospital. It's a shame you couldn't have been here, it was hilarious! It ended up No Report – neither of them wanted to do anything – and them yelling at me. But if you arrested everyone you *should* arrest in a division like this, you'd never get anything done. You can't do things totally by the book here.

What's the ratio of black officers?

About fifty–fifty.

And outside, on the streets?

In our division it's ninety per cent black, maybe five per cent Mexican and five per cent oriental. No whites. You've got all the extremes. You've got a wealthy black neighbourhood who look down on the black people, even in this division. You've got to change your whole way of thinking when you come down here. There's a big class structure even amongst blacks, and in fact the biggest support in LA for the police is in this particular neighbourhood, in the black community. Ninety per cent is probably the most supportive for the police you're going to find anywhere in the world. It's the other per cent that are very very violent.

This South West is the toughest Division in the LAPD area?

Probably in America. Definitely the toughest in Los Angeles.

Wouldn't you rather be in Hollywood or Beverly Hills, looking after the film stars?

When I came here I wanted to work in the worst area. It's part of my personality. I've always believed you should go where there's fear to tread, so I came here and I've never left. It's like my home now. I've been to three murders this week. It's a different world here than England, a far more violent society. People say to me all the time, 'How do you feel about carrying a gun?' You'd be crazy *not* to carry one.

So you walked in here as an ex-bobby, like Dixon of Dock Green; how was your first night on patrol?

I was working through to midnight, and my first radio call was: Shooting in progress! In London you just don't hear that sort of thing. We get there – a hamburger stand with about a hundred people outside, and there's a guy lying there been shot about six times, obviously dead. I run up and my partner grabs me and says, 'You *never* run,' he says, 'You walk up,' and he calmly handles the situation.

We're trying to get things under control and I hear two shots going off about a hundred yards away. I dive down. When I look up, I'm the *only* person on the ground – everyone else is still eating their hamburgers! My partner says, 'I'll wander down there and find out what's happening,' and there was another homicide just down the street. As we were dealing with that – this is a true story – about another hundred yards away there was *another* murder! Three murders in the course of half an hour of being out on the street! That got me going a little bit, but after five years I've seen probably close to two thousand homicides, so I know how to handle them now.

What do you expect on one night here?

The maximum I've seen in this particular division is eight homicides in a night. On an average you can expect one or two. Shootings, probably ten or eleven. Stabbings we don't even keep *count* ...

This is all drug-related, is it?

Eighty per cent of it's drug-related. Then we have family dispute problems. Five per cent of our murders are family disputes. We have to go in there and try and solve someone's marriage that's been on the rocks for five or six years. Nine times out of ten they'll turn on us.

Of course. So how do you handle things?

You get there and the first thing you do is you want to find out what the weapons are. A lot of times they've got the gun in their hand, or a knife, so you try and take the weapons off them as nice as you can, and you sit them down. I've often had them going at each other for about ten minutes. You use different techniques and turn their animosity towards you – then normally they call you all the names under the sun and when you walk out they're hugging and kissing! They all hate us, but it seems to work.

If you go into a house here it's not unusual to see ten kids. You say, 'Where's the father of the children?' not 'Where's your husband?' If you come out with something like that straight away you've *lost* it right there and then, because they know you're new and they'd be on top of you.

A lot of cops go through their whole career and never have to draw their guns. . . .

Yes, but I've had to. We had this individual called Legs Diamond. He was quite comical. I like the guy actually, but he's shot three policemen in his career. He's an ex-Black Panther and he sets policemen up. You get a lot of that here. He called us to his home for a family dispute and when we got there he opened straight up on us with a gun. We had this big shoot-out and I missed, my bullets went about twenty feet in the air.

What happened to him?

SWAT got him out. When they went in he was cooking marshmallows over the fire. He's back on the streets now. But it's safer than London in many respects because of the way we do it here. I think in LA we're probably the best in the country. San Francisco's not in the same class as us as far as the safe way we do it, the way we constantly train, whereas in London you stop a car, you roll up and say, 'Excuse me, sir, I saw you go through that red light.' In this division you don't do that. You stop the car and you get the person to come back to you. I don't care if it's an eighty-year-old – I've been shot at by seventy-eight-year-olds in this division.

When you go to a house you stop about three houses down, you get out, you look around. . . . After a while you feel a lot safer because you do things the way we're trained. Whereas in England they had two policemen shot while I was there about a month ago, and that wouldn't have happened in this division. You're ready for it here. These two policemen in London stopped a van and walked right up to it. When I stop a van I get the driver out and turn him around – I don't care if he's the President.... At night I'd be on the loudspeaker saying, 'Step out of the car.'

You could point a gun at me and if I've got my hand in my pocket I could kill you before you could pull the trigger. If someone has a gun on your partner we've already trained what we're going to do. He gives me a code and within three seconds I'm going to start shooting – and that's three seconds for him to do something, to get out of the way ... things like that you'd never think in London.

You've got your issue .38 Special and a back-up gun and a shot-gun under the seat?

And we take them out about two times a night. We have a helicopter here the whole time. A typical call is: 'Shooting in progress, there are two people down.' When I'm going there, there'll be the helicopter telling me what's going on, saying, 'Two people down ... guy outside with a rifle.' I'm no hero, but in some ways it's safer because we're geared to the violence.

What's the call sign for a policeman in trouble?

Help!

Not a number?

I still get all my numbers confused. Everything's geared to numbers, but even to this day, especially under stress ... I forget.

I remember when I spent a month on patrol with the San Francisco Police what I appreciated very much was, whenever there was a Policeman-in-Trouble call, every car in the city would put on its lights and siren and converge flat-out, like some avenging horde....

You don't care *what* you're doing. I can be at one shoot-out and if the person's going to live I'll leave him on the ground....

How many officers are there?

It's got to be close to three hundred in South West Division. That's off the top of my head – that's with the detectives and Drug Squad. The Olympics was held just down the street here. We hit that neighbourhood beforehand because that Coliseum area, you just normally don't go there. You go in for a pop concert or something, but you wouldn't walk round there at night. We hit that neighbourhood for three months.

I'm almost a client of yours because I've just had my attaché-case stolen at San Francisco airport, so I'm going to be picked up for driving a car without a licence on me, which I know is a heinous offence in the States....

Just tell them you're English. I get stopped all the time. The speed limit's fifty-five here and I still keep to the English speed limit. I tell them I'm a police officer and they say, 'Yeah, I'm Henry VIII.' I've been dragged out of my car so many times.

But you've got a badge, haven't you?

Normally you have different signs to let them know you're a policeman. You put both hands up on the steering wheel, and you try giving them different hints: 'Do you want me to get my gun from the glove compartment?'

You've been married twice – how do you get the time? I thought being in the police force was death to a marriage?

I work sometimes seven days and get four days off. My life away from here is completely different – no one knows I'm a policeman. I'm just an English tourist to anyone who asks me, and that's the way I like to keep it.

One of the compensations of coming here and facing all this action every day must be the pay – it has to be good?

It's very very high: I earn $36,000 a year. When I first started it was $26,000. With overtime this year I've got $38,000.

That's almost £35,000 a year ... they must envy you, back at Notting Hill! At least they're also doing well with overtime during the miners' strike, though about fourteen hundred of them have been injured by Scargill's pickets, so far....

I used to be in the shed at Chelsea and I know about that sort of violence. They wouldn't get away with it *once* over here, I guarantee you. The order would be given for shotguns to come out. They wouldn't get away with it, they really wouldn't.

There was a piece in the LA *Times* yesterday saying that in the old days a policeman would stand and take abuse if someone was giving him a hard time, but the young officers now coming in *won't* take it.

23

No they won't. I take more than most of them do. I still do a lot of things the old English way....

Hello hello hello what's goin' on 'ere, what seems to be the trouble, sir?

Yes, and I try and make tea for people, even though they don't *have* tea. It amazes them. They're not used to that. I don't think any English policemen earn the money I do, or have the lifestyle I have. I have a boat, I have a house with a swimming pool. I go home and my family and friends all get in the jacuzzi – you just couldn't do that in Bethnal Green!

That's true. But then, the chances of getting your head blown off in Bethnal Green are a little bit less than here.

A little bit less. I *earn* my money here. I've had my moments – but I'm living proof that not every policeman gets shot in America!

The people you're dealing with are very different from the people you were dealing with in Bethnal Green?

I can take you to a place round here where you can buy guns in supermarkets. When you have that situation, it's very very volatile. In England you can't buy a gun. Even as a policeman I wouldn't have known where to get a gun. Here kids growing up know how to get guns – they see murder and it doesn't mean that much to them. I've been to homicides where ten-year-olds have killed people. I treat a kid exactly as I would anyone else. *Anyone* can take you, here. You treat everyone the same, you have to. The whole way of thinking as a police officer has to be different than England, because you only get one chance here, whereas in England you get in a pub fight and you just get bruised. I've got a bulletproof vest on, you *have* to wear one here.

That's mandatory?

It's mandatory, but my head can get shot. Nothing's one hundred per cent, but it's pretty good.

What about these new Teflon-coated bullets?

These bullets will just go through this vest like a knife through butter. We're trying to get 'em stopped by law.

So you might as well not wear it?

Back at square one, might as well not. Hopefully the average person won't get hold of them, but if someone wants to do you, they're going to get hold of these bullets. You know in this division, especially New Year's Eve, we get snipered-on in this station when we're leaving. At night I vary my route out because it's happened, we've had policemen get snipered, so I change my route. We have three different ways out of here.

You mean somebody might be picking on you?

Yeah, it happens. I've had threats. Your whole way of thinking here is geared to survival.

As a bobby, you were used to being respected. Here I suspect you're not?

No, there's no respect for the police here. They don't like you. I'm not just talking about this neighbourhood, I'm talking about everywhere in America, the general consensus is lack of respect for the police.

They think you're bent, you're crooked, you're taking money?

More than that, they think we're *brutal*. It's not really like that, you know, especially corruptionwise. In this particular department there's very little corruption, and brutalitywise we could kill a lot more people than we do. In our training we hold back, but the public don't even realize it. I could have shot probably ten people last week, but the fact that I didn't doesn't get in the newspaper.

Also when you do hold back, when it's Gentlemen of the French Guards fire first . . . you're putting your own life on the line?

Whatever you do you're gonna get questioned. You've got three seconds to make a decision, less than that, and everyone's gonna second-guess you. But in this department we have a saying, 'I'd rather be tried by twelve than carried out by six.' My family's more important to me than this job.

Everything you're telling me makes being a copper in Notting Hill sound better. . . .

Well, I've told you the bad things. We have the fun times here too. It's not all like that. There's a lot of fun to this job. We have our lunatics, we have a woman here who believes she's got ghosts in her attic, got another one and the only person she'll see is me and she tries to rape me every time I go in there. There's a fun side of it. But I always have a gun on me.

Off duty, unless it's a major situation, I wouldn't get involved. It's too dangerous, it really is. If I saw another policeman getting injured or shot, then I'd step in – but with the lack of respect here I have to be careful, even carrying my ID, because if a store gets robbed when I'm in it and they take my wallet out and find I'm a police officer – it's the *end*. They'd kill me. Off-duty I try and stay well away from it. Luckily with my accent the way it is, most people have no idea I'm a police officer.

About two weeks ago on the way home, looking forward to a nice beer, I went into my liquor store. I rolled in there and a guy had a gun. I thought, Oh *no* – here we go.... As I looked in my mirror a police car was pulling in, so I obviously had to do something. I was out of uniform, had my shorts, my T-shirt which I come to work in.

I pointed my gun at the guy and got the gun out of his hand. He gave up. My partner had a big gun with him. As it worked out, the guy was wanted in Texas for the murder of a police officer. He was about to rob the liquor store and he'd have probably dumped the policeman as he came in. That's about the only time I think off-duty I've got involved. Normally I won't.

You'd walk away, would you?

Yeah. People start cursing the police out and I have to go along with them, curse them as well. I haven't got the heart to tell them I'm a police officer. My wife never tells anyone what I do. We keep it to ourselves.

As though it's a guilty secret?

This is a very violent station, and when I leave this I want to switch off from it altogether. My whole personality changes. In our house we don't even discuss what I do during the day – in fact she watches the news and normally my station's on the news once a night, so she knows more about it than I do. I get home and she tells me of a big murder that happened here.

When you're on patrol here at night, what on average would you see, what would happen?

You can probably guarantee a homicide – at least one. Shootings and stabbings come out all the time. When I drive along you see drug sales going down, you're gonna have PCP suspects going off, family disputes, robberies – we have *so* many robberies you can't even get to most of them.

A lot of people get lost coming out of LA airport: you can easily wander into this neighbourhood. I was driving along and I saw this rented car at 60th and Vermont, which is a very bad neighbourhood. They shouldn't have been there. I can tell English people miles away – they always travel on the plane with a tie on. I put the lights on and pulled them over and saw this guy get out, obviously nervous. I said, 'What are you doing in this area?' And this northern accent said, 'What t' bloody 'ell are you doing 'ere?' I said, 'You know we get murders round here?' In the end I gave them a tour round the division and escorted him to Century Boulevard.

A year ago a German tourist got out to ask the way and a guy just stuck a gun in his mouth and blew his head off. He was going to rob him. It can happen. If you spend a couple of weeks here you realize after a while that with homicide, there's no reasons.

Last Christmas Day I was at a family dispute where two kids got in an argument over a turkey bone. One got up behind the other and put a knife right through his throat. Then you've got the odd crazies on the loose. A city like LA, which isn't *that* big – London's eight and a half million, LA's only three million – last year the county of LA had 2,300 murders.

It's drugs, plus a short fuse?

Yes. It's hard to stab someone or strangle someone, but it's not that hard to *shoot* someone. It's a very impersonalized way of doing it and if you've got the short fuse which most Americans have, you can go *boom*, and it's over and done with. In England you can get into an argument with someone ... over here on the freeway when you go home if someone yells at you, you've got to be very very careful. If you're going to yell back you've got to start thinking, Has he got a gun?

What's the law here? In Texas you can carry a gun in your glovebox ...

You can't have any concealed weapon in California. You can have it if it's not loaded.

But *everyone's* got one!

Everyone's got one.

So you can have the empty gun in one pocket and the bullets in the other?

That's right, and that would be legal. Or you can have it on your hip. You *can* do it, but we get them for other things. We have a few minor laws in LA, Brandishing and things like that, and we can get round it. But people aren't that stupid, they know if they've got a gun like that, the chances of a policeman shooting them are probably very very high.

But in your home, it's legit?

Yes. When you go to a house on a call you knock on the door and the first question you ask is, 'Are there any guns in the house?' 'Yes.' 'Where are they?' Say *you've* been victimized, you've been burglarized, you're the victim. If you go into the bathroom, I would go there with you. Once I'm in that house I'm never going to take my eyes off you.

Why?

You could set me up. It happens in this country, they get policemen in and kill them.

To what end? Apart from not liking policemen, what's the point?

It's status, in some gangs around here. To be *in* a gang you've got to at least take on a cop. We've probably got about twenty gangs and they all live and die for their street. There's streets around here where you can see guns coming out of the wall. They're not really after you, they're looking for other narcotic dealers coming in to take over.

What about the clean-up of hoodlums LA had last week?

It's the tip of the iceberg. In England you haven't got the poverty level you have in the United States. You've got a higher middle class here than you have in England and you've probably got more millionaires, but in England, in Hartlepool or Bradford or even the East End of London where I was born, you haven't got the poverty.... Here I'll take you to houses where you have twenty Mexicans living in a small room, and life is extremely cheap. They don't talk about hitting someone here, it's 'I wanna kill the sonofabitch.... I wanna kill the MF....'

The language is different, and I have to speak like that. I still find it hard because I come from a Catholic family in England and I wasn't used to swearing, but sometimes I have to relate differently because it's the only way to get across, if I'm talking to somebody, say a gangbanger....

They train in prisons here how to take a policeman's gun. They'll talk to you, and try to get closer. A lot of new police officers won't think about it but as soon as someone gets close to me I say, 'Step over there!' My gun leg will always be back so they're going to have to reach across.... I have my back-up gun under my shirt, so if I get in a fight and someone's trying to get it, first of all I'm going to hang on to it and my hand's going to come in here.... I don't like it down in the sock because it's a long way to go. Some policemen do carry it down there but I want mine within reaching distance.

28

Presumably villains all know you've got a back-up gun. . . .

They know, but they don't know *where* you've got it, luckily. A guy who's been in the joint, as I say, they train how to take your gun, so they're walking backwards and firing it. That's why it's different from London. At the London Police Academy in Hendon the whole month's training was in public relations and that sort of thing, whereas here you train on *survival*. In roll-calls we're constantly talking about barricaded suspects, what do we do? It's a constant training factor. Violence is a way of life. We know guns are out there, we know they're in every house and if you walk up to a door here they're likely to kick your ass. If they see you positioning the car the wrong way they'll jump on you. There's really no second chances in this country. . . .

As soon as I get a new probationer I'll take him in the park and we'll go over certain things. If someone has a gun to my head – which's happened, someone's taken my gun – my partner will have a gun pointed at both of us, and what we do is, we'll exchange names. My name's Peter and his name's John. I'll say, 'Peter, give him your gun.' That's the clue that in three seconds I'm going to drop to the ground because I know he's going to open up on both of us. That's what he's trained to do and he *must* do that.

I've got three seconds to drop or get out of the way ... because he's going to come in and take that guy's head off. If the probationer doesn't do that, or he *can't* do it, then he'll be out of a job. We have a lot of policemen leave because they get in a situation where they suddenly have to pull that trigger, and they can't do it.

On Patrol

Right here in this building on my left – looks like a chicken stand – they're selling PCP, cocaine, marijuana. Not a lot you can do really. This guy on the corner looks like an old blind guy but he's probably a look-out. If I was gonna do a Stop here I'd even search him – he could have a gun.

If that blind guy's a look-out, he's not earning his money. . . .

He looks as if he's asleep but he knows exactly what I'm doing. All these people know there's a police car around, especially when there's other people in the car. Most of them, you've got to remember, see us every day. They know if I'm likely to make a narcotics arrest – then they'll all go in. They know us better than we know them.

Around here you probably take your gun out two or three times a night. You don't fire it, but you go to a lot of situations where the shotgun will come out and just the *noise* of cocking it could do the trick.

You've been in Notting Hill, in Brixton, but life is on a much higher voltage here?

Everything's faster. You have to adjust to it.

There's more violence and less understanding?

That's correct, violence here is just a way of life. Most of these people will sell you a gun if you want one, and the way of solving an argument is still like the Old West days, having a shoot-out.

Do you find the people you're dealing with are frightened of you, or do they just hate you?

A mixture of both. We *have* to have an element of fear because if they don't have that fear, then they would take us on all the time. They do fear us. Most times people call us when they need us, but they don't like us.

After a few nights on patrol it must be difficult to keep those nice liberal British instincts?

I still try and keep a lot of them, but I've had to adjust. I do things a certain way but I still try and treat people like human beings – which most policemen do, even in this country.

Do they understand what you're saying, with that Limey accent?

When I first came to this division it was hilarious, I'd say, 'Put your hands on the bonnet!' and they'd say, *'Bonnet?'* and you'd lose control of the whole situation! They think I'm from France, Germany, Australia. Eventually when I'm telling them I'm from England, they love it – except if I've got a gun pointed at 'em, they don't really care *what* accent I have!

They might blow your head off of course, there's always that?

You have to live with that. We're trained to deal with most violent situations, so if it happens it happens, but I can't think about it every day or I'll end up in a mental home.

A lot of these houses look nice, but inside you have six or seven families living in them. We have a big problem at the moment with blacks and Mexicans shooting each other just because they're black or Mexican. We're caught in the middle.

Most of these liquor stores get robbed every day ... quite the done thing. This shop is closed down: he was robbed about ten times in a week so he went and got himself a gun and a ten or eleven-year-old kid came in and robbed the place and the guy just blew the boy's head off. He'd just had enough of it.

We're heading a little bit east into what we call the Jungle, which is a very, very dangerous area. It's ninety per cent drugs. We have murders there every night. I've never seen a white man in there, except police officers, so if you went in chances are you wouldn't come out, or if you did you wouldn't have anything left. There are parts of LA where you can walk around twenty-four hours a day, then you go two blocks either way and you're in trouble. Round here for about a ten-mile radius you just can't go *anywhere*.

Most of us – specially white officers – are conscious we work in Watts, in a black area. We try and adapt to the culture as much as we can, even though they don't like you trying to make out you're black. You've got to let them know that you have respect for them being black, and that's as far as it goes – they think you're having fun with them if you try and push it too far. You just try and show as much respect as you can. The bulk of the people here are really nice and there's not an us-and-them situation, but with the criminal element it *is* us-and-them. They'll kill you whether you're a black policeman, a white policeman or whatever – in fact a lot of people round here don't like black police officers. I've been in some situations where they won't *talk* to a black policeman, they'll call him an Uncle Tom.

Why's it called the Jungle, this place?

When they originally built the Jungle it was an upper-class area and they put palm trees and various items like that to give it an African appearance – twenty years ago this was a predominantly white neighbourhood. Life inside here *is* a bit like a jungle, we have more murders than anywhere else in the city. Just by looking at it it's hard to see why, but most of these apartment buildings sell narcotics and have wars with each other. It's not unusual to have big shootings around here on a daily basis.

Is there any area here where you wouldn't go?

There's an alleyway used to be called Shome Alley. They're all drug dealers and they guard that with shotguns, machine guns and various other weapons. If we went in there it was normally because a murder went down and we'd have to go in with seven or eight police cars. I can come here now, but at night even I wouldn't. I'd get at least another police car. You see, the word has gone round there's a car in the neighbourhood now, and you find people disappearing off the street.

Most of these kids have taken drugs before they're ten years of age. They see these Cadillacs driving around because some people are making big money out of drugs, but they don't see the people who aren't, so that's what they gear their heroes to. You try speaking to them and they think you're crazy half the time. Probably one in six cars you see here is stolen. The danger about these houses when you approach them, there can be guns anywhere. At night time there's cars parked along here and they're all selling cocaine to each other.

We pay the police to do jobs we don't want to do ourselves, but you can't solve *all* society's problems. . . .

All I'm here for really is to try and keep the violence down, and when a violent crime or a murder goes down, to try and stop it escalating from one murder to two. We just try somehow to keep a lid on it – and some of us wonder if we ever do *that*!

You can't become a policeman and think you're gonna solve anything, because you won't. You deal with each situation as it arises and you don't get socially involved. Even here most of the people want a police department because they know without it, it'd be a complete war zone. At least when we roll up the battle stops for half an hour, while we're here. . . .

THE SUPERWOMAN

*Few men can tolerate women who move at
the same speed....*

Jane Deknatel, a silver-haired forty-ish divorcee from Oxford, is the quintessential career woman. Elegant, powerful and pithy, she lives with two daughters in a pleasantly disorganized house in Santa Monica; as we dined under the trees on her moonlit patio a large opossum crept past our table and slipped into the kitchen, upsetting my appetite.

Her father was a Communist trade union organizer who lived in the US during the Depression and supported himself by playing professional football. He died when she was ten, having urged her to go to America one day: 'The only place to be free.'

After marriage at twenty-five she had two daughters, but proved a failure as a wife – her first and last diversion from a career. She walked out after five years, became an executive with CBS, with NBC, then with the successful American cable company Home Box Office, as senior vice-president wielding a budget of $85 million. Now independent, she produces films from a high-rise office in Century City – and complains that none of her dates takes her to dinner without producing a script....

She came on my *Whicker!* talk show with Professor John Kenneth Galbraith and Peter Marsh, an extremely voluble English advertising man. While the males radiated hostility at each other across this cool and stylish centrepiece, she recalled an intimate dinner in Paris with an attractive friend who confessed he was at that moment having a fantasy about her – but was too embarrassed to elaborate. With visions of some erotic sexual adventure, she persuaded her shy suitor to reveal his hidden dream. Finally he stammered, 'Could you ... would you ever consider ... going into *business* with me?'

═══

What brought you to America?

Several things. First of all, when I was at university somebody said, 'If you can fill a plane with students, I'll give you a free ticket,' so I couldn't turn down a challenge! Those were the days when with three months' summer holiday we all said, 'Go to America, work for six weeks, hitch-hike across to California for six weeks, and come home again.' The year before everyone had gone to India in a Land-Rover, I think. But more seriously, my Father had been here before the Depression and had come back to England quite radicalized. He always said the United States was the only place to be truly free, and that one day when I'd finished college I would get a trip to America. So it was always waiting there. Then I married an American, had two children and got divorced, rather quickly.

You felt you could move faster without him?

I never thought about moving at all, I just thought about being rather unhappy, and having to do something about it. I was quite unhappy being alone at home in a suburban American environment, which I found very isolating.

Inadequately occupied?

Right. Very busy, but inadequately occupied. So I found myself divorced with two small children who were one and three, with very little income and nowhere to live, and realized that I'd better get up and get myself a job. In those days I went to a very chic exercise class, so I walked in and did the unforgivable: I said to half a dozen women I worked-out with, I need a job. Please go home and tell your husbands – all of whom ran various companies, corporations or whatever – that I need a job. They said, 'Don't be ridiculous, your ex-husband or *somebody* will take care of you, dear.' I said, 'No one's going to take care of me, please tell them I need a job.' So indeed they did.

One man called me next day and said, 'I work for a large consulting company in the oil and gas business, I'm an economist and engineer and I need someone to help me on a project and I understand you have good organizational skills.' I said, 'Yes but I can't do mathematics and chemistry and physics – I'm absolutely retarded in those areas.' He said, 'Do come.' I was terrified. He called me every day for four days, and finally in my gym clothes I went over – and found myself that night on a plane to Dallas to meet a client. I was there for two and a half years.

You finished up as senior vice-president of Home Box Office; you became a powerful lady in a marketplace where there are a lot of powerful ladies, as opposed to in England, where they're rare?

I don't think there are a lot in America. There are a few who're very visible; and fewer still, obviously, in England. In the last two or three years the numbers are dwindling. I think we're in a real backlash period. These are the moments when women disappear from the marketplace.

34

You mean the men are striking back, the pendulum is swinging?

Absolutely.

If it's swinging here, imagine what's happening in England! Over there, would you have become an executive or remained a suburban housewife?

I certainly wouldn't have remained a suburban housewife, but I doubt very much if I ever would have had the opportunity to become powerful. Here, once I seriously started thinking about what I was going to do, I decided it made no sense to use the same kind of energy on being someone's secretary. I might as well use that energy to accomplish something for myself. Plus, I'm not very good at taking orders. I'm not very good at making coffee, either!

Los Angeles is a very energized city. I think it's vulgar, it's crude, it's exciting, it's the kind of life and the kind of work where as long as you're working hard and in the middle of everything that's going on, it's wonderful. One has a sense of power and a sense of excitement. It's difficult to relax here, it's difficult to have a family life, an intimate life, a social life outside of what you do. I think that's true in general of the entertainment business. It may be true of other businesses too.

Everybody's running fast. Also it is such a business of magic-in-a-bottle that it's difficult to have any kind of encounter with anybody that couldn't be *useful*. You're always thinking of a potentially useful conversation – doesn't matter whether you're having dinner or playing tennis or taking a walk on the beach, this could be somebody who could be helpful or instrumental a month from now or a year from now. That makes it impossible to meet people outside of what you do. In England I have a lot of friends who're in the business, but when we see each other we don't necessarily *talk* about business; when we socialize we talk about many other things. I think life is slower in England, which makes it more pleasant – but you can't have it both ways.

You are *Cosmopolitan*'s idea of the successful woman, and one wonders whether even in California you *can* have it all?

I don't think so. The definition of having it all is having a family, having a man in your life, having a successful business. I think there are very few men who can tolerate women who move at the same speed as they move. It's very disruptive of family life. You have to have whole new contracts in terms of what relationships mean at home. I'm not just talking about who does the dishes or who does the washing. Presumably if you're successful you can always have some kind of help in those areas, but for example can you imagine sitting home on Sunday night, both of you with your calendars, and saying, 'When will we see each other this week?' 'These are the business dinners I have, will you come with me to this?' 'Well, no darling, I have to go to *this*.' Do you toss a penny? I'm sure you can work those things out, but I don't think there are a whole load of people who ever get to the stage of even *wanting* to work them out.

So do your children have to make an appointment to see you?

They used to. We used to see each other whenever we could, obviously, but we had set dinners each week when they were required to be home and I was required to block off an evening. Two evenings a week, seven breakfasts a week, without fail. I never even *met* anybody before I had breakfast with my children! Breakfast means one hour sitting down to a proper meal, and talking. Now I'm in my own business my hours are more flexible and I tend to have meetings at home and do more entertaining, so I'm there more often.

I was going to ask you, is there sex after success?

(Laughs) I don't think so.

A sad thought. . . .

Yes. Yes.

I had dinner with a friend of mine last night, an Englishman who's splitting up with his girlfriend – a very beautiful model – because when they go out she always wants to pay. In a restaurant, she reaches for the bill. She's a feminist, she's gorgeous, she earns her own money, and she *insists*. He's very affronted.

I went through that period. My feeling is that one should try and aim for a peer relationship.

That means going Dutch, does it?

Not at all. I think that's quite gross. I hate going Dutch. I think there's nothing more offensive in a restaurant than everyone emptying their pockets and putting a pile in the middle of the table. But I do think that paying for someone's meal in a restaurant is *only* an indication on some level of wanting to say, I'm your equal.

I used to live with someone who got very upset in a restaurant when I ordered the wine. It was my feeling I knew *much* more about wine than he did, which he acknowledged. He didn't mind me buying the wine for the house, but I wasn't supposed to do it in front of anybody else. The issue was, at home nobody could see that we were peers, but in public I was supposed to acknowledge he was the superior person in the relationship. I think that's what galls women, not who pays the bill, I think that's irrelevant. If you can both afford to pay, who *cares* who pays for dinner? What is really relevant is that through certain customs women now feel as though their power is being taken away from them. Why can't I pay for your dinner? Why is it so affronting? Why does he get so upset – because it takes the power away from him?

I never meet these women who fight for the bill, it's maddening – they must be around somewhere! The thing I notice is that American men don't seem to *like* women very much. . . .

American men are scared of women, and I think something has happened here that hasn't yet happened in the rest of the world: the women's movement twenty years ago hit America with a great deal of force and has accomplished, some of us think, a *little* change. Some people say, a great deal of change – but change indeed has taken place. We are in the workforce in very large numbers, and some of us are creeping up through to the top. American men have had their consciousness raised in a way men in England and in Europe have not.

American men used to be very conscious about not saying 'girl', being conscious at a business lunch not to reach for the cheque if it was the other person who'd invited them – after all it's two *companies* having lunch, not two people having lunch! As a result of watching their Ps and Qs – and I think most people now do it without thinking about it – there was a distance put between men and women.

I also think women have had the opportunity to do something men have not had to do. Women were trained to stay at home, be nurturing, creative, take care of children. Then they went into the business world and learned how to take care of business. So most women who are successful are quite well-developed in both areas. Most men are not. Most men are little boys who are taught 'You have to go out there, be successful and take care of a family financially.' There are a lot of men who do not take care of their families *emotionally*, and a great chasm has grown up.

I think it's finally beginning to change. You're beginning to see American men saying, 'Wait a minute, I can be a parent too, why shouldn't I get off work and go home and see my kids? Why do I have to move sixteen times in ten years for the company? I won't do it, it's too dislocating for my family, therefore for me and my relationship.' I think the criteria for success is changing as a result of that. But the women's movement started it and we have a whole generation, maybe two generations of men and women that have suffered because of it. Those of us in our forties have experienced that again and again and again.

Yet you're still meeting resistance in the business world because you're a woman?

Absolutely no question about it. Men don't want women in the workplace, and the closer you get to the top the more scary it is. One by one they all get knocked off: fired, contracts not renewed, business changes. I really believe that women are never allowed on a team, anyway. One is allowed to function as a satellite around the sun, but you're never actually allowed on the team. You can shine, you can be a star, but stars always have to perform all the time. You're never allowed to make a mistake, you're never allowed to have a day when you're not quite up to par. Women have to be better at what they do, more talented, work harder.

My experience is that men become part of the club: after you pay your dues for a certain number of years, it doesn't matter any more how incompetent you are or how ordinary you are or how average you are – you're part of the club, everybody knows you, and men get sort of carried from job to job. That's not true for women, unless women are prepared to play the game.

In England we're all brought up to be modest and self-deprecating, aren't we?

Yes, to a fault. Absolutely.

So how did you become a success here?

How did I become immodest? (Laughs). Painfully, one learns how. I had dinner in England a few months ago with an old friend of mine I went to college with, who was actually quite successful. She runs a big clinic in London and she commented on the fact that she's become more English and more internal, turning inwards. In England even one's body language is more closed in. Twenty years of living in America has done the opposite to me, because here if you want to be successful or make yourself heard in a country with 250 million people, you can't be quiet and expect the culture to recognize you. If you want it, you have to take it.

James Clavell, the novelist, when he was writing *Shogun* for NBC and I was working on it, once said to me when we were having lunch, 'Why do you think you're successful?' and I said, 'Because I'm very good at what I do.' He said, 'That's rubbish – there are many people who're very good at what they do, and in this town there are many talented people.' He said, 'The reality is that we're just pirates, and the English have always been the *best* pirates.' I said, 'James, what does that mean?' 'That you walk into a room, see a pile of gold in the middle of it and say very politely, "Excuse me, everybody," and you walk to the front of the queue and take it – and before anybody notices you walk out of the room again.' Which was his description of those of us that are English who are successful here. I think it's true but I don't think one is necessarily polite when one does it. One may be charming but I think you have to *learn* to become very aggressive.

If you're modest in America, you finish up with a modest job?

If you *don't* walk in to your boss and say, 'I know there's a promotion available, I would like that job and these are the reasons why you should give it to me,' you're not going to get it. No one is going to notice you sitting there if you don't tell them you want it.

Success in England can be a slightly dirty word, like cheating at games – a bit unsporting?

Absolutely. At the same time, you're supposed to be successful.

Or a gallant failure! In England, that's quite a suitable thing to be. It's rather gentlemanly *almost* to make it: Bad luck, old chap!

Well that's very nice if somebody else is paying the bills, but it *is* acceptable. I also think in England you are acceptable because of your family, you're acceptable because of the club you belong to, you're acceptable because you play a good game of something or other. That's not true here, especially not true in this business, and very especially not true in Los Angeles.

But conversely, confidence and energy seem to be more important in America than intellect and ability. If you've got a good front, you get away with it?

I disagree with that. To be successful you have to have the intellect and the talent. I don't think it's possible to be successful and be stupid. The English often feel that if you have what we call in America, a lot of top-spin, it covers the fact that you don't know what you're doing. I mean people always used to say to me, 'Oh well, you winged it again.' Winging is walking into a meeting when you don't quite know what you're doing.... Occasionally we all wing it, but most of the time you have to know what you're doing. You might make it *look* as though you're winging it – it might make other people more comfortable to think that.

But you are judged by the amount of money you have?

In Los Angeles, in the movie business, you're judged by success in terms of money and your ability to generate a product that an audience want to see, which of course makes you rich because it sells. But yes, I think in essence, money.

You *are* what you earn?

To a very large extent.

That can be a sad consummation of a life, I suppose?

On some level, it's sad. On the other hand to be able to build yourself a mock Tudor house and drive a pink Rolls-Royce would horrify you or horrify me, but it's nice that you're able to do that – along with somebody who would have, in our judgement, better taste. If you're smart enough and you work hard enough to make a lot of money, why not be able to spend in any way you choose? Why have to conform to some other person's notion of what is OK?

Are you sweeping your children along with you – do they look upon England, for example, as a quaint place over the seas or as Mother's homeland?

It's interesting – my eldest daughter who's just turned fifteen spent one month in England and one month in France this summer. She loved England and can't wait to go back. The whole point of sending her was so she understood that her mother was a refugee who came to this country from another place for the same reason *everybody* comes to America – which is to find a better kind of life than they were able to have in their own country. I was certainly no exception to that. So I hope that by the time their education is finished and they leave home, which'll be within the next five years, they'll have some understanding that England is very much a part of their heritage, and who they are.

Can you see yourself escaping the fearful race and going back to England?

No, I don't think I could ever live in England again. I would find it too claustrophobic.

Because we're not striving all the time?

Because it's too hard to do business in England. On a day-to-day basis I would find it very frustrating. I'm used to picking up the phone and making things happen. To make things happen in England you have to be more patient and do things slowly. Patience is not my strong suit, and I'm not very good at doing things slowly.

You make it sound as though business is a substitute for living – there's more to life than doing business, surely?

Life is about doing business and life is about living it. Most successful people have what they do entwined in their life in such a way it's very difficult to separate them. That's the difference between people in England and people here. People in England do manage to lead very good separate lives, very interesting lives outside their work lives. I know a lot of people whose life is much more important than what they do. What they do, they *have* to do – because somebody has to pay the bills. That's not true on the whole for successful people, and it's less true in America. You need an enormous amount of energy to succeed here, and in England people don't have that level of energy. As you said before, it's not acceptable, it isn't polite. I'm sure if I went back to England I would not be considered very ladylike.

You're always reaching for the bill, that's your trouble!

I don't reach for the bill any more in England, I've become quite well-mannered! (Laughs.) I had a lot of business in Italy last year and the third day I was there I went to a dinner given by the people I was working with, and the interpreter stood on the doorstep and said, 'I want to tell you a quick story. The day you arrived they said, "My God, they've sent a woman." The second day they said, "Well she's OK, she's as good as the men." Today they said, "Three men." ' When I confronted them about this, jokingly, they said, 'You're really quite European until you do business, and then you become a very tough American businessman.' I found this stunning because I don't think I'm any different in my personal life than I am in my business life – though I think they *meant* it as a compliment.

But you want it both ways?

Of course, yes. I would like to be perceived as successful and straightforward and charming and feminine. That's all....

THE ENIGMA

I obeyed the church and, like poor Princess Margaret,
I suffered. . . .

Of all the many thousands of Britons who've settled in the United States, Dawn Langley Simmons has had perhaps the most unusual life. Born Gordon Langley Hall, her father was chauffeur to Vita Sackville-West and Harold Nicolson. Gordon left home for Canada and taught Indian children on the Ojibway Reservation; then in New York became a professional writer. He was penniless and ill in hospital when rescued by a distant, wealthy and eccentric cousin, Isabel Whitney, then in her seventies. For six years he lived in her forty-room mansion in New York; after her death she left him $2 million and the house on West 10th Street.

He bought a pink stucco villa in Charleston, South Carolina, and was 'adopted' by the actress Dame Margaret Rutherford and her husband Stringer Davis – thenceforward referred to as 'Mother Rutherford, Father Stringer'. He was still Gordon then, but after living as a man for more than thirty years, had a sex-change operation and was accepted by Charleston society as Dawn Pepita Hall. Her first lover was an aristocratic married neighbour, but she then fell in love with her cook's black boyfriend, a young mechanic called John-Paul Simmons.

Theirs was the first legal mixed marriage in South Carolina. British Sunday newspaper headlines said 'Royal Biographer Weds Black Butler'. Locals threatened to burn down the church, and she believes a contract was taken out on her life. She later discovered a white man trying to knife Natasha, the daughter to whom she says she had by then given birth.

She escaped Charleston's anger and went north; her black husband, with a history of mental illness, deserted her and ran off with a woman who had shot her own husband. He sold Dawn's paintings and antiques, dispersed or destroyed all her possessions. Penniless again, she moved to New York State where her divorced and schizophrenic husband returned to live with her in the small town of Hudson.

In dreams 'Mother' Margaret Rutherford, now dead, came to her on three nights saying, 'Help Lemuel, he's innocent.' The message meant nothing. Then three days later she saw a newspaper picture of Lemuel Smith, also black, a convicted murderer awaiting the electric chair on Death Row. She wrote, visited him in jail, became convinced of his innocence, started to hunt for clues to help defend his case like some Miss Marple – and is now engaged to marry him. . . .

I confess Mrs Dawn Pepita Manigault-Simmons was hard to assess. Having lived as a man for so long she must have fantasized a lot – and who can tell how many daydreams have now become reality? She has an air of sharp innocence, nobly tilting at social injustice – or perhaps merely lacking judgement and common sense. . . .

She arrived for dinner looking frail and old and walking rather carefully, but appeared – apart from faint five o'clock shadow – unassailably feminine. Natasha, a bright thirteen-year-old, did not resemble her; she had purple eyeshadow around alert pale eyes, and the remains of black nail polish. It seemed she took most of the household decisions.

Their home in Hudson, once a handsome townhouse, was a crumbling red-brick pile at the poorer end of town. One room downstairs was furnished with worn rugs, broken armchairs, knick-knacks and mementos in glass cabinets. The other rooms were unfurnished: rotting floorboards, peeling walls, sagging doors. The smell of animals was overpowering. When I asked for a loo I was directed to a railway station two blocks away. . . .

Later Dawn Langley Simmons, established and successful author freshly back-combed from the hairdresser, sat in her decaying old house and name-dropped happily. A large black man shambled in, asking for his coffee; this was the disturbed John-Paul. Natasha dealt with him sternly, like a nanny, handed over a battered copper kettle and sent him upstairs to his room.

That house has now been sold, Mrs Langley Simmons writes; she has bought 'a fully-restored Federal townhouse in Charleston complete with Mr James my old butler and Joannie, the maid who looks like a lady prize-fighter. . . .'

═══

When I was born the midwife simply didn't know how to register this poor child. My natural mother's brother had kicked her in the stomach before I was born. We had this great history of twins; I should have been twins. The midwife didn't know if it was a little boy or a little girl and in England the law was, you automatically registered the child as a boy – with dire results.

It wasn't too bad when I was small, but as I grew older and went to school I could never go to the bathroom like other children, I used to run home. My voice never broke and I liked dolls. At a certain age there was this very irregular menstruation. When I was seventeen I sold up everything

– I had an apartment of antiques because I've always been a great one for buying stuff – and got enough money to go to America. It was either that or look after my Aunt Gertrude Hall, and everybody was afraid of her – she was the one who on her golden wedding day announced she was still a virgin, and broke up the entire party!

I came to this country and I was going to my much-married aunt in Detroit. I got as far as the border and my uncle was killed that night in a hit-and-run accident. I had no sponsor and was stranded in Windsor, Ontario. I didn't want to go back to England and become a failure, having to send for the fare home because I'd only got a one-way ticket. By putting my age on I managed to get a job as a teacher on an Indian reservation, and out of that came *Me Papoose Sitter* and three Indian books.

Just like Vita Sackville-West, I go into my writing room at ten o'clock in the morning. Harold Nicolson told me when I was six years old to apply my bottom to the seat of a chair, and I would work just as Vita worked until one o'clock, and then I ate. Then I'd do some gardening, or in Hudson I usually trot up the street and see one or two of my friends. I haven't done that much lately because I've become very controversial.

Miss Whitney left you a house and $2 million, most of it invested in property – how did you get through it all?

Well a great deal of the money was in the big house in New York and what happened was, Isabel had the habit of employing people that she almost picked up on the street. This major-domo she had, this Sicilian had worked for a big auction gallery in New York and came down to the Whitney house to hang tapestries, and she decided that he should be my bodyguard and run things for us. He took over the entire house and when she died he made my life so miserable. I couldn't have anybody to the house – he was always saying they were after my money, or something like that. I went to Charleston almost in desperation. I left him in the big house I was converting into apartments and I don't know how we lost that house, but we did.

In Charleston most of the money was in the property. I bought the house down there with the money from my best-seller, *Golden Boats from Burma*, and then when John-Paul came along, he had four boats, three motor cars. I'd be away on a trip and come back and he'd been selling things out of the house, once he caught on to it. That place was like a museum – you'd only got to take a miniature off the wall and go out and get a thousand dollars. When we went down to Mosquito Creek, which is where the black people kept their boats, one of the men said, 'John-Paul came down with this marvellous boat on Friday and on Sunday it was all smashed up.' I was very much in love with John-Paul.

How long before you realized he was schizophrenic?

I realized what John-Paul was before I married him. We came up to New York and they dug all the engagement pictures and showed them on TV. We stayed at a hotel where I had stayed for years and all the staff were black and John-Paul had a terrible to-do there, whether he was on drugs I don't know, but he hit me and kicked me in front of everybody, and a lot of the money disappeared from the room. He blamed people at the hotel. It was awful. Then he'd buy his mother all this furniture, he'd furnish her house and I would get a call from a store in Charleston to say, 'You've got to co-sign.' They had me over a barrel. One of my friends gave me a motor car as a wedding present and two days later I asked John-Paul, 'Where's my car?' and he said, 'Oh Brother Joe wanted it so I gave it to him, I didn't think you needed it – you don't drive.' What did Brother Joe do? He went and traded it in for a Cadillac.

But it must have been registered in your name? It's not as though you were bedridden or incapable?

No, but I hadn't had much experience with men.

Come on, you were full-grown, you'd travelled. . . .

No, I lived mostly in my books. I wrote on the top floor. Isabel never gave you any money unless she found it in a secret drawer. Everything had to be kind of Jane Eyre.

What sort of a person was Miss Whitney?

She was an ageless lady, a very good painter and she'd been a suffragette. The man who wanted to marry her was the richest man in the world, Mr Gulbenkian, who founded the museum in Lisbon. Her sister wouldn't allow her to marry him because she said his name reminded her of oranges.

I saw everybody as a character in a book, and John-Paul was a charmer. Physically it was a good marriage. Even when he was living with Mrs Benson, every time Natasha went to Sunday school he was right down at my house wanting to go to bed with me – that wasn't the trouble. I think it's very sad to see him now, he has no interest in sex, he lies in bed most of the day. He's got very fat and people say to me they can't believe it because he was so good-looking. You have to talk to him sometimes half a dozen times before it registers. It's sad – I mean, there *had* to be something there. He's been twenty-one times to the mental hospital. He's been in jail.

He used to get in people's houses in Catskill and paint pictures of nude ladies and gentlemen on people's dining-room walls, and they'd haul him off to jail.

Your daughter is enchanting, but is she your natural daughter? She's not adopted?

She was born in Philadelphia. There's the wonderful scene in Mother Rutherford's biography in which Nurse Hardy, the Catholic nurse who was present, says that she was sent up to be private nurse for Gordon Langley and when she went into the room and pulled back the sheet – there was the body of a beautiful woman! She thought she'd seen a miracle, it was as simple as that.

You're obviously comfortable, living as a woman....

I think I've been a good mother. I think Natasha is proof. She grew up properly.

In marrying a black you were perhaps ahead of your time?

It would be nothing today. Nothing. Now there are plenty of mixed marriages but when I married John-Paul and went to get the licence the Jewish registrar had two filing cabinets, one was black and the other white, and he said, 'Now I suppose I'll have to start another one for you!' He said, 'My dear, I've *always* been in the minority – welcome to the minority!' After the marriage I had to go into another hospital because I had to have a surgical operation. There were four other women there with the same thing and I remember the black nurse looking at me and saying, 'Honey, no man is worth it.' I've often thought of that!

I was going through such awful things with this racial thing in the South and I was trying to keep myself alive and keep this child alive. Natasha was born in '71. The Simmons family had never had a light-skinned child in their family and when she was born she had blue eyes! I won't tell you what John-Paul said! He's always been very outspoken and he said, 'Whoever did see a blue-eyed nigger?'

In England you'd just be a face that doesn't quite fit, but here your position's been quite perilous?

It *was* in Charleston of course, and it has been in Hudson after coming out for Lemuel Smith. I was threatened on the streets of Hudson by people saying, 'Did I want to end up like Karen Silkwood? Did I want to be another woman pushed under a train?' Natasha was threatened at St Mary's Academy where she went to school – a Catholic school. When Lemuel was on Death Row, a boy at school told her they should put Lemuel in the electric chair and sit her mother on his lap and kill them both at the same time. The child used to come home with these stories.

Then last January I was in Mr Tanner's antique shop and he said, 'It's slippery, don't walk home in the road,' and I didn't, but I was found on the sidewalk close to a house with a Correction Officer still in uniform bending over me. I had a broken shoulder, a broken arm. A reporter from the *Times Union* in Albany came along just at that moment in his sports car and I think he saved my life because he followed the ambulance and everything. Really it has been *very* dangerous coming out for this man, because a lot of people have said that this little housewife could bring down the whole of the New York State Department of Correction.

You believe that was an attempt on your life?

Oh yes, I think so. It's been very frightening. A few weeks ago the Mayor of Charleston wrote to me and said, 'Wasn't it time I ended my exile and came home?'

All is forgiven, down South? He's a black man, is he?

No he's white, but the Police Chief is now black – he rides around Charleston on roller skates. Charleston has changed very much in the last ten years.

So it would seem.

Natasha and I go there all the time for vacations and she cannot understand why in Charleston people, black and white, run out to me for autographs. I'm sort of a celebrity down there, and very well thought of by black people.

In fact you've made a helluva mess of things, one way and another?

Well I have and I haven't. Look at Natasha, you wouldn't say she was a mess. I've been a good mother. All I ever wanted to be was a housewife and a mother. I have a stepson in Charleston who is older than Natasha. His mother was a chronic alcoholic and still is. I had to go and see her in hospital and she was in an oxygen tent and I was so upset for this illegitimate baby I said, 'He has to have someone's name.' My mother-in-law who's a minister's wife said to me, 'Dawn Pepita, you should leave that child on the street where it belongs.' I looked at her and I said, 'I'm British, I couldn't *possibly* do that.'

I went and had his name made officially Simmons. You can do that over here. So years later Dear Abby in her column was writing about stepmothers. All these stepmothers were complaining, so I wrote her a letter and said that Barry had been a great blessing to me, he was an adorable boy. I went to see him every time I went to Charleston. So Dear Abby wrote, 'This is one stepmother who has earned her place in heaven.' I thought it was very beautiful.

In my personal life maybe I loved not wisely but too well. Everybody thinks I'm crazy but I'm taking John-Paul back and putting him in a trailer caravan and giving him the first down-payment. He has money from the Government every month and there's no reason why he shouldn't be able to survive.

You've had a most extraordinary life here in the States. It seems you've broken every taboo – crossing racial lines and sexual barriers. Was marrying a black your worst infringement of the rules?

It was, in Charleston, but it wasn't to Mother Rutherford. She said a man worth lying down with was worth standing up for. I obeyed the church and, like poor Princess Margaret, I suffered. As simple as that.

You suffered ostracism?

Yes, in a way. The women's clinic in Baltimore where I was going to get my mind prepared for a possible marriage said that the thing most necessary for me was to fall in love with somebody who'd give a quiet and a balanced Severn. Somebody said the other day, 'Whatever happens to you you always seem to have the last laugh.' It's been that kind of life.

You've always bounced back – yet much of what's happened may have been your own fault ...

Yes, in a way. The women's clinic in Baltimore where I was going to get my mind prepared for a possible marriage said that the thing most necessary for me was to fall in love with somebody who'd give a quiet and a balance life. . . . I'd been a romantic all my life. I was brought up on the classics but of course I didn't have a normal life as a child and so I've never fallen in love with the people that conventionally I *should* have fallen in love with.

I don't quite understand why, when you didn't know where to go, you came north to this cold, mountainous area?

I was desperate. The Simmonses were threatening to kidnap the baby – they'd never had a white-skinned baby in the family and they wanted her. My money was going and they didn't want me without the money, they'd all had everything they could out of me.

I'd always been very independent and I certainly wasn't going home to

England to have my family support us. Mother was dying – she died when Natasha was a small baby, and Father Stringer died of a broken heart, you might say. I was desperate to know what to do, and they had this contract on my life and Suellen Austin came to me and said, 'You've got to get out of Charleston, they're going to kill you.' I said, 'They've got the house, they've got everything.' That night I heard a crash upstairs and I went up and there was a man with a knife over the baby.

You do seem to have a behaviour pattern here, do you not? Two black men, both unbalanced in a sort of way, one after the other. You're chasing impossible causes?

In the beginning, Mother Rutherford came to me in a dream and said, 'Go and help Lemuel, he's innocent.' The only Lemuel was in the Book of Proverbs and in *Gulliver's Travels*. She was absolutely fascinated with Correction Officers and guards, she went to prison every Sunday to read to them. Then when I met Lemuel it was the only kindness I'd known for such a long time. When we first knew him in jail it was like visiting somebody in a cafeteria. He was so good to Natasha – they had this wonderful repartee. Then of course when he got on Death Row it was more like a meeting of minds. He'll never come out, I know that, but I shall do what I can for him.

With American justice, as Harold Nicolson once said to me, 'Don't ever try to understand it, you never will,' and although they struck down the death penalty in this State and he's off Death Row, he was then sentenced in the kangaroo court to fifteen years with loss of all privileges. He couldn't get a cigarette, he can't even get soap, he can't get anything. And now he's coming up to re-sentencing again and the prosecutor is coming back into the story and trying to get the death penalty back. So he could be back on Death Row. It's an impossible situation, but I will help him to the end.

Meanwhile here in Hudson you're living, let's face it, in some squalor?

Yes.

This room isn't too bad but I've been upstairs and the smell of those animals made my eyes water. . . .

Unfortunately when we took over this house, I mean it was like going to Sissinghurst. . . .

Well, not *quite*!

In the beginning it *was* like going to Sissinghurst, I mean this is a fine Federal house and I'll do very well with it when we re-sell and go back to

Charleston, where I have my own butler to run things. I just can't write books and do everything and have a mentally sick person in the house with whom I cannot cope. My ex-husband has his own apartment because no one else would have him, so I just had to do the best I could for him.

So the Southerners were quite unkind to you, you came up to the North – the liberal North – and they've been even *more* unkind?

Yes, everything is different in the North. The Southern blacks are very different to the Northern blacks. The Southern blacks want to buy their own houses in Charleston and they're always working. Up here, unfortunately, so many black families have been on Welfare for three generations, with no intention of working. I was the only white woman who worked with Mrs Martin Luther King in the nurses' strike down there, and Charleston never forgave me. I was also the first white woman in Charleston to insist that her cook pay Social Security. When I said to her, 'Where's your Social Security card?' the woman didn't know what I was talking about! And I was told by Peter Manigault's mother that all I had to do was give them twelve dollars a week, and they would take what they wanted out of the refrigerator. But that wasn't the way I'd been brought up, and I clashed from the moment that I went down there. So when I see a young black man messed up with drugs and things I want to give him a good shaking and say, 'Look, I didn't get broken shoulders and arms and things for the likes of you, so shape up!' It makes me very cross, but if I go down there now it's different – all the black people are getting wonderful jobs in hotels.

So you think you've been treated badly in America?

I could have been treated better, but in Charleston I *did* break their rules and Charleston is still living in the seventeenth century. It's changed now a great deal because it's one of the few cities in America that really is in the black; all the construction is coming in, all the tourists are coming in. Ten years ago you would never see a tourist in the street in a bikini, but I did last year.

You've had your triumphs and your tragedies but nevertheless, taken for all in all, you'd rather stay here than go back to England?

I wish I *had* thought of going back to England. I'd have gone back when Mother Rutherford had been so sick and Father Stringer was struggling to nurse her. I wish that it had been possible to have gone, but I was fighting this thing in Charleston to save my home and my furniture. I had a husband who was never home, who was always in somebody else's bed, and Natasha came and my in-laws were threatening to kidnap her. I was trying to keep myself going, just as Mother and Father were trying to do the same thing at Elm Close, and none of us really succeeded.

Sometimes when I'm lonely, I long for the sea, I long for Hastings – I mean I was married to John-Paul the second time in Hastings. I want to take Natasha home and show her Heathfield Market and things like that – that was always my great joy on Tuesdays. When I go back I'll stay in Hastings and go up to the market. My godmother lives in Brighton. Flora Robson, who died in Brighton, she wrote me such a lovely piece about Mother. And I have the stuffed kangaroo that the people of Australia gave to Mother, it's sitting in an armchair. I've been a fish out of water in Hudson for two and a half years. I did think of going back when Natasha was a child, but it would have meant living a bit on my family and I'm too proud to do that. I remembered that my sister came down to the little house I'd found and said, 'We'll hang a curtain here,' and 'I've got the right curtains to put *there*.' I'm a person in my own right and I wasn't ready to have somebody tell me what to do. Of course Natasha is the image of my sister, she's very self-opinionated.

She's much older and more responsible than you, isn't she?

Yes she's getting very responsible, she knows just what clothes to wear and everything. She's running me very well.

I'm out of step, but a lot of people think Tony Benn is out of step. I don't, but other people do. He's Mother's cousin, he always writes to me and begins 'Dear cousin Dawn'. I send him clippings on American politics and that, to the House of Commons. He's been extremely kind to me.

What would you do differently, the second time around?

Well I couldn't have had better parents, they were wonderful. Sometimes I wish I'd married into Charleston society, because I would have revolutionized it. That's the only thing that I wish I had done – I would have been a female Tony Benn down there! But when I go home to Charleston I'm going to lead a very different life. I'm going to write the book about the fourteen months on Death Row. I'm going to let Mr James run things while I sit at the typewriter. Mr James is my old butler. He's in Charleston waiting for the old Missis to come home.

He hasn't been sentenced to death, has he?

Oh no, he's a deacon of the church. When he served the soup his watch chain used to go backwards and forwards, backwards and forwards. Oh, he's a character!

How would John-Paul get on with Lemuel, should you get him off?

Well, he wouldn't. John-Paul finally realized that the other day, and said, 'Are you really going to marry him?' I'm one of these people who seem to finish up with ministers' sons. . . .

And lost causes?

Lost causes, this whole social reformer bit comes out at certain times, but I'm happiest polishing and dusting and working with antiques and writing.

You were a man who became a woman; do you find that as an author you grow to believe your own fantasies?

I think I always had fantasies, because I *had* to live in a fantasy. The first thing I ever wrote, which was never published, was called *The Green Orchard*, but it was really me. I was always the ugly sister with the beautiful mother who did not want to grow old. . . .

THE ENTREPRENEUR

*About half-a-million dollars in cash
went through my bed. . . .*

Richard Wrigley is small, smiling and unnoticeable. He grew up in Manchester, had a paper-round at thirteen, left school at sixteen; now thirty-eight, he still seems an ingratiating and rumpled teenager with tousled red hair who's slept in his clothes. All his possessions move around the world in one battered suitcase. To join me for dinner he was braced to visit a boutique for a new outfit – but just in time found some old clothes in a friend's flat which fitted adequately. . . .

With no financial background and no visible means of support other than his bouncy enthusiasm, he has created a vast million-dollar real-ale brewery in Manhattan's Soho, just off Broadway, and runs the new $11-million ice rink in Central Park. I'm still not *quite* sure how he's done it. . . .

═══

The weather was so perfect I thought: maybe I'll make another film – I'll wander round New York and film bodies and buildings. It seemed a very *physical* city. So I got hold of a Bolex, because it's the only one I know how to operate, and wandered round New York filming and came across this skating rink in Central Park which wasn't being used in the summer. I decided to organize a roller-skating party – it sort of typified everything I wanted to show about New York.

I rang the Commissioner of Parks and got on well with him. He decided I was just what he needed because he had too many roller-skaters in Central Park. He decided to encourage me, but only allowed me to have my party if I would do six weeks of roller skating at this rink, thereby getting all the skaters off the paths in the park.

So I commuted backwards and forwards about ten times during June and July and opened at the end of July and did this series of events. People like Gloria Gaynor came down. I got a lot of musical people, I had a very good sound system, I put up big theatrical lighting round the rink and it became the biggest open roller-disco in the world. This was in '79. It actually started the roller-skating boom, quite inadvertently. After that about ten roller-discos sprang up in New York and scattered around the world.

53

That turned out to be a money-loser because the weather was awful. It kept raining, but in between the rain we had these wonderful events. And it was my money – I'd rented it from them, plus I paid for all this lighting and stuff. I'd just sold my house in London, in Fulham – actually, my girlfriend had taken me to court and forced the sale of the property, so I took the money. At that time you couldn't take money out of England so I got all the cash, put it in a big paper bag, got a plane and arrived in New York with this carrier-bag full of notes.

I went down Park Avenue and thought, Well I'd better put this in a bank. I went to about five banks, wandered in and they sat me down and said, 'How can we help you?' I showed them my bag and said, I'd like to deposit this cash. *Boomf* – I was out the door! They thought I'd robbed a bank somewhere. I was astonished, I was very offended. I ended up staying with a friend, stuck the money under the bed, used it for this roller-skating thing, *lost* it in the roller skating and was stuck in New York with about fifty pence to my name. I was cheating on the subways, I was so broke.

In the meantime the Commissioner of Parks was impressed by the way I'd run these events. I'd paid everybody off and I owed nothing. People don't *do* that in New York. If you're losing money you just disappear – but I paid everybody! He got such good reports about the atmosphere, because normally in New York people are very segregated. You don't get different types of people mixing very easily, although you see every type of person you could imagine, but they don't really mix very well – there's quite a subtle hierarchy.

They're not very good at *running* things because they think security is something you do with force. They don't think it's something you do by organizing yourself well, so if you've got an event like I had where you get maybe several thousand kids skating, they'd have big bouncers all round the place. I didn't do that. If somebody did something that I didn't like I just went up and tapped them on the shoulder and said, 'Look I'm sorry but this is my rink and I really don't think that's what you should be doing.' And they responded.

With a punch in the mouth?

No – but we used to take guns and knives off people! I remember once we had an all-night party going; at one o'clock in the morning forty kids arrived from the Bronx on their skates and started climbing the fence. We were full and the security people came to me and said, 'We're not staying there, it's too dangerous, we're going.' I'm very naïve, so I said, 'That's not happening in *my* rink!'

I toddled down there and stood in front of the fence these kids are coming over and said, 'I'm sorry – you can't come in.' They started screaming at me in Spanish and I said, 'Look, I don't understand Spanish' – though I did actually – 'if you'd care to speak English I'll discuss it, but you're not coming in.' I stood there for twenty minutes just reiterating my point, holding my ground and after a while their girlfriends at the back are tapping them on the shoulders saying, 'He doesn't speak Spanish.' They all stood there and looked at me. I said, 'We're really very full, it's dangerous.' Then the kids that'd climbed in started climbing out: they toddled off into the night. They just went.

I remember one night coming out when I had a few thousand dollars in my pocket, because even when I ran the rink I didn't have a bank account. Because I'd started without a bank account I couldn't *open* a bank account, so about half a million dollars in cash went through by bed!

I had a friend visiting from England and I asked him to take a carrier-bag for me as I had so many to carry. We got to a restaurant and he said, 'What's in that?' I said, '$20,000.' He just about fainted on the spot! Point is, I couldn't put it in a bank 'cos the bank wouldn't open an account for me because I didn't *exist*.

So one night I had a few thousand dollars in my back pocket and I went out of the back end of the rink, which I never did. It was raining and the ground was quite slippery. As I walked down to the bottom of the path a big black guy came up and said, 'You got any money?' I thought, Oh God, this is it, no one'll see me here. But I also thought, Well I'm not going to give it to him. So I said, 'No!'

He said, 'You motherfuckin' white pig.' I was so surprised he'd been rude to me I said, 'Are you talking about me specifically or the white race in general?' It just floored him! He started cursing and swearing. I walked on slowly – I couldn't run, it was quite wet and I had rubber shoes on. We engaged in this conversation and I walked out of the park, with him walking along beside me.

Discussing semantics?

He was cursing, but in actual fact he'd completely forgotten that he'd wanted money. A couple of hundred yards on a police car cruised by – and he was gone like a shadow, back into the bushes. The police said, 'You've got a guardian angel on your shoulder.' I've always had luck. I have this certain naïvety, I'll walk right into the middle of something because I believe I'll be able to work it out.

But Central Park at midnight is pushing it a bit, isn't it? It's like breezing into Brixton on a Saturday night and assuming all will be well!

I didn't think about it. It just worked. Afterwards I thought – that was a really good atmosphere. Parents would come up to me and say, 'We don't mind sending our daughter to your rink.' A lot of young kids would come at night and the parents were very calm about it. I realized afterwards there's so much paranoia about violence in New York, and the violence is actually very predictable. They respond so quickly to the most elementary discipline here, it's amazing. They're just used to having *no* discipline.

I then did a season of ice skating. I was stuck in the city, I didn't have any money – not even the money to go home because I'd blown it all, really. The Commissioner said, 'Would you like to take over the rink permanently, or try ice skating?' He didn't know I had no money, he thought I was some sort of eccentric English millionaire. They think everyone's related to the Queen.

So they wanted me to take the rink over. We were having these big discussions. Finally I took it over on a very good deal for both of us, with no money, and borrowed about $5,000 off a couple of friends. It was ten days before Christmas. I took over on a Saturday morning. There were forty-six staff, so I fired them, re-employed eighteen who I thought knew what they were doing. I'd never run an ice-skating rink and I had a huge battle with the unions who tried to stick sugar in the petrol tank of the ice-scraper and do everything they could to wreck it. It was the municipal civil servants-type union. I'd fired them from the rink but they didn't lose their jobs, they just got redeployed. While I was doing this I discovered the Commissioner's no fool, he knew I'd fire them when he *couldn't* fire them. Before I took the rink over, the staff were pretty appalling, the majority were ex-Vietnam war vets and were either on drugs or on a drug to get them *off* drugs. They were extremely erratic. They'd come in in the morning completely high and by the afternoon they'd be absolutely crazy....

And these were the good guys?

These were the good guys! The policy of the city was to employ people like that – and they were actually all nice guys but they were the victims of rather severe circumstances, and the supervisors were drunk all the time.

The year before there'd been shootings going on at the rink and in one fell swoop I'd just cleared it out. I went through this month of horrendous battles where everybody from every corner was coming at me – but the rink doubled its turnover, doubled its attendance. I cut prices for kids, did all sorts of strange things, had all sorts of events going, put on good music. I had Senators coming down saying, 'The Commissioner says he's going to give you the whole of Central Park!'

Did you have to put out a lot of money?

No all I did was – I had this lighting equipment from the roller skating that I'd made my last payment on, and it'd cleaned me out of money, so I just painted it myself with a couple of the guys. We were in there at nights, painting. I went to various concerts here to see the way they organized things. I saw the way they did it: they have these big guys and if some kid does something wrong, about five bouncers would converge and pulverize him. Often they'd get the wrong person – *that* was their idea of organizing a concert!

The big promoter of concerts used to come down to the rink, because every summer we put on concerts there. Effectively, I had got rid of him by coming in, and he's the biggest promoter, he's got a hold on New York. No rock concert can go into Madison Square Garden without him. He used to come down and say 'Anybody bothering you?' And I'd say, 'Well.....' And he'd say, 'Fifty dollars and they're gone!'

How would he have spent that fifty dollars?

He'd get some heavy to do it. He's a little guy – you go into his office and there's his six-foot portrait behind the desk.

The only problem I had with the rink were the white kids from middle-class families in Queens. The black kids would come in and shout and scream, but they were ok. The Puerto Rican kids had no brains, but were totally predictable. The white kids were dangerous because for some reason you assumed they had *some* sort of sense, or brains – maybe because I'm English and we're generally white – but in fact they're worse. They get drunk more, they do more drugs, they're brainless beyond belief. It's just that the parents of these kids have had everything, and they'd been doing pot since they were twelve.

We had a fire ... some of these kids would come and skate and we'd throw them out and they'd come back after setting fire to us and say, 'We'd like to skate again.' One night one of them had a litre bottle and threw it off the balcony outside the park, straight into the middle of the rink where the skaters were. I chased him out of the park and I said to the kids, 'If you ever see him again....' After a while you know who they are. You look at their eyes and you know, this kid's up to something.

I used to wander round the terraces and I'd see a kid with a certain look and I'd know he'd stolen something, so I'd get a skate-guard to tab him and then go into the back toilets and find a wallet floating around in the loo. I think sometimes if you're used to dealing with the public you develop a sixth sense. You tend to know what's going on, you can predict it. The whole point is, every gang has a leader, so you separate them. I'd train the skate-guards to spot the leader and then just take him away and sort of deal with him. Then the rest of them are just very very meek and mild.

One occasion we had two girls, very well dressed, very respectable-looking girls and they just wouldn't conform to anything, so I told them, 'If you don't leave the rink now I'm going to stop everyone skating and I'm going to announce on the public address system your names and *why* I've stopped everybody skating.' They just laughed and said, 'You wouldn't do it,' and off they went and carried on doing their thing. So I stopped all the skating and ordered everybody off the ice. I very politely explained who the people were that were responsible. The two girls absolutely died, they were scream-ing at me, and they left the rink. They came back a week later and apol-ogized and said they realized I did the right thing. I was really quite touched. I thought, Well, it sort of paid off. It had an effect with the public because they realized you can't mess with this person, he's going to do what he says he's going to do, so it established a certain order of respect and it also established that I was the boss in the rink, I wasn't some anonymous government person you could mess around with.

But you're the antithesis of a heavy, of a marine sergeant-major: you're small and affable and smiling and foreign.

Right, right, right! I think what you do is, you establish a set of rules and you follow those rules, and people tend to respond. My Father was very good at that, he was a specialist at problem children and maybe I picked up a little bit from him.

Have you ever been injured?

I got attacked once, at another rink in Brooklyn. . . .

Tends to be a bit permanent, the way they attack you here?

It was actually twice in Brooklyn, and within three days. I went to help somebody out at the rink there. I was talking to a white girl and I felt this tap on my shoulder. I turned round and it was this foaming six-foot-six black giant. If he'd had a weapon I'd have been killed.

What was his worry?

It was his girlfriend and she was having an affair with a white fellow. He saw me talking to her and it was like – This is the guy, so *kill!* That's how violence is in New York – it just sort of happens suddenly.

Spontaneous combustion?

Right – straight between the eyes. Insanity is so close to the surface here. You won't see it in London but here you can walk down the street and people will just start screaming. It isn't that they're insane, it's the *environ-ment* that's insane – they just happen to be a weak link. It's like the eruption of a volcano; it could be a perfectly sane person but the veneer is too thin and they explode.

The Cop: Peter Vanson

The Superwoman: Jane Deknatel

The Enigma: Dawn Langley Simmons

The Entrepreneur: Richard Wrigley

The Poker Player: Mike Haywood

The *Vogue* Editor: Shirley Lord

The Tycoon: Sir Gordon White

The Phenomenon: Joan Collins

The Actress: Edana Romney

The Ecologist: Dr Geoffrey Stanford

The Personality: Pamela Mason

In London you'd care for him and call an ambulance, but here he's just another of those flaky people?

That's right. I mean every evening you can step over poor people. When I first came here if somebody asked for money I'd go through a whole dilemma because I felt an obligation to give them what I had – and then I realized in one instance the same chap with the same rags on and with the same story asked me every day, and he was making a fortune. Unfortunately it colours your whole view because there might be a genuine case. I know one chap in the park stopped me and I just felt he was genuine so I gave him a few dollars to get some breakfast and said, 'If you'd like to work you can come back to the rink later.' He showed up, worked for four days. He was called Billy. We paid him, and he disappeared. Then a year later I bumped into him again. He didn't remember me but he had the same story. He just lived in Central Park.

I was attacked by an Irishman once who cornered me in the back of a building. I'd never fought anybody in my life. I can be very aggressive verbally but I've never seen the point in belting somebody. Fortunately neither the Irishman nor the black had weapons. The Irishman was working for me and I'd paid him; he'd given me a quote that he was going to lose money on, but it was a fixed-price job. He just couldn't deal with the situation he'd got himself into, so instead of talking about it . . . he picked me up and threw me down a flight of stairs. Fortunately I just bounced on my feet.

With the black guy I don't know what happened, but two other black guys came and hauled him off. I find the black communities within themselves are very good. They take care of themselves, they're actually a lot easier to deal with than the whites. They've got much more respect, they're much more family-oriented, they're really OK with whites. If you just treat them as real people, they're no problem. A lot of them are very aware they have limitations. I have two black guys working for me on the building and one of them, Tim, will come and say, 'Look, if you just explain so I can understand, I'll try, I'll get it. . . .'

The white kids'll just stomp around and they don't try to learn. They haven't learned *how* to learn. The West Indians are all very good here. There's even the hierarchy within the black communities, because the West Indians think they have class and the black Americans don't have class. You have these little differences in the black community.

The Puerto Ricans are incredible. They're so dumb, it's ridiculous. A lot of them don't speak English, they don't even speak Spanish properly. Their vocabulary consists of about twenty-five words. You stand there and watch one of them try to communicate and you can see his brain start to boil. He can't get it out in Spanish, he can't get it out in English. They have this macho thing where all that counts is your body. You're not a man if you haven't got a gun. A sixteen-year-old carries a .22 pistol, a seventeen-year-old's got a .38, the eighteen-year-old's got a .357 magnum. They shoot themselves in the knees and feet half the time. They go to the dance halls and give their guns to girlfriends who put them in their bags, because girls generally aren't stopped and checked.

I used to go out with a Dominican girl called Gigi, and it was kind of bizarre. She was from the Upper West Side, from the real Spanish side, and I was seduced by these big brown eyes and beautiful black hair. She looked like a Brazilian. She was a great ice-skater, so in the midst of all the madness that was going on, this little angel appeared.

She came to England with me and went to pieces because people were too relaxed, too calm, there was no music. She had to have music all the time. My friends were too nice, the country was too green, she just absolutely flipped. People were too relaxed, too quiet, too attentive, too willing to talk without all the madness going on. She got very unnerved by it all, so I put her on a plane and sent her back. Her family locked her up for three weeks because she'd disgraced them by not coming back with me. It was a big dishonour.

I came back to New York, and after the three weeks two punk friends of mine arrived from London: one was a fashion designer and one a fabric designer with pink and green hair and so on. I decided I was going round to see Gigi to try and sort this out, and without thinking I took these two girls with me. Her parents didn't know what had hit them, with these two punkettes. We took a couple of bottles of champagne to try and relax the tension, and of course the parents had never had champagne in their lives and got quite drunk. Gigi slipped out the back way and went to dance at Roseland with somebody else, so I decided to go to Roseland and talk to her. I took my two punk friends and we were the only whites among two thousand Puerto Ricans! When they dance it's incredible. The next day we were walking up Columbus Avenue and all these Puerto Rican kids stopped us and said, 'Hey man, you were great! Wish we could dance like you!' Next day at the rink some kids said to me, 'Hey man, I gotta get some bucks – how do you *get* those women! Wow!' Dancing really is their only means of expression.

Gigi's whole family ended up working for me in the rink. I could trust them with cash or anything because they were a family. They were Dominicans and they considered themselves very different from the Puerto Ricans, who seem to go crazy when they're presented with materiality. They have five TVs, six cameras, ten hi-fis. They have to have these material things.

There's now a greater percentage of blacks and Puerto Ricans and Spanish in New York than whites, so the balance has gone over. Kennedy decided he wanted to appeal to the Third World, so they have progressively made it easier for Central Americans to get in and harder for Europeans. That's why there's this massive influx. Then Castro dropped off all his weirdos from the jails and hospitals. It's a major problem because they all end up in New York. Now they go backwards and forwards between Miami and New York, according to the weather. They reckon that half a million El Salvadoreans have come into Greater New York and the area just can't handle this influx. In the old days you had the different immigrant communities: Russians, Italian, Irish. The blacks consider themselves considerably above the Puerto Ricans. The upper middle-class blacks try to emulate your middle-class whites so even within the black community they get rejected by a lot of other blacks because they get this order of lighter skins. You'll still get a black business guy who's got his hair straightened out; he dresses very well – but he's really emulating your white stockbroker.

I don't like living here. I enjoy my involvement, but this is not a city in which to live – it's an insane asylum. It's wonderful to visit crazy people, but you don't want it *all* the time. I've never had a job, I've never had a routine. I'm thirty-eight, I've never gone through the normal things people go through, I don't have any concept of time in that sense. I've travelled enormously and I've been in eighty-five countries since I was sixteen. I've been constantly roaming around the world.

You travel light, I suspect?

I'll give you a classic example: none of these clothes I'm wearing are mine. I didn't have time to go home so I popped round the corner to a friend, dived in the shower and he turned out to be exactly the same size as me.... I was going to a boutique down the road to buy a set of clothes. That's how I tend to accumulate clothes. Everything I possess will literally go in one suitcase. As an individual, I'm completely mobile.

America actually needs people like me. They need more small breweries to start up in the States. I'm absolutely no threat – though I've got the biggest horses, Shire horses. We're the Manhattan Brewing Company. The beer's going to be called Manhattan Gold. The first brewery ever built in the States was built in Lower Manhattan in 1632 so I'm re-creating the art of brewing in America at the source. I'm going to build a hundred breweries. I have this master plan.

My partner is a chap from Brooklyn, but America's a funny place because you actually don't *need* money here. I can prove that because I blew my money in the first few weeks and started from nothing. You need perseverance and you need to pay attention to detail. You must *not* use advertising agencies, PR consultants or any professionals – they'll kill you because they'll invent such God-awful explanations as to why you are doing what you're doing that they'll so distort the facts you'll get lost and never be able to live through it. Do it yourself. Don't get involved.

I've never really lost anybody any money. I've lost my own money, but I've made it work as well. I blew my money in Central Park but then again I didn't, because they've just built this skating rink for me, which I designed. So I may have blown some money but the fact is, they've spent $10 million – $11 million actually. I don't have to pay a penny of it back, I just pay rent.

And it's not a high rent. It'll be adjusted by about three per cent a year. My final contract was the last thing the Commissioner signed before he went.

Suddenly he's out on the street, without a job!

Yes, that can happen. But I suppose it's like any political appointment in England, while the civil servants continue.

Do you know anything about beer – or have you just started reading about it?

I've been involved in this for three years so, when I took my brewer to Germany I got involved with German breweries and discovered they know a lot of things English brewers don't know. The English brewers just don't know how to brew lager. The brewing engineering companies have sold them a package of equipment to brew lager – expensive equipment, but not the best way to brew lager. Very few of them have ever been to Germany or Czechoslovakia and seen how they *actually* brew it.

What do you reckon this brewery is going to cost you – what sort of money are you using?

About one million dollars. It was a transformer station and it was sold some years ago to a property company. They tore the inside out, the machinery they sold, but the window frames are all copper. They were going to sell it but when they found out what I wanted to do they so loved the idea they wouldn't sell it, only rent it. They wanted to be able to say, 'We own this building!'
When we started off I just started looking for money – about $1.2 million. I don't know *how* I got it, to be honest. We still don't have it all. We go along day to day, week to week and juggle, and then suddenly we get some more money from somewhere. We have a couple of banks involved, but it's all Catch 22 because one bank won't lend unless the other bank lends, so you have to run backwards and forwards, and eventually they feel confident enough to give you the money. The actual private capital is about $400,000, that's actual hard cash you could say. We go through about $10,000, $12,000 a week on the payroll.

These are people who think your track record inspires them to lend you money?

There's just two of us in the venture. The other day we had CBS Television down here and he said that I was a great con man. I was completely and utterly insulted, because a con man is not the way I consider myself – I think I have good ideas and I've worked hard to put them together. But over here to call you a good con man is a compliment. I was ready to hit him. The bankers like to invest in people who've got that sort of reputation: that you can pull off the gamble. When I started this three years ago I knew absolutely nothing. All I knew was that I liked good beer and there wasn't any in the States.

I'm trying to think of a polite word for American beer – it's like drinking, er, cold water, isn't it?

When some of my guys came over they took their first American beer and they looked at it and their faces dropped and they said, 'Perrier'. It was just carbonated water.

Whereas this stuff is going to be . . . ?

This is the real thing. In England you'd call it real ale, it's unpasteurized, unfiltered, all natural ingredients. Even the lagers that we're going to do will be completely different from any English lager.

I always like to have a master plan of whatever I do, so my master plan would be to build a hundred breweries and to have Whitbread send six people over here, on and off, for three months – because all the English brewers have thought, How can we get into America? In England they're used to having brewery pubs controlling the trade. That's illegal over here, but there's nothing to stop you owning a hundred breweries with a hundred pubs. You are allowed one pub or bar or restaurant providing it's within the premises of the brewery. You could run a chain of breweries across the States.

Of course Whitbread, Watney's, Bass, they all sent people over here to talk to me but fortunately none of them could do it because they're so incompetent. They would have destroyed me just by the sheer number of people they would hit me with. But I learnt a lot from talking to them: costs, and how to operate. So my master plan is, right, Manhattan Brewing Company, Boston Brewing Company, Philadelphia Brewing Company, Bermuda Brewing Company. . . .

America has national brand products. Budweiser is the classic American beer, and it's the same beer right across the country. It doesn't take into account any regional differences in people. The English breweries went the same way. Watney's were the classic: Red Barrel was a national brand product that almost destroyed Watney's in the end because it wasn't a good beer.

How did you get your brewmaster?

I went up to Samuel Smith's, a brewery in the north of England, because they have a very old way of fermenting. The old ways intrigue me. I always

63

remember my childhood in the north of England in a cotton town and being fascinated by the machines and everything that went on. I had a very happy childhood and I've always regretted the way the world has gone so impersonal. I hate computers. Something in me loves machines – when they *were* machines, and turned. I went to Bass, in Burton on Trent, a fantastic brewery with a museum and a very old method of brewing. From the inception they fermented in big oak casks and it was a unique method called the Burton Union System. I saw somewhere that they'd closed their No. 1 Brew House, that the last Burton Union System had closed down, so I immediately phoned and said, I'm going to build this thing in New York and I'd really love to preserve your method. I wandered round the place – they'd just built a computerized big modern brewery. The brewmaster thought I was completely nuts, but he showed me how it worked. I chatted to him for a year, on and off, as I progressed and they agreed they'd let me have some bits and pieces for my museum. Then he took me to one side and said, 'I'm seriously considering taking early retirement. My Father was a brewmaster and I've been head brewman of thirteen breweries and this computerized brewery just isn't beer any more.' This man is one of the best brewers in Britain! I was so privileged that a man like that would want to participate in my idea. That's what makes it worth while.

The dray horses cost £2½ thousand each and it cost £4,000 to fly them over on Flying Tigers. You pay approximately a pound in money for a pound in flesh. They're Shires. The colour is blue roan and they've white feathered legs and they're about 17.3 hands. The cart's an old Whitbread one, used for pulling beer to the docks in London. It's been restored and they're repainting it at the moment.

Are American businessmen hard to deal with?

The odd thing I've noticed in Manhattan is that there's very little ethics. It's not an honourable place to do business – and I've found they're not very bright. They don't *expect* anybody to be honest, they don't expect anybody to do what they say they're going to do, and they don't have much intention themselves of doing what they say they're going to do. And they're terribly insecure, because they don't expect to be in their job very long. You're dealing with a completely unstable situation.

Everybody thinks American banks are fantastic, easy to deal with, but they're so disorganized, they change the terms. You can go in and negotiate something – and they change. You get *that* set up, and they change again, and continue to change. At the end of the day you have no idea where you stand.

What about the efficiency of your average executive?

64

It's just an appearance. I don't find them very efficient – it's all a show. American executives have such a short life in any company – I think on average they're fired after six months. Your chief executive is in a hopeless position, he's got to create a change and effect a result because he's being *judged*, so he's very nervous, obviously. It makes them difficult to deal with.

How do they cope with you, looking like an eighteen-year-old hippie, when you stroll into their office and say you're going to build a million-dollar brewery?

They really don't know how to deal with me – and it works to my advantage.

Do they take you seriously? I mean, even I don't take you too seriously – so how can they?

I'm very persistent. After a while they realize I'm serious. I wasn't able to open a bank account when I came here, so everything that was done had to be done with cash. That's a bad situation to be in, in America, because you're supposed to have bank loans and owe money and have accounts, and I didn't. It was very hard when I started because people wanted to know, 'What is your track record?' I'd say, 'Go and look at Central Park.' They'd say, 'Yes but your track record is a credit card.' I don't have a credit card, it's a little piece of plastic. The fact that there's a $12-million thing being built in Central Park is *not* what they consider a track record, so it caused me a lot of problems.

In my life I just do everything myself. You'll notice that virtually everything to do with the brewery has been done in England or Germany – because I know that there I can meet people and go away and know that things will progress in a certain way. With this particular building I got so tired of talking to the owners I moved in and started demolition before I signed the lease.

It's very hard to build anything, because nobody actually knows what the rules are. I had the Chief Superintendent of Buildings come in, ordering us to stop all work. I said I couldn't stop because I'd got a concrete truck arriving. He said, 'Well stop, and when I walk out of the building you can start again.' He didn't want any money or anything. I'm sure most Americans would have offered – they start pulling out the notes.... But he was completely honest. He said, 'There's somebody in the neighbourhood who's complained, they're giving us some pressure, and this piece has come out in the *Daily News* so I've got to work to rule with you.' Then he said, 'You know New York isn't what it used to be. This place stinks!'

So I shouted: 'Stop work – stop work!' All the guys sat down. He walked out of the building and I said, 'Right, close the doors, start work!'

My business formula is called *fait accompli*. You work it out to the best of your ability, and you *do* it. Nobody actually knows what the rules really are, so if you have a sensible plan and do it, then they have to come along and prove what you've done is wrong. If you go and ask them, you're presenting them with a problem. Then you've got the whole bureaucratic machinery to tackle and everything gets thrown at you, but in America if you just do it and you're fairly confident, you'll get away with it.

What about corruption – chaps coming round and saying 'You can't do that' when all they're looking for is a backhander?

Only twice have I been exposed to it, and I didn't even realize it was going on, to begin with. An official comes along, creates a problem, and I get angry. One of my chaps went and paid the fellow off after I'd virtually threatened to demolish him in the street.

I've never been directly approached, and of course I deal with the city a lot. People presume that you have to pay somebody off substantially. The original permit for the demolition and gutting of the building we got in ten days, which apparently was a record in New York. People presumed it was a matter of paying somebody else, but it wasn't.

Marvellous to hear New Yorkers can be as honest as you suggest – that's a *new* New York to me!

The biggest problem in New York is the reputation of New York – and the fact that New Yorkers play up to that reputation.

My life comprises having ideas and then taking on the task and challenge of actually creating the idea. To me this is a painting: the horses, the arch, the copper kettles.... When it's finished, it's a *working* painting. Once it's brewing beer and people say, 'This is good beer,' I've finished, and I can go on and do something else. Whether that's building ten more or doing something totally different, I just don't know at this stage.

You're a sort of enthusiastic innocent, aren't you?

Right. That's exactly it.

What about the water shortage, rodent control, noise abatement, zoning....

All of these people are individuals in a madhouse. This city is a madhouse. They basically want to live in a sane environment, you feel it coming out of them. I've never had a problem dealing with an official in the city.

You're riding high at the moment, but in New York you can be a celebrity one day and bumming bus fares the next....

Most of New York's just a big show. People open a club and really intend to skim everything they can get off it in the first few months; cheat on their taxes, grab the cash and run. What I've done is to build very real things. The skating rink has been there for twenty-five years and it'll be there for another twenty-five years. The brewery is intended to last for the next fifty to one hundred years.

Are you going to keep a penthouse in all your breweries?

Well I have a tent up there, actually. I haven't erected it yet. I'm planning on moving in shortly.

If you've been living out of a suitcase and borrowing clothes, living in a penthouse is going to be unaccustomed luxury isn't it?

I honestly don't know how I'm going to deal with it. I know one thing: I'm going to be a target in New York: women in particular are very, very keen on people who have a name, publicity, money and all the trappings. There are really very few genuine relationships here, so you become a target. Already I've noticed that when we started doing this building, let's say I had normal appeal; now I've been on the News a few times, when I talk to a girl it's like *zump*, she's ready, you know, tune in!

Can't be bad?

Well, it's disconcerting in a way because it's nice to talk to somebody genuinely and not feel the only reason that person is talking to you is because you happen to have something that they want.

Which is a brewery?

A brewery or money or whatever it is. I mean *you* may encounter that as a known person – people approach you differently than just somebody who is a regular person?

So you're a moving target at the moment – an available male in New York where there's a considerable shortage of non-gay marriageable men.

I know, it's a problem also because I'm setting up two businesses which are rather large, and under American laws divorce proceedings get very nasty – so I could fall in love with a girl, lose my head, marry her – and a year later be in court and lose half of what I've spent years putting together.

She'd have half a brewery. . . .

It's a very precarious situation. I know a chap here who's a playwright and his wife is suing him for divorce. She wants fifty per cent of everything he's got, she wants fifty per cent of future earnings of the plays he wrote while they were married and she wants fifty per cent of the earnings of all *future* plays that he might write.... This is a mind-boggling situation over here.

When we were going through the process of looking for money for the brewery I had two potential partners: one was a known television presenter here, and just at the point where we'd agreed everything his wife sued him for divorce. They've been locked in court for two years now, trying to sort it out. A lawyer gets involved and he's taking thirty per cent of whatever he gets for the wife.

So it's no longer ambulance-chasing, it's unhappy-wife-chasing?

Right, it makes life very very difficult. One of the hardest things I've found working here is the legal profession, because you have an impression from England that a solicitor is somebody who's got a certain honour. You trust him like a doctor. It's hard to realize that over here they don't represent you, they're in business strictly for themselves. There is no such thing as trust or confidence with a lawyer. You could have a simple disagreement with your wife that got sticky, a lawyer gets involved and the next thing you know it's a knock-down battle and she's not talking to you. It's strictly what the lawyer can make for himself.

There must be *something* good to be said about the relationship between the sexes here, but you're making it hard to think what it is....

It's very physical, it's horizontal jogging. To be fit here you've got to jog, eat health food, see an analyst, make love regularly and energetically. That's the approach to life. It's very funny because when you meet a girl here there's no delicate moment of going out for dinners and romance. Courtship doesn't exist. It's like, 'OK, my place or your place?' And often that question isn't even asked, it's just taken for granted. Sensitivity in relationships doesn't exist.

There's one of the chaps working on the site here and an American girl has taken a great fancy to him. They went out of the bar one night and when they got back to the apartment, she just got in the bed. After a while he decided this really wasn't what he wanted. She'd arrive at the job looking for him, or she'd go to bars. He said, 'Stop following me.' She said, 'Look, I don't want to talk to you, I don't want to sit in the bar with you, I just want sex with you.'

Couldn't he say he had a headache?

It's like, 'What's wrong with you – you want *feelings?*' It's rather like making love to a human vibrator here sometimes. I have another friend who's very very attractive, yet she just couldn't get a worth-while relationship with a man. She decided she wanted to have a baby and went through this whole dilemma. She decided maybe she should just head out to all the best discotheques and spend the evening looking for the best-looking guy, spend fifteen minutes talking to see if he had any intelligence, then get him to bed. She didn't want to know his name.

She went through this dilemma for three months, and used to discuss it with me. She ended up marrying a dentist who she didn't love, didn't like, but she decided he was good-looking, reasonably intelligent, would make a good father – and he'd got money.

And she'd known him longer than fifteen minutes!

She'd known him for about three weeks when she decided to marry him.

Could she not have gone to a sperm bank and drawn out a small deposit?

That's what her mother recommended – artificial insemination. But Manhattan's really Singlesland, it's individuals who come here just looking for fame, fortune, sex, money, whatever you want to call it.

Like you?

Like me, yes, I'm a typical case. A typical case.

New York women all want to be abused. There is a definite desire to be mistreated. That is normal. Normal, is to be mistreated. A girl I was good friends with I used to phone up and she'd be really upset: *Why* was I calling her? I said, 'Just checking to see how you are.' 'I can't talk to you!' A few days later I asked her what was wrong, but she wouldn't tell me. It was as though she didn't believe that friends were there to help, because if you showed your weaknesses you could be exploited. You don't get it off your chest to friends – you go to your analyst. You can't just be natural and show your weaknesses, you've got to hide it all. She was terribly sensitive – she taught art to children – and I just had this feeling she really wanted to be abused. She was raped last weekend by her ex-boyfriend who broke the door down, beat her up, raped her and locked her in the bathroom for five and a half hours. She rang me up and said, 'I must talk to you, you're the only sane person I know and I've got to get this sorted out, there's something wrong with me.' I said, 'Get out of New York, go somewhere where people are not under the pressures they are here, and then think about it.'

This guy who beat her up was a carpenter. She went out with a couple of English fellows because they all think, I must go out with a European – they've got class. Believe me there are some pretty loony English people over here who've come out of England because they want the drugs and this and that. In London maybe they're an accountant and there's not much going to happen, and they come to New York where being English has a tremendous advantage. Some of them are a disgrace. They're very obviously using the fact that they're English. They play up the English accent, play up the way they dress and that's really all they've got. Americans are very gullible and they'll take them in.

You get women who want to be professional and equal to men, but they feel inferior. You know they have a Masters in this or that, they're lawyers, they dress in business suits and get terribly frustrated because they may have financial success but an equally intelligent successful man wants a very pretty girl on his arm, and he can *buy* that girl. His credit card and his money will get him that girl.

They're very much into the *image* of things, they're not much into the depth. The guy's concerned with the image he projects – I'm successful, so I've got to have a good-looking girl. A successful businessgirl, very nice, very intelligent, has no chance with a man in her own sphere, unless he's ugly.

I've found with the girls the only thing they respond to is sex as physical exercise. Sex has no meaning, no caring. It's been drilled into them that you have to have a good, healthy sex life to be mentally in good shape and to be physically fit. Sex is jogging, no different. You're just jogging in bed.

The singles bars are astonishing because when you go in initially you think, Oh what a lot of nice people, all the guys dressed up like advertisements in *Esquire*. They look quite good, their hair's clipped back, ties on, jackets are good. Then you watch them and everything they do is a movement and they're checking the mirror all the time. Every movement is rehearsed. And then suddenly you realise all these chaps are girls in drag. They're all the same, there's no individuality.

You sit down and talk to them, they'll say something I find I don't believe, so I'll disagree and give my viewpoint – and they instantly agree. They have no viewpoint. They can't argue, they can't question. They've been brought up on media, on not thinking. They honestly have never been told to think.

Another thing that's hit me is that in my own age group I don't know anybody, male or female, who's had a happy childhood. They hate their parents. I try to find out what happened. Nothing. Nothing actually happened. They weren't beaten, they weren't abused, nothing you can grasp. It's, 'My Father wasn't a man enough.' They can't just say, 'I've had my childhood, it's over....' They're hung up by it. They live at home, so a kid could be twenty-four and he's still living off his parents, whereas I left school at sixteen. From thirteen I was doing my paper-round, I was earning my money. In the north of England you had to work things out for yourself.

If you go to a party in Beverly Hills and talk to a girl, I've noticed they snap into their Analyst Syndrome and start pouring it out to you. The next thing, if you're not careful, is they're inviting you into the bedroom. It makes you wonder what these analysts really *do*! This is why I'm saying they like to be abused.

It's like standing in line to get into a restaurant or a club. When I first came over, I was considered to be a noted person or something because *People* magazine had written this article. There was this club called the Mud Club which was the *in* punk place and I was invited down there. I said, 'Can I bring a couple of friends?' No problem, names at the door. So we went down there and there were crowds of people waiting in the street and I thought, This must be a great place.... I always like Sixties rock-and-roll bars and it looked that sort of neighbourhood so I fought my way through the crowd and said, 'I'm Richard Wrigley and I've two guests.' He said, '*You* can go in, but your two guests will have to wait fifteen minutes.' So I thought, Well it must be really jammed in there, and I walked in.

Six people! The place was completely empty, and they're fighting out in the street. I was completely bemused. Then this girl in a green catsuit came up to me and said, 'Hi, who're you?' I said, 'I'm Richard Wrigley....' And she said, 'You wanna fuck?'

I was completely flabbergasted. She said, 'Well do you or don't you?' And I said, 'No, not right now, I'm not really in the mood.' She said, 'What's wrong?' I said, 'Nothing, I'm waiting for two friends who're outside.' And she steamed off. And she came back to me all the evening – 'Well?' Really angry that I wouldn't....

Sometimes New York is surprising and exciting and stimulating, other times one walks out into these steaming streets amongst all these people who want to break your neck or rob you, and like Captain Scott you think, My God, this is a *dreadful* place. What impact does it have upon you?

The first thing is that it's just so *old*. You think of New York as being the super modern city, because all you see are the big skylines, but in actual fact if you look at these old brick buildings, sort of half falling down, you could be in Amsterdam, or Paris.

Can you see yourself spending the rest of your life here?

No, I absolutely couldn't. I can see myself visiting New York regularly for the rest of my life but there's no way that I could see myself living here, I think I'd jump from the building, or at some point I'd go and get a machine gun and run out into the street.

Because?

71

The noise. There's no peace, there's no quiet, you can never relax here. And it isn't that you're rushing around having such a fantastic time – the city just doesn't sleep, in a literal sense. You can't switch off and prepare for another day, so after three weeks you're mentally exhausted by the sheer fact of being here.

There is also something about always being braced to defend yourself, either against people who're being rude to you or against violence; I'm never *totally* relaxed here.

Right, your space is continually invaded. I find that in New York I can walk down the street and sense the tensions. You see a group of Chinese, a group of Puerto Ricans and it's wonderful, the colours and shapes, the bodies, but actually you sense a certain tension between these groups. It's a very very racial city in a way that perhaps we don't understand in Europe, because we see all these different nationalities living together, but after a hundred years the Italians are still in their little quarter, the Chinese in their quarter, the Greeks in theirs. It's a very fragmented city and the vibrations that exist between them are not always the most wonderful.

It's not a good city in which to feel yourself vulnerable – I'm thinking also in terms of personal relationships; you've got to be fairly hard. . . .

You're on your defence all the time. I think that's why people are so busily projecting images here. You go into a bar and when you talk to somebody you're not really talking to them, you're talking to an Yves St Laurent commercial or a Gloria Vanderbilt or a Budweiser commercial. They're afraid to expose themselves and so they wear designer clothes and come over as television characters, not as the real people.

It's, Why be yourself when there are so many better characters available?

Right, you have a catalogue. Another funny thing is that very very rarely will people invite you to their homes. They'd much rather take you to a restaurant, because there you can programme the impression you want to create and you're not exposing yourself the way you *really* are. I have friends I've known for five years and I have no idea what their apartment looks like. It wouldn't occur to them to say, 'Come home and have some tea.'

It's also the relationship between the sexes, isn't it? Women feel themselves vulnerable, which presumably may be why they come on so strong, as you're suggesting.

I found it's funny being English here because on the one hand your accent immediately opens certain doors, but on the other hand because we're much more accustomed to talking and relating to women. I get on with women in a way American men can't – in fact American men say it's the homosexual side of me because I talk to women a lot and I have women friends. There is a strong homosexual side to me. They can't understand that a man and a woman can just have a conversation, be friends, relate together without this sexual aspect, you see, so it's a confusing environment. I don't have many men friends here because of that fact. I find them very difficult to talk to because they're very strong in their images. It's machismo. It's because the classic American idea of the strong silent man who goes west and makes his fortune is that he's a man of few words. Today very few American men actually have very much to say. Maybe that's why Reagan is so popular: he doesn't have anything to *say*. . . .

THE POKER PLAYER

You seduce, you cajole, you bully, you shout
and you whisper . . . .

Some three thousand full-time career gamblers live in Nevada. One of them used to work at Aldermaston: Mike Haywood, professional poker player, is in his late forties but looks younger – lean and studied and worried about what he eats. He lives in a small hotel, paying the weekly rate, and works four hours a day. On the side he writes Runyonesque sin-city vignettes of Las Vegas life, which is full and flavoured.

At lunch he was boyish and exuberant, but as he settled down at the table his face closed up and, in the shadow of the large cap with 'London' on it, the eyes grew cold and watchful. He does not talk or react to the usual Vegas exotica around him: a Gucci cowboy, an elderly gambler with dead eyes peering out from a blond wig, a professional who's also a jewellery salesman with a strongbox under his chair, ready for somebody's big win. . . . Dealers, changing every twenty minutes, ranged from the brooding Central-Casting heavy to a cheerful blonde with breasts so big they pushed over her stacks of chips. . . .

═══

You've been a scientist and a sewing-machine salesman, which is an odd background for a professional poker player – though come to that, I'm not sure what would be a good background for a professional poker player?

There isn't one. This town is full of computer programmers and costume designers, and they're all poker players.

Along with doctors and cab drivers and psychology professors . . . ?

The top player, I suppose, is Pug Pearson who's Tennessee, dirt poor, no education whatsoever – and he's one of the best poker players in the world. On the other side of the coin last year's world champion, Tom McEvoy, is an ex-accountant. Brunson was a two-time world champion; I think he was a basketball coach. I went from being a scientist, at which I wasn't terribly

74

successful, to a sewing-machine salesman, at which I was *quite* successful, much to my surprise. I ended up in sales promotion with a couple of large American agencies based in England. Then one day I just got tired of the backbiting and backstabbing and being grey-faced eleven months of the year and I thought, Well I've played poker on Friday nights like most people, why don't I go to the mecca and see how it goes? I came for two weeks and I've been here four years.

When I first arrived I stayed at a very small hotel with a very small bedroom, and the poker-room managers and dealers introduced me to the Vegas rules; they're all good friends of mine still, which is rather nice. I thought I might see if I was good enough to take them on, and at the end of the two weeks I decided that I probably *wasn't* good enough, but why not work at it?

Were you ahead of the game, by then?

Yes, I got lucky, but I played very badly. When you play for a living you can't just rely on luck, you have to play good all the time.

You play the percentages, do you?

Not necessarily. I know what the percentages are. I tend to play the player, and the sequence of cards. If a player is losing, then you'll go after him. If a player's winning, you'll avoid him like the plague. It's a combination of a lot of different things, but basically you've got to play good card structures. It comes down to money management, really. It's not the amount you win, it's the amount you lose.

Do you find you can frighten people out of the game?

Yes I'll make moves, as we call it here, because other people are going to make moves on me.

And do they work?

There's nobody in this town who's better than me – there are a lot that are richer than me.

A professional poker player sounds like a turn-of-the-century riverboat man. Are you playing a role, are you being James Bond and Paul Newman and Steve McQueen?

No, I wish I was. I just go to work and I happen to work as a poker player. I don't play a part. Steve McQueen was the Cincinnati Kid and he played that hand so badly he deserved to lose! We do something slightly

75

different, we pick the hours that we do it, but basically I just pop in to work four or five hours a day.

Vegas divides into three shifts: day, swing and graveyard. At the moment I'm working days, which means two in the afternoon through about six. I don't like to work more than four hours a day: first of all your concentration starts to go because you're looking at forty-five hands an hour – whether you play them or not doesn't really matter. You're looking at them and you're concentrating on other people's play, the way they bet, the way they act. It's high-concentration effort for a short period of time. So more than four hours and I get a bit tired and sleepy and start making mistakes, and that's expensive.

It's feast or famine, your life?

It is for a lot of players. My life is partially feast, rarely famine.

You almost always win, is that what you're saying?

You don't work on a daily basis, you work on a monthly or a yearly basis, and when I tot my figures up at the end of the month I know how I've done.

Strange to find a professional poker player going home to double-entry bookkeeping . . .

I know that, but I keep very good books. My win rate is forty-three dollars an hour. My basic expenses run about thirty dollars a day, my percentages are: transport forty per cent, rent twenty-eight per cent and so forth. I just keep good books – all poker players do, actually.

Have you a target? You win a certain amount and then you quit?

Depends on the game, because one of the nice things about poker is that there are too many variables for it to be an exact science. Basically I aim for somewhere between two hundred and four hundred dollars a day win – or a loss of two hundred dollars.

Then you get up and go?

Yeah, because I know I'm running bad or I'm playing bad or things aren't right. There's always tomorrow, because Vegas is open twenty-four hours a day and there'll be a game somewhere.

There are lucky streaks and losing streaks – you pursue a win and you cut your losses?

What we call, hitting the deck. When the deck hits you, any manner of cards you play will win, but that happens once a year and I have to earn money every day, so luck plays a minor part. Everybody has the same amount of luck – cashing in on it is the trick. Most of the time it's a matter of the numbers of players in a hand which'll result in you winning a huge pile. With one player in, you're going to win a moderate pot with the same hand – so there's a little element of luck. If a number of people all have playing hands at the same time, you're talking in terms of a thousand-dollar pot instead of a two-hundred-dollar pot. It's quite simple.

So you're not making your own luck?

No. You make decisions on how you're going to play a certain type of hand at a very early stage, whether it's Texas Hold 'Em, which is a favourite game here, or seven-card stud, which is the basic staple of American poker. Once you've made that decision, the way you bet and the way you raise or check-raise a hand will be totally dependent on what the other players have.

Just because there are pros in this town doesn't mean that the visitors don't win. Visitors run all over a game every now and then. They come to have a good time, they come to roll five dollars or six-hundred dollars. There's nobody in this town that hasn't been beaten, that's the nice part of it.

How many of the people you're playing against are going to be pros?

I hope there're about fifty per cent, because that gives your balanced game. Half local, who'll show you respect, and half tourist, who are happily drinking – and hopefully not getting too lucky!

Do the tourists know you're a pro?

No. If anybody asks me, then Yes – they rather enjoy taking down a professional. They come with a different attitude. They come to enjoy themselves and if they beat the local pro they can dine out on that story for weeks. And I'm a target anyway at all times, that's why I wear the hat. I set myself up because the locals know me, so they know it's only camouflage – but the visitor doesn't. And Americans love beating Englishmen – I win very large pots sometimes because of that.

You set yourself up as a dummy?

I'm a terribly honest player but I give the impression, partly because of my youthful look and partly because of my attitude, that maybe I'm a relatively easy person to beat, and I'm not.

77

Isn't it the case that unlimited money will frighten most people out of a game?

Only in a no-limit game. Most of the games here are limit structures, so you can't bet more than a certain amount. This is good for the house because the games are fast and the rake is regular. These rules aren't for my benefit, they put them here for *their* benefit.

And what's a record pot?

It can go to $300 million. Sort of, pick a figure. Some of the money in this town is so enormous, you just can't be in that league. So you pick a level at which you're comfortable and at which your bankroll is comfortable.

Are you a worrier, at the end of the day? Do you go home and wonder how you're going to pay for the baby's boots?

If you start worrying about it you're in real trouble. What happens is, you talk it out with a fellow sufferer, another poker player. We have a thing called the Bad Beat Story – which is how this man caught this impossible card and beat me! Everybody has a zillion of them and they're very boring, they *have* to be boring because it's always, He beat me! But you talk them out of the system so when you go home it's like coming back from work – you're happy to put your feet up and watch television or read a book or whatever. You have to separate the two; if you let poker dominate your life, you're in real trouble.

But one of these days when you buy that cottage in Sussex it would be nice to be able to do it easily, so do you think of rainy days ahead ...?

I'm a modest player, so I'm looking at a target of $60,000 tax-free a year – and with the pound the way it is at the moment that'll probably buy me Berkshire, won't it?

Have you been ahead every year since you arrived?

I was stuck the first year, broke even the second year, a little bit ahead the third year, and this year it's going pretty good. I figured it would take me about four years because, first of all, I'm a slow learner and my mental faculties are not as fast as they were when I was twenty-three – so I *think* a little slower. You're very aware of it when you're playing poker. I've noticed a couple of times I'm slowing down. That's the only fear I have really, losing the mental bit, because I've always been a fairly fast thinker.

Yet bridge would seem to be the ultimate game and the best bridge players are quite old, are they not? It suggests that although we're losing our brain cells as we get older, experience in some way compensates for that?

Yes, hopefully. Somebody once said, 'There is no substitute for experience,' because it's a nice cliché sound. The thing about bridge, which is a game I don't play, is that all the decisions are made very early on in the hand and the rest of it is relatively automatic, but in poker the decisions are made as every card comes down. If you're playing seven-card stud, the first three cards which are basically free should tell you pretty well what everybody else has got – a trick I learnt from my mother, who was one of the great whist players of her day. I would lead one card and then she would read out the rest of my hand, with minor variations.

ESP?

She was just bloody good at it. It is ESP, to a certain degree. It's easy to confuse experience and ESP, but the more you play poker the greater you develop your ESP on a situation. It's not foolproof by any means, but if I'm not right ninety-five per cent of the time then I'm really running rather badly. When I first came to town I was probably running about sixty per cent, so it *has* heightened in that instance. But also, as you say, it's experience as well. It's an instinct. It's like anybody who's good at their job, they have a sort of instinct for what's right and what's wrong. You don't have to explain it to them, they just know.

Everybody gets the same amount of luck issued at the beginning of life, making your own and getting lucky. If you play very bad cards, unconnected cards, unsuited cards, you may happen to make a marvellous hand like a guy did against me once: he was a beautiful man, he came from Phoenix and he was on his seventeenth or eighteenth dry martini and he was having a ball. He started with a Jack, five, deuce off-suit – and made four eights against my three aces. Now that's luck, that's pure luck, the percentages are forty-nine million to one.

There's nothing done here that hasn't been done before. In a card-room you'll see on average three straight flushes and a couple of royal flushes a day, and lots of four-of-a-kind – which in your home game you wouldn't see in ten years.

Why is that?

We deal two thousand hands a day, and you're also playing very selective cards – so the chances of getting good hands are that much higher. In a home game the boys'll sit down about eight o'clock and it's got to be over by one because we've all got work tomorrow, so we're going to play rubbish. Here the place is always open. I throw away a lot of hands.

Because you're playing the percentages, but the amateurs are not?

That's right, but I only worry about me. I only play a certain type of hand in a certain type of position. There are hands that you won't play in one position but you would in another because you're looking for pot percentages. You can try to make a flush, which is patently a long shot, but you're putting more into the pot than it's worth.

Do you talk while you're playing?

Americans talk a lot – I don't. It spoils my concentration. I'm not a talker. They like to talk because the American poker game is the old style – they all sit around the table bullshitting and smoking cigars. The question I'm most often asked is, 'You're not *allowed* to talk in England?' This is true in certain clubs. It was to stop the Arabs, because they were telling each other what they had in Arabic which made it rather difficult, so in England they stopped it.

You'll find the best mechanics in the world here, but they can spot each other. It's not good for the casino if somebody's caught cheating. The biggest problem we used to have were team players, two or three guys working together in a game, and a dealer working with them.

Always with a dealer?

Always a dealer. But they change every twenty minutes, they rotate them, just like in the pit.

How do the management look upon you pros – is it a love-hate relationship?

I suppose poker players are the lowest form of life in town.

You're not putting enough in the pot for them?

We keep them in jobs. Poker players keep an awful lot of people employed. In the first year your aim is to earn enough to break even, and in the second year your aim is to earn enough to beat what a dealer earns, and in the third year to try and top what a cocktail waitress earns. That's about right because we actually give cocktail waitresses money, we give dealers money . . . in toke forms. Because of the structure of the system, everybody is on a basic wage here so they live on tokes, which means tokens of appreciation, tips. . . . So when I win I give the dealer something out of the pot. The higher the limit, the less likely the dealer is to get anything, that's the way this town is. In the lower-limit games people play to enjoy themselves and there's a tendency to give the dealer 50 cents, but when you're up in the higher limits that I play, you may be putting $100,000 in the pot and the professionals have worked out that toking costs you a minimum of $6,000 a year.

If you don't toke the cocktail waitress she'll probably put something very strange in your tea, and some of them do. So you're supporting a $150,000-a-year cocktail waitress and a $75,000-a-year dealer, and you're earning $60,000. There's something wrong here, but it's OK because that's the system.

How can a cocktail waitress be getting $150,000 a year?

She carries twelve drinks to a tray, she'll probably pick up something between three and six dollars per tray and she works an eight-hour shift four or five days a week. In the bigger units like Caesar's, if you give a girl a fifty cent piece she almost spits at you because she's used to the redbird, which is a five-dollar, or a green, which is a twenty-five dollar. They're the elite, or at least they believe they are, at Caesar's.

How do they get a job there?

You've got to have big tits, long legs and blonde hair. They like that. Most of the cocktail waitresses are a bit bent out of shape within the first year. They fall in with a not-terribly-nice person.... A lot of guys live off their cocktail waitresses.

But they're surely not on the game, because they're doing well enough with their trays?

Yes, but they're suffering mental problems because their boyfriends are screwing around and beating them up. It's a pretty brutal town, which you have to stay a little bit above....

Are you superstitious?

Not at all. As long as I've got my rabbit's foot and my horseshoe, I don't care.... I have a preference for seats, but that's because of the view it gives me of the table. I want to be in the third seat because that gives me a view of every other player. The two-seat or the three-seat are the key seats. It also means I'm at the front end, because of the way cards are dealt here. There's the Vegas shuffle which is very fast and tends to put cards in certain sequences, not exactly so you could say, 'Ah, the ace of clubs!' but basically they get bunched a little, especially with a bad dealer, so you want to be in a situation where when you see your first card, you have an indication as to what type of cards are coming down next.

Isn't it best to sit on the left of the big money?

No. If you're scared of the money, then you shouldn't sit down. You're always watching where the money is, but it moves round so much. About four weeks ago a guy came to the table with more chips than the remaining seven and I ended up winning the tournament because he'd acquired these chips a little bit by accident, in the sense that he'd got lucky early and it didn't take long to discover that he couldn't play. And so I bullied him out of his chips. Chips in big volume in front of a guy doesn't mean too much. A lot of people like a lot of chips in front of them, because if they're losing they like to appear a winner to a newcomer at the table. But you can tell from their attitude and their expression. . . .

What about *your* expression?

I glare at people but I don't speak, and then they don't know where I am.

Yet you're an ingratiating sort of guy. . . .

Not at the table, I'm not. ·

Is there any person you won't play with – a drunk must be tiresome?

The only time you avoid a drunk is when he starts winning, because there's no way you're ever going to beat him. I don't care how subtle you are in your knowledge of poker, if the guy's drunk and not looking at your cards, whatever you do he's going to turn over *something*. Never try to bluff a drunk.

Are there some players who make you think, Oh boy, I'm going to clean up today! Can you tell?

Not really. We have a saying in Vegas: If you look round the table for the Live One, it's probably *you* – you're the sucker, the easy mark!
I walk in quietly, I take my seat quietly, I'm a very quiet person. As I sit down I don't do anything except look, watch, observe. It's an old story that when you're *not* in a hand, you learn the most. I probably won't play the first couple of hands anyway, irrespective of what I have, because I want to see where the money is, I want to see who's losing or who's winning, I want to see what the opposition is like. Ideally if I'm looking at a game, I

like to see four locals and four tourists, because then the balance is right. You can't beat seven tourists, no way, because all the cards are going to hit *some* of them. You've only got one hand, and they're all shooting at you. Tourists don't worry – I mean they come here to enjoy themselves, to lose some money. They love beating pros. I know one guy who comes to town specially, he doesn't do anything else, he just comes to the MGM card room and sits and waits for people like me.

We English are quiet, retiring, conservative – so this would suggest we're predictable players?

I am – I'm totally bloody ruthless, and that's the only prediction anybody can make about me. I'm a Gemini by birth so I have at least two person-alities going for me. That helps, funnily enough, because I appear to be conservative and then I'll make a move on a pot and everybody will assume I have the hand that I'm representing I have, when in fact I haven't – I've got nuttin'!

Don't you think Americans find you easy to beat because as a Brit they know how you're going to play a hand?

They have no idea. Americans play Americans, so a Brit is a novelty factor – and they really *love* beating us. They've never forgiven us for the Colonies! So they make me a target, and one of the reasons why I wear this hat is to set myself up as a target. I want them to know I'm just off the bus – although I've been here four years.

You're playing dumb bunny, are you?

Slightly, until they find out. I must have the edge on my side of the table – then I have them. It doesn't *always* work out like that!

But we Brits aren't naturally aggressive – we don't have that American craving to win, do we?

I think we do. What about Backs-to-the-wall in 1940 and all that?

But that's fighting-back . . .

Well that's what I do here because, you see, there are more Americans than there are me.

But you need a killer instinct to be a poker player – have you got that?

I think Brits have that. I think they've lost it in England now, which is one of the reasons I've left, but here you've got to have it otherwise you will not survive the day. I have a killer instinct – I go for the throat. No point in playing otherwise. It's not friendly, you know, there's a lovely line which says 'If poker is such a friendly game, why play it for money?' and I agree. This is how I earn my livelihood.

It's the psychology of poker players that fascinates me – if they're scared, if they're bluffing . . .

Yes, ninety-five per cent of the time you should be able to read a player, otherwise you shouldn't be doing this for a living. The five per cent is when you make your error – that's when you start being human again!

Can you be friendly with the people you're playing with regularly?

Not at the table. Away from the table we're all poker players and we all share the same disasters, we all have bad days and good days, but at the table it's battle royal. Away from the table I've got four or five good friends.

Most people think of poker as you used to, as something you do on Friday nights – but that's comparing a pussy cat to a tiger; how much money's going over these tables?

Depends on the limit, Alan. For every two hundred dollars you put down, you're probably going to turn round eight hundred dollars, one way or the other. So if you multiply that by eight, it'll give you some idea. The money turnover per year is enormous. To win $60,000 you're probably turning over somewhere around half a million.

So perhaps it helps to be a phlegmatic unemotional Brit?

I hope so, although I try to be imaginative sometimes; you use all the ploys we all use in every aspect of life. If you're chatting up a girl you use a certain number of techniques, and with poker you do the same: you seduce, you cajole, you bully, you shout and you whisper . . . and you do it with cards. The cards and the chips are our tools of trade, the rest of it is up to us.

Sometimes you bully, but if you never over-exaggerate you're going to have a much more effective role as a poker player. So you don't attack, you just push. There's a way of putting a bet into a pot, and there's a way of *not* putting a bet into a pot. It's an old technique, but if you want somebody to call, you *slow* the bet in. If you're bluffing, you *fast* the bet in. Now all the poker professionals know this, so you reverse it when you're playing them. . . .

Last night in a tournament I actually had three kings showing, and I had the fourth so I couldn't be beaten no matter what happened. I raised the pot to give the impression that I had maybe a full house or something, and I got called. That made the difference of sixty or seventy dollars that I wouldn't have earned if I'd have played it any other way. You use techniques just as you use techniques in any industry you care to name.

What are the disadvantages of this life you've chosen?

It's lonely. It's a life where if you're winning you have people who are interested in you, and if you're losing nobody wants to speak to you too much, because nobody likes losers. I think that's the same anywhere. The winning way and the American way are the same thing.

We don't mind losers in England – we've got too many of them! There's a lot of us about, you know. . . .

But the British're interesting, you see. American losers are *not* very interesting people – they get very depressed and they jump off the Hilton.

They do that sort of thing in Vegas, do they – like gamblers shooting themselves on the balcony at Monte Carlo?

Oh sure, they do it all the time. It doesn't make the press because it's not good news for Vegas, but people get very depressed. They get into the drug scene, which is horrendous in this city, and there's no fun in not having any money in your pocket, you know. I've been there and I didn't like it.

You kept off the top floor, did you?

I live on the second floor. Even if I fell out the window I couldn't hurt myself.

You're living in a totally unnatural society, are you not?

It seems that to a visitor. It's actually the most natural society in the world because nothing is hidden, whereas in a big city like London or New York people hide themselves away, hide their personalities and hide what they really think. Everything is up front in Vegas. Instead of daggers coming in from the back, they come in from the *front* – so you see them coming. Yes, a brutal and glittergulch city but it's very real to all the people who live here and earn their living here.

It's a place of instant gratification? You get married and divorced on the same day, your money comes across the table instantly and you've got it in your hand – you haven't had to work for it . . .

You've had to work very hard for maybe thirty seconds. Or lose it in that thirty seconds, and *that's* the key – there's no monthly cheque, there's no Social Security, no protection, you're on your own. It's rather like being a genuine maverick.

It's still Wild West?

Nevada is the Old West, population's a million. I don't know how big the State is but I think England would fit into it several times.

When you go back to London and you see your old girlfriends, do they fall about?

Laughing, usually, because I've put on weight or lost some teeth . . . or something like that.

Don't they realize you're a big-time gambler?

Good friends in England I've known since I was in business over there, they dine out on me. In fact I was invited to a wedding a couple of years ago and the mother of the bride knew I was a professional but added 'tennis player' in her own mind, so when I arrived with my sheepskin jacket and jeans – because I'd literally got off the plane to get to this wedding – she was a little put back by the whole situation.

But when you pulled out that thick roll of dollars and threw it on the bar, she was reconciled?

I had about three quid, I think. I was poor.

Are you going to spend the rest of your life here, pushing chips across the green baize?

I don't know. Life is a little adventure anyway, isn't it? I've been terribly lucky, I've eaten in the best restaurants and I've visited lots of different countries. I've done lots of different things and I've met some gorgeous women in my life. When I was born poor I didn't actually expect to ever leave that street, so it's all bonus-time.

What do you hope to earn at the end of this year?

Target's about $60,000, that would be my net. That'll be after expenses, and that's fairly modest.

But it's more than you'd make selling sewing machines?

It's also more than I got as managing director of a company – but then England does pay bad. This is still the land of opportunity, it really is. If you have limited skills at anything, there's a way in which you can achieve something here in spite of taxes and all that.

And what about that tax man – do you have to declare?

No, I'm not a registered professional, I'm still an alien visitor awaiting residence, which is due in about a couple of months, so the only taxes I pay are on the articles I write for *Poker Player* and such profits as I make from my book, which are minimal.

What are the advantages of living in Las Vegas, apart from a tax-free $60,000?

Forty-five minutes that way is all the skiing you would ever want, twenty-two miles *that* way is the second-largest man-made lake in the world for boating, fishing. You've got pretty good weather eleven months of the year, you've got the sun all day, you've got a city that's open twenty-four hours a day, so whatever time you wake up you go to work.

Are there any normal people living here?

A hell of a lot, the nine-to-five people we never meet. We're two societies, us and them. *Them* run banks and businesses and never the twain shall meet, but we are the real Vegas. The rest of it's just window dressing, people living off us. We're the reason Vegas is here – the gamblers. . . .

THE *VOGUE* EDITOR

To see a man carrying the woman's handbag,
it absolutely turns my stomach . . .

Shirley Lord was a £3-a-week typist living in a council flat with a good view of the gasometer in Leyton E10, and determined to break into print. She finally reached Fleet Street on a No. 6 bus from Hackney Wick and a few fruitful years later, left in a Rolls. . . . Once upon a time, you see, she had gone to interview Cyril Lord, the tiny tycoon who brought us those carpets we could afford – which, it transpired, he couldn't. He said he'd give her twenty minutes but in fact gave her fourteen years – during which they married, went bankrupt, moved to Barbados, and divorced.

Later she married the man who had built their Caribbean home, went to work in New York, became Vice-President of the Helena Rubinstein cosmetic empire, was widowed – and is now Special Projects Editor for American *Vogue*. Friendly and brisk, she lives in some style on the twenty-second floor of an exclusive block on Central Park South, and in a house on Long Island. Her first novel, a steamy 500 pages, met critical resistance; she's now writing another with the highly improbable theme of a young journalist – you're not going to believe this – who marries the millionaire she's been sent to interview!

People who come here for the first time, particularly from England, say, 'What *is* that?' and I say, 'That's Central Park'. (Laughs). They can never believe it's as large or as beautiful. The man who actually kept these eight hundred acres would've had a Knighthood in our country, that's for sure.

Do you use the park – do you jog?

Yes. Well I don't jog, I fast-walk. I don't believe in jogging – the man who propagated it, Jim Fixx, dropped dead! But I'll tell you one thing: I had an early-morning plane to catch as I often do, so I went out to do my thing in pitch black and I was a little apprehensive because you have to be careful who's out there – and I was nearly knocked down by the rush into the park! I mean, people run in the *dark!*

So you can stand here on your own balcony and watch people down there being mugged?

Having already been robbed in this apartment, I don't. I came home on Easter Sunday to find a wonderful hunting knife in my bedroom, and I'd lost quite a lot of jewellery. The police seemed to think it was a cat burglar. I said, 'On the twenty-second floor – it *has* to be an inside job!' They said, 'Well it's either an inside job or a cat burglar.'

But you've got guards in the lobby downstairs, the liftmen, the porters ...?

Exactly – it's twenty-four hour security. It's supposed to be a very secure building. They say it's the first robbery in the building in ten years – but they *always* say that. They're very PR people in America.

They took a lot of jewellery. No fingerprints. The police told me to go to West 45th Street, I've forgotten the number, where there's a whole lot of little jewellery shops, and it would probably be there. Then tell the shop, 'I like that but I must discuss it with my husband,' go out, call the police and they'd go in and take it back. It would have taken hours and hours and I thought, I'm not going to do that. I didn't.

It's a price you pay, I suppose, for living rather grandly in a place like this. Are you scared, a woman alone?

I would say I'm suitably apprehensive – which I would be anywhere, living alone. In New York perhaps a little more apprehensive – but not frightened or paranoid.

You're not alone tonight – you're giving a dinner party?

I'm very rarely alone, and I entertain from time to time. Not too often, because it's a lot of work. Twenty-two tonight – that's all I can fit in. I call it my nightclub in the sky. I've got some of my special beauty people, Estée Lauder and Bernard Laser, who's my friend and also the Managing Director of all the European *Vogue*s. It's really in his honour. I've got that nice Princess Elizabeth of Yugoslavia. ...

Did you fall on your feet and arrive at this premier position when you first came to America?

No, I was in the Mayfair Hotel, just across there. It was seedy when I came here thirteen years ago – but then I never intended to stay. I had at that particular moment very little money, it was all kind of cut off or blocked off. I remember my son coming for the weekend and he was moaning and groaning because I'd come to live in New York from Barbados, which has sunfish and all that kind of thing. He came out of the bedroom and said, 'The ceiling's fallen down.' I said, 'Mark, will you *stop* your ridiculous remarks,' because he'd been very sarcastic. I walked in and the ceiling *had* fallen down. (Laughs). It was all over the bed.

I've had three apartments in this building, going up all the time. This is the twenty-second floor and there are twenty-four. New York real estate is truly rollercoaster: it goes up and down all the time. This recently went co-op, but luckily it has a clause which means I can't be turned out because the insider price was $495,000 and I was told that tomorrow I could sell it for $700,000. I said, 'But where do I go?' Because now the rollercoaster's up, so I pay rent and can't be turfed out. I don't think. A non-eviction clause: I like the sound of it.

Providing you behave yourself, I suppose?

I behave myself.

You have a demanding job, you've got two homes, two sons, in the evening you write novels. What do you do in your spare time?

Try to sleep! I really do run all the time and I think America *encourages* you to run, because the profits are there. I've always been a bit of a workaholic, a livaholic.

I always believed you'd be a success here because you've got confidence, you're self-generating and you enjoy entertaining – you're really a natural New Yorker.

I'm not really, because I'm often asked 'Do you miss England?' and I say, 'Only when I'm *there*!' Sounds a funny thing to say, but when I'm there I always wonder what I'm doing somewhere else. New York, particularly now that my husband has died, New York emphasizes loneliness even though you can be with lots and lots of people. It's a hostile city and for the first time in my life, really the first time, I have felt extraordinarily lonely even though I keep myself incredibly busy. And I'm lucky because the boys are here and they're always checking up on me and seeing who I'm going out with. They're both wonderful sons – I'm very lucky in that.

If it's so lonely, have you not thought of going back to England?

Yes I *have* thought about it, but I have to admit that I feel people work much harder here and I just wonder whether I would fit in again in England, because I suppose I might be demanding. I mean I'm not demanding here, because *everybody* is! If you want, you can get – if you go after it. In England I used to laugh about people having breakfast meetings and things like that; I used to say, how ridiculous all those Americans are. Now I never think anything about it. I don't think anything about working Saturdays, Sundays, holidays, anytime. I used to say how lucky I was to be paid for what I loved to do, but I don't say that here – because they take you at your word and don't pay you!

You see you're so confident, which is very good for a lone woman – I've watched you striding into nightclubs and ordering them around. A lot of people couldn't do that.

I suppose I *do* have confidence. I've had some good teachers, you know. I've been with a lot of confident people in my life.

So you came here, happily married, to be Number Two in the Helena Rubinstein organization. Then your job disintegrated and your husband suddenly died.

I was there five years and learnt an enormous amount and don't regret it at all, but it was very *very* tough. I realized as time went on that I much preferred a typewriter to a calculator. No journalist usually operates a budget; I had a huge one and I was terrified of overspending it or under-spending it and I was always working out figures. I was not really happy in the job, but I was determined not to be fired because so many creative people go into that world and don't make it, and I was *determined* to make it.

Then Colgate decided they didn't want to be in the cosmetic business, but they had by then unfortunately renewed my contract. I was earning a great deal of money and they made life very uncomfortable for me. I used to feel when I went in maybe my phone was tapped or something. It was a real squeeze-situation, but I was *not* going to be squeezed out, so I did everything that I had to do – but looked around. My husband, who was alive then bless his heart, always thought I could be Estée Lauder or Helena Rubinstein. In fact I registered the name of a company which I'm now using in my second novel called 'Ready to Change' for a cosmetic company. I had the money, I had the warehouse, I had the chemist and when I had it all and he was saying 'Wonderful, off you go!' I was profoundly miserable because I knew really that was *not* what I wanted. I am a creative animal – my favourite hours are with the typewriter. So I went back to *Vogue* and I was absolutely right to do that.

The sudden death of your husband knocked the bottom out of your success?

It sure did. That was a really bitter blow and it took me at least a year to realize that I'd never lived alone. That's probably been the hardest thing to overcome because I went from my parents to be married, to be married, to be married – but I never dated. I had three husbands and I was very in love for thirty years. It took about the year, thank God, before Americans started to say, 'Are you dating, who are you dating, have *we* got someone for you!' You know ... horrendous! Awful!

But I thought a single woman was unpopular here because she's a threat to marriages?

I'm not.

You're nice to the ladies, are you?

I think I'm really too work-oriented. I know a lot of people say there are no men in New York but I think that's ridiculous. Look out of the window – I mean they're everywhere. But I don't go out looking for dates. I like to meet men when we have a lot in common – companionship and all that kind of thing.

Yes, I've heard about that.

(Laughs) I thought you might have.

But it's a lonely place for a woman suddenly single. ...

I've gone back to having a bottle of witch-hazel in the fridge. It's pretty disgusting. Today I couldn't offer you very much, I'm ashamed to say. Tomorrow when the party gets under way everything will be bulging, coming in from the caterer. I don't look after myself really, because I go out all the time. I have a diet drink in the morning for breakfast, a cup of coffee and off I go. Or I'm at one of my famous breakfasts that I've already talked about. So in a sense it's a bit like living how a man lives, and not perhaps as a woman should live.

Women are not wary of you, fearing you're going to pinch their husbands?

Oh no no no no no no no I don't think so. You say I'm confident – well my friends are *very* confident. Betty Bacall said, 'You clone your friends,' and I think that's very true. I think you choose friends from people who are similar to yourself, with similar tastes, and if confident is what I am, confident is what my friends are.

Women here are very competitive and career-minded, so clones are not hard to find?

I don't think you belong in New York unless you're working, and I mean that for women too – it's a very tough city. If I were here as the wife of a very successful man or a not-so-successful man but as a wife and mother, I think it would be difficult because you're doing what's expected of you, and waiting for the phone to ring to make arrangements to go out and fill your time. I couldn't do it.

The other thing is, this is a second-chance city – or in your case a third- or fourth-chance city . . . People *do* start again.

Absolutely, oh you see it all the time. I think if you know what you're doing, there's nowhere that you can't go in America.

It's no place for a shrinking violet though, is it?

You learn not to be – or maybe you *can* be a shrinking violet, which is very attractive too, but you're not really. On the top you're shrinking, but underneath you're really a full-blooded orchid!

A steel butterfly?

Yes, yes.

You would seem to be *Vogue*'s ideal woman. . . . You've got a career, men friends, money, position, you have this apartment on the park, you have a house on Long Island – what haven't you got?

I'd like to find a husband. (Laughs). But I'd have to say *the* husband, not a husband. I am very very particular. I thought frankly when David died that I would not ever again want to share my life, but I think when you're *used* to sharing it as I am, then it's hard not to.

And New York is a good place to find a fourth husband?

I haven't been looking. Honestly, I promise you I really haven't – I'm too busy. I must say I like Englishmen, I really do – I'm not just saying this because there's a hell of a lot of men who are going to get on a plane and come and find me on Central Park South. In general terms when I look at my really close friends in America, the people I feel comfortable with, they're *all* European. I'm including England in that.

93

Do you think you stand a better chance in the hurly-burly of New York than you would back in Mayfair?

I prefer Englishmen to American men. I was brought up in England and I thought my life was over when I was married to Cyril and he said we were going to leave England. I truly thought it was over – when of course it was just beginning! Nevertheless I know that it may be totally phoney-baloney, and you'll laugh, but I like to look up to a man. There's something masterful about an Englishman, whether it's the public school system or whatever it is. I think American men truly are a little soft and a little wet. I shouldn't say that because I'm going to have a hell of a time now, but I like that kind of autocratic man – I suppose because I'm a strong lady, maybe. You've already said I'm confident – that's another word for strong. I don't want to be kicked in the you-know-what or anything like that, but I certainly like the approach of a man I can look up to, and somehow they happen to be English.

American men are dominated by their womenfolk?

That's always been the story. I thought it was a fallacy but when I observe, I wouldn't say it's domination but on the surface it's almost like – All right, Mother. After a certain age, it's quite nauseating you know.

Like a stereotype, it's got a germ of truth in it: the women do kick them around a bit. . . .

They do. I mean to see a man carrying the woman's handbag, it absolutely turns my stomach – I think it's terrible. And another thing: the language. I mean I love the fact that when I meet really terrific English friends, English men friends, I love to say, 'Let's have a cup of cocoa,' or 'Have you rubbed your chest with Vick,' or whatever. I mean, I love the language – it means home. Perhaps I should have said that first. Sense of humour, irreverence. It's a totally different sense of humour here. Totally.

Yet you've gone striding out as an executive here and done extraordinarily well.

If a woman loves her work – *particularly* a woman – this is the place to be. There's just no question about that. If we're talking about professional behaviour, really getting things done, this is it. If you're talking about your emotions and making your life with a man, that's a whole other thing.

I had it all. I had a British husband who I loved and loved me very much, who was the most fantastic foundation . . . *and* a wonderful career – so as you said, I had it all. And you know because I had it all, I want it again!

It would seem this is the place to grab it . . .?

I don't know. I think probably it's in London or Australia or somewhere, who knows? The other thing about America is that this is a place where you have to appear rich, even if you're not. This is no place to be poor and not to be successful. I mean I'm not rich, I'm not poor. I don't believe in flaunting it, but I think that people evaluate other people in terms of money. . . .

If you're not rich you're *imitation* rich – you'd pass as monied!

Average. Comfortable. It's called comfortably off.

Comfortably orf?

I mean rich here is richer than anything you can possibly imagine. I do think it's unfortunate that women here are very conscious of labels. I remember an English friend of mine came for dinner and she looked very elegant and I said, 'Oh Connie that's so nice, whose is it?' And she said, 'Mine, you fool,' and I said, 'You're absolutely right – I've become *American!*' Labels, where you sit in restaurants – that's all to do with rich in a sense, and that's very unattractive I think. I don't like that.

Do you get much time to be Mother Earth to your two boys?

We see each other a lot and we're on the phone. My eldest son and I talk every day, without fail. Richard when I can find him somewhere in the nether regions of the Fish Market.

Mark has just got married so you're about to be, if you'll pardon the expression, a grandmother?

I feel like Shirley Maclaine said: 'What makes you think I want to be a grandmother?' But I probably will like it – a very *young* grandmother, of course. . . .

THE TYCOON

I have at the moment 185 lawsuits. . . .

Sir Gordon White's last purchase of any consequence was US Industries – which he picked up for $530 million, cash. In his private 1-11 executive airliner he pops over to California to look for another house; while I was there he was considering a standard Beverly Hills pad for around $10 million – yet in 1973 he'd arrived in New York from London with $3,000! Laconic, lanky, elegant and slightly deaf, Sir Gordon has all the right interests for a self-made Yorkshireman: ladies, horseracing – and taking the natives for a ride.

Perhaps our most successful empire-builder, he operates out of a twentieth-floor think-tank on Park, and a superb apartment just up the Avenue. He is the transatlantic end of the phenomenally successful Hanson Trust, Britain's eleventh-largest company with a market capitalization of £2.2 billion; his Hanson Industries, already America's 150th-biggest company, is now slightly larger than its London-based parent.

A good party-man, he wears his responsibilities lightly: 'Does he *ever* do any work?' I was asked. One of his directors was better informed: 'You never lose money with Gordon. ...' To me it seemed extraordinary he could create an industrial holding company of such magnitude – food service, garden tools, shops, furniture, clothing, sausages – without ever *seeing* what he was buying. He does it all from the balance sheets: 'I've never gone to look, never visited a plant or headquarters. I don't believe in royal visits.'

Knighted in 1979 for services to British interests in the US, he owns and breeds racehorses – Hanson Trust sponsors the Derby and the Oaks. He has broken a few bones on the hunting field, his neck on the Cresta run, and still appears more often in the gossip columns than the financial press.

═══

As many Britons coming over here to do business find out, they book into the Waldorf and they start to do a deal. They think they've *got* a deal. They've been in the Waldorf for the week and it's time to go home. They go home – and then suddenly they find that the lawyers have brought up an objection! So they come back again. By the time they've been back five or six times they're desperate to *do* the deal, and they start to give way on all those points a lawyer can bring up.

I've seen sixteen lawyers closeted in one room for twenty-four hours, all earning a couple of hundred dollars an hour, and when I went in to try and find out why we weren't closing the deal – which was in fact buying some stock from Banque Paris Bas – the representatives of this very good law firm said, 'But imagine if the stock is phoney. ....' It's ridiculous! They wanted to carry it on and roll it on further. Lawyers here can't make money without litigation, so they're quite happy to see you in a situation where you've got to litigate.

But you find here that most things *are* settled. Two of the heads of the most prominent legal firms in the corporate world have breakfast together every morning. They're on opposite sides on every major takeover in this country – and they have breakfast together every morning in the Regency!

You can't really fiddle around with British institutions, as you can here. If you have a political debt, the Mayor in New York appoints the judges. Now if you've been a very nice kind fellow to the Mayor when he was looking for a little money, then of course he would perhaps intervene for you with the judge and help you along the way. You see, if you provide a politician or a judge with money up front for his campaign, that's a campaign contribution – but if you give him money *after* he's been elected, that's a bribe.

But you came over here as a simple Yorkshire businessman – you weren't into bribing judges!

I still haven't got into it because, first of all, there's a law here against foreigners contributing to political parties. And the other thing is that I was too naïve. It's very funny here: you go down the line to a contract level, the contract is signed – and they will go by the *letter* of that contract, not the spirit. As you know, most contracts underline the spirit.

Take the political systems here, take Concorde – which I had a little bit to do with. You have two presidents, Nixon and Ford: both had agreed that there would be no problem in flying Concorde into the United States, as indeed the British, the French hadn't raised any problems flying the 707 and the 747 into France and Britain – in both cases having to lengthen runways and change the noise regulations. So what happened? Carter takes over and says, 'I don't want any part of this,' so he passes it to Washington. Then it comes to Governor Carey, who passes it down to the Port Authority.

Governor Carey said to me, 'Sue them! You don't expect me as a politician to grant the right for Concorde to fly into New York and lose two hundred thousand voters down at Kennedy Airport? Sue 'em.' You see, in this country you can sue the Government, you can sue the State, you can sue any public official.

I had lunch with Carey's wife the other day – a Greek lady who's into property with a splendid office opposite the cathedral.

There was a bit of trouble about her: her first husband was supposed to be dead, but he turned up alive. Carey was a super pragmatic politician, and that was the advice he gave me. So the Concorde flew into New York eventually, and has been flying ever since. Nixon approved it, Ford approved it, Washington approved it ... but Carter reneged on his predecessors' promises. Whatever anyone in politics in this country says today means *nothing* when they go out of office. They do not pick up on promises made by predecessors.

The Russians have learned how to play. We haven't – we're not as clever at playing the system. De Gaulle learned how to play – he did well for France. We've always been considered to be a good friend of the United States, so we don't play that game.

The system is now swinging back to a first-class capitalist system, from the liberal left-wing approach. Listen to the rubbish talked by somebody like Carter, who in fact destroyed his ally the Shah and happily stands up at the Democratic Convention and says, 'Nothing's changed, I'm still for human rights,' forgetting of course that what had happened in Iran was directly his fault.

What was the background to your arrival here?

The general breakdown of capitalism after that speech by Mr Ted Heath, who actually was mainly responsible for the collapse of the British economy. Heath coined the phrase 'the unacceptable face of capitalism', which had put him in power. ... The unacceptable face of capitalism was something which Heath knew nothing about. After the Barber rush for growth, when they unloaded the vaults and spewed money out at the rate of five per cent interest, and of course the miners' strike, you'd got a Socialist government. At which point Socialists were turning totally away from what apparently had been the rush for growth, which was the unloading of cheap money. Property developers were supposed to have made millions and millions. The Socialist platform wasn't going to stop it.

In fact what had happened was that Mr Barber and Mr Heath had screwed up the whole country. Six and seven generations of money had gone down the tube because of this easy borrowing power and these low interest rates, and most of the people that made those millions went down the drain. Slater's empire collapsed and there were dozens of others. The lifeboat came out from the Bank of England.

And then you had the petrol crisis, at which point the British Index reached 150. The day after Dunkirk it was 350! So you can imagine the over-compensation for this sudden increase in petrol prices: the whole of

Britain collapsed, from a financial point of view. The change of government happened about that time.

Hanson Industries was one of the few companies that was doing tolerably well – you weren't in trouble?

No, we weren't in trouble. We had cash because I insisted we got out of property. You'd see a property sold one day for a million pounds, a week later for a million five, two weeks later for three million ... and suddenly you realized the world had gone mad. This was the Barber–Heath rush for growth. We got out of property, so when the crash came. ...

You were right in the short term, but not in the long term?

Yes, quite. Because you can always stay with property, but it wasn't really our business – we'd gone into it as a sideline. We were not under any pressure at Hanson Trust; I think the year I left England we made £7 million pre-tax profit. Last year we made £90 million!

But it was obvious after the Barber rush-for-growth, Heath going back to the country and – I can't quite remember the timing – then the Labour Government got in. Then Mr Healey, who was not of course aware the unacceptable face of capitalism had been well kicked in the arse and there was not much in it left, he said he'd squeeze the rich until the pips squeaked. At the same time we were about to do a merger with Bowater on a friendly basis and it was referred to the Office of Fair Trading ... at which point we said, 'Forget it! Four years of Socialist rule on top of what we've got now, the country's finished! I must go and try to increase the fortunes of Hanson Trust, rather than my own, somewhere else.' And so I came to the United States.

You're so aggressively British I'm amazed you could ever bring yourself to leave Britain!

Alan, that's true. If someone had said to me in the August of 1973 when I had just finished my ultimate house, that I would leave England ... I'd have sent them along to the nearest psychiatrist. I had no intention of leaving, but I could see we were in for a very tough time. I'd also been considering the United States. I hadn't got starry-eyed about it but at the same time I thought there were opportunities over here, because in the main the Americans coming to Britain didn't understand British methods of doing business.

It broke my heart to leave England, it really did, but I comforted myself with the thought that really I was working for England, because whatever I could build up here would belong to the shareholders of Hanson Trust and those shareholders were all British.

Hanson was an affluent trust, even then – did you arrive in New York with a sack of gold?

No, we didn't have any money. We had some cash but of course you couldn't bring money out of England because of Exchange Control regulations. I came over and started the company with three thousand dollars, but I was fortunate enough to persuade the people from whom I bought the first business – this fishing company down the Gulf of Mexico – to take my paper, secured on the assets of their business. This today is known as the leverage buy-out – where you're actually using the assets of the company you're buying to secure the money to buy it with.

You came over with three thousand dollars and bought your first company with paper. What is this part of Hanson Trust in the States worth now?

Just under a billion dollars, I'd say.

How many years did this take?

Ten. This is our tenth anniversary.

So it *can* be done?

It can be done. You need a lot of luck, you need to study the American business philosophy – which is devil take the hindmost. Whenever you feel the warm comforting arm around your shoulder from some American businessmen, particularly New York men, shortly after that you feel the pain as the knife goes in. It's tough, it's very tough. They only understand excellence in this country – you cannot get by with mediocrity, which you can still do in Britain to a great degree.

I had money for expenses, I booked into the Hotel Pierre with an old friend of mine, Eddie Collins, an American who's not a businessman but a very good contact man, and we opened up our office in a suite, a very small one. We were there for a year. They eventually got angry with us because one day they logged about a hundred telephone calls and said we were using the hotel as a business.

Which you were?

Of course. Then we got a letter from their lawyer – everything immediately goes to the lawyers – so we had to think about getting an office, but by that time we had a fairly good business. The fishing company was doing terribly well. That's where the luck comes in, you see.

So you've come from a telephone in a hotel room to a $2.3 billion sales volume in ten years? I find this hard to understand.

Sometimes I can't believe it myself – I mean after all I'm not really very clever, but I did know one thing: a lot of people arrive here thinking the streets are paved with gold. I didn't. They didn't know who I was and they really didn't care until I won a strike in a business we'd bought, and the unions recognized our right to manage. The men went back to work and I sold that foundry to a group of local businessmen and paid back the bank, and so created a rapport with the Chemical Bank. They were very pleased to get their money back because they thought they'd lost it all. So then I had someone to talk to, as far as buying something else was concerned and borrowing the money, because I still couldn't bring money out from Britain.

The next thing that happened was I bought thirty-five per cent of a company called United Artists Theatre Circuit. There was a little fight going on between two sisters and two brothers, and the sisters decided to sell, so I bought their shares and hoped to buy the rest on a very friendly basis, but there wasn't a lot of friendliness as far as the brothers were concerned. The next thing I and James Hanson knew was at Christmas of 1974 we were both sued for $10 million each. It's what they call over here a scattergun lawsuit: they sue you for everything that you can think of and then they begin to harass you by getting you into court, taking depositions and generally messing you about. So again it was a learning process, dealing with American lawyers. I have at the moment one hundred and eighty-five lawsuits. (Laughs).

I've got one settled quite recently: this was a black man who was working in one of our depots and he had a lady supervisor. She couldn't get on with him, and one morning when she came in he was in the loo, so she went in – these American loos have got an opening at the bottom of the doors – she went along looking underneath and saw his feet and banged on the door. The door wasn't locked, it opened, he jumped to his feet – and she fired him for indecent exposure! (Laughs).

So he sued the company for damages – a million dollars for sexual harassment! Now really it had nothing to do with us, but we understood his problem and we offered him another job somewhere else. We offered to move her. Eventually we settled for $7,500. You *have* to settle because it's very expensive for us to fight a legal battle. So all of this is part of the learning process of doing business here.

If you've got a hundred and eighty-five lawsuits, are you sleeping easy?

Oh yes – most of them are garbage. But you see they're throwing out about six thousand lawyers a year. They hang up their shingles and they follow ambulances looking for anybody who might've been hit by a car.

The system works on the basis that you *don't* pay your own legal fees. A lawyer here can work on a contingency and if you lose, that's it. If you win, the lawyer gets half the money.

You escaped from this scattergunning?

We sold them back their shares, making a very handsome profit, and moved on to another deal.

Now you've just bought US Industries – that was the second biggest buy of the entire year in the States?

If we were a public company we would be the 150th-biggest company in the United States. We're the thirteenth-largest foreign investor in the United States and we've never invested a penny! It's all been American money, borrowed. . . .

It's all been paper?

No, it got to be using-money after a while, but on the leverage buy-out basis. When I bought US Industries I went to the bank and said, 'I want $550 million, secured on the assets of US Industries.' I think the company I used as the vehicle for that operation had a net worth of $50 million, so their banks were actually looking at a loan of $500 million that couldn't be secured until we owned one hundred per cent of the company, but that's a leverage buy-out and it works very well.

American banks are very aggressive, they're of course always looking for what they call the three Cs: Character, Capability and Credibility. Character is the most important thing you have to establish, because they want to know that if everything goes wrong, you're going to maintain your endeavours to pay back the money they've lent to you. So I created this rapport with the Chemical Bank as lead bank to a point where they no longer really need to examine a proposition that I take to them, because they know that I've done all the work necessary to make sure I'm buying the right thing.

You have a good reference – but then you've still got to pay the interest; the bank's not going to do you any favours?

Oh no no no.

So what's the interest on $530 million?

At present-day rates it's something near $68 million. But the company made $67 million in the year before we bought it under *their* management, and they had a head office that was costing $24 million a year which wasn't needed because there are thirty companies all over the United States in everything from ladies' shoes, cowboy boots and electric light fittings to oil-well servicing in Texas. It's an enormous company – it doubled the size of Hanson Industries.

When you're talking in mega-millions, as you are, how do you keep a sense of perspective? It becomes Monopoly money, doesn't it?

Yes.

So if you go out for a haircut and it only costs ten dollars, do you give them a hundred dollars and leave the change?

No no no. My Father always used to tell me that any fool could sell, but it does take a clever man to buy. The real secret, I suppose, is that I can see where something is the right price. If you buy at the right price you're not going to make a mistake. The major problem that most people make – particularly coming over here – is that they pay too much, like Imperial Group paid $670 million for Howard Johnson's and it was probably worth about $400 million.

I was told *you* paid too much for US Industries?

On the face of it it looks like that, because it's a conglomerate, and conglomerates in this country are a dirty word. James Hanson and I have managed to prove to the investment world in Britain that an industrial holding company, or an industrial management company, has got a greater chance of surviving a recession than a one-product company, or a two-product company. Our record now is twenty years of unbroken growth.

You're sitting here in this think-tank and you're looking for companies to buy?

All the time. I read all the papers on any possible company, the financial records – and there are various parameters, you know. The important thing is the cash flow – how much money they've spent on the company in the preceding few years, which brings you to the depreciation, which is part of the cash flow. Take US Industries: it was making $67 million pre-tax and it had a depreciation charge of $40 million. You knock the tax off and you come up with a cash flow of nearly $70 million a year. Now if I can improve that output – and it seemed to me there wasn't going to be too much of a problem because the company was badly managed. It was badly managed because it didn't *need* managing – the people out there in the field are the ones that are making the money, not the fellows in the head office. That's why we have a very small entity. Our main office in New Jersey has only about twenty-three people in it; they had a hundred and eighty-seven.

So it's all done from a balance sheet – you never look at the companies you're going to buy?

Physically? Oh no – particularly if you're making a hostile tender. They don't look too kindly on you knocking on their door. You wouldn't get in to see them.

What I don't understand is, how is it all your frogs turn into princes?

Well, I have only one thought: I'm not interested in what we can make, I'm only interested in what we can *lose*. The down-side risk is something that I constantly hammer home to any of my people involved in a smaller way in acquisitions. I say, 'Don't worry about how much you can make, how much can you lose?' That has turned me away from some very big companies. I could have bought Avis from IT&T very cheaply. It was a major one-product company – second-biggest car rental company in the world – but if it had gone wrong it would have busted us.

So that's really the way it works. A very simple formula: it's hands-off management who are working in the field, no royal visits from head office. All the people that work for me, other than one man, are American. I have no trouble relating to Americans.

The mistake people make is to come over here and think when they're talking to an American, they're talking to an Englishman with a funny accent. That is totally untrue. Their thinking processes differ from ours, their stamina is different to ours. They're trained to work very *very* hard. I'm not saying that we haven't got good people, we certainly have, but here they often use stamina to break down your resistance.

Are they more ruthless?

The Americans? Incredibly ruthless. They're not going to look at someone getting a golden handshake of millions of dollars if they take over a company – he's just going to get fired! They might pay him six months' salary – and away he goes. They're very tough indeed.

I'm not saying they're better than we are in a lot of regards, but the one thing they will do, if things start to go badly – as you've seen with the motor industry in this country – is a little help from the Government squeezing Japanese imports, and out come General Motors making billions, Chrysler recovers and they get down to it.

The unions take a view of self-interest: it's no good putting a company into bankruptcy, otherwise we'll all be out of work, so the unions are prepared to join with management. They can read a balance sheet just as well as management can and they know exactly what they can afford to ask for, so they do a deal.

The days of John L. Lewis holding up the whole country to ransom for nine months in World War II, and then again for a year in 1950, are all over. Now you've got a wonderful coal industry here employing probably less people than we employ in Britain. They've just finished for the first time in history wage negotiations – and no strike. General Motors settled their wage negotiations, no strike. Their union leaders are of much higher standard than our people, who keep rabbiting on about what happened in 1926....

This is an exciting environment to work in. I've taken some strikes here but they haven't lasted long. I closed a place down in Stormlake, Iowa which was the entire income of the town, but we couldn't keep it going whilst it was losing money. We had a go with the union and said if they would take a very big cut we'd keep it going. We couldn't reach an agreement so we just closed it down – but then someone bought it and started up the same business at lower rates by *not* dealing with the union.

So you're learning some of the American ruthlessness?

I'm not very ruthless because I don't think it's necessary. Once you've made up your mind you must be totally ruthless in the *decision* you make, but then you can be compassionate in its execution, therefore you can treat very kindly people you may have to make redundant.

At the time I arrived in the US – talk about being a Briton and you got a faint smile of condescension. They just didn't think of us as being anything but those poor cousins across the Atlantic. I walked into a bank here to cash some sterling traveller's cheques, and they wouldn't cash them. And when I went to talk to one or two banks they would keep me waiting for a couple of hours in the waiting room and then I would see some snotty-nosed kid who didn't know anything at all and had just been sent out to get rid of me.

Then I got lucky and found out about this company that was for sale – a fishing company called Seacoast. How on earth I ever bought that and made a profit I'll never know! But it was a stroke of luck because right after I agreed to buy it protein went out of sight, so the company made $17 million the first year I bought it, and I only paid $32 million for it – in paper of course – and I was able to pay off that paper.

But the banks must have been friendly?

No, it wasn't covered by the banks. After I'd bought the company and the money started coming in I discovered we had $14 million in the bank, and they were banking with Morgan Guaranty. So I asked to go and see somebody there and I arrived at this banking hall down in Wall Street on a bitterly cold day. In front of the door there's all these desks and I sit in front of the first desk in front of the draughty door – so I know I'm actually talking to the fellow who joined the bank *yesterday*.

I'm trying to find out how to do my next acquisition. We did have some sterling in England and I wanted to do what was called a back-to-back, but after a couple of minutes I knew this fellow didn't know what I was talking about – that if I put up £10 million in England and we took the exchange risk, would they grant us credit for £10 million here, which is a straightforward thing.

Anyway he said he'd think about it and I said, 'Well don't think about it, I'd like to see your vice-president.' So I got an appointment for two or three days later. I sent for one of our young accountants from England and we arrived and we again sit outside this door and wait half an hour, and then we're sent for. We go into a nice office and there are three young chaps sitting around.

We pass the time of day and nothing much happens and then this much older man comes in and sits behind the desk and he says, 'Now what can I do for you?' So I said, 'I'd like to know what would happen if we put up £10 million in Britain and took the exchange risk and you lent us the equivalent of £10 million, what would be your charge?'

So he took our balance sheet – which was not the most impressive sight, this Hanson Trust balance – and starts to go through it.

He said, 'I don't like your equity rate here. I'm not at all happy about this.' By then I'd been putting up with this arrogance for quite a long time, and the fact that being British meant you were an arse-hole. So I said, 'Just a minute – would you mind telling me how much we've got on deposit in your bank?' He said, 'You have money here?' I said, 'Yes we do, would you mind finding out?' So he gets on the telephone, and there's about five minutes of silence. These three young men, my accountant, myself, we sit there until finally he said, 'You've got $14,150,000 on deposit.'

And I said, 'No sir, we *had*. I'm about to close the account. But before I leave, as you used me as a model to teach your three young men the banking business, I'm going to add to their lesson.

'Number one,' I said, 'it's extremely rude as a moneylender, which is all you are, to keep a client waiting for half an hour outside in a draughty waiting room. Secondly, it's even more rude not to offer him a cup of coffee. Thirdly, it's a disaster if you don't know how much money he's got in his account. And I hope these three young fellows will never *never* run into the same problem that you've run into – you've just lost the best account you might ever have had!' And I closed the account. I told that story to Hartley Shawcross and three Morgan Guaranty people in London – they've been trying to get our account back ever since!

How did you hear about the fishing company?

I wrote to a lot of merchant banks saying I'm looking for something and they just sent me, among other things, this company that had been turned down by everybody. And I have to say it was an enormous stroke of luck that it wasn't a tremendous disaster.

I just sold it this year. I think we must have had about $16 million out of that company and I sold it to Zapata for $30 million, so it wasn't a bad buy at the end of the day.

If that had been your very first disaster . . . back home to Mother?

No I wouldn't have gone home, I'd have had to fight it out. But God knows I'd have been wearing a sou'wester and fishing in the Gulf of Mexico! I'd have had to go and put it right if it'd gone wrong.

I got terribly ill too, I got sinusitis, I got flu, the whole thing, back and forth to Wall Street. Freezing. It's about twenty below, and I'd go down to Wall Street every day and back again.

Funnily enough, I put a lot of faith in people and the young man running this company, David Clark, it was his family business. I trusted him. We struck up a rapport, so that was why it was a success. Now David Clark is the President of Hanson Industries – he's running the whole thing. This is my think-tank office – our real office is in Iselin, New Jersey. David's very young, I suppose, by our standards. I'm the Chairman and Chief Executive Officer.

President sounds more important?

Yes it does, but it isn't. You see in this country, they're very keen on titles. Titles are so important. The chairman is always the chairman. You have a president: he's managing director. You have chief executive officer, chief operating officer. You have senior vice-president in charge of this, you have vice-president in charge of that, the ratio of titles is very important and the first thing that happens if you get a group of Americans in here, they'll immediately give you a pile of visiting cards.

Titles are so important that when I was having this takeover for US Industries and Gordon Walker was suggesting he might stay on, the first question he asked was, 'Who will be reporting to me?' So I said, 'You're wrong chum, it isn't who's going to be reporting to you, it's who *you're* going to be reporting to!' He said, 'Well I can't report to David Clark.' I said, 'You must be joking. David Clark is the President of Hanson Industries which is just about to pay $530 million for your company, so I don't think there's anyone else you're about to report to unless you want to report to one of the cleaners. . . .'

Curious that in this easy-going democracy, face should matter so much?

Face is very important, titles are very important, and yet they're incredibly pragmatic. You'll get a man who's been with a company for fifteen years and he'll get booted out overnight. He'll take it, and go.

You're part of the brain drain, the talent drain; are there many others behind you?

Very few people have come to this country and made a success. I was having lunch with the No. 2 man of City Bank, one of the most aggressive banks here, and he told me that ninety per cent of the foreigners who come over here to buy something or open something new . . . fail.

Becoming Sir Gordon must have eased the way?

Definitely – there's a romantic touch to the Americans. They still hanker after knights on white horses. . . .

They think you're going to swash your buckle, do they?

That's right, they particularly like that. Then as you get more successful, they love you more than *anything*. If you're successful, you immediately become a demi-god. I mean, take Joan Collins – Joan made sixty films, was a so-called movie star for years and years and years, comes over here on television – and becomes a *megastar*! Her book crept out in England and sold about forty copies. She's just been paid $1,200,000 for the paperback rights for that very same book, because Joan has achieved what all Americans really want: they want to be successful, so they love her for being successful, they love her for being rich. But if you're a knight they'll ask you if you've got a castle – which of course I haven't.

It's almost the only thing you haven't got! How many homes do you have?

Well I've got four, I suppose; not bad for a bachelor is it? But I really haven't *got* a home – I haven't had one for a long time. Talking about houses is one thing. I've got my nine-year-old son and I've got to take him somewhere for a holiday, but I can't bring him to New York – there's not much fun for a kid here. He's seen the Empire State Building, he's done all that, he's on his second passport – and he's only nine! He's been everywhere in the world.

How were you treated when you first arrived here?

Very casually. I'm not a brash human being, you know, I'm a sort of low-tone operator and therefore perhaps I didn't impress them very much.

But you're fairly tough, are you not – you go in on your own?

Yes. Then I play dumb bunny. I don't want to be smart or clever. Everyone has their own negotiating style and mine's always been very low-tone.

When you play dumb bunny, how do you do that?

Well, my ears don't grow! I just sort of lounge around and make jokes and generally appear rather a playboy, you know. And then if they say something I say, 'Oh dear,' or 'Explain that to me, I don't quite understand it.' By the time you've been there for a while they think they've got your measure. I know one or two people that do play a very smart game, but they're so much cleverer than I am. Jim Slater was brilliant, but after about five minutes your eyes have glazed over because you think you're in the wrong division. He's in the First Division, and you're lucky to be playing with Watford – or are Watford now in the First Division?

How much money do you need to have before you're regarded as being comfortably off in America?

The list of four hundred richest people starts with Gordon Getty at about three billion dollars and works its way down the scale. I don't think you can get into that list unless you've got a hundred and fifty million. I remember a story that Lance Reventlow, the son of the Woolworth heiress, used to tell when he was asked about his wealth: 'It must be about ten million,' and they said, 'Then you're very rich and powerful?' He said, 'No – rich but *not* powerful. Onassis is powerful because he has three or four hundred million dollars.' So the measure of money is the measure of power, and in this country that power is really absolute. But for an ordinary fella I suppose anything over a million dollars begins to put a man into the category of being rich.

You're a very social guy and you like to party, you like to enjoy yourself, so New York and LA are OK, but I can't see you being a tycoon in Lagos and Johannesburg?

I can't stand the winters in New York. I'm getting old now and when the wind begins to howl down these canyons. ... If my sinuses go, I'm in trouble, so I think Los Angeles for the winter – January, February and March.

Los Angeles for the sinus, New York for the fun?

It's all here. This is the most vital city in the world, as you know.

Yet New York cost you your second marriage, did it not?

It did indeed. You see the pressure in this town is so great. ... It really was a winning thing that I was doing, and I was devoting a lot of time to it. Then one began to develop a social life, which meant burning the candle at both ends. When I went off to the office in the morning Virginia was at home and she had nothing to do. She was basically not able to fill in her day, because American women are achievers and they're trained from an early age to work. She was not trained to work and so therefore her days were very boring. I would come home racked out and then go on a social round. It caused the erosion of her spirit – not mine, because *I* found it tremendously exciting. I was totally wrapped up in it and I thought, like every man thinks, if a woman has a baby then he's done his bit, right – but it isn't enough. It wasn't enough for her. She didn't like New York. She found it a very cold and soulless place.

Still, Lady White has a certain cachet here?

That didn't come until later; that was five years ago.

She left too early to enjoy it?

I don't think she really cared that much about it. She couldn't cope with New York. We were living in this small hotel suite at the Pierre. Four or five people would come and see me, and she'd be in the bedroom – and suddenly the door would open and everyone's trooping into the loo. That was a major problem, which is part of the stressful side of American living. That's why they've got the highest divorce statistics in the world.

This is a tremendously tough city, Alan, you can't compare it with any other in the world. Someone once said every city has its day, and I believe in the Fifties Paris was the place – it certainly was in the Twenties. Rome had a bit of a swing, and then London in the Sixties. Now it's New York. This is the centre of the world, the most exciting city – if you don't want to go to bed, you don't have to. It's open twenty-four hours a day, there's always something going on.

If it's so stimulating, shouldn't she have enjoyed that?

If she'd had a function, if she'd been able to fit in to the type of life. ... I've never involved the woman in my life with my business – it's terribly boring for women. I adore women and I would never expose them to a lot of boring business people, so I never did ask her to do any of that. We'd go to the theatre, dinner parties, whatever, but in the morning when I got up to leave, her day stretched before her. She wasn't really equipped, you see, because in London you've got that wonderful thing where all the girls get together. They have lunch at San Lorenzo or Harry's Bar and it's a very casual life. . . . So that was the end of my marriage and I was back on my third tour of operations as a bachelor! But it was very traumatic because I had a little son, who's a character. I just sort of took up where I left off before I got married, I suppose.

But it's a curiously lonely place, don't you find?

It is, very lonely.

The parties are good, there are a lot of attractive people and you have a lot of laughs . . . but then you go back to your apartment and start worrying about the figures, the balance sheet?

If you're in a growth operation like we are and have a twenty-five-year record of success, I particularly cannot *bear* to fail. When I took my helicopter flying lessons there were two young guys with me and we bet who would solo first. One was Bill Shand-Kydd, who's ridden the National a couple of times, and the other was Peter Blond who competed in the twenty-four-hour race at Le Mans. I think he came in third. They were both a lot younger than I, but I soloed first. I guess I'm driven, in some way.

I've always been a playboy at heart. At one point I'd say I had a Peter Pan complex – but then some girl gave me a book on the Peter Pan complex which says it's somebody who doesn't want to grow up, so I decided I'd drop that and just be immature. . . .

You seem very relaxed and laid back, not only socially but also in business. Are you in truth like that – or are you working on an ulcer?

I'm very laid back. I couldn't care less about business, other than the fact that I feel it's like boarding a ship, robbing all the men and raping all the women. It's an adventure, as long as it's fun. It *has* to be fun if you're going to tilt against the Establishment or, and particularly in this country, you're going into a very tough fight. Every time you have to gird up your loins to get in there and kill 'em because if not, they'll kill you.

In this environment if you go to have lunch at a bank, they'll ask you for 12.30, don't offer you a drink, tell you not to smoke and sling you out at 1.30! You go to a bank in London, you've got sherry before lunch, a lovely wine with it, brandy after lunch – and away you go in an alcoholic haze. Not here – you want to muddle up your brains with a little booze, and they'll take your knickers!

You're psyched up because you're on your guard the whole time. I'll give you an example: I went to a cocktail party and there was a fellow I like very much and I was talking about a property I had in California and wanted to sell. He was a broker, and he said, 'I'll buy it from you,' so I said,

'Well, I was only mentioning it.' ... Next morning I received a letter from him with a cheque for $50,000, buying the property he'd never seen. I really hadn't done anything other than mention it! So I rang him up and said, 'You're mad.' He said, 'I've bought that property, I'm going to sue you,' and in no time at all I find myself in a lawsuit. (Laughs).

If it's such a tough place and you're putting so much into it and you're hyped up all the time, aren't you going to burn out early?

Burn-out here is usually at forty, forty-five. I didn't come here until I was forty-nine – and I'm *still* forty-nine and fighting burn-out! You can burn out here in short order, and a lot of people do.

Are you going to spend the rest of your days on Park Avenue, or are you going back to Yorkshire?

Never back to Yorkshire. You can't go backwards. I mean England to me represents everything that I believe in, you know, honour. ... The first deal I ever did, I did on a handshake, and I've always believed that a man's word was something you could take. If you have to surround yourself with twenty lawyers to ensure that the man's word is being kept, it's not really very good – but that's what you have to do here.

But in spite of all the awful things that have happened to me, I still have faith in human nature. I still am a crusader. I will go to war for things that are really nothing more than a matter of principle. When Hanson's lost its aircraft – it was the first aircraft that was hijacked years ago – the British Government at that time were doing nothing about it and we had our two pilots in prison in Algeria. They'd been there for days and I was fuming. ...

Anyway we finally got a meeting at the Foreign Office, with the Permanent Under-Secretary of State, and he said, 'You must understand we can't do anything about this.' And I said, 'Well I'm not surprised, this place stinks of decadence – it's rotten to the bloody core.' I said, 'You've got two Englishmen sitting in jail out there with British passports who've been hijacked and we've got George Brown wandering around the Committee Rooms of the House of Commons saying, "There's no way you can hijack an aeroplane. All you have to do is pull the stick back, then everybody can jump on the hijacker."' He said, 'I do not have to be responsible for my political masters.'

I was horrified. Eventually I got hold of Chapman Pincher of the *Daily Express*. I was very psyched up – in fact if he was sitting here now he'd say, 'Oh yes I remember him, I thought he was round the bend.' But he then started a press campaign, headlines in the *Express*: '79 Days' – '80 Days' – '81 Days' ... and finally something was done about it. They released our two pilots, but we didn't get the plane back for ten months.

Did you get financial recompense?

No, the insurance company said, 'We would pay out under the Piracy Act, but as it's not been destroyed and it's still sitting there, you still own it.' So as I'm saying, nobody wanted to do anything about it. It's my sort of a crusading attitude to injustice, and so whilst one can have the attitude of a playboy, I guess that's what's been driving me. I feel like a hamster in one of those cages that goes running round.

Is your anchor so securely dropped that when you go back to your Park Avenue apartment this evening you'll know you're home? Or do you feel you're just here temporarily, and home is really in Chelsea?

I feel some great sense of rage when I go back to Britain. I feel incensed that a man like Scargill can operate. I feel incensed that the injustices that are being perpetrated on the long-suffering British people *continue* to be perpetrated. I cannot bear the Liberals, their attitude to life – that whole thing infuriates me. I think the British working man is as good as anyone, anywhere. I think Margaret Thatcher has done the most tremendous things for Britain. She's given Britain what Ronald Reagan has given the United States: its self-respect. When she took on the Falklands war I think she brought Britain forward twenty-five years and I believe this last spin around the wheel with Mr Scargill, hopefully, will see the end of those barons of the unions because they to a great degree misuse power. Eventually it became the unions' turn and they, I hope, are running out of steam.

The thing in *this* country which is appealing is where you get a bi-partisan approach to a problem. I'm not saying in all cases, but when Reagan was taking on those air traffic controllers, it was not that maudlin cloth-cap technique of the Twenties which the Labour politicians go on spouting – that garbage! They're living in the backwoods – they don't understand. Mitterrand could have studied Britain. De Gaulle took France and shoved it ten years ahead of Britain, from being twenty-five years behind.

Mr Mitterrand discounts Harold Wilson's government with two devaluations of the pound. He discounts how, every time you say, I'm going to squeeze the rich, the money leaves, the brain leaves, and here are these lunatics in England still doing the same thing. Kinnock isn't going to come out and slam the table and say, 'Scargill must go!' He doesn't give a damn shit that the country is being affected by this, because he's preaching something that no self-respecting human being would believe for one second can work, and therefore he'll eventually get stabbed in the back by his left-wing colleagues.

I love going back and I *will* go back. I'll probably be some blimpish individual being pushed up and down Brighton Pier in a wheelchair saying, 'It wasn't like this in the old days!'

You have a home here in New York, you're about to have a home in LA, you've got a home in London, a home in Bermuda, a home in Marbella. . . .

Yes but I haven't been back there for five years. It's like the Duke of Westminster who said, 'I only want to sleep in my own bed.' He was shooting up in Norway, bought a castle – and never went back! I suppose homes are really property investments. I don't consider that I'm running five homes.

It's an amazing thing how, as you said, you do worry. One sees devaluations of currencies, stock markets falling out of bed, gold going up through the roof and you suddenly begin to think: My God, all that you've worked for all of your life can go overnight. Whereas if you'd been reasonably well off in the late Thirties or even the early Forties and Fifties, you could have said, 'Well, interest rates at five per cent, inflation very small and we've no fear'. That's really why I think property, as far as I'm concerned, is a good investment. At least I'll have somewhere to rest my head if the shit hits the fan.

The difference between working in this country and working in the United Kingdom, is the attitude. There's this business of everything being reasonably accessible. If I wanted to see the Mayor or the Governor I could see him. It might take twenty-four hours, but he would see me and he'd give me a good hearing.

But now you're Sir Gordon White of Park Avenue – when you were just Gordon White in the Pierre, it took you half a day to see your own banker!

Yes, well it was much more difficult then. But as I say this is a country of achievement. This isn't a country where if you've got a Rolls-Royce they want to kick the shit out of it. They all look and say, 'He must be somebody.' This is a country where they aspire to achieve. There isn't the jealousy. Though they may try to mug you!

Normally in New York I use limousines, they're easier, but I've never had anyone go ... you know ... up yours! This is just not the place to have a motor car. It's a town where you walk. I wouldn't take a Rolls-Royce to Paris with a driver because you're going to get the finger if you stop at the traffic lights. You're going to get them giving you a hard time. I would not be happy to take a Rolls-Royce out in London and park it in the West End somewhere. It'll get done over.

If you're in the residential districts in London you're OK. Of course you're going to get a yobbo everywhere, but in the main they're not envious of your having a snazzy-looking motor car here. When I say here, I mean the whole of the US and not just New York City. They're very happy to see you succeed and I've never had any real problem with that. I find they try harder.

Again you see, you've got service in this country now. Years ago I remember talking to Harold Wilson about service, and the trouble with Britain being that iniquitous Selective Employment Tax that they brought in where you would feather-bed the manufacturing industries and penalize the service industries.

And I think the ratio today of people is sixty-five per cent manufacturing to thirty-five per cent service in Britain, and in this country it's the other way around. If you go back to your hotel and you want a bottle of scotch from your local liquor shop you can call up and they'll deliver it to your door. You're not going to be charged anything extra for it. Now that fellow's earning a lot more money than his counterpart in Britain will be earning. Service here is the basis of the country operating.

What about the calibre of the executives?

They are not as apt to go off for long lunches as their British counterparts, but then I'm again only relating it to London.

I've got this luncheon coming up in Washington: 'John Macmillion is pleased that you will attend our 12.15 p.m. September 10 Board luncheon in the Capitol, S207 the Manfield Room.' The first meeting of the international committee will be convened at one-thirty, immediately following the luncheon. Now that's not much time, is it? And this is honouring a man who's done quite a lot, so if you were to take the American approach and the British approach, I think you'll find that the Americans tend to work in a slightly different way, longer hours. They push more paper around than we do. I don't think they're any more efficient, other than that they will cut through red tape. If you go back to the war the Americans were quite prepared to swap a Jeep for something else that they might require, and the hell with what might happen afterwards.

When you think, we won the war and the Americans squandered the peace and we found ourselves in 1951 – reckoning the war broke out in '39 – still with petrol coupons, food coupons and God knows what else, one Socialist government after another, and then MacMillan for thirteen years and You've Never Had it So Good and nobody doing a bloody thing for the British working man.

I'm not going to criticize, but there isn't any way that one can begin to believe *that* is the spirit of Britain which conquered the world. Is it still there?

One of the most difficult things in running an empire this size, or any other size, is whether you're lucky enough to be a committee of one, because if you're prepared to make the decision, then you have an enormous advantage over your adversaries, your contemporaries or anyone else. You're not sitting around a table talking about something for hours and hours, and usually leaving without making a decision. I believe there isn't anything that's needed in this organization that would demand a decision I wouldn't give in very short order. I don't need to have meetings to discuss it. If they run into a problem where a decision needs to be made – somebody wants $15 million to build a new factory – it'll eventually land on my desk and I will assess the value. . . .

I operate here with Eddie and very little paperwork. James Hanson and I don't operate by committee. Normally a British company in the United States, if they run into a problem or they want to do something, they'll go back to Britain where they'll have a board meeting and discuss it, and then send answers back. You get a problem over *here* and somebody in Britain's trying to sort it out – it doesn't make sense.

My job as Chairman and Chief Executive Officer of Hanson Industries is, I am responsible for the bottom line. I believe my responsibility is to make money. We have a lot of people working for us making cowboy boots, hot dogs, furniture, food service, ladies' dresses, six hundred shoe shops . . . there must be about sixty-five companies. You name it, we've got it. We make about twenty-five per cent return on capital employed, which is extremely high.

Of course there are two ways to make money: one is to keep your capital employed low, that way you're getting a high return. You do away with all the lush offices and the whole thing. US Industries, for instance, that we've just taken over – their head office costs were twenty million dollars a year. I reckon we can run it for one and a half million dollars. We'll get rid of all those people who're not doing any work. Then there's a magnificent office, eighty thousand square feet of building and five thousand dollars a month to cut the bloody grass! It's all unnecessary. The lads who're making the money are those out in the field.

Why is it that so few Brits make it here?

Because it's tough. They are different people. Their whole sense of doing business is entirely different. Also you're not dealing entirely with Anglo-Saxons. There's an enormous proportion of Jews here, particularly in the legal profession. The Jews have always been very hot on education. They're also very liberal. Most of them are Democrats.

Until Mr Jackson . . .?

In any other country in the world Mr Jackson would be laughed out of town. . . . In no other country of the world would you find them cheering and shouting that they've elected a woman as a possible vice-president. All she knows is about Queens. I doubt she's ever been on a foreign trip anywhere.

I'm not a chauvinist. I would have voted for Margaret Thatcher with bells on because the man she replaced was not even a man! He'd do very well over here in the Democratic Party, not in the Conservative Party.

Why doesn't someone like Gerald Ronson come over here?

Gerald's not a businessman, in terms of running a company, but he's a very tough cookie. Robert Maxwell hasn't time to come over here. The sell is softer in England you know – much softer. The erosion of spirit here doing a deal. ... I mean everything that goes wrong – the arguments, the fights, places where you think you've got a deal and the next thing you get a call from a lawyer who says, 'No, you didn't have a deal,' and that wasn't said and this wasn't said. ... And then all the hookers try to climb on the bandwagon and make something out of it.

Are you feeling a bit burnt out now?

We've had a hot summer, I've just finished the biggest deal we've ever done, $530 million, despite a $7 million lawyer's bill. This merely confirms what I already knew would happen, so I already deducted that from the price, but it still pisses me off to think I'm going to have to fight them all. That's a mass of work – there's fifteen different people involved in that lot.

You're talking about ...?

Lawsuits, fights with each one of them. Yes I'll fight them myself. What I would like to do, and might even do at the end of the day, is expose the whole obscenity by persuading the *Wall Street Journal* to run it as an article. I mean it, because I believe that these people should be exposed – the people who're working for the company that we've bought.

So you inherited them and they say, 'This is the end of the line anyway, so what the hell ...?'

That's right – send the bill to him! We were lucky, by the way, we put a stop on all the cheques before they got paid. They're like a bunch of carrion crows round a dead body.

But these are very reputable lawyers and accountants?

Of course they are, but that doesn't mean anything. They're in the business for making money. You see, so much depends on whether or not you can chuck overboard your Britishness when you get here.

But you haven't ...

I have, really. I don't think I've chucked it over to *you*, because you're British too, but if I was dealing with an American you wouldn't be hearing anything smart from me. I would be asking him to repeat what he was saying a couple of times and I would be being very casual and very dumb, and then wait for him to take advantage of me. Oh yes, it's a game. But what happens is, you get bored with the game. . . .

It's all poker?

If you would like to buy this cigarette lighter from me, I know I would take five dollars for it, but I ask you fifty dollars. Now you could turn round and say, 'Goodbye,' at which point you wouldn't get to the door before I reduce the price to forty-five dollars or whatever, and then slowly. . . . I find all that incredibly degrading. I can do it, but I don't like doing it.

I do my negotiating on the basis of listening to what the man is saying, what the whole thing's about. I'm not about to knock what I'm trying to buy, or pump up what I'm trying to sell. I don't want to waste a lot of time, so if I'm selling something I'll say, 'These are the figures,' and I can either say, 'Make me an offer,' or 'I want X amount of money for it and that doesn't mean Y.' Well he won't believe me, so then we'll start to haggle to get the price down and I'll just sit there. I'll say, 'You're wasting your time, son, I don't want to start at a hundred and get paid up at fifty, so let's get ourselves straight.'

If you know what you're doing and you go in expecting that, you can dance the light fantastic and play according to the rules, but I don't even take any lawyers with me. I prefer to be alone and I don't mind if they've got twenty people.

When I sold this fishing company quite recently, the fellows had all gone round our fishing fleet, thirty vessels, and they came up with a portfolio, all beautifully presented, of photographs of little holes that they'd found, rust marks and so on, and this fellow then says, 'Your fishing fleet is nowhere near as good as ours, it's not worth what's in the books.'

I said, 'You shouldn't have gone to so much trouble to knock our fleet. We catch twenty-five per cent more fish per vessel than you do. Our captains earn more money than yours do.' And he said, 'We couldn't have these ships with our flag the way they look.' I said, 'Well then, you're obviously in the shipping business and not in the fishing business. You can buy these ships and paint them up – but they won't catch as many fish as they're catching now. If you don't want to buy my business I'll buy *your* business.' Anyway I sold mine, thank God.

You can't say that was a terribly bright fellow, but he'd gone to all that trouble to knock the product. I was always brought up to believe that you should not knock somebody else's choice. If you're shoving motor cars and a fellow drives up in a Cadillac, you don't say, 'God have *you* got a bag of worms, you should have a Rolls-Royce' – because straight away you've insulted the fellow's intelligence and his perspicacity.

I've walked into a room with twenty people, exchanged four words, and walked out. I went round and shook hands with each one of them, and then I walked out. They'd got me there under false pretences. I wasn't going to sit there and listen to a lot of rubbish. I did the deal eventually, but in fact they'd just got me there to kick the shit out of me. They weren't ready to do a deal.

Leverage! We call it gearing. Means the same thing. Who said, 'Give me a big enough lever and I'll shift the world?' Archimedes. Leverage is borrowed money. So let's say you put up ten dollars equity and borrow ninety dollars, you've now got a hundred dollars to work with instead of ten dollars. And that ninety dollars is the leverage. Or gearing.

The other thing here is that the tax laws are incredibly helpful. Like the initial deal I told you about where I paid with paper, you'd say, 'Why would they take your paper?' The reason was there were five different families, all of them quite old, and one who was quite sick. I was paying them $32 million for the business. I gave him $32 million of paper, IOUs. Each of the IOUs was for nine per cent interest, payable over three years. I took the business to pay off the notes, and I secured the notes with the business.

Their business secured my notes; their money paid them off, but the reason they did it was because if you take paper, you don't pay any taxes. If I'd been paying them in cash, Uncle Sam would have taken his half right away, so by paying him in paper they would pay tax on the dividend interest, nine per cent interest, but they would not pay on the principal amounts until they were paid in cash.

In the meantime if any of them had died, they wouldn't have been taxed twice because a note is valueless, effectively. If they'd taken cash they would have paid tax on the cash, and then if one of them had died afterwards, the cash that was left would have been charged as estate duty, just the same as Britain.

So this is where you get the leverage principle working, and I was lucky enough to run into a group of five dissenting family members, all of them very old, all of them wanting to get out of the business, and prepared to take the notes from what looked like an honourable fellow – me!

A Gordon White promissory note is just an IOU?

That's right, that's all they are. And that's what the bank has right now, for $530 million.

You didn't pay them the commitment fee?

No I didn't pay it and it's quite unique. Where on earth can you ring up and in twenty-four hours get $530 million! But that is the extent of my credibility here, after nine years. I've never put a deal to them that they had to turn down. I've lost a number of deals that we didn't get, and every one of them went for three or four times the money I wanted to pay for it. They have this feeling that they can trust me implicitly. In fact I said, with arrogance, You know you couldn't afford to employ me so why bother to second guess one of my deals?

Who were you dealing with – what sort of level?

Chief lending manager. Now they're asking me to bring in a couple of other banks because they're reaching their legal lending limit. Banks are in the business of selling money; they're greedy and not very good-quality people in a lot of ways – and lazy, bone lazy.

So imagine lending $530 million to one customer, one set of accounts, one legal document to be drawn up, instead of a hundred borrowing $5 million. Imagine the paperwork! If they can find someone they can trust for $500 million or a billion, they're happy.

I was Chairman of Operation Drake, a round-the-world thing, and I've always been fascinated by Francis Drake because when he finally got up against it he executed the gentleman adventurer who was trying to persuade him to turn back. You can't turn back once you've set out on this type of venture.

I have no more goals in my life, other than developing what I would like to see as the biggest British company in the United States. That's really what motivates me, because I haven't got anything *else* to motivate me. I think once one has enough money, you can only have so many suits, so many watches. Money is a commodity – it's there to be spent. Personal money is not something that's driving me, but I *would* like to have a real presence in this country. I think we saved this country, you see. The Battle of Britain, when we stood alone. Basically if it hadn't been for Britain, Hitler would probably have conquered the world, and during that time there was a thing called Cash and Carry, where all of the British assets in this country were sold off: pay cash and come and fetch it. I think that's all Roosevelt could handle with Congress, as it was at the time. Britain owned about twenty per cent of this country. It was all sold off and it paid for us to fight that war up until that moment that the Americans were forced in, in 1941, by which time we'd been fighting alone for two years.

I'd like to have all that back again. I was fascinated to buy back a company called the English Linen Thread Company, an old company that had been sold off during the war.

I believe Britain is now the biggest investor in the United States. We've always been investing overseas and we *have* to invest in the United States. This is the biggest economy in the world, it's the greatest challenge and the rewards are the greatest.

How do you think you are regarded at home?

A lot of people say I'm a tax exile, which is absolute rubbish. I pay American taxes, I'm an American resident. When I first went out of England

I became a Bermudan resident and I'm still domiciled in Bermuda, but it wasn't really anything to do with tax. It was just my terrible fear that if I did make any money, that the Socialists were going to take it away from me or from my children, so I got a reputation of being a tax exile.

I'm not a tax exile, I'm a crusader. As a matter of fact, I did something really rather important at one point, because I couldn't understand why we couldn't bring money out of England. Back in 1939, 1940 when they decided this Cash and Carry thing would work, every Briton had to turn his assets over to the country and you were repaid in sterling. That is why they created Exchange Control regulations; so you found a situation like Lester Piggott being arrested at the airport for having seventy quid in his pocket when you were only allowed to take out thirty-five pounds in business allowances. God knows, I couldn't get any money *out* of Britain, so I employed the *Economist* Intelligence Unit to go into what this whole thing was about, going back to 1940 when it was introduced. They discovered that nobody had ever looked at it, or ever thought about it. Then of course when the Thatcher Government came into power, the Prime Minister must have done a parallel scene. They decided to scrub it out because it was ridiculous – all these people stopping travellers going through Customs with thirty-five pounds in their pocket, when if you wanted to buy a 747 for $50 million and you had the money, you could get it.

I feel that Britain should redevelop her overseas assets, but we have to develop them in countries that are stable. We had masses of money in Africa, South America, the Argentine – the railroads were built by the British. We colonized the world, and then slowly all of that adventurous spirit disappeared as these assets were swallowed up by nationalization. I think the United States is the country where we can develop a major empire, for the benefit of the British shareholders. . . .

THE PHENOMENON

I truly listen to what Joan thinks and believes. . . .

Joan Collins was a good old trouper for many years, though her show-biz rollercoaster never paused long enough at the top: it kept swooping her down again, into obscurity. Then after appearing with some desperation in such indelicate British B-films as *The Bitch* and *The Stud*, she joined Hollywood's *Dynasty* as a tentative Alexis Carrington – and became the world's most famous, sensual woman; not merely a star in a night-time Soap of little merit, but an international phenomenon bringing reassurance to every woman over fifty-two who could see how, with a little luck, everything can be held together. . . .

With Joan it was not so much luck as application, determination, discipline and ferocious ambition. With looks the lens adores, she cannot take a bad picture: large eyes, large cheekbones, large teeth, large mouth, large chest – everything perfectly proportioned for the camera. The extraordinary *Dynasty* clothes in fierce colours may look tawdry in real life with their glitter and swansdown and beading, but on the small screen show a sort of Sunset Boulevard style.

Joan–Alexis adds an enviable glitz to everything she promotes – not only herself, but Cinzano, Revlon's 'Scoundrel', Cannon Mills towels, fur coats. . . . Far more significant, she has brought hope to watching generations: 'You may be here today and gone tomorrow – but you could be back the day *after*!'

———

I get all the English Sunday papers first thing Monday morning so I know what's going on, and I must say I do miss it terribly. Believe it or not, I miss the weather, I miss the change of seasons. I miss the sort of *reality* of it. I miss the buses down the street, the look of London, the look of the English countryside. Los Angeles is a very barren sort of place, and when you're locked into a sound stage as I am three or four days a week you don't get to see any sun and wind and moon and rain, and people walking down the street. Looking at people just walking down Oxford Street or Park Lane, just looking at people in action. Here everybody's in their cars, and of course when you're in your car you have to close everything up and lock the doors because this is not a terribly safe place, particularly if you're very well known. You go everywhere by car. I hardly ever walk along the street

122

at all. I did the other day along Rodeo Drive and because I'm rather sort of obvious and well known, it was kind of difficult. I couldn't be private. People kept on coming up and talking to me.

But wouldn't they do that in Bond Street?

Yes (laughs) that's true, but not so much. In fact English people have a tendency to leave you alone a lot more than Americans do. Americans are more outgoing, so if you come into their living rooms every Wednesday night they think you're their friend and they have a sort of *right* to come and say Hello, and how much they liked the show, whereas of course we in England are more laid back, if that's the word.

So if they decided to film *Dynasty* at Pinewood, would you be delighted?

Oh I'd be *thrillllld*! I'd be overjoyed. I'd love to go back to Pinewood in any case, it's the most wonderful studio.

Yet the British press has on occasion given you rather a hard time?

That's for sure. Yes. Well I think I'm probably a sort of controversial, notorious or colourful character, and I think people like to read about my life, what I'm doing. So often i've found that what they write about is a gross exaggeration and often downright absolute fabrication, but there's not much I can do about it other than grit my teeth and not let it bother me too much.

You're selling those supermarket tabloids, aren't you? Every time one sees a headline it's another of your adventures. I suppose that's a sort of validation of your success?

It is, in a way. It's strange because it used to be that film stars, movie actors were the sort of crème de la crème of show business, but it's changed now. Television has become such a major force you're finding the biggest stars of stage and screen coming on to television – in fact, *desperate* to get on to the hit shows, so the television stars have become more important. People are avid to read about what we're doing. Beats me why!

You've also become a sort of whipping girl for the press?

It's very interesting because I think there's something the press like to do on both sides of the pond: they build somebody up and say they're wonderful – and then take knocks at them. I found the other day to my horror that they were actually taking knocks at Princess Diana, because of her hairstyles. They've been saying how wonderful she is for four years and now all of a sudden they're knocking her. If they can do that to her, they can do it to anybody – and they do!

How then does life over here differ – is it easier?

In terms of work, in terms of being an actress ... for the very first time in my life, I'm secure.

Financially, you mean?

Financially yes. I suppose that is as important as knowing I'm going to be employed in *something* – first of all that I love doing and secondly, quite lucratively, for at least another two years, because the show is No. 1, vying with *Dallas*. Sometimes it's No. 2. That is an enormous security for an actor, because this is the most insecure of professions. Whenever you start any job actors are always wondering when it finishes in five weeks or ten weeks, What are we going to do next? There's no security as an actor, none at all. I've had quite a bit of that, so this is quite gratifying.

You've always lived the gypsy life – would this then be the best place to come to rest?

Well, I'm not really resting Alan, I've never been so busy in my life. Never. I mean it's a good thing I've got a lot of energy, because I actually never stop. Not only am I doing *Dynasty* but I brought out my book, I've got my own line of jewellery I'm bringing out, I'm associated with various other things. ...

Scent and towels and ... you name it?

Yes, Revlon ..., Well, not towels, that was just a sort of one-shot thing, but lots of things. I want to become more of a businesswoman because I adore fashion and I'd like to have my own line of dresses, evening dresses or sportswear. I'm blessed with an abundance of energy, so I'm not exactly slowing down. I'm getting faster.

From a business point of view America is obviously better, but what about your social life – is it happiness to be in Beverly Hills?

I've got a wonderful house and a swimming pool and the weather of course is very nice. It's great for entertaining, but of course I never have time to entertain. One goes to Palm Springs if you really want to get a tan, but the whole thing is that there isn't that much time, because these clothes don't just *happen*. I don't normally dress like this – I've come straight off the set. They take a lot of work, they take a lot of talking about, a lot of fittings. *Everything* takes a lot of time. I don't wake up looking like this! I mean, the make-up's got to be done, the hair's got to be done, the lines have got to be learned, the scripts have got to be studied. You have to talk to the producer, the director, the writer about various things that have to be changed, because I'm a bit of a perfectionist.

I realized finally in my life that I know a *great* deal better than anybody else about what I'm doing. I've always listened too much to what other people have told me – agents and directors and producers and everybody. Now I listen to myself. I truly listen to what *Joan* thinks and believes in, and that turns out nine times out of ten to be correct – for me.

You first came here in the Fifties, and since then you seem to have taken part in all the American rituals – you even went to a psychiatrist?

I did for a short period of time. I really did that because at that particular time I was under contract and I was bored during the day. There wasn't much to do when I wasn't working, and everybody else was doing it so I figured, Well it's the *in* thing to do. I also did the thing that everybody else did, which was take a business manager and a personal manager and press agent. All the things one is supposed to do. But I don't do any of that now, I don't have any of those people.

Did the shrink help? You were a well-balanced girl from Maida Vale, so was it useful?

Yes, it was quite interesting. It made me get in touch with some of my past a bit more and gave me a certain realization of what created me.

You also did Actualization therapy at one time – this is like EST, isn't it? I had a friend here who put his wife and his girlfriend into EST, which was the worst thing he ever did because they came out and gave him a hard time. Did it do something to your character? You were pretty strong to start with. . . .

No, no, I wasn't. I'm actually quite shy – when I was younger. I couldn't say boo to a goose, I really couldn't. I think Actualization in a way helped me get in touch with my own opinions, helped me raise my own self-esteem because I realized that I was responsible, in the final analysis, for myself. And nobody else was. It was useless for me going around and expecting this agent to do that and this person to do this. The only person who could do it was *me*. That's one of the things that helped me quite a bit.

It seems that in this place, more than anywhere else, they *do* like a winner. I remember Peter Sellers telling me that when he did a couple of bad movies, people crossed the road to avoid talking to him. They were frightened it was going to rub off. . . .

Oh that's terrible. And I can't believe it, I think there's a lot of exaggeration about this place, I really do.

Well what about 'Joan Who' – you did that!

That was my little joke. That was when I was in my episodic TV period, which was when I was on *everything* from *Mission Impossible* to *Batman* to *Star Trek*. I would go into the studio and say, Joan Collins come to report for *Policewoman*, and they'd say, 'Joan *who?*' So I finally got a licence plate with Joan Who on it.

Great! It seems that generally Americans are more ambitious than we are. You're an exception – you were obviously ambitious and determined, but Americans show much more drive. . . .

I think, Alan, one of the reasons is that the American is brought up to believe he can become President of the United States, he can become President of General Motors. A great many people are brought up to believe that you can do *anything* in this country. There's no class barrier, it doesn't matter where you're born, where your parents are from. The self-made man has proliferated all over the place. And I think that's possibly one of the reasons why there is this driving ambition with so many people, because they know that if they apply themselves, they can make it. And they do. Often.

You're becoming, in a way, the quintessential dream figure for American women, are you not? You go into *Playboy* and it sells an extra million copies. . . . Women are buying the tabloids to find out how you've done it?

I'm quite popular with American women, I think, because I typify in a way in the character that I play. . . .

But you're playing a bitch?

Yes, but she's not really, you see. If she was just that. . . .

A bitch with a heart of gold?

Not even that. No, she's much more complex, because I don't think people are just black and white. You see a lot of bitches on television and they're just black and they're just boring. What Alexis has I think is this tremendous drive, this competitive spirit in which she will not be downtrodden by anybody. This feeling that nobody is going to say No to her, absolutely nobody, and this strong sense of survival in a man's world. I think this is what a lot of women like and identify with.

It seems to me there are only two kinds of women on television, the bitch or the wimp. There's nothing in between. It's rather pathetic. Women are so categorized there's this and then there's that, and there shouldn't be – they should be able to cross over, they should be able to be both because nobody is just one thing. If Alexis was a man they wouldn't call him a bitch. They wouldn't *dare* call him a bastard, because you can't say that word on TV. They'd probably say a strong, tough, aggressive man, isn't that wonderful. . . . But because I'm a woman, she's a bitch.

It does seem you've tapped something because so many American women want to be you, or want to be Alexis. . . .

Quite a few. There's the thing about being over forty and still not sitting knitting an antimacassar – that's quite appealing! I think that trend which started some years ago of the woman being over forty and still being acceptable and attractive has become extremely prevalent. Practically every actress nowadays is over forty, in any case.

A few years ago an over-thirty leading lady didn't exist.

Not when I came into the business. I came under contract to Fox when I was twenty, for six years, because quite clearly they felt that by the time an actress was twenty-six or twenty-seven she was past her prime, the bloom was off her and nobody would want to look at her. That went on for *years*, from the Twenties up until the Seventies, really. Actresses were sort of discarded like so much old Kleenex by the time they got to thirty-five. Go back to the old stars, the Hedy Lamarrs, the Norma Shearers, the Joan Crawfords, they got into playing grandma parts when they were in their late thirties. It's really amazing how it changed. I think it's great!

Americans are curiously puritanical, so you must have given them a few shocks, one way or another?

Well there's this sort of double standard, isn't there? I was watching cable TV last night just as I was about to fall asleep and I suddenly sat bolt upright because I was seeing a very explicit sex scene on Channel 14 or 16, one of the cable channels. I don't think they're as puritanical as they make out.

I was watching television last night too and there was one programme that was showing European television commercials and they screened a warning: Parental Guidance Advised! They were advising people to guard their children from a British commercial advertising jeans! The girls had their breasts whited-out!

It's a bit silly – when the kids are buying their comics they can see copies of men's magazines with very blatant sexual attitudes on the cover. It's strange double standard.

It seems that the theme of rich people being unhappy, which is *Dynasty*, is a winner here.

Oh yes, yes – it's wonderful! Everybody loves to see rich people suffering. And the better-dressed they are, the more expensive the Rolls and the Bentley, the more lavish the chandeliers, the accoutrements, the better they like it.

Are you going to stay here and suffer, or do you see Highgate looming large? Is it back to Maida Vale . . .?

Maida Vale? Oh I don't know if I want to go back to Maida Vale, it's where I was born. I've got very strong ties to England. Really strong, I've got great friends and a lot of family there. I think that I would love to be able to have my cake and eat it too, to live between England and America and spend perhaps an equal amount of time in both places. It's very difficult because Katy, my twelve-year-old, is at school, and I can't yank her out. So basically I see myself here for a few years, and after that I don't know. I may decide to go and live on an island. Ibiza, who knows – near Ibiza, at least.

So the future is another couple of years of *Dynasty* – and then?

I've already formed my own production company and in April I'm going to be doing a television movie which I'm producing, which I've been involved with from the beginning. I want to get more into doing what I *want* to do, choosing the subjects.

Your own life would be a hell of a good television series wouldn't it – it's got lots of drama, sex, men, success, failure. . . .

I'd rather do a fictionalized version of various things, I don't want to do my own life. Enough is written about it already. I try very hard to keep a private life. When I go into my house and close the doors, that's it. Nobody knows what's going on. And I want to keep it that way.

What about your nude pictures in *Playboy?*

They weren't *that* nude, actually.

Nude-ish?

Nude-ish. I suppose they would shock a lot of people, but well – not *that* many. They were quite tastefully done. . . .

THE ACTRESS

*These women do not realize they're really
making men impotent . . . .*

In the Forties Edana Romney was with the BBC Repertory company. In the Fifties she appeared in films like *Corridor of Mirrors*, produced by her husband John Woolf. In the Sixties she was on BBC television as an early agony-aunt: in *Is This Your Problem?* homosexuals, drug addicts and beaten wives would sit before the camera – protected by a winged armchair – and confess their traumas to Edana and Edgar Lustgarten. Then in the mid-Sixties she suddenly flew to California on a visit – and stayed.

She took her elderly mother, her elderly butler Freddie and most of the furnishings of a Hyde Park Street flat and a cottage in Kent . . . to an elderly house on Summitridge, high above the Los Angeles smog-line in Beverly Hills. They could not drive, so amid the automania of Los Angeles had no car. Sometimes friends would come up the winding roads to their rescue, and perhaps stay for tea. A wise woman and a great friend, Edana transported her world unscathed from Rose Cottage, Somerhill, to the unreal atmosphere of Beverly Hills.

═══

Was it an instant love affair when you arrived here in the Sixties?

You know those old movies when they get off a plane and they suddenly hear harps and lutes and things like that? It's the most extraordinary thing considering how ugly LA airport is, but I suddenly felt incredibly happy and knew at that moment that I'd not return. I didn't, for years. I was frightened in case I was pulled back to stay – in case the magic that brought me here would go. That's no disloyalty to England because what I feel about this country is what you feel for a lover, and what I feel about England is what you feel for a parent.

After those fourteen hours, or whatever it is when you fly here, I found such an incredible change. I might have dropped out of Mars, manwise. It took me at least a couple of years to understand Hollywood-American men, as opposed to other American men. In England you grow up with the friends you know, and you expect to be led up the garden path – but the garden path has roses. Here it's instant sex, like it's instant coffee. I don't mind that, but I *do* mind it from strangers who I have no intention of having sex with. I found it very difficult to cope with.

In Europe you meet a Frenchman or a Spaniard, and something in your computer says, This is the way you behave towards a Frenchman or a Spaniard. Here because it's such a homogeneous world, you don't realize that behind that dark man you're meeting – who might be called Mr Brown – is an Italian; therefore you can't change the switch and adjust your reaction. Frenchmen are supposed to be very flirtatious and so and so, and you understand that and flirt with them, but if a man is named Brown, your whole attitude is different – yet he really *is* French. It's total confusion! In the Arab world they all wear different turbans to denote what sects they belong to, so that you should know. Here they don't wear the hats or turbans you expect.

Everything here is based on money. In England if you have money, you should hide it. Here it's the reverse. They immediately want to know who you are and how much you've got. If you said you were down to your last penny, they'd think you were down to your last million. The only way I cope with that, as I haven't anything, is to live entirely as I lived in England.

This particular community of Beverly Hills is very generous, very kind, and was absolutely marvellous to me. Obviously if they hadn't been, I wouldn't have stayed. It was wonderful being a foreigner, with no one knowing your past. They only know what they see. That was very exciting then – but now I miss people knowing my past, and feel lonely.

It's curious that you've been so comfortable and happy in an area where a single woman is at a disadvantage – and a single woman without a lot of money would normally be at an insurmountable disadvantage!

I live exactly as I lived at my cottage in Kent. I live in a farmhouse sort of way, which they found eccentric and unusual. I always collected around me interesting people from all walks of life. Here they're terrified of knowing or meeting anyone who's out of what they consider their class, so when they come to my teas or my At Homes or Twelfth Nights or whatever, they're fascinated by this extraordinary mixture of people. Different people are attracted to bits and pieces of one. That's why I have this liquorice-allsorts group of friends, because each one of them appeals to a particular side of me.

I've always believed, Don't wait to be asked: *do!* If your home becomes known to have interesting people coming to it, you're never alone because whatever happens they're going to invite you ... to be invited back. Americans are much more generous than the British. At the drop of a hat they'll give a party for you, they're going to entertain you.

People have told me that in Beverly Hills you only meet an architect if you hire one, otherwise you only meet *other* actors, *other* doctors .... You do seem to keep to your little groups?

There are two hundred people, I would say, in Beverly Hills proper, and you can go from party to party to party of tremendous wealth, great catered affairs – all sorts of presents given to the women – and you'll meet precisely the same people. They very rarely give little affairs where you can *talk* to people. But I've grown out of all that, I'm being much more selective now. When you first come to a foreign country you're not selective because you don't know who to select.

The telephone is a lifeline here and I know you have your daily hook-ups. No one wants to listen to your problems, they want to tell you theirs – so you must be unique as a sympathetic listener in an area where no one ever listens....

Absolutely. There are no ears around here, they never listen to *my* problems. I find that women in their thirties, forties, fifties, are very lonely, very insecure. When I first came here I had to get the telephone wired up as I had a radio show then. I phoned a repair man and said, 'Could you come early, at about seven o'clock, because I've got to go off.' This man arrived ready to pop into bed! He was a lovely blond Scandinavian. I said, 'How *dare* you assume a thing like that, you're a telephone man!' He said, 'We almost pay to work in this area. My friend's had this particular lady for the last three years, and I just assumed when you asked me to come at seven that's what you meant.'

So women are lonely, and they don't *do* very much – I don't know many single women who entertain, they're all waiting to be *asked*. They wait and they wait and they wait. I've never felt alone, I've never felt lonely, ever in my whole life. I've felt bereaved, if you like, but not lonely. I never see myself that way.

Many English women make their homes a centre – here when a woman is single her first thing is, 'How am I going to get another man?' I don't mean just as a boyfriend or a lover, it's, 'I've got to get someone else, I've *got* to be Mrs again.' They're in absolute terror of being alone, and therefore they'll accept anything. They're chosen, they do not choose.

One of the most terrifying things of all is that these women do not realize they're really making men impotent. The natural thing for a man is to be the aggressor – I don't mean socially, but sexually. If you stop that aggression, you're going to stop the sexual urge – and here are these women who *pounce*! I've spoken to many men who're absolutely terrified because they're now being judged by their sexual prowess, apart from anything else: 'That's *not* how it's done on page seven!' Here the only weapon a woman has is sex.

The other day a girl told me she'd met a man and was absolutely crazy about him, but he hadn't phoned her for three weeks. Having had an affair already, she phoned him and he was very ho-hum about it all and finally she said, 'Well, should I come?' to wherever he was, and he said 'Why not?' Now if someone had said that to me, I'd have been dead. It's very possible that one is old-fashioned and doesn't understand, but there's no wooing any more, there's no one sending flowers. Well for me, they'd have to because I would not be able to function as a sexual person if I felt I had to be aggressive to get that man. But I think that's an upbringing; it's what one's used to.

Do you find relationships over here are often curiously shallow, compared to affairs and friendships at home?

People are frightened of ever letting their hair down. I don't mean you're going to tell all, I don't mean that. What I mean is, the openness and honesty in the relationship of friends. People are constantly surprised when chums come over, like yourselves, who I've known for years – and that they're exactly the same as they were when I left. They have not got those sorts of friends. If you take Elizabeth Taylor, Sinatra or whoever, they have this sort of rat-pack around them, their hairdressers, their secretaries. They're the people they go about with – they need them for protection. None of them have deep friendships, except with those people.

It's a character thing, too. There are all sorts of people who're always looking over your shoulder – that's why I very rarely go to a cocktail party. That's why I give tea parties – they can't look over my shoulder with a cup in their hand. It's a much homelier thing. When people are sitting, they're different from standing and seeing who they can interrupt.

In America people seem to be using others all the time – everybody's got something to sell or promote, whether it's their bodies or their minds.... On every level, every acquaintanceship's a bit suspect. At home we have friends we don't want anything from and they don't expect anything of us – we're just pleased to see each other; yet that doesn't seem to happen here. Everybody's thinking, Perhaps this guy will help me....

I don't actually agree about that: I think we should want things from our friends. Friendship is based on deep memories of what you've shared. If you haven't got those things, then the person becomes an acquaintance. When I went back to London there were people who were quite good friends, saying, 'We haven't got a maid, do come and have a drink.' A drink! I've gone all those miles to meet an old friend and they can't be bothered to do something for me! It hasn't got to be a big Do, or anything special.... They wouldn't be like that here. When anyone's about to go anywhere, they're given big farewell parties; at the Bistro there's always a table for somebody's birthday. I hadn't had a birthday party given to me in my life, until I came here...

Beverly Hills is a collection of some of the most extravagant houses, the most ostentatious wealth you can find anywhere in the world: every store on Rodeo would supply a whole town anywhere else with luxury, yet here there're scores clustered together – just another Giorgio, another Lapidus.... I don't know where else there's such a concentration of conspicuous expenditure.

And yet when you go around with the creative people here, the writers and the directors, when you're with them there's this chummy feeling because of the communication of ideas. Most other people talk about what was on *Dynasty* yesterday, what was on the telly, whether they've bought a new dress.... Heard any dirt this week? It's never to do with an exchange of ideas, because everyone's camouflaged.

Joan Collins has done an enormous amount for all women – nothing to do with being an actress. In some way she represents the most important breakthrough in the last twenty years – she's given great hope to a lot of women. Men look at women differently now. In France women have young lovers and the mature woman is absolutely worshipped and adored because she has an exoticism and a strangeness that someone wants to find out about. Here there are very few mistresses – those wonderful *femmes fatales* – because they're all giving it away for nothing! Here they can look in the tabloids and find what everybody else is doing – it's made sex terribly common. They haven't realized that to be sexually exciting there must be the atmosphere of excitement long before the person's even arrived in your home.

People have talked about the *Is This Your Problem?* programmes I did in England and asked what's the difference here, what was the American problem I *never* met in all those hundreds of people who wrote to me. There were two very definite problems I didn't get in England: one was the fear of a man who'd had a heart attack, and when would he be able to make love again? The man who feared, and the woman who didn't know how to cope with that. The other was the total disregard for parents here. I heard so many problems about the loneliness of parents and how badly they were treated by their children. We never *once* had that problem with the BBC.

Pack them off to Sun City...?

Quite. No children have grandparents any more – and a grandparent in the family is terribly important. The breakfast table's important. There's no breakfast table here, there's no dinner table. People sit round the TV with

TV dinners and there's none of those wonderful exchanges between parents and children that there are in English homes.

So what's the view of England from here?

Oh it's wonderful: a special kind of feeling. . . .

Little country pubs and Portobello Road?

Right. Also this Princess has done an enormous amount – people were up all night for that wedding! They have a great feeling about the Royal Family and about Royalty and Ladies and Gents – they just adore titles. That's why so many people invent titles when they come here. Von this, and the Baron something. They accept acting here in every sense of the word.

Roderick Mann told me that as soon as he was away from Beverly Hills it instantly disappeared – whereas wherever he was, London *never* disappeared. . . .

That's very true, that is absolutely so. England is full of sounds. I don't mean country sounds, I mean sounds of busy-ness, bustle, moving. . . . The sounds here are sirens, police cars, ambulances – or silence. There you can walk from Marylebone into Piccadilly and there's always a different kind of sound taking over. Here, because you never walk, you don't pass anything. You get into your car and no one chats to you on the way anywhere. When I walk with my dog down to the shops people point and think it's a *very* strange thing to be doing with a dog. . . .

When I lived in England I'd escape from London and go to the cottage every weekend. Here I'm in a countryhouse in town; within five minutes I'm downtown in an urban situation. I don't know why people have always got to *become* what the town is. . . . For example, when you do programmes you're always yourself, looking at people. You don't change. People get American accents very quickly here.

This house is no different from the cottage in Kent, and of course everything's *from* the cottage. I've always lived as if I were a snail with a shell on my back. As long as I have my little things around me that I've collected, I can be put anywhere – in the middle of the desert I'd be at home. But women are lazy. . . . They're terrified, for example, of going to a party alone, of going *anywhere* alone. It's as if it's a stigma: something must be the matter with you – so of course they pick up with all the gays in the world.

When I go back to London I find that nothing has changed. It's almost as if there's a time warp and everyone is just about to put their cup down, where they've picked it up. I find women look very matronly. There are *no* matronly women here – they haven't got a trademark that says: You're this age, you're a grandmother. Maybe some of them have had dozens of facelifts, that doesn't matter. What's the difference between dozens of facelifts or going three times a week to Arden's? It's just more permanent. Palm Beach is much older: they're eighty being sixty, and here they're sixty being forty. They're much richer there, I think. That's an old-age home for the wealthy, and this is still a very creative town.

An enormous number of men have facelifts here, and quite right. There's a terror of looking your age.... But what *is* your age? Your age is what someone sees you as – and that's important for a television career or a film career, very very important.

Here they do *anything!* They have this fantastic false erection thing, have you heard about that? A girlfriend of mine's husband arrived back with this contraption. There are two types: one is the type you press from the hip – and up it goes! Another is the type that is permanently up. On the *Donahue Show*, they brought it out. It's pretty revolting, like a couple of Tampax. He was dangling this thing and the doctor was showing how it all worked. I could think of nothing more terrible – the man isn't going to be *feeling* any different. That's an operation that's done in Chicago – it might be done here now – and I'm talking about something that's on television for all to see at three o'clock in the afternoon. This sort of thing's got nothing to do with reality, and nothing to do with sex. It's to do with contraptions....

THE ECOLOGIST

More people die in the USA being bitten by their children than die being bitten by snakes

Dr Geoffrey Stanford, an affable and enthusiastic eccentric with a shock of white hair, stands out in the Texas prairie like an early version of Dr Who on the moon. He is Director of the Greenhills Environmental Center, staffed by volunteers and founded in 1975 'at the interface of town and country' just outside Dallas. To the non-Texan this nature reserve seems merely an expanse of scrubland and low hills, but to Dr Stanford it is 'uniquely beautiful'; certainly it is a welcome green interruption in the ever-encroaching ticky-tacky development of the Dallas–Fort Worth conurbation. Dr Stanford lives by himself at the Center, cooking his own meals, worrying about Doomsday – and tackling the Texan establishment with fine spirit.

Dr Stanford I presume? May I ask what you're doing here?

I'm saving Texas for the Texans mostly. For future generations, anyway. This is all going to be covered with houses and we're going to run a road all the way as far as you can see, practically.

Just a minute – you're not saving Texas by building a road, are you? Texas has enough roads.

No I'm not building the road, I'm *saving* what I can, because when the road goes down it'll destroy quite a number of these nice young trees. So I'm marking the trees and then the engineers will either put the road around them, or dig them up and move them – and bring them back when they've built the road. This is the first developer who's ever asked me to advise them. The previous one did, but the advice got ignored. I've got three of them on this land. They need not take my advice, but they might. Next time they probably will, or the time after.

So at least this owner's a thoughtful progressive man?

137

Not necessarily. We shall see whether he is or not, because developers historically say sweet things until they've got what they want, and then they renege. That goes on all the time, so my Board is more cynical than I am because they've been bashed more often. They deal with these people more often.

Does this area *deserve* to be saved for the Texans? You've got a housing estate up there, you've got these ugly power lines – it's not the Lake District or the Harz Mountains, is it?

It's the nearest they have – this is the finest stretch of hillside in the whole of Texas, and whereas it's been built on all over the north of us and all over the south of us, the present owners who're doing the development want to save what little they can for future generations. That's what I'm here for, to help them. I've been here ten years waiting to save this stretch of land because it's so beautiful. There's nothing like it anywhere else, nowhere. The escarpment, the cliff edge runs all the way from Denton in the north right through to San Antonio in the south. It's seventy million years old or so, and it goes up and down, sometimes buried and sometimes up. Here it's up. And wherever you go it's built on, so when the new lake goes in over there the people on the lake will just see a hillside and trees – that's what the idea is about.

I have to say, Doctor, it's all relative; this is just a bit of scrubland to me and *not* particularly attractive.

You see these same trees, about a thousand or two thousand miles further north, are three times as high. We've had a drought continuously here since April. We've had two inches of rain. The droughts here are extreme and very very hot. Most of the prairie plants, the first six inches doesn't have any roots.

If you know Ullswater you couldn't really class *this* as beautiful, could you? Or even the Hog's Back.... Where do you come from, Doctor?

London. Ipswich, actually, but London.

Any one of those little Suffolk villages has to be prettier than this, surely?

Well you see they've got 1066 and all that, eight hundred years of civilization. This country's had about a hundred and twenty years – 1860 was when this country was built on. It's been logged quite extensively for firewood. But as you say, it's relative. This is the finest land they have around here bar none and well worth saving, very much so.

We had five thousand schoolchildren through last spring, teaching them. We have about ten thousand visitors at weekends over the year, and gasoline is going to get rarer so they're not going to be able to travel so far. This is going to become the middle of the great Dallas-to-Houston metroplex; you've got a hundred or two hundred acres, it's well worth it. Think of New York without Grand Central Park, think of London without Hyde Park.

The schoolchildren must love it here – for starters, *you* look like a former Dr Who! Are you familiar with him?

Yes, vaguely, but not very.

He's another magician you know, always doing wonderful things.

I'm a Doolittle man, that was my generation.

But by the standards of a national park in England or America, it's not very beautiful here.

It's not meant to be. There's plenty of parks in Dallas, magnificent parks, huge flower beds, lots of mowing. Nothing happens here at all. We don't *do* anything. If a tree falls down we say, 'Hmmm, it fell down, how interesting! I wonder how long it'll take to vanish?' The answer is, about one hundred years. We say to the children, 'If a tree falls down you can look at its roots because they're sticking up and you can think, Oh I wonder why that fell down, and you can look at the animals on it and you can realize that if you don't leave it there but tidy it up, nothing can live on the bark because it's gone, the dead bark, so the birds that live on beetles in dead bark won't be here.' You've got to have the total ecosystem to teach ecology. So we just do nothing.

When I first came here eight years ago this was a bog. Now it's completely dry. I wonder why? Will it ever flow again? When I came here it was bare, bare chalk from over-grazing. It's carpeted with flowers now. Further on it's becoming quite a nice little prairie, so now after eight years I'm beginning to re-introduce the plants which I know for sure used to be here, and have died out. We're forming a genetic pool, a reserve, and when people want a new gene for one of their crops or whatever, we've got it. So we're doing multiple things. If you want to build a windmill, come and build a windmill, have fun. You can't do it anywhere else that I know of in Dallas.

You're mildly eccentric – Americans have to import their eccentrics, it seems?

No not eccentric, just Renaissance. Ren-*ay*-sance they call it. I translate as I go, because I'm forgetting I'm talking to an Englishman.

How long have you been in the US, Doctor?

I came here for three months in 1970, and never left. I was invited in a January for a visiting professorship in California. You'd go too, wouldn't you, in January? I was in environmental issues, even then.

Texas obviously needed you! Couldn't the state have protected this land if it's so important, and left you without developers to worry about?

That's not a technical question, that's a political one and I really can't comment. That's the way they do things here, and I do what I can to preserve the finer aspects of the land. When you think of it, England has destroyed her natural life, we've destroyed the whole of Scotland, Snowdonia's not what it was, *we* can't point a finger. . . . We have all our experience behind us. I come out here and explain to them what they're in danger of doing. If they listen to me, I can feel delighted. I mean, we're saving this escarpment – what more could you want?

They *are* listening, are they?

Oh yes rather. This is going to be saved, I'm sure – that's what's so wonderful. That's what we tell all our schoolchildren. We break them up into groups and Liz, my colleague, hands each ten to a volunteer teacher whom she has trained and they go off on the trails and see what's going on. And they're terrified, absolutely terrified.

Of what?

Nothing, just wild trees. A little boy says, 'Why are those trees planted so untidily?' I mean, they're *that* basic! If they're not actually terrified and want to go home, they don't like to picnic out in the roots, they want to picnic inside a house or on the road. Another one said, 'Who puts away all the birds at night?' They have no concept of what goes on in the country. Of course we had that when we had the evacuation of London at the beginning of the war, the town children came up and wouldn't eat a cabbage out of the fields because it was nasty – it had to come off a bench. Urbanism is a creeping disease and I've always said that urban people are actually lunatic and don't know it. It's the country folk who are normal and they *do* know the urban folk are loonies, so it's all right. They tolerate each other.

Have you got snakes here?

Ooh, rather – rattlesnakes and coralheads and all kinds of lovely things.

Lost any children yet?

No no no. More people die in the USA being bitten by their children than die by being bitten by snakes. It's the saliva which is venomous.

I always suspected American children were dangerous! It's about 90 today – but it's been worse, presumably?

Oh yes, 103, 105 degrees. By then you don't notice it – it's just hotter than hot. Our worst problem here is chiggers. They're little teeny-weeny creatures, you can just see them if you're good at it. They're colourless and they live in long grass. They're looking for a cow and you come by and they mistake you for it and bite their way through your skin, they burrow in. When they realize they've made a mistake, they can't get out. They die under your skin and you itch for weeks. It's horrible.

So you're exposing these happily innocent urban people to nature in the raw, right?

They've had chiggers for three million years, since man evolved. One more day won't hurt them.

And what about these children who bite snakes – how do *they* get on with chiggers?

We put sulphur on them before they leave. You rub sulphur dust on their socks and round their tummy and they're fine.

So lots of little yellow moppets leave here?

Yes that's right. But it's good for the grass – a bit of sulphur does it good!

Once you've convinced them the trees weren't planted by a gardener and the birds are not tame, what are you telling them?

You try and relate the thing they're looking at – what they see, and what they don't see behind it. The difference between a grass and a tree they don't understand. One of our courses is the difference between a reptile and a snake. We've got a big boa constrictor – they love playing with that. They wrap it round themselves. We use a parakeet and a rabbit and they can see the difference between these different types of animals, and fish. That's quite basic and you'd think they understood it, but they don't. It's a revelation to them. Then when they've been here and had all this teaching, three or four weeks later the children come back with their parents and drag the whole family round, teaching them what they've just learnt. They're so joyous and happy. That's what we're at, we're giving the urban people a bit of the heritage which they've forgotten. I mean three million years of heritage is nothing to throw away.

You say, 'If you don't bite the snake it won't bite you' – and it doesn't. A snake will always go away if you give it a chance. You teach them those kind of things. I always try to give them something to eat as soon as they arrive, something wild. 'That's wild, can I eat it?' 'Yes, try it, yes.' 'Gosh. Well perhaps I won't, it's nasty.' But some of them do and then the others follow and then they relate once they've eaten something. We say, 'Lie down on your tummy – now what's in front of your eyes?' They've never done that before, looked at ants and little tiny things wobbling about.

We don't see all that many animals. We know they're there and we teach them about spores and what they're looking at, the footpads and so on. They enjoy that, in the stream bottoms, but by and large the birds are out mostly in the dawn and the dusk, you don't see an awful lot of them. The coyotes aren't out except during the night, and the armadillos sometimes. We've got a bobcat, we know that by its spores. We've never seen it. The deer no longer come here, but we're going to get this under control and then bring back some of these animals. I want to bring back prairie hounds, prairie foxes. Squirrels – that would be nice, and they're great fun to watch. As soon as we get those back then of course the birds of prey will come in. We've got buzzards and you can tell the time of day by where they are. They circle in a fixed daily pattern. I don't know why because you'd think the animals, knowing they're up there, would stay away that time of day, but apparently they find it the right way to behave.

Marvellous to have a Londoner doing such evangelical work!

Put it the other way: I haven't been able to do this in England – they're destroying stuff too fast there. No one wants to listen. Any innovation in England hasn't a hope in hell, in my opinion, but here it *has* a hope – whether it's got success-potential is quite a different matter, but it certainly has a hope.

The one thing they're *not* short of in Texas, it would seem, is land?

Once again you're on to a political, commercial matter, the way money is made. When I arrived here this land was worth $480 an acre and I could've bought it for that if I'd had $480 to rub together. Now it's reaching $45,000 an acre. It's going to reach $5 a square foot. Speculation in land is a very peculiar thing and it's universal throughout USA and much worse in the Third World. I mean we don't know what speculation *is* here, compared to Manila or Singapore.

You don't do a Mr Deeds Goes To Town – go and pound on the desks in Washington?

I do a modest amount of that when it's a technical matter on which I can give expert opinion, but I don't do it because it's my opinion and I don't like *your* opinion – that seems to lay me open to attack and my technical expertise to questioning. The media are owned by the developers and speculators, as is the city council.

This is a country where you buy and sell land for profit, that's how the system runs – if I don't like it I can leave. But I can talk to them and say, 'While you're doing the developing, you can develop it either badly or well.' They're very keen to listen to me because doing it well is actually more profitable to them. If we keep this piece really nice, then the land both sides of it is worth up to fifty per cent more. If it's all run over, it isn't, so I'm working on their receptive spot. It's a different viewpoint.

I don't think we've got room in this tiny world for antagonism. We've got to have outright co-operation, understand each other. I'm living in a society where profit is respectable. Money is a commodity, not a topic for discussion. There's nothing else to talk about, except money. When you meet at any gathering they're ready to tell you how much something cost or how much it's going to cost. That's the common parlance, it's *the* topic of conversation, except sport – which is money-oriented. But if I like to live here, that's fine.

Is the enormous wealth of Texas a help or a hindrance in such a sanctuary?

I find it absolutely staggering that the house many people live in here and consider a tract-home would have been a *palace* in England in 1945. They do not appreciate their fantastic wealth. When they talk about the poor, the poor here have got a washing machine and a TV set – otherwise they're destitute. Come to Manila, come up in the hills of Guatemala if you want to see poverty.

So Texan wealth in general doesn't rub off on places like this?

I think it will, in time. It's a hard row to hoe, and at my age I wonder if I'll make the grade. They want what they call 'a bang for the buck', they want to see and be seen. There'll be intense rivalry and jealousy if it's understood that you were with me here, and not *them*.

In one of the expensive restaurants you have to be wearing the right clothes at the right time in the right company, and be seen and recorded and appear in magazines. That's what they do with their money, and really quite sincerely I think they're as miserable as hell with it! I have much more fun without *any*, than they have with.

There's one lady I know whose husband died four years ago, and her entire daytime is spent sitting in a chair looking at TV – but she's *not* looking at it, she's looking at the clock and when the clock says half past the hour, that's the time to take the next pill. She lives from pill to pill, day to day, and she's destitute – on only $150,000 a month! She's worried she's so poor....

The thing that distinguishes Americans for me is their absolute tunnel vision – money! They'll leave the price on a bottle of wine so you'll know how expensive it was. They have no other criteria. They are uneducated, untrained, uncivilized. The only index they have is money.

One of the things I've also wanted to do, and I've thought about it seriously, is drop this job, advertise in the *Wall Street Journal*: 'I Will Spend Your Money With You' and take out this $150,000 woman for a month and give her a menu and say, 'Which of these things shall we do this month?' She's only about sixty-three, she's made herself a neurotic wreck and of course the doctors all tell her how sick she is. She has to go and visit several of them once a month – she comes to Dallas to see her four doctors. So if I took her out and said, 'This month we're going to really investigate the granite industry of Texas, and next month we'll do ports, we'll go to Portugal ...' her life would change, and it wouldn't cost her twenty thousand dollars a month.

All her life she's been married to a farmer who had oil and got richer and richer and never left his farm and never took her anywhere. She doesn't know how to enjoy life. She's terrified of leaving her TV set. And what about her medicines? She couldn't get them, they'd get disordered on her tray. She wouldn't come to me in case I was after her money, which of course I am.

At one of these Texas super-parties one lady was saying to another, 'It's a shame the Symphony's got to close', and a third lady said, 'What's that?' 'Oh, hadn't you heard my dear, the Symphony's run out of money.' 'How much do they need?' 'About five million dollars to see them through.' So she hauled into her handbag and wrote a cheque for five million dollars and said, 'Give that to them would you, sweetie?' This is not an apocryphal story, it's true

There must be, I would think, fifty people in Dallas at this moment, each of who'd give us five million dollars and deduct it from their income tax and not even know they'd done it – but you have to find them....

So you're preserving a natural environment for *un*natural and uncaring people?

No I'm not, I'm preserving it for their great-great-grandchildren, who hopefully will become natural again. You see when the oil runs out and you can't bring stuff from California and Florida and you've got to live and take your pleasures on your own land, by then we ought to have in place good sewage treatment with a reflux back to the agricultural land that's left, growing our own vegetables locally and having our own forests and woodlands to walk in.

Then rapid transit's going to come out to here, so people will get access. Imagine five million people having access to this! It's worth it. Now when you say how can we enlist the sympathy and support of people – Dallas has half the billionaires of the nation, but there's no way I can talk to them. I don't mix in their circles. I can't get in to say, Hi! They're protected by layers of assistants.

Well I talk to them and I'm not *half* as personable as you are. . . .

Ah but you're BBC and you contain enough potential for glamour and for ostentation. When a thing's as dicey as this, is the public going to accept it? They don't want to be seen associating with an environmentalist.

But there's never been any question of your going home?

What would I do there? I couldn't get a piece of land like this and live on it and work on it. I'm doing a lot of research here, I'm noticing that we've got an astonishing amount of Mexican Plum, it's a very difficult thing to grow in a nursery. Here it's growing on absolutely bare, virgin chalk, so I've got to change all my plans for growing Mexican Plum and plant my seeds in chalk. Every day I learn something – it's wonderful. You see some people go around collecting money, and the more money they've got the happier they are. Some people go around collecting knowledge and distributing it and the more they've got the happier they are, so I'm the knowledge-gainer.

You're doing all this in one of the most unnatural areas in the world, a place of audioanimatronic animals and fibreglass trees. . . .

I don't see this. My lifetime of a hundred years is like the flash of a glow-worm in the night, it has no significance at all to the overall illumination of the world. If you take that viewpoint, this sort of thing you see so vividly passes me by. I'm living in the last ten thousand years and the next five hundred every moment.

Across America, especially in Texas, you find shopping malls with artificial ponds and artificial trees; Americans are not deeply *in* to nature. . . .

Well I'm working on the shopping mall people, saying to them, 'Why don't you put up wisteria and vines so that the cars can park underneath them. Their response is, 'They drip honey.' So I say, 'Well yes but they also shade.' I'm trying to persuade them to put down perforated bricks which grow grass, and the honey will come down on to the bricks, on to the grasses and they'll grow lushly and mop up all that oil. You can't take any one problem and try and solve it like an engineer does, you've got to look at the whole spectrum. It's a vast interconnected network. It's like a bowl of spaghetti. Everything connects to everything else. You have to reckon that the ants which are biting the hell out of me right now only grow to my knowledge near a roadway. Ragwort, which is a pest here, only grows along the roadside. All the cedar elms in the town, in the suburbs, are being bitten and eaten away by animals which don't eat them here – that's a very interesting observation. It's quite a nice tree, so how can we get those cedar elms in the city to resist this bug? The answer is almost certainly to get the paving off them and to let the air in. Then you have this strange potato grower in Idaho who irrigates his potatoes underground. He's discovered that if he pumps water through them one day and pumps air through them the next, he gets an enormous yield. So maybe all we've got to do is to pump air through the free roots of our trees in our cities and get very big trees again. Then perhaps they can cope. I mean all these things are part of my daily thinking.

One feels that in America, in the world in which you are now, that there's *not* much money in nature, while there's money in development, there's money in concrete?

That is entirely true. You can't make money by *saving* money. You make money by spending too much and creaming off too much. That's holding up a lot of progress here, progress in my terms. I mean every civilization you've ever read of is a means of impoverishing the poor and enriching the rich, and if you know that's happening you can't get too excited about it.

What is the educational level of the people you're dealing with? They were telling me in the New Orleans Zoo that they had to write the descriptions of the animals in terms a thirteen-year-old would understand.

They overstated the case. If you aim for *six*-year-olds, you're doing much better. Six-year-olds are very bright, by thirteen they've become quite dim. They've been taught to be dim. Any intelligence is thrashed out of them by, 'Oh Johnny do shut up, don't keep on asking questions, listen to what I'm telling you.' So the child doesn't ask any more questions, and if it doesn't ask any questions how can it learn? You've got to answer questions. All of this generation was taught by people who were children during the war, when education was bad. They're being taught by uneducated people. It's very very bad here, education, we all know that. Children from England who come here find that they're three, four, *five* years in advance.

Has television something to do with that?

I think so – children actually spend more time in front of television than they do in the classroom, up to the age of seven or eight. The stuff on television for adults is pretty pathetic so for children it's infantile, because it's adults talking *down* to infants. You see we're moving out of a literate society into a visual society and into a computer world, the children upgrading themselves in spite of their teachers. The teachers can't keep up with them.

I was in one single classroom last week where they had eighty fully equipped IBM computers. *Eighty* of them, in one class! I don't know what they've got in the other buildings. But you can't talk about anything serious or advanced. They can't conceptualize – they've never been asked to.

I'm told – I haven't checked it out – that forty-five per cent of army entrants can't read at all. They've just had a great inquiry in Texas, and in other States too, and they find they're being graduated at age eighteen and they've had twelve years in school, $18,000 spent on each of them – and they can't read, half of them. You can't use long words, you can't use a vocabulary. I think we're the first generation that's ever brought up our children more ignorant than we are. We have taught them *less* than we know, and we've left them to fend for themselves, to find out what they can. We've left them an intolerable legacy of poisons, short-term, mid-term and long-term which will persist twenty-five million years ahead – and we don't give a damn. I think we're absolutely beyond the pale, as a generation. I carry a load of guilt constantly about what my peers are doing to my, your, their great-great-grandchildren. It's dreadful – including not educating them to understand it. There are lots of good books but they're not available in schools because they upset the business world.

Yet with all this, Doctor, you'd still never consider going back to London?

I personally wouldn't unless I was given a lot of guarantees that I would be given the freedom to do my thing, and the salary to do it with.

It sounds as though you haven't got all that much freedom here because of the developers, and not all that much salary because of the lack of charity towards nature?

I've chosen to work in this field and not to work in money-making. If I wanted to make money I could become excessively rich exceedingly fast, but it doesn't interest me. I'm more interested in doing what I'm doing here and playing my part for posterity. I may be mad, but at least I'm honest. I think people respect me. They think I'm a lunatic but they still respect the lunacy I have.

I'm entirely on my own. The money ethos is so deeply ingrained that I have no close friends. There's no one I know of who can conduct an intelligent conversation, outside the university faculty, and all *they* do is talk about university faculty matters, politics. That's why I left the university – you couldn't get any work done because you were always doing politics.

But there are so many ecologists here I would have thought you were leading a trend, rather than being isolated and solitary?

People don't like to associate with other people, other than on a purely financial level. They look at you, they know what your income is – and that's who they talk to, the people in their own income bracket. I'm in the income bracket that a garbage collector would look down on, so I have no friends.

But what you're doing is so socially acceptable that your multi-millionaire property developer would earn some Brownie points merely by associating with you?

He gets his Brownie points by telling his publicity agent to publish a report about us, showing how clever he is in following me. He's got to spend every waking moment of entertainment time entertaining potential clients – he can't afford to waste a meal on one of his employees. I'm so appalling, I'm unacceptable in any decent society, and they daren't invite me to their home because I might call them up again.

That's obviously not true – you're an Englishman and they're reputed to like the English, you're an academic, which gives you even more kudos. . . .

No! If you're an academic who makes money, that's a plus, but a rather dangerous plus.

I would have thought you could have been their blue-eyed boy, even as a performing seal! Do come to dinner, you must meet Dr Stanford, he's *so* quaint. . . .

They don't have those elegant tea parties of the 1840s where society hostesses brought in the leading men of the time and they'd talk to each other and entertain you: what happens here is, you go to the golf club on Sunday after church. The real socializing, friendliness as it were, is done at the church level and at the country club. If you don't have a country club and you don't have a church, you've got nothing.

The church is an interesting phenomenon here. I'm beginning to find out what it does. In the olden days before the motor car, each village was really its own entity. The motor car split that up and the churches have become a village diffused throughout the megalopolis. All people in one church are a village, scattered all round, but they keep the village thing together and they trade actively amongst themselves.

But if five thousand kids go home and say, 'We had a great time,' you should have ten thousand parents on your side, at least?

No, they've disavowed the upbringing of their children. They don't want to know. A respectable family has two children, or five, or whatever the street goes for, and they pay taxes and it's the *school's* job to raise the children, not theirs. They have abrogated all their rights and their responsibilities towards their children almost entirely. Three little boys come up here most evenings for their parents say, 'Get the hell out of here and don't come back 'til seven.' Don't know where they are. Don't care.

This society that I'm now in has become urbanized to the extent that they don't want to recognize; they feel uncomfortable with nature. When I qualified I lived in Ipswich and I knew a gentleman who was seventy-seven or so. He was raising rabbits and he knew about their needs. He was raising piglets, thirteen to a litter. He could drive a steam tractor, a diesel tractor, a gasoline tractor, he could drive mules and horses, he could pleach a hedge, he could be doing something in the fields and say, 'It's going to rain in five minutes' time, I'd better do something else.' An *enormously* skilled man, I mean really skilled, highly trained – and they talk about ignorant peasants!

After your fifteen years here how do you feel about the American way of living? Have they conquered that difficult art?

Oh no no no no. They're in a horrible mess, they're destroying their trees, they are absolutely ruining their land. We estmate that the total biomass productivity of the land before the white man ever came here, before 1520, was *eight* times what it is today using the very best techniques of farming. Eight times! Now the catch is that that's the total above-ground dry weight of growth per year, not the total above-ground dry weight of *edible* growth. We're getting much more edible growth than in those days, but much less growth. We've swung the whole system into commercial growth, economic growth.

There's a classical paper written called 'The Tragedy of the Commons' which says that land in public ownership gets spoiled, but land in private ownership gets ruined. This is something akin to population pressure, coupled with greed. There's no other word in the language for it. Here it's called the spirit of enterprise, or healthy competition – but that's greed with a good name.

The whole system, ever since people stopped being nomadic or working in groups of forty to one hundred people as a little tribe wandering around in their own territory, the whole system once you urbanize, once you get organized into hierarchies or rank, is a system designed to make the few at the top richer and the mass at the bottom poorer. You had a break in that tradition with the rise of the industrial revolution in the last century, when the poor could get rich quickly if they were clever enough to match the landowners by amassing capital in the form of savings.

I think the whole of the Thatcherism and the Reaganism and the dictatorships around the world are the swing back to the really rich getting control once more. Democracy is virtually dead, I think, as a trend, as an historical trend, and we're going back to dictatorship – enhanced rape, if you want to use those words. I don't use them except that they're shorthand and everyone understands them, whereas if I use more technical terms they don't.

We're going to kill ourselves off quite soon. You see we used to do things at a national level, a territorial level. Europe or Mayan civilization or Rome or Genghis Khan or whatever it was, they ruined their society. We're the first civilization that's ruining the total whole *globe*. We're the first ones that've had the chance to do it and we're doing a very good job, both short-term by desertization and long-term by nuclear power. So I think we're in for the death of the race, the death of life probably. Maybe fifty billion years from now it will all start up again. . . .

There's an argument going on now, which is well documented, that we presently have about ten to a hundred times more nuclear warheads than are required to bring the permanent death of our climate. A permanent, nuclear winter. Therefore we could afford to reduce our nuclear warheads by ninety per cent and then we would have reduced the present risks. The present risk from the nuclear warheads exploding by accident somewhere, man-made or just mechanical failure, is greater than the risk of some politician pushing a button. So if we can at least reduce that by destroying nine-tenths we'd be none the worse off because we'd still be on the brink, on the threshold to a nuclear winter, but at least we've only got two men to talk to, to stop it. That seems to me a compelling reason, so anybody who goes to the polls in any country to do anything other than destroy nuclear warheads is just being simple-minded, head in the sand, ostrich-like.

You ask what I'm doing here. I'm *living* here. People tolerate this kind of talk, and I'm free to tell it to you. I mean in Russia or any other country I went to, someone would split on me and put me into jail for life. I'm very very fortunate – I can still preach, talk common sense, and no one cares.

You've had no antagonism since you've been here from people outside?

They got to tolerate me and now they've got to think that I might be worth listening to. I've made my case and I've stuck it out.

You're on the side of the angels?

No, I'm on the side of their great-great-grandchildren. I talked to a man who's working for an oil company and he's heavily into nuclear power and I said, 'How many of your grandchildren will not be born because they're exposed to radiation? He hadn't thought of it, but he said, 'Well, my daughter died of leukaemia.' It's an uncomfortable question to put to him because the leukaemia rate is rising. All these birth defects are rising. It takes a bacterium four and a half hours on a hundred-cycle basis to mutate out of a drug. It takes man two thousand years, a hundred generations, twenty years each, to mutate out of the same drug. So we shan't know for two thousand years what DDT is doing to you and me. Well, you and I won't know. These are important questions, and I talk about them all over the place. No one listens. . . .

THE PERSONALITY

I'd be shot *before I'd go back....*

Pamela Mason divorced cameraman Roy Kellino to marry James Mason, the Yorkshire film actor. When it came in due course, theirs was an early big-headline divorce. She did not remarry but lived on in their large crumbling house on Pamela Way, so named after she had granted Beverly Hills permission to build a small road on her property. Her daughter Portland, an early *enfant terrible*, wore make-up and mink in days when children were not small adults. Her son Morgan was an assistant to President Reagan. A notable animal lover, her home is still alive with cats: dishes of cat food stand in sitting rooms, along with cans of air-freshener.

A woman of strong and instant opinions, Pamela had her own radio show, briefly became a besieged businesswoman when her father willed her some Yorkshire woollen mills, and is today a provocative addition to any television chat show.

I didn't like New York much, but the minute I saw California I fell in love. I made up my mind when I came here that I would never go back, for serious reasons. One, most important, was that there's a quarantine law in England for animals, and when we came we brought with us five cats and a dog – so we knew that it was *for ever* because I would never put my animals in quarantine, and we wouldn't leave them behind. It wasn't a question of coming and testing – I knew I could never go back.

Another reason was that all during the war I'd been a chicken farmer – that was to keep out of being in a factory – and I was allowed to entertain for ENSA, ten weeks a year I think it was, and the last year we entertained where the American troops were just coming in. I'd never known any Americans, except once meeting Constance Bennett and Sylvia Sidney and one or two wonderful people like that. I didn't know Americans, but suddenly we were working at RAF camps where American soldiers were, and they were *so* lively and enthusiastic and full of fun and well fed, and they had cans of Spam and Hershey bars, cigarettes, silk stockings, and they were adorable. We just flipped over them, so we managed to get into the American Red Cross and go to Paris as soon as the war ended in Europe, and entertained troops there. We were the only English-speaking act because they had no time to bring others over from America, and so they adored us. We'd never been so loved in our lives, so naturally we responded. We thought, Oh this is *it*!

In England everybody had sort of sneered at our doing *Gaslight* – men in the army hate these dreary serious plays. *Man and Superman* we were asked to do, things that people who are just about to be killed are not that crazy about seeing. For the Americans we had a little zippy revue sketch, and they adored us. We went to Frankfurt, we went to Wiesbaden, the head-quarters of the American Army, stayed there for six months, and we just couldn't imagine settling down in England again without all this love and Spam – so *that* really made up our minds!

It wasn't just coming to Hollywood, although I'd grown up watching movies with Rudolph Valentino and all of those things and knowing that everyone who worked in America as a secretary had an apartment as big as the Beverly Hills Hotel – I'd *seen* it on the MGM films! Everything always looked terribly desirable – they all wore satin nightgowns as they walked about their apartments. Everything was wonderful in the movies, so I had that sort of old-fashioned attitude about America, and it didn't die as I grew up – failed to grow up, I should say – so when I became an adult, sup-posedly, I still was stuck with all those little phobias I dreamed would be so wonderful in America.

It lived up to all those dreams?

It did. We were on the maiden voyage after the *Queen Elizabeth* stopped being a troop carrier, and it was one *heck* of a voyage, I mean the boat went whoops and whoops and they lost ten thousand dollars' worth of china on the first whoops.... It was just a ghastly trip, but still as it sailed into New York harbour and we saw the Statue of Liberty ... I've never forgotten it. The sight, with the sun on it, I started to cry and I thought it's the most beautiful thing I've ever seen in my life: I want to *belong*. And I felt I belonged, I don't know why, because I'm not really a patriotic person in any direction, you know. I would fight on the beaches of Malibu if somebody landed there, but I wouldn't *go* anywhere to fight them!

You didn't feel sad at leaving the Palace of Westminster and Tra-falgar Square and Piccadilly Circus?

Ohhh I *longed* to leave! It was having bombs dropped on it, buzz bombs and things like that when I left, and queues of cold miserable people wrapped up in coats waiting to get coal or a piece of fish. Everything was so terrible during the war.

What about today? What's the view of England from Beverly Hills?

I've had to go back to England for rotten reasons. First of all I was divorced twenty years ago. I went back because my Father died and left me as executor of his estate, where I was double-crossed, screwed – I can't *think* of the number of awful things that were done to me by the lawyers and the mechanics of British jurisprudence.

I know it's not that much better here, but it is a *little* better – at least I could handle it better here. There I was absolutely devastated, I became four feet shorter and much smaller and crippled and old. I got to be like that in England. Also it's very cold all the time and here – look at it! November, and the sun is out. The sun is *always* out – that makes an awful difference to me.

How about earthquakes and violence and robberies and. . . .

I never notice the earthquakes – I hardly wake up for them. The only reason I know we have earthquakes is because the pictures all go *that* way! You can tell when you come downstairs and all your pictures are out of position. You think, Oh whatever's that? I just thought I must have had one too many! But it was over so fast I realized it couldn't be *that*. I don't worry about earthquakes because every moment of one's life anything can happen. I've lived through the buzz bombs and the V2s and all those things, and I travelled with people firing at our trains – and after all, they're dropping bombs in Harrod's. . . .

Don't you look back at Britain with *any* affection at all?

No. I don't remember being happy at all in England. I don't know why I don't.

You were brought up in England, your father lived there, you were married there?

Yes, but my Father and Mother were divorced when I was eleven. My Mother was divorced for adultery, which as you know is very *un*chic in England, or was then, and so she was sort of banished to the South of France – which I wouldn't call *too* bad! My Father continued to live in England and sort of claim custody. He didn't know what to do with us and would send us back to France to her for a while with no money to support us, then bring us back to England in the lap of luxury. So I had what I call a horrible upbringing, and I was determined that when I had children, if I did, they wouldn't have that kind of an upbringing. Divorce or no divorce, they would have one parent who was steady and was *there*.

What's interesting about America is such a mixture of things. I kind of sympathize with the way they always beat their own breasts and complain about themselves first! American politics are so absurd; if they made a mistake they never seem to cover it up, they have open inquiry after inquiry after inquiry. They can't wait to say how *wrong* they've been and 'Look what we've done,' and so on. Any other country would either shoot them quietly and have them buried and say it was a car crash, or they'd be quiet about it. The Americans seem to have a guilty conscience. The puritanical influence is still there – and that's rather sweet and naïve in a way, and kind of lovable.

I understand why they love Ronald Reagan so, because they want terribly to love their flag and the country – which is so huge and vast it's almost impossible to know what country it *is*. He's a believer, you know. My son worked for him for three years and said that he is *so* sincere that, right or wrong, nobody can say he doesn't mean it. When he puts on one of those funny little caps and becomes a Legionnaire, tears come into his eyes – he *means* it. He feels it, he's proud as can be and thinks it's wonderful he's all wrapped in the flag, and people *want* that. They don't want to hear that it'd be sensible to knock down the overdraft or whatever. It means nothing to them – when it gets to be billions, who cares – it's too silly. It's no good talking to me about billions; talk about hundreds and I'll understand.

Talking of millions, this is a nation of 240 million rather disparate people of every nationality congealed together, whereas the Brits are still mainly Anglo-Saxon are they not?

Well, not at the moment! The last time I was in London it looked to me like they were all Indian. As a matter of fact I had a horrifying experience: I was staying at the Hilton Hotel, picked up the telephone and asked for something and they couldn't *understand* me!

Your American accent, you see.

(Laughs). I don't *have* an American accent! They don't speak English in most of England any more. I lived in London, or below London, let's say, in the south of England: Folkestone, Broadstairs. I never went north except on tour once or twice in a play with James. He never took me to Huddersfield because he didn't want me to see it – he said it'd be too depressing. He showed it to me once out of a train window and indeed it *did* look depressing, so I've never been there.

My Father had run the British textile industry for years, from London and Ascot and the South of France. He'd never been north. He called a sheep a wool. He said, 'I think there's a lot of wools there.' He knew nothing about it. He was a commodity man, but he didn't understand farming by any means. I went up to those areas and I must say it was a most depressing, sad, gloomy thing. I felt the people were quite different from Londoners and southerners. They talked with different accents and they are very much more narrow-minded than people from London, at least so it seemed to me.

They were bigoted against the whole world. They still believed that we had the Empire, and we were *it*.

When I was a girl in school we had a great big map on the wall and I was shown that pink on the map was all ours. Now pink on the map you can't find, it's just England. We lost it all! Clumsiness, oafishness, wars, I don't know.

I told my daughter that sometimes when I read of terrible things happening in countries where children are starving to death, I comfort myself with the thought that I learned in an English school, which is: It doesn't matter, because those sorts of people don't love their children like we do, because they're not British. The British had a very superior attitude, and the Americans don't have that attitude. They don't teach in their schools that we are the only people that feel anything. But I was taught, what little schooling I had, that we are the ones who feel, and the rest of the world don't because they are less intelligent and less emotional and less realistic and less whatever, and it stayed with me. I felt that it was a cold country, not only cold because of the wind and the weather, but cold emotionally. And I did marry two Englishmen and they were cold emotionally, compared with better luck I've had since then.

As an ex-wife of a famous film star, did you find fitting into life here at all difficult?

Well I loved it, so I suppose I wouldn't have noticed anyway. I'm a great believer in, you make your own life. A lot of women hang on to their husbands and make their lives off them, but I'm a very social woman. I love people and I love mixing and I'm easy to talk to. I love to meet new people, and I don't care what they earn. It doesn't make any difference to me 'cause we can't all afford to go to somewhere smart, so we'll go to Hamburger Hamlet – which is getting very expensive, by the way!

You can always make a social life, no matter where your money is. I had always made a lot of friends. James was a very cool and aloof person and only interested in his career, and so when he went I still had all the friends I'd made. I suppose I lost a certain number of people who would have been after me to get to *him*, to see if he would do a film or something, but I didn't notice it because I was working. I always worked, all the time I've been out here, on television or radio or something, I always had a job of some sort. Never equal to anything he was doing, but it always kept me busy and kept me known locally, so I can't complain I had the same situation of a woman who's never done anything. On top of that I had this fascinating life because I had all these animals. I wrote, I had a wonderful daughter, I had a darling baby boy growing up around me and I was rather relieved to have complete control of them after being with a husband who was not that interested in children.

He had found himself at fifty, you know, he'd discovered the new boy in him and he got one of those fast cars and started to whisk around, do all of the things he hadn't done when he was young. I didn't like being divorced, because I could perfectly well have put up with it and had my life on the side – which I could do very well because I was clever at that. I learned it from my Mother!

It's much more to do with whether you give out. My Mother always used to say, 'Don't go to somebody's dinner party and just eat. They didn't ask you just to fill your face. Entertain!' So I know that I must paddle my own canoe: don't arrive there and hang on to the hostess like grim death and make yourself a burden. Make yourself an opportunity, and work for it. I consider going out to other people's houses the same as I do going on a television show. I must be as light and entertaining as possible, as interested in other people's problems as they want me to be, and in doing that I never found I was cut off or made to feel lonely.

Yours was Hollywood's first big-money divorce, was it not?

That's what my lawyer chose to say, and he exaggerated somewhat! Yes, I found Marvin Mitchelson, I invented him. He's my proud invention and we are still great, great friends. It was just a bit of luck. I'd fired two lawyers for being crooks and I was going to conduct my own case, because I figured at least I know what my case *is*. My case is, I must have custody of the children. I don't want them sent to school in Switzerland. I must have the house, because of all my cats, and I felt that I could persuade a judge to see this necessity.

Both the lawyers immediately went to James's lawyer and got paid off, and then they came back to me and said, 'There's no way, you know, it's committed property, you have to split the children six months of the year,' and all that stuff. So I felt, Well I'll go in and plead my own case, and I was very worried about it but I thought, I'll be on the covers of *Life* and *Time*, I'll be famous, I'll probably have a good show all over the country, make a better living than I have been making – so it may pay off. But it was nerve-wracking because I really don't know the law that well.

I happened to go to a dinner party and I was sitting next to Marvin, a young lawyer, and we got to talking and I could see that he was a bad hat, you know, he had his wife with him and he went to the phone – so obviously he was talking to a girl. I thought, Here's a man I can talk to! I called him the next day and he came over and I told him my problems. I said, 'If you double-cross me I shall take you before the Bar and I will expose you'. He took the case and he won it, hands down.

These days, if you meet the occasional Brit out here, do your hackles rise?

I have dozens of English friends – I don't blame them for being born the same place I was. Britain's changed a lot and I don't think it's changed for the better. I was born just after World War I and I grew up in those leisurely lovely times of the Thirties and the Savoy Grill every night and lunch at the Ivy... Things are not like that any more. I had the experience of six years of war there, which were not pleasant. So did everybody else for that matter, but then I had the opportunity to come to a country where the sun came out, so that in itself was rather wonderful. If the sun had ever come out while I was in England I'd have felt differently, but it never has, and as far as I remember you always had to have the electric light on 'til at least eleven o'clock in the morning, because it's *always* dark. I find that depressing. The climate's depressing.

I'm all for Mrs Thatcher, I think she's wonderful and I think it's incredible that a chauvinistic country like England had the guts to put in a good great woman. I'm very proud of them for that...

Nothing makes you feel you might one day return?

No, nothing. Nothing would make me go back. I'd be *shot* before I'd go back. I couldn't go back – I'd rather die. I absolutely belong here, I feel so rooted here. I'm a cat by nature, so I don't like to leave my hearthrug...

UP-MARKET EDITOR

They ran after me shouting, 'You're a nobody . . . .'

Harold Evans, prince of journalists, made the classic ascent in our craft: reporter on the *Guardian*, assistant editor of the *Manchester Evening News*. A slight hiccup in 1961 when the Westminster Press decided he didn't have *quite* the right accent to be editor of the *Oxford Mail* – but as a consolation, made him editor of the far superior *Northern Echo*. Then, accent and all, to London to edit the *Sunday Times*. Finally, the summit: editor of *The Times*. There he confronted Rupert Murdoch and made the classic descent: he was fired.

Pausing only to write a weighty book about that episode, Harry left Printing House Square for America. His wife Tina Brown was already editor of *Vanity Fair*, an almost too-smart New York glossy. He became editor of a publishing company and then editorial director of *US News and World Report*, a magazine published from splendidly lush offices in Washington where staff pad along deep-carpeted corridors amid a rarefied atmosphere of paintings and backlit statuary.

When I arrived he'd been there a week, and was the only executive without an elegant office. Nevertheless, freed from the bonds of Fleet Street's Luddite unions he was already in shirtsleeves in a sort of cupboard, facing up to his computers with the assurance of a Yorkshire newspaperman who knows *exactly* what he's about. . . .

══

Accommodation is fantastically expensive – people think nothing of having to pay half their net salary on accommodation in New York. Many of my friends are paying $20,000 rent, and $30,000 is not unusual. Then in addition to that, you can't move unless you're ready to tip everybody. Living in New York, the first thing you have to realize is its Hassle Factor. It diminishes your salary by X because with apartment living, everything's a hassle. You stand on your twenty-third floor waiting for your elevator kicking your heels, pass the time of day with the elevator man. If he's carrying your bag you may want to tip him. Get past the guards on the door who're waiting with machine guns in case someone tries to raid you, then go out and face the traffic congestion. That's the Hassle Factor. . . .

But don't let me be defeatist. I absolutely adored my time in New York. I worked in a Mies van der Rohe building, the Seagram Building with these great fountains coming up. Travelled up to the thirty-eighth floor, looking out at the vast panorama of the city. ... The most exciting thing of all was to find how much I could get done in a day, which is why all these people flee at the weekends. You can almost get more than you *want* to get done in one day in New York because of the compactness of it, because the publishing industry is very closely located, and because of the intensity of exchanges. I can do more work in one day in New York than three days in London or two days in Washington.

If somebody says, 'Are you interested in so-and-so?' and you say, Yes – the manuscript's on your desk the next minute. In London it's more difficult to organize, there are bigger distances. Then they ring you back the next day: 'Do you want to make an offer?' 'Well, give me another day.' 'This afternoon at four o'clock?' I find all that terrific. If you don't take it too seriously, it's stimulating. They're all thrusters.

If you look round the city you see it's mainly female. My experiences of hiring a secretary in New York: Secretary, Day 1 – I gave her dictation and her typing was absolutely hopeless. 'Don't bother to come back.' Tried another next day, absolutely hopeless. Third one, third day, all temps – London temps are terrific. Third day the girl was pretty good on the typing and shorthand but there was something slightly awkward about her. At lunch-time I said, 'Get me a copy of *US News*, and *Newsweek*.' 'No.' I said, '*What?*' She said, 'No, it's not in my schedule of duties.' So I said, 'Well don't come back tomorrow.' 'Very well.' And she didn't come back tomorrow.

The office manager said, 'Mr Evans you have to understand it's rather important that people are employed for those duties for which we ask them to be employed, and we didn't specify doing errands and messages. We have messengers for that.'

Imagine if you'd asked her to make a cup of coffee!

Oh I wouldn't do that – I don't mind making my own coffee. Let me explain some of the business things in publishing: you dial 411 and you can get in touch with almost anybody – but you try to find Evans in London! You go through Enquiries and twenty minutes later you're still there, waiting for it. It's much quicker for me to direct-dial somebody in London and ask *them* to look in the telephone book, because the London exchanges are absolutely useless, hopeless. They're a laughing-stock over here. You send an ambassador, an intelligent, cultivated man, you give him a Rolls-Royce and he's seen by – or influences perhaps – fifteen or twenty thousand people. You have *millions* of business people in the US dialling Directory Enquiries in London, ring ring, ring ring. ... So they immediately think England's finished. Can't get the telephone answered in England. That's nationalized industries, they say. Socialism, they say. So their picture of England is of a quaint, sleepy country, a little like Portugal or Spain was some years ago, torn by a kind of incipient civil war between the upper class and the lower class.

But what about *their* post office – seven days to get a letter from London....

You don't use the post office, you see. I hope none of us are going to be ideological about this, but in fact it's very easy to get things quickly about the place with Federal Express and these private organizations – you learn how to use the system.

What do you do about your own transport through the congestion – have you got a limo and chauffeur?

I have if I want it, but I feel embarrassed. There's something wrong with me – I don't particularly *care* for being driven around. You avoid the stretched limo, the gangster scene, because it's just a ridiculous waste of time, and it's slow as well. You take an account with a limo service which your company will pay for, which is very efficient.

We've been paying forty dollars an hour.

That's about right. I must tell you one of the dangers of having a stretched limo. I was in the 21 Club with Sid Perelman and as we were coming out Frank Sinatra joined us. We had a chat standing on the steps, whereupon a crowd of black lads gathered around my car which happened that day to be a stretched limo. They were all saying, 'That's Frank Sinatra's.' But *I* got into this limo and the black kids all looked at me and wondered who I was. They finally ran down the street after me pointing and shouting, 'You're a nobody, you're a nobody!' I thought that was marvellous!

I must say I love living in Washington. It seems to have most of the efficiencies of New York. I can walk from my apartment near the office into Georgetown, which is super. The houses are lovely, there's two or three main streets and it's so pretty. I'm going to buy a house there.

How will your wife feel about Washington, because it's not a woman's place?

She's not going to live here, she's living in New York.

When your *Times* drama ended in March '82, you then wondered what the hell to do?

Curiously enough I was invited to the United States immediately by quite a lot of people. I came to Florida to an academic journalistic institute, and then I went back to London and, as you say, wondered what to do. I joined Goldcrest to do twenty-four-hour television news, which unfortunately was a premature idea – at least for my time-scale. Because my book was a success I'd already been invited to be a professor at a couple of universities. I decided I'd try Duke University in North Carolina, teaching Ethics, Law and the Press, and it was absolutely fabulous. It was I think one of the happiest times of my life, going down to this blossom-filled land with these kids, all eager as hell to learn, talking about journalism – and bringing in politicians and journalists and so on, that was a marvellous time for me. At the end of that I had to decide whether to stay in academic life or write another book. I've been funded to write a book on the press on the American election, so I started to collect material.

The Making of the President . . .?

Yes, but basically concentrating on how television and the press reported it. I was also asked to edit various other books and the Goldcrest thing was still interesting, but that's really more feature films and I'm basically a news journalist.

Then Mortimer Zucherman said, 'Come and run the Atlantic Book Company,' and that really excited me. Straight away I said, 'Yes I'll do it.' He's a wonderful guy. He's the second good-Canadian-fairy in my life, Roy Thompson being one; third, if you count Ken Thompson. His father was a candy and tobacco wholesaler, he went to Montreal University where he was pretty distinguished in the sense that one day he saw an accident in which the police were involved and offered to testify for the civilian, whereupon he was beaten up and flung into a police cell. Then he came to Harvard and taught Finance and Planning. He went to a Boston law firm and did some very good deals for them, but they didn't pay the commission due to him. Since he was Jewish and they were Anglo-Saxon they took a poor view of this man qualifying to earn $5 million from a land transaction. So he sued them and won the $5 million, but by that time he was already well established as a property developer. He now owns sixty-two buildings in the US. He's worth about $200 million and in 1978 he bought the *Atlantic Magazine*. He's building two skycrapers in New York. He's forty-six. There's no Mrs Zucherman – he wants to get married and have a family. His girlfriend's Gloria Steinem at the moment. So he asked me to run the book company for him. We have a lot of fun together – he's very witty, a very funny man, very well informed, sensitive. In 1978 I was editing the *Sunday Times* and there was no paper because it was strike-bound. He came to London and said, 'Would you be interested in editing the *Atlantic Magazine?*'

But you're not a magazine man?

The *Atlantic* I could have done. You can think of the *Sunday Times* as a weekly news magazine, really.

Of course you could do it because you're brilliant, but your forte is news, journalism.

Maybe you're right. I'm interested in literature and ideas, but it's not what makes me go. It's the same as being a professor – I don't have the natural originality. I'd rather be a journalist finding out what the hell goes on. In fact I was beginning to enjoy my role in disguise as a gentleman publisher. I felt I was masquerading. The day I walked into the office to take up the job Zucherman said, 'I've just bought *US News and World Report* for $166 million.' The next day I saw him he said, 'Oh my God, what have I done!' It's a very significant and important magazine here.

It hasn't changed for twenty-five years....

It's changed a bit, Alan, because it's less ideological. It used to be quite right-wing and reds-under-the-beds, rather like *Now!* magazine and the late Sir James Goldsmith. So it has changed a bit. The question is, How much further should it change, or can it change, without losing ten million readers? And my concept of it at the moment is to monitor power more effectively, possibly by doing some investigative stuff, and improve the writing and presentation. But we'll see. I've only had seven days. There's two hundred people that I've got to try and understand.

How do they feel about you?

Trepidation.

I bet you sold an extra two hundred copies of your book?

I did, *and* my other books – they all went like hotcakes, mandatory reading.

They're probably even reading *Vanity Fair*.

That's right – it's Marked for Advancement if you're seen reading *Vanity Fair!* At the end of one week one of the older men said, 'You're a Brit and you've been here a week – so what's *wrong* with this magazine?' I said, 'I don't see there's any logical connection between the two, it's premature.' He said, 'But you must have thought about it, since you've come from over there.' He was the only one who was offensive, most of the others had been very nice.

I took the lift, no, the elevator – I'm trying to get out of that yet I don't actually see why I *should* since it's a better word. I say, 'Where's the lift?' and thirty seconds are wasted while they go ... 'Huh?' I asked my brother who became a Canadian and spoke Canadian if it was an affectation, but it's not, it's simply to get through the small change of life quicker. Anyhow, I go down in the elevator and there's another accent I recognize; he's from Sussex and he's one of the seventy-six reporters on the magazine.

You have a few nights-of-long-knives ahead of you – do you look forward to a fight like that, even if you are fond of your proprietor?

I can trust him. I don't want to talk about my previous proprietor particularly, but if you've got a decent man at the top you can actually make change without agony. It depends on the ethic of the place and the attitudes of people. I was fourteen years at the *Sunday Times* and made enormous changes. It's fantastic when you look back on it, but because of the character of Denis Hamilton it was possible to do that without long knives. If it's necessary for long knives to come out, somebody else will have to do most of it. On the *Sunday Times* they used to say I was the man with the rubber hatchet.

You have a strong personality ...

I wouldn't say that. I've strong desire for what I want to do.

... yet you're a bit of a softy I suspect, when it comes to firing anybody. ...

Well I've done it, but I did it with reluctance. I may have to do that. What I try to do always – I did it at *The Times* and I think I succeeded – is to get people to do things slightly differently. The marvellous thing here is, they haven't got a union! The contrast with Britain is agonizing. In 1976 I came to this country and went back to Times Newspapers and wrote a report saying, 'We must have photo-composition and electronic technology.' The Board was already half-convinced anyway. They bought the machinery, but it has never been used in the way it was intended to be used, even in 1984, eight years on. I can go into the Middle East and Africa, never mind this country, and find the equipment which we bought in '76 being used four or five times as efficiently as it's used in London at the moment. There's a certain frustration about that, especially when you know the poor old country is economically slipping slowly into the English Channel.

Here in the US I walk into a completely new thing at *US News*. I said, 'I want to plug in to your system,' and I can look at all their copy on an electronic screen. I can alter it on the electronic screen, I write my own memos on an electronic screen. None of these things would even be remotely possible in London. Why I should be denied access to one of the great inventions of the twentieth century, the computer, is ridiculous, absurd!

So you don't have the unions and even when you have them here they're not as stupid and greedy as the British unions. I really feel *they* are betrayers of the working classes. They're not members of the working class – they're members of a little oligarchy, a kind of Mafia.

Better leadership in the industry means people taking chances, setting up new publications. The existing Fleet Street proprietors will never change anything. We have the unions that we deserve because we've got the proprietors that we have.

I have two computers in this office, and of course in England I wouldn't be allowed to have a single one, or even to do this. This would be an act which would bring the whole of the British printing industry to a stop, if I did it in London! But here, everybody's delighted.

This is my personal computer on which I do memoranda, store comments and letters, and shortly they'll be fixing a jack in there so I can send memos directly to Boston and New York, to my offices there, the book company and the chairman, and they'll be able to write to me. We'll be able to amend balance sheets and whatever it may be. That's what I do on this personal computer, but I have another computer where I can watch what's going on in *US News and World Report*. For instance, I can read the story 'Does Mondale have a chance?' or 'Insurance companies cannot base their car insurance rates on sex' – sounds interesting. I can go through the whole of what's being readied for *US News* here, and with the right commands I can change their stories and send them back to the desk. So I've got a picture here of what's going on throughout the entire editorial operations of *US News*.

This is what you were fighting for at *The Times?*

Yes, exactly. This is what's exhilarating here. It's used in a very primitive manner at Times Newspapers today. No journalist can touch it, only various members of the printing unions. There's a lot of duplication and a lot of unnecessary waste in the way it's used in Britain. It's tragic really. Journalists shouldn't be denied that kind of access. You can do it in darkest Africa and brownest Middle East, you can do it in Kuwait – anywhere in the world except in Britain.

Obviously we must have had lousy management, so people in your position have done wrong in the past?

Yes.

And we've had stroppy unions?

Yes.

Because it's the last gravy train?

It's the last gravy train, and it's sad because the public would be better off and the industry itself would be much better off, there'd be better newspapers. It would have been nice if these things could have been in London at *The Times*. Of course at the end of the day, as many of my colleagues would say – including you I suspect – having a toy like this doesn't necessarily improve the journalism or the writing. You still have to have curiosity and persistence, you still have to have the good reporter.

What about the calibre of the people working on this magazine, compared to those who worked for you on *The Times?*

They're enormously capable, they come from a diversity of cultures, which is one element where they're stronger than the great intellects and extremely well-educated people on *The Times* and *Sunday Times*. Here, coming from all parts of the world and all parts of this country, there's a diversity of culture which is a strength. You have to learn to speak a different language, of course.

The difference between Britain and America in business and in many other ways, in my judgement, is that the Americans construct superb programmes and people operate them. Britain operates on individuality – much more quirky and eccentric. In the United States there are three layers. There's the great layer at the bottom of young women who do perfect work in banks and publishing houses, providing you press the right button. They're like clockwork then, but if you ask something *slightly* out of the ordinary the machine goes, 'Blink, blink, blink, blink – that is a problem.' So you have to go to the next layer of women. Very important in the USA, women – they've had greater advancement and opportunities than in Britain, which is very exciting. So you reach a superbly groomed woman of about thirty-three who's been trained to deal with the problems the robotic layer can't cope with. Then at the top there's this thin cream of men getting into their stretched limos.

Chaps in waistcoats?

I don't get into stretched limos – and the waistcoat is a gesture to *you* today!

It seems that here you have to know how to sell yourself?

You do – it's a country of fantastic salesmanship.

Can you do it – you're rather a quiet sort of chap, aren't you?

If quietly or noisily you can show them that you can do something, whether it's a British micro-biologist or civil servant or journalist, then they treat you just like anybody else – since most of them *come* from somewhere else. I often think as I go around New York that none of the people I see in the streets were there when I was there in 1956. They're *all* newcomers – a Moscow Jew, a Pakistani, an Afghan, a man from Milwaukie ... all newcomers trying to get up that ladder in New York.

There's a lot of cameraderie in our craft – a lot of friendship. Here there's no El Vino's and one feels they're a bit short on friendship?

That may be true, due to the competition, which is tremendous. However there's one big difference: they have no El Vino's but they have a much more serious attitude to journalism. Professional matters are discussed in a way which in Britain you'd be regarded as Being Rather Pompous, old boy. There's none of the Fleet Street cynicism here, but endless discussions about the propriety of invading privacy and that kind of thing. Of course it's a much more open society, and the press being taken more seriously – not necessarily for the right reasons – takes *itself* much more seriously than we do. There's very little of the entertainment or pop press here. If I wanted to I could call up the Secretary of State and he would immediately be available. In Britain you'd have to cut through a swathe of private secretaries and offices.

This office is an experience in gracious living – I've never seen such splendour – those carpets, the statues, the lighting, the pictures, the *hush!* Somebody was suggesting they were going to use Muzak in the lifts and it would be the sound of typewriters and people shouting, 'Hold the front page!'

To me it's kind of confusing. Going into any newspaper in Britain, or in this country until a few years ago, you'd go into a clackety-clack, noise, men in shirtsleeves. You can't see anything like this today, and you wonder what's going on. The magazine is produced by stealth, as it were. It's all these electronic snakes awinding their way through the building.

It's unnerving, actually.

Yes, it *is* unnerving. I sometimes think that if they screwed the light pinewood down I'd wake up and find I was in my coffin. But why should you be subjected to all the hysteria: The Front Page and Hildy Johnson ... and so on. Though one misses it.

Yes – a bit.

A bit. American offices, when they're well done, are superb....

How does an American office take to a Limey coming in as numero uno, as editorial director, the ultimate hire-and-fire man?

With a certain amount of suspicion: Whadda *you* know, anyway?

And whadda *you* tell 'em?

Well (laughs) the best thing is not to say anything and, as you work your way into the operation, show them that you have been around before and that there's no difference at the end of the day between the nature of journalism. Some people would dispute that – there's certainly a difference in the American sensibility; on a very serious and important magazine like this I'm going to go exceedingly slowly....

Having edited *The Times* I don't know what you do, journalistically, for an encore?

After editing *The Times* you can come to the United States, because there's nothing else you can do in Britain. That's one of the reasons I'm here.

What about editing the *Washington Post?*

No I wouldn't think of that. I think frankly that the position I'm in here, editorial director, is almost a Cloud 8 position. I'm taking a strategic over-view of the whole magazine, its place in America, what kind of service we should offer the reader, should we do investigative journalism, what *kind* of investigative journalism? What should we do about the design of the magazine? How should we cover the world? What is the American reader's interest and response? Our responsibility in serving it and giving it news, say, from Peking. Should we have a man in Peking or an extra man in London or one in Cairo? The United States I find is very insular – Britain being internationally-minded I think it's helpful to me to come from some-where at the crossroads of the world.

Here readers are primarily interested in trivia and gossip?

New York's a city where things are very hot and cold. They keep saying, 'This is the hot magazine, the hot person, the hot show,' and so fashions – and freakish fashions – come and go very very quickly. One has to hold on to one's sense of what's worth while.

You're a peppy and alert sort of chap, as you have been all your life, so you would take to that style of life quite easily. A lot of English people, I suspect, wouldn't....

They wouldn't take to it. And I sometimes don't.

What about rewards – you must be earning an enormous amount now?

One doesn't bother to count because the Inland Revenue here is quite as efficient as the British Inland Revenue. Yes I *am* well paid, very well paid indeed. If I translate into pounds I don't think I'd dare go out into the street in case someone was going to rob me! One is well paid – it's an expensive business and the amount of disposable income is much higher.

What's more, Mrs Evans is also pulling in a quid or two?

Yes Tina Brown, editor of *Vanity Fair*, is earning quite well too. But one isn't here just to earn money, really, although it *is* quite useful to be able to pay one's creditors.

This is a place to make money – is it a place to live?

There are many seductive aspects of life in America, because the play-grounds are accessible. I first came here in 1956 and lived in New York for a time and always said New York must be the worst place in the world to live unless you can insulate yourself from some of the pressures by dollar bills. It's marvellous – I have a house on Long Island at a beach. It takes me two hours on one of those wonderful American trains, hooting away, somebody serving you drinks. It's very delightful if you're well off and it's not all that *hard* to be well off as a professional or middle-class person here. You can live a very good life indeed. A far better and more comfortable life than in Britain.

I feel angry and proud about Britain, both ways at the same time, and although one can do these things, there are many aspects of British life that I miss. I miss the politeness, I miss the tranquillity – but here nobody cares about Britain or *thinks* about Britain. It's a very great shock arriving here and turning to the paper and after a week you realize you haven't read a single story about Britain. Nothing has happened in Britain that week! If you go across the USA you may go months and months without finding a single story about Britain except 'Woman of 78 drives at 100 mph'. They're into the kind of stories about Britain that the *Daily Express* used to do about America: Americans are people who eat plastic flowers – that kind of para-graph would appear in the *Express* in the Fifties and Sixties. We're relegated to that kind of curiosity. They're quite interested in Lady Di and the Queen, quite interested in Mrs Thatcher when she's brave and stands up.

So what do they think of *us* here, Harry?

As a small interesting polite off-shore island like Quemoy or Matsu. An island they've almost forgotten about, apart from the Queen and the occasional violence. You get very little news, but a lot of distortion on occasions, which angers me. The IRA isn't treated in the way it ought to be treated. NBC television gave equal time to the IRA spokesman or the NORAID spokesman after the Brighton bombing. That's an obscenity. So America is very insular, not interested in Europe at all. As the leaders of the free world I find this rather discommoding and hope I can do something about it as a journalist here.

So today, where do you think of as home?

Probably my house in Ponsonby Terrace in London, but I think more and more it'll come to be the house in Long Island, which is going to get so much affection. We married in Ben Bradley's garden in Long Island. It's a summer place and we're getting it ready for winter, which means we've got to put central heating in. It's already nicely furnished.

But that *drive*, all the way out there. . . .

Forget the drive, think of the railway! Think of a Winston Link photograph in sharp black and white of a rural American railway station with the white woodwork and the scalloped edges of the roof, think of the noise and the hoot of an approaching train, think of the light coming towards you. Stand on the station at Westhampton after a superb weekend, or stand in Pennsylvania Station and go out that way.

The actual train is an additional superb experience. I just love the romance, because the hoot of that train spells the forty-niners crossing New Mexico and all that kind of thing. The drive – the uniting of the country. My Father was a steam-engine driver which is perhaps why I'm excessively romantic about trains. But even Tina feels it. Every time we're on the station and we hear this noise and see the big headlight coming, this great cowcatcher, with about forty-five locomotives pulling a hundred and ninety-two coaches, snaking their way round – it's very very dramatic.

I could have bought a place in Connecticut, but decided to buy this partly because you could get there very easily and quickly by rail, so I do beseech you to think about it in those terms. If you're thinking in terms of Long Island Expressway you'll go out of your mind, because that's just murder. Not only that, if you think in terms of East Hampton – which is New York by the sea – you can't walk down the main street without finding the deal you thought you'd half finished on Friday has to be renegotiated on Saturday. That's a nightmare.

So I don't want to go to East Hampton, although I got married there.

Where I am at Quogue they're very snooty. I went to the local club to play tennis and they said, 'Who're *you*?' Everybody has made it clear they don't want to know us, which is absolutely wonderful because we don't want to know anybody! We want to be there in seclusion. We don't want to know Philip Kingsley – he might be in danger of inviting us for drinks or something.

So the anchor's firmly dropped here?

Yes it is. I've got a three- or four-year course at least on *US News*, and with the book company. I'm going to be a permanent resident here.

You can save your life financially by coming here, but you can lose your individuality?

You do tend to. American companies work superbly well because there's a system for everything, like this computer here. There's a format for it and once you can work your way into it, it works perfectly well. The society isn't really built for the eccentric, the individualist. The English are brilliant at innovation – this is a familiar observation – and the Americans are very good at execution. If you're going to make a contribution here and you're not really a systems person, you have to find some way for the egocentric, crazy innovative aspects of the British temperament or culture to fit into the system. The Americans don't work on inspiration and impulse, they work on programs!

So you're going native?

Yes I'm going native – programs innovator, the lot! But let's not forget, civilization here was basically Anglo-Saxon when it was started. They've made differences with the written Constitution but in respect for the rule of law and regard for civil liberties they've gone further than we have, because we have no written Constitution. Personal rights are more greatly protected in many ways in the USA than they are in Britain, where it's ad hoc, it's all improvisation. Depends on what judge is on the Bench on a particular day, whether the press is free or less free. Here they're always coming up against the Constitution, which is written down.

At the end of the day, though, you've got to leave your home and walk down the street....

I've never had any difficulties, but I think it would be ridiculous to pretend it was as safe to do so in the USA as it is in London. It's not. One is always walking down a street in New York with that extra alertness – eyes everywhere – which is not very relaxing. . . . It's edgy enough in the office without that, so there *are* many aspects of British life that one misses.

The terrible thing about England is the little conspiracies between the comfortable extremely rich City, the concentric circle of press barons and others which overlap, and the corrupt trade unions. There's that Olympic three-circles that to me represents the worst about England. Most of it's concentrated in London and south of the river. North of the river and the north country I exempt from all my criticisms, basically. Mind you, Scargill is a nightmare and he's north of the river but he's part of it, bred in these conditions. I get angry about it. It's not a question of Left or Right. Many of the virtues of the working classes are resident in Margaret Thatcher: certain fortitudes, strength of purpose, honesty of purpose and so on, whatever political disagreements one may have.

These corrupt fringes represent the worst of some kind of eighteenth-century French philosophical throwback to me. I don't know how they got into English culture. The Germans shed their Marxist inheritance, the French have not quite shed it – they're going through traumas – but the British still have this little incubus, eating away. . . .

DOWN-MARKET EDITOR

Mothers Eating Babies are out, but Sex-mad Monsters are still in. . . .

Bill Burt was on the *Daily Mail* in Glasgow, but in 1967 escaped Britain's troubled newspapers and went to the Toronto *Telegram*. He moved south to Florida as an early British import of the *National Enquirer*, first and most successful of America's flagrantly sensational supermarket tabloids. As its Los Angeles bureau chief he became aware of the paper's reputation as a pestilential parasite among Hollywood people upon whose peccadillos it flourished: 'I told everybody I was from the London *Observer*!' The film world is now biting back, with Burt Lancaster playing the unscrupulous publisher in *Scandal Sheet*, which specializes in celebrity sex, fad diets and headlines like 'I ate my Baby'.

Burt moved to the *Enquirer*'s clone, the smaller *National Examiner*, and as I arrived in West Palm Beach had just been made its editor. His modern office was bright and sunlit, his seafront penthouse a long way from the Gorbals. . . . Small and jocular, Bill walks with a stick after a stroke two years ago: 'If I swam ten laps every morning and did some exercises I wouldn't limp, but I'm too lazy.'

Mildly irritated by their remorseless cheapjack journalism, I was indignant that the craft should be outraged by this lowest form of newspaper life, where any imagination goes into the headlines. Bill and his colleagues replied with such mischievous delight at their own cheek, at what they could get away with, that as they conspiratorially recounted each outrageous story in ascending order of unforgivable exaggeration, I reluctantly began to share the joke and see their papers for what they are: silly comics for almost-adults.

===

Why is it that the British are so successful in your sort of tabloid journalism?

When British journalists started coming here in the late 1960s they brought little elements of the old *Daily Sketch*, of the *News of the World*. They brought elements of *Reveille* and *Titbits* and magazines like *Picture Post*, *John Bull*, *Everybody's*. They brought all these human-interest elements into a weekly newspaper – a kind which had never been seen in the United States before.

British journalists have a talent for this sort of clever trash?

One of the main things is that they've got very fertile imaginations. You'll find most journalists today go to journalism schools, while in my time we didn't *have* such things. I spent my early days walking up tenements and banging on doors and getting punched in the mouth – you know, the school of life.... Also, we've had more experience with tabloid papers. There are not many in the United States – there's one in Denver, two in New York and that's about it. The other tabloids are the weekly fun tabloids, most of them produced in South Florida, which is a non-union State, where we are today.

The *National Enquirer* used to bring British journalists out by the job lot – planeloads of willing lads from Fleet Street?

In the mid-Seventies they did, yes. I went over there myself, scalp-hunting up and down the pubs of Fleet Street, dangling dollars in front of their faces. I bagged twelve in one week. The success rate was about twenty-five per cent, Alan. Could they adapt – that was the problem.

We are a little more sensationally articulate – we can be sensational but credible. In other words if we were writing a ridiculous story, we would dress the skeleton with the scenario that's plausible. It might be all bumshit. They all came out on try-outs and if they didn't pass the Pope scrutiny after three or four weeks, they were out. If Generoso Pope discovered anybody on his staff had faked or phonied a story or a quote, their feet wouldn't touch the ground – he'd fire them. But sitting back and thinking about it now, they're not being fired because they faked a story, they're being fired because they got *caught* at it...!

When I joined the *Enquirer* it had a circulation of 1.1 million. It bounced up to the five million a week it sells today through the supermarket to the lowest common denominator of intelligence, pardon the expression, to Mrs Smith from Kansas City, wife of a gas-pump attendant. They were paying the editor, Ian Calder, $450,000 a year! He's the same age as me.

That's above Fleet Street minimum anyway ... What about the *Examiner?*

I'm getting paid as much as a senior reporter would get at the *Enquirer*; I was an articles editor eight years ago, and they were paying me seventy-five thousand dollars a year.

So you all brought over here the ultimate in printed sensation, which has little to do with truth – it's just titillation and amusement?

It would be ridiculous for us to be pompous and say we were searchers for the truth, that we were crusading journalists – we're in the entertainment business. If you want to find out what's happening in the financial world, get the *Financial Times* from London; get the *Wall Street Journal* from New York. If you want to find out what's happening in the realm of international affairs, buy *Newsweek*, buy *Time* magazine. But if you want a relaxing chuckle and a good read, buy the *National Examiner*.

How many Brits are working for you here?

I've got twenty-seven editorial. Brian Hogan over there's Australian. Carl Lewis is ex-*Sunday Mirror*. Sheila Donovan, formerly of the Press Association. . . . Freelance, about sixty. The *Enquirer* have got about a hundred and twenty editorial and a thousand on the stringer list.

They're all prostituting their art, earning a fortune and living happily ever after in Florida?

Breaks my heart to say it, but it's true.

What is your particular talent as editor – an ability to be outrageous?

I think after fifteen years in American tabloids I *do* have an ability to be outrageous, he said in all modesty. . . .

But all the stories you're printing could be made up in a pub – down at your local El Vino's you could sit and dream up the lot!

Yes, but that's not the challenge. The challenge is to put together a story with a kernel or a *core* of truth, that's the real challenge.

You're punctilious about that bit, are you?

Yes, yes – at least have *some* substance in the story. You can't plug *Snow White and the Seven Dwarfs*, you know – we couldn't publish that.

If you gave it a really jazzy title, you could.

You find a woman living with seven dwarfs and we'll come up with a good headline.

Headlines *are* the most important of all, for this is supermarket journalism – people pass the payout desk, see a good headline and buy it?

It's a box of cornflakes. All cornflakes taste the same but the boxes look different.

This is your first full week as editor – are you going to last? Aren't they liable to go for your scalp in this ruthless business if the circulation doesn't go up next week?

Naturally. If I was publisher and I wasn't producing, I wouldn't have me here. That's to be expected.

Do you enjoy living here as much as living in London?

I think it's fantastic. I thought once I got to my forties I'd start getting more sober-sided, but the reverse has happened. I'm getting more juvenile! I don't think I'll leave Florida. I did what most of the other people have done – I've bought myself a few houses for a rainy day. We've got a little plan in a month's time – a group of us here have booked about fourteen cabins in a cruise ship and we're heading to Nassau, to Freeport for the weekend. Where else in the world could you just suddenly cruise off to the Bahamas? Plus Disney World just up the road – although we've got much the same elements of Disney World *here*!

Rupert Murdoch had something to do with the revolution, I suppose?

No, Rupert came over and spotted that Generoso Pope, the chairman of the *National Enquirer*, was a very very rich man – somewhere in the neighbourhood of $150 and $200 million. Rupert decided that was a profitable market and copied Pope. Now the second-largest tabloid is owned by Mr Murdoch.

There's a theory that no one ever lost money underestimating public intelligence...?

That is true – but there's something else: the other publications, for goodness' sake, they're far too serious. If the whole world was doomed to read only the *Sunday Times* and the *Sunday Times* magazine, can you imagine what a dull world it would be? No, there's room for these fun papers. I'm sorry that there's not too many of them left in Britain, although I must admit the *Sun* gets very funny occasionally. Even we get a chuckle out of the *Sun*.

And apart from chuckling, you're lifting stories from everywhere and rewriting them?

It wouldn't be tactful for me to say that we steal stories, but we do latch on to certain ideas and develop them ourselves.

I would take great care that you never saw *my* autobiography, because you'd find one single sentence and the headline would say: Cannibal Chief gives Whicker wife. . . .

That's a bit tame. I don't think that would go down very well.

You mean, I'm safe?

Yes – unless you were involved in any demonic rites lately?

That was *last* week! Demons are sellers, right?

Demons are great, and possession. Ever since the *Exorcist*, which is eight, nine years ago, we're into exorcists, we're into reincarnation. People don't want to die these days, they want to come back.

They don't want to die, but they want to read about *Princess* Di. She's your saviour, isn't she?

She's tapering off a little bit. On our board of front pages you'll see how she peaked, and then tapered off. She's still very much admired, she's the Royal Family the United States never had.

I think to get the flavour of your paper properly I should look at all the covers you've got up in your office. These are your creations?

Although this is my first week as editor, I did spend two years as executive editor. I plead guilty.

To all these? 'My Sexy Husband has Two Heads'?

Isn't that a delightful headline?

'JFK and Jackie Reunited'. . . . 'Grace Kelly is Alive'. . . . 'I Saw a UFO Murder'. . . .

'I Saw UFO Murder – police officer's horrifying ordeal.' In America about a dozen UFO publications come out every month. We read them all. A police officer claimed that he saw somebody being murdered by little green men

177

coming off a UFO. Now that's what the policeman claims, so rather than hide his magnificent sighting, we put it on the front page.

'Drinking-Straws Make Woman Pregnant'?

That's a story from Australia. There were many cases of women using drinking-straws in a very clinical way to impregnate themselves.

'Elvis and Lennon Speak'?

There are many, many psychics in the United States who talk to Elvis Presley regularly – and of course since John Lennon's assassination even Yoko's been talking to John.

'JFK Alive'?

A psychic story. The man started receiving vibes and discovered that JFK was in fact alive and living in a modern hideaway.

'Alien Seduced Girl Astronaut'?

Er . . .

Are you stumped?

Do you know, I believe for once you might have got me without an answer on that one. I don't know what the scenario was.

It has to be true?

Oh good Lord yes – it wouldn't be on the wall, would it, if it wasn't!

'Wife was too perfect so Doc removed part of her brain'. . . . 'I Married a UFO Alien'. . . . UFO is a buzz-word here, obviously?

That comes from a couple in Denver, Colorado. The man who married the UFO alien claims his wife is what they call 'a space person' – in other words, wasn't born on this earth. She just suddenly appeared here. The marriage is very successful because he also claims *he's* one too, so it's probably the world's most compatible marriage.

What you're doing is taking bonkers people and giving them the serious treatment?

No, we don't discriminate. We're a platform where all persons, regardless of their beliefs or intelligence....

'I Sold my Baby to UFO Aliens'?

Well that young girl claims that happened to her. She probably put it up for adoption, but that's the story she told the UFO investigators.

'Girl, Five, Gives Birth to Baby'?

That story is perfectly true, one hundred per cent copperbottomed.

Like 'The Sexy Husband with Two Heads', right?

One hundred per cent true – you notice we don't say *when* it happened? That was about the turn of the century when the original Siamese twins – Chang and Ing – were brought to the United States by Phineas Barnum, the greatest showman on earth. It's worthwhile copying the greatest showman on earth. When they retired they went to North Carolina and married two sisters and spent two weeks at one house and two weeks at the other house, and of course they were all in bed together, so if the woman turned over on the pillow, there would be her husband and of course she would see two heads. Very sexy, because they had seventeen children between them. The headline is one hundred per cent accurate.

'Di's Abortion Dilemma' – now *that's* not!

That came from London and I was *very* surprised to see it – I believe it was in one of the heavy papers. It was a doctor in London who suggested Princess Di and Charles should set an example for population control by getting fixed.

What you're doing is finding one sentence somewhere down a long story in a women's magazine a putting it up to the headline?

We will look for the giggling bit. We will look for the fascinating bit. We will look for the bit that the other papers are scared to put in the headline but *should* be doing – and we'll do it. I'm glad they don't, because it gives us a great opportunity. I'm sure when you're doing your own programmes you're always looking for a real good nugget to hold interest? For far too long the British papers and some of the American papers have got that good nugget, that inside story, but they're scared to project that as the headline. We'll take that, throw out all the rest of the garbage and build that up. If Princess Di burst into tears, that made into a story that she's upset about going to watch Charles play polo and running away from the photographers. The headline: Di's Nervous Breakdown Threat. There's nothing wrong with that. I do think it's naughty, but it's not wrong.

'JFK Bugged Jackie's Bra'? JFK appears almost as often as aliens?

I believe he will be selling in twenty, thirty, forty years' time – the man's a legend.

Elvis is also still there, at fifty?

Elvis doesn't sell as much now – he's beginning to taper off a little bit.

Like Princess Di?

Like Princess Di – if she'd had twins, she would have been good for another couple of years! And you notice we did have a story somewhere – 'Di's New Baby is a Girl'. That was on July 19th.

That's about as accurate as *most* of your material!

And then here, 'Di, It's Twins'. Now we took these stories from prestigious British newspapers so if *we* get accused of being sensational ...! We took these stories in good faith, so somebody's telling lies. You know Marilyn Monroe escaped from that government asylum in Alaska where they've been keeping her for twenty-two years? She's not really dead. Bobby Kennedy and JFK arranged for her to get spirited away to this special government asylum in Alaska. She escaped and they couldn't find her. One of our wonderful stories. . . .

Diets also seem to be in? 'Honey and Vinegar Melts Flabby Thighs.' Is there any medical background to all this?

It all boils down to, don't eat any more than twelve hundred calories per day. But you put in the buzz word! There's a wonderful word that will help you in diets. For example: 'Melt Ugly Bulges with Garlic, Vinegar and Honey.' You get the bitter with the sweet. But if you say, 'Melt Ugly Bulges by not Eating as Much', who would want to buy the paper? Would *you* want to eat a lot if you sat down to a plate of garlic, vinegar and honey? Wouldn't that put you off eating?

Anytime we mention the word garlic it will sell papers. Over one million people bought that paper because they want to know how something as lousy as garlic can cure everything, banish pain and have miracle healing powers. We also use it as a diet.

Now is there anything that you wouldn't *use? Do you draw the line anywhere?*

We'd never get into clinical-type sexual things, er . . .

Your enthusiasm for Kraft is Ebbing, right?

Fifty years ago the tabloids used to have front pages with the most horrific pictures of men being crushed between street cars, and headless torsos. We would never do that because we want our paper to be taken into every household in the United States, where people are much more puritanical than they are in Britain. If they left a paper lying around the house with a naughty headline or a horrific picture that the kids could see, they'd stop buying it.

So you're into clean *sex?*

Clean sex is the way! We call it kissing. 'Top Scientists Discover Key to Health and Happiness is Kissing', and then just a few issues along you'll see 'Love', in delightful pink. Now what we're trying to say is that if you get right down to it, if you have sexual intercourse you'll be happy, you'll be slim, you'll have wealth, but we don't put it that way. We never say 'Sex!' Kissing and love – I'll leave the people to say nudge, nudge, wink, wink. So there's nothing blatantly sexy in any of the headlines. They look sensational, Alan, but they're perfectly harmless. We wouldn't print a story that would cause someone to travel thousands of miles seeking a cure for cancer, or something like that. You won't find that on the board. Say someone asked us, 'Could I get in touch with one of the doctors who's got a cure for arthritis?' we would not put that person in touch with the doctor, we would say, 'That's what he *claims.*' Because quite frankly, we only report – we don't necessarily believe.

Your paper's really just a comic?

It's fun. Our reader is the mature woman with the headscarf and curlers who goes through the supermarket and sees it and wonders, 'Joan Collins, how *do* you look half your age?' If she's turned fifty she wants to look like Joan, so she whips it off the shelf and sticks it in her shopping basket.

The strange thing is, you're aiming at women yet you don't have any men on your covers – men don't sell, evidently?

Men don't sell.

Why not Burt Lancaster, Robert Redford, why not Paul Newman? Is it because they're all suing you?

No, we don't get sued.

Not much!

We don't, we really don't. We're very tame. But Americans are so naïve sometimes – there *are* people who take it too seriously. You know who we've got a lawsuit from this week? Mr T, from *The A-Team*! We're saying he was going to have a sex-change operation ... and he's suing us! Some people have got no sense of humour. The psychic who predicted that was Sven Petersen, who you've probably heard of. You can never get hold of him, he's continually travelling the world giving lectures, but he phones in every time he gets something. There's no such guy. It's *me*!

The *Enquirer* gets a million-dollar lawsuit every other day, from what I read?

The *Enquirer* has a circulation of five million copies. I'm thinking about what they spend on the celebrity budget. They go after the biggies, so if you play with the big boys, you'll get hurt. At one stage I believe there was in excess of a dozen lawsuits against them, for millions and millions.

And a lot of them, I believe, are being won? Hollywood is up in arms. You were writing for the *Enquirer* in Hollywood at one time when you were their show-biz correspondent. Didn't the stars take out a contract on you?

They didn't like me very much. I'll tell you a funny story. I was in the Beverly Wilshire Hotel one time, very new to Los Angeles, and being a bureau chief you feel you can wield some sort of power. So I walk up to the bar – in fact it was the El Padrino lounge – and I ordered myself a beer and announced to the barman and the couple of people at each side that I was from the *National Enquirer*. (Laughs). It was as if I had AIDS. The bar cleared!
When I was working for the *Enquirer* we ordered a Christmas story once; it was when the author was still alive, and we wanted good fiction. Now I've seen it used elsewhere: it's called 'The Swan' and it's a very delicately written story. We'd hired this stringer in New York, called Paul Gallico. We're sitting at a mini-meeting in Generoso Pope's office, which is a big enormous hall. He sits at the top of the office and says, 'I don't like the ending.' Then he says, 'Rewrite the ending, Burt.' And I said 'I'm not rewriting the ending of a Paul Gallico short story, it's sacrilege.' 'OK, then we won't use it!' They paid him, ten thousand dollars and sent it back to him. Said it was garbage.

Who makes the decision that it's rubbish? Was it always Pope – no one below?

Everyone below agrees and says, 'Oh yes yes, rubbish . . . .'

He's paying enormous salaries?

Yes he's bought you, body and soul.

Was it you who wrote that story about a woman giving birth to a fish?

No – that was seventeen rabbits! If you read the story, somewhere maybe down in the tenth paragraph you'll find this was perpetrated in the nine-teenth century, but it was believed by royal physicians. It was in England, it came out of a book and it was of course a hoax, but 'Woman Claims I Gave Birth to Seventeen Rabbits' makes a real grabbing headline. . . .

So now, after 'Mother Ate her Baby' . . . what's left to do?

Mothers Eating Babies are out, but Sex-mad Monsters are still in. . . .

THE SIKH

My mother thinks I'm a bloody wog....

When Victor Briggs, lead guitar of The Animals, got weary of the pop world he became a yoga-teaching vegetarian Sikh called Vikram Khalsa. He also became a plumber. His present ashram is within a little white house in a pleasant San Diego suburb. The city has perhaps the best climate and amenities in the world – far superior to the slopes of the Himalayas in the Punjab where he is despatching his daughters, aged eight and eleven, to attend a Sikh school for several years. Their mother Kirsten was born in New Zealand of Danish parents, appeared in Hammer films as a vampire and is now a school librarian. They are a striking family.

Southern California is the home of many cults and religious sects, all seeking Peace and Truth in their various ways; but that solemn little group of chanting Sikhs in quiet Myrtle Avenue is reassuringly far from the Moonies, the Hari Krishnas, the horrific Charles Manson freaks, the Jesus People.... Not *too* many plumbers get up at 4 a.m. every day to lead three hours of prayer.

———

The neighbours got a little bit out of shape about our arrival, because this is rather a nice neighbourhood – we have some million-dollar homes just down the block. We started making a deal, and one of the neighbours approached me. The guy's a psychiatrist, and he's also Jewish – not that I have anything against Jews. In this country Jews are normally very liberal and this man was a very liberal type, you know. He said, 'I'm approaching you on behalf of a consortium of neighbours; we'd like to make you an offer for the house.' I said, 'How can you come over here and say that to me? I think it's totally *disgusting*!'

Anyhow we went to work on the house and when we got it looking good and put the lawn in, the neighbours had a total change of attitude. Now they're very very supportive. We get on very well with them.

So how did Vic Briggs of Shepherd's Bush become an Animal?

I was born in Twickenham and lived in Feltham until I was twenty-one or twenty-two. I went to Hampton Grammar School. I'm forty in February, so I started there in '56 – which was just before you started on the *Tonight* show, wasn't it? When I was about sixteen or so I really wanted to be in the music business. I had several bad years and finally my big break came: I joined Dusty Springfield's back-up band called The Echoes in 1965, and from there I got an opportunity to join Brian Auger and the Trinity with Julie Driscoll, Long John Baldry and Rod Stewart. At the time they were all nobodies, all of them – but right after that they started to become famous, one by one!

I joined Dusty in February and left in September or October to join Brian Auger, with Rod, Long John and Julie. At the time the whole thing was called The Steampacket. It was the era of Swinging London, Carnaby Street and all that.... Then after about a year and a half we went to Paris to do a show with Johnny Halliday, who for many years had been the biggest thing in France. I was a lead guitar player. Also in the show was a brand new comer called Jimmy Hendrix! His manager was the manager of the Animals, a guy called Mike Jefferies, who later died in an air crash over the Pyrenees. He approached me in this little café near the Olympia Theatre in Paris and said, ' Would you like to join The Animals?'

They were already big then, but they'd broken up. They had the original band with Alan Price and those guys, and Eric Burden wanted to have a psychedelic group. This was October 1966, so I joined The Animals and we came over here in February of '67 and made a world tour and swept through the United States, New Zealand, Australia. We were doing really well, having hit records, but in England we were getting too West Coast, too psychedelic.

So three of us settled here, touring the States and Canada. Then after a while, I guess it was the summer of '68, I really wanted to get into the studios in Los Angeles and be a producer and an arranger. Also the sex, drugs and rock-and-roll were just getting to be too much.

It was total self-destruction time...?

Yes it was, it really was. I was just starting to get out of it. We had an agreement to disagree with Eric, and I left in August '68 and got a job with Capitol Records – who were paying a lot of money at that time – doing sessions. I was arranging and producing, and it was really incredible because I was working with guys who were famous names to me, you know, like musicians' musicians.

You were the token hippy in the recording studio?

I remember one time somebody said that if I ever wore socks to work they wouldn't trust anything I said any more! It was easier to go in with sandals and bare feet. They were doing record dates for me and I was going out with them and for a while it was just fantastic. I achieved a certain amount of success and I was doing well financially. I had a girlfriend who used to live with me, I pretty much had everything. But in 1969 the whole thing just started to depress me. I'd had enough.

You'd been in to the drug scene, which was very heavy at that time ...?

Oh yeah – not heroin or anything like that, just hash. But I was getting out of it and I realized that what I wanted more than anything else was spirituality. I was brought up Church of England, but it was non-practising: they'd drop me off at Sunday school and go off on a Sunday afternoon ride and come back and pick me up. But even so I'd had no awareness of God in my life, because in England you don't *talk* about stuff like that, you keep it to yourself. But that awareness was there.

I'd literally done almost everything I wanted to in the music business, I had plenty of money, I had a nice house, a fast car, but still things were totally empty for me. I didn't know what to do. I didn't want to leave my job, because I was getting a lot of money.... Then something very interesting happened: I got fired! Capitol Records decided they didn't want me, so they fired me just before Christmas of '69. You know the way they do things in this country? They bring in a new guy at the top and the guy feels he has to kick a little you-know-what – a new broom sweeps clean, and all that.

I'm sure you've heard of Timothy Leary? Richard Alpert, who became Baba Ram Das? Well Alpert was one of the guys who was with him in Boston. He went to India and became a Holy Man, and came back to this country and started teaching. I went to hear him speak and I said, 'My God *this* is what I want, I want to be a Holy Man. Where do I start?'

So I said, 'The first thing I do is become a vegetarian.' This was just three days before Christmas, I'd already ordered my organic turkey, I'd already got the wine in and Capitol Records gave all its employees a ham for Christmas. We had friends over on Christmas Day and we had the turkey and the ham and the wine, and the next day we finished off the cold turkey and the ham and the last bottle of wine, and I said, 'That's it – now I'm a vegetarian!'

So there I was, a vegetarian – and I wasn't quite sure what to *do*. I thought, I'll just see what happens. About two or three weeks after that I saw a thing in the paper that said: Yoga Class. I went there and the room filled up and all of a sudden this Indian came in. He was about six-foot-four inches tall, wearing a white turban and white clothes. He was huge. We did one exercise after the other and I thought I was going to die. I was in pain and suffering and I said, 'My God I'm never going to come here again.'

The next day I came back to the next class, and the day after that and the day after that. Then after about four or five days just by chance I happened to go to this man's house and when I walked in he said, 'I've

The Up-market Editor: Harold Evans

The Down-market Editor: Bill Burt

The Sikh: Vikram Khalsa (Victor Briggs)

The Abandoned: Joan Norris

The Marriage Director: Mavis Okerlund

The Kicker: Mick Luckhurst

The Model: Vanessa Angel

The Professor: Marcus Cunliffe

The Vendeuse: Pamela Symes

The Spokesman: John Hughes

The Dancers: Jill Marshall, Rachel Davies and Suzanne Lunn

been waiting for you to come for a long time.' He said, 'You're a very old soul, your soul is a very very high soul but in your last lifetime you totally blew it – that's why you had to come back. Otherwise you would never have come back to this earth, but you're here now and you've got to make amends.'

I'm thinking, What's this guy talking about? He said, 'People come to this path, people go from this path, but you're here for the rest of your life, so you might as well forget it.' I said, 'For many years now I've wanted to play the sirode' – that's a classical music instrument something like the sitar. I might add that I'd never sung, though I've always been a musician. And I said, 'Will I ever be able to play the sirode and be a really good player?' He said, 'When you sing the dead will rise from their graves, people will come thousands of miles to hear you. I'll show you, sit down and close your eyes.' I closed my eyes. A friend of mine who was in the room said all he did was point his finger at my forehead, and I just felt this incredible energy inside me and saw this beautiful light and heard these angelic voices and tears came into my eyes. Then he said, 'I just wanted to give you a little taste of what your life was like before.' So that was it.

I started doing yoga very heavily. I'd given up meat, fish, eggs, intoxicants. I'm *trying* to give up anger, rage, hypocrisy, intolerance, things like that. After six or nine months of studying, it came into my head that I should go back to England and teach this kind of yoga. I had a few royalties coming in. I wasn't working, just living on my capital, but I came back to England in November 1970 and started a yoga centre in St Stephen's Gardens, near Notting Hill Gate. I wasn't really a Sikh, but after a while I put on a turban and started going to the Sikh temples in London.

I was teaching yoga to mostly hippy types – there were still a few in London at that time, and we did quite well. I still had the same girlfriend, by the way. She was American and she loved England, but our relationship started getting very rocky over there. Vegetarianism wasn't a problem, but as soon as I started becoming a Sikh that freaked her out. She couldn't handle that.

Things started getting really heavy, because when you teach spirituality you always become tested. As people learn to be spiritual, doubts and negativity grow in their minds. It's a thing people have to go through. So everybody kind of turned against me. When people learn spiritual practices they learn a certain amount of power. They reach a point where their own ego becomes very strong, and they either have to go through their ego and leave it behind, or else they get totally *into* their ego. Spirituality does that for you. They look to the teacher and start to see his imperfections. They say, 'This guy's teaching me all this stuff, but when he goes to the bathroom it stinks just like when I go to the bathroom, it's really no different.'

They see your faults very clearly, because they develop more perception. So there was a big break-up and a lot of people left the ashram. I really got kind of burned-out over there. It had been a traumatic time. It's hard to do stuff like that in England, believe me. The English don't take too kindly to things like that.

Yet we're supposed to tolerate and appreciate eccentrics – and all that might be considered eccentric...?

The English do like eccentrics, but if the eccentrics ask them to *participate* it becomes a whole different kettle of fish! That's my opinion in this situation.

Anyway I decided I wanted to come back to the States, so the central authority for the teachings sent somebody else to take over, and I came back. The yoga teaching arm is called 3HO: stands for Healthy, Happy, Holy Organization. The religious part of it is called Sikh Dharma of the Western Hemisphere. The yoga side is financed by donations from the people we teach, holding special courses and that type of thing. The Sikh Dharma is financed by offerings to the temple, and also by tithing. By and large the people who run the centres round the world, we don't receive salaries. We work, as well as leading the centres.

But one very important thing happened before I came back to the States. There was a lady coming to my yoga class, and we became very friendly. When I came back to the States she decided she wanted to come and study yoga. I must say that as a Sikh it was very painful for me at the time, my whole stature as yoga teacher and a spiritual man meant I'm not really supposed to have wild affairs and that kind of stuff, but this lady and I fell very much in love.

It's not required that you be celibate?

We haven't got to be celibate, but we have to maintain a certain amount of decorum and not be promiscuous. When we came back my teacher, the six-foot-four man, picked up immediately what was going on and said, 'You two better get married.' So we did. She was born in Denmark, brought up in New Zealand. This is my wife in these cuttings from '69–'77, she was in some of those Hammer films. See the headlines! 'The Vampire Girl who shows her teeth at parties....' She's now working in my children's school as a librarian.

The children are eight and eleven. My two daughters and myself all have the same birthday – Valentine's Day! We went and settled up in San Raphael, in Marin County, and she became pregnant almost immediately after we got married, so I had to find a job. My father was a GI, so I didn't have any Green Card problems.

When I was a child I could tell my family were very unhappy. They didn't enjoy their lives very much. It seemed after they came home from work they were always unhappy, so somewhere along the line I made the unconscious decision that there was no way I was going to work for a living and do an eight-to-five job, regular hours. The music thing and the whole hippy

lifestyle had fitted right in, so I started doing odd jobs and slipped into
plumbing repairs and things like that. I became a plumber, I just taught
myself.

That's the best-paid job in America – harder to get a plumber than
a doctor, I'm told!

Oh I wouldn't say that – it was a real struggle. I really didn't want to
work with my hands, but now I have a fairly successful company. My
partner and one of the employees are Sikhs, but the other two guys are
non-Sikhs. We specialize in doing restaurants, mostly fast-food type, Burger
Kings and Macdonalds. We've just done Café Casino, a chain of cafeterias out
of France.

I've changed my mind about a few things, like now I believe in wearing
nice clothes and working for a living and things like that, but still my
idealism has remained the same, I haven't lost it. I feel good about that –
it's very easy in this day and age to lose all your idealism.

My father was killed just after they crossed the Rhine into Germany – a
shell burst outside his company HQ. He was one of the heroes of the invasion
on D-Day, and decorated by General Eisenhower. He was killed in November
1944 and I was born in February 1945. My mother never remarried. She's
now come to terms with her life. She has a small factory between Ashford
and Staines, she drives a Mercedes and her partner has a flat in Majorca
and they seem to enjoy life.

By the time I got to be an Animal she was really happy, because I was
famous and travelling the world, but she's still not too happy about my
lifestyle. She thinks I'm a bloody wog! She's unhappy about the fact that I
wear a turban and have this lifestyle.

And how about your being a Sikh?

That's worse!

Because it's exotic – and the money's not as good as being an
Animal?

(Laughs) I guess so. She just said she doesn't understand. She doesn't
want to understand, so what can one do?

Is this an ashram, or a home?

Well it's a home, but it's part of the ashram. An ashram is really a centre
the community revolves around. Some things are communal: we pool our
money for rents and utilities and that kind of thing, but we don't eat

together very much any more. There's about fifteen adults and seven children in this one.

Why are you sending your two little girls away to India?

Because I think that's a place where they can learn values. I feel this country is missing a sense of values, that families are breaking up and children are not being brought up with discipline and a sense of self-worth. Self-esteem is non-existent.

Mrs Khalsa, you're working in their school at the moment, so you know about the prevalence of sex and the drugs.... Is this why you want your children out of the way?

Yes. They feel very good about it, they have so many friends at the school in India who send letters speaking so highly of their experience there that they're looking forward to it. Of course they're a little apprehensive also.

You're sending the children away to protect them?

It's especially for girls – they *need* protection: but also to gain strength, to have a chance to learn self-esteem, to learn who they are, so they can face anything. Not to get them away from bad things, because life is full of bad things. We want to teach them to learn how to deal gracefully and powerfully with that stuff, not to take them away from it.
We don't take ourselves away from those things – if I wanted to do that I would still be back in New Zealand enjoying a peaceful suburban lifestyle, but I want a challenge in my life; I want it to change. A life of spirituality is a life of continuous challenge, because we have to change ourselves all the time, to learn who we are and why it is we have problems with people.

How do you think two little girls brought up among all the amenities of middle-class America are going to accept life in the remote Himalayas for so many years?

Without already knowing that after a short time they become very happy because of the numbers of children already over there, I would be very concerned. Since I already know that, I'm not at all concerned. I'm sure it'll be hard at first.

Vikram, did you ever think of sending them to a school back in Shepherd's Bush?

I'm glad I went to school in England. I learned a lot and I enjoyed the discipline, but I wouldn't want my children to go to school there – I think it's

hard. It was difficult for me growing up in England. I appreciate the discipline, I appreciate the sense of culture but I think English children tend to
be somewhat cruel to each other. It's hard to be in a minority. I had some
difficult times when I was at school, particularly when I'd just come back
from America after a visit and spoke with an American accent. The kids did
somewhat ostracize me because I was a little bit different. It was hard.

They should see you today!

I'm *really* different now! (Laughs). You know in the United States they
have these high-school reunions every ten or fifteen years? I thought I'd like
to meet some of my old classmates and see how *they're* doing. . . .

THE ABANDONED

There is Charity Hospital, so I've somewhere to go....

Around the world it's generally believed that when a marriage splits up in America, the wife heads for the hills with everything her exhausted husband possesses. I once filmed a *Whicker's World* in a divorce lawyer's office as the wife issued her instructions: 'I wanna leave the bastard so he hasn't got a pot to piss in....'

It is not always so. In a charming little street in the Old Quarter of New Orleans a small hole-in-the-wall called 'The Useful Shop' is run by Joan Norris, once of Ruislip, an Oxford graduate whose first job was in the spy-centre at Cheltenham. In 1975 her English husband left her and their two children destitute in Louisiana: 'He's living with some woman who's got a hacienda in Ecuador, near Quito. There was no point in doing anything about him, because he hadn't got a penny.'

After nine years' struggle her son is in Alaska with the US Coastguard, her daughter has a B.Sc. in biology and works as a waitress while searching for the right sort of animals to look after, and Mrs Norris – neither resentful nor bitter, just matter-of-fact – goes on selling hardware in the Vieux Carré....

———

Your story is the inverse of the traditional American-marriage story, where wives are always supposed to take their husbands to the cleaners?

I sort of ended up the other way around. My husband left me with no money and debts and vanished into South America, and here I was with the kids and no papers and didn't dare work because I knew I'd be deported.

Are there any safety nets here? It must be hard to be destitute and preserve your pride?

Well, that's it. It *is* difficult, but I still feel very English in lots of ways and it didn't really occur to me that we didn't have any money. I mean it was a nuisance, but I didn't feel like an American would feel about it. It didn't really bother me. Lack of money to me isn't really a humiliating thing, it's just a damn nuisance. One has money, one doesn't have money, but one doesn't actually feel any different.

So how does a lone woman with no money handle that situation?

My friends were very good, my landlady let me stay on – it was rather an expensive place and I'd run up a big bill before we realized my husband wasn't coming back. Fortunately I'd furnished with antiques, and *they* paid the rent. I sold my furniture and that left me with a hundred and fifty dollars which was enough to pay the rent for the sort of rat-hole in which we lived for about three years. Susan was twelve and Harry was fifteen, and the only thing that upset them was that they were in this school for bright kids from all over the city and because they were bright they tended to be from rather good homes. There is a free school-meal programme here and you apply for tickets, which we did, but they were the *only* kids, both of them, who had tickets. They were terribly ashamed of having to present lunch-tickets when everybody else was paying. They just hated it.

How did the other kids treat them? If my daddy's got a Cadillac and yours hasn't . . . did they give them a hard time?

No no, that doesn't happen in New Orleans because there's a tremendous mix of money. They were from all over the city, and fortunately we lived in the Quarter, so although we were living in what I would consider a rat-hole, other kids thought it was *marvellous* to come down and see how people lived. The Quarter is considered rather dangerous by a lot of parents, so they don't bring children down here much. They weren't familiar with the Quarter, the younger ones, and they thought it was an immense joke to come down and scoot on my floor in a sleeping bag. I mean we'd be stepping over each other, we couldn't get to the bathroom. They just thought the place I lived in was probably the way *everyone* lived in the Quarter and the whole thing was a great new experience, they loved it. There's a lot of people with no money in the Quarter, there's a lot of very wealthy people. Money here really doesn't matter.

I looked for a job, and of course I kept on being overqualified. I'm not exactly young and I don't type worth a damn. The whole thing was really very humiliating. It was horrible. My only Oxford job that I held for about five years was at GCHQ at Cheltenham; they were still in London, and then we moved to Cheltenham. Then I was sent to Australia to the Defence

Department. I was just an analyst of the stuff that came in. I don't think they use analysts now like they did, because they've got computers to do it.

You'd got a degree from Oxford?

Yes, but in Greats. What good is history, philosophy, Latin and stuff for trying to earn a living? It doesn't mean anything in this country, I mean no one has ever *heard* of it – all they want to know is, Can you type? I kept on having to do typing classes. Now it takes me ten minutes to do what any competent typist can type in five seconds. I sat at one place and typed a thing about the Panama Telescope. I couldn't even find the backstop, because it was one of these complicated IBM things. The lady whose typewriter I was borrowing, and who was even older than me, eventually said to the Boss, 'You know this lady has obviously been used to having a typist....' Which was true.

As you say, Greats is not a marketable commodity here....

No of course not – I don't even know if it's a marketable commodity in England any more. In this country if one can't type about the only other thing left is some form of shop work. I had originally, when a girl, done the retailing training in Lewis's in Manchester, because I thought I wanted to be a buyer – that's before I was with the Foreign Office. The job I was finally offered was with a firm that sold uniforms. I put an inventory system in for them – I think that saved my sanity, because it was something to do other than standing around waiting for customers.

You couldn't get Social Security?

That's right, I wasn't resident at that time, my papers were going through but they weren't finished. I couldn't get food stamps for the same reason. So charity and friends helped out, the church helped out. It aggravated the hell out of my American friends because they said, 'My God, here we're paying taxes and we import Cubans and you're white and English and you can't get food?' And I said, 'No I can't....' Nobody could quite believe this.

Harry needed glasses badly – it suddenly turned out he had no middle vision and couldn't see the blackboard. They were supplied very kindly by the Lions Club, who supply glasses to poor children who can't afford things like that. The church lent me money and I just sort of did bits of cleaning for people, but there were times I felt like jumping off the bridge.

How about going back to England?

The problem was that the kids had by great good fortune got themselves into a very good school, a State school that's nationally famous, and I knew that they wouldn't be able to get into such a school in England. I didn't want to uproot them and give them more troubles. I've practically no family in England and it was mid-winter and we didn't have any winter clothes and I would have needed an assisted passage and whatnot. I wouldn't have been able to take anything with me, not even the sheets. It seemed to me we were better off here, and it was worth fighting to try and stay.

When did you decide to open The Useful Shop?

I decided I was too old to be ordered around, and also it seemed I could be fired at any minute, which was rather alarming, so we all went on starving for another couple of years and saving money, and then I opened this.

It's most improbable for an Oxford graduate to be running a hardware store in the Vieux Carré?

Ah well you see, this is the value of Greats! It's supposed to fit you for anything – so why not for running a hardware store?

Don't you find most of your customers know more about what you're selling than you do?

Not now – but they did. *Everybody* knew more than I did when I opened the shop, but now I find it's only the professional plumbers and electricians who know a lot more. It's called The Useful Shop because people kept saying, 'What sort of a shop?' and I said, 'Well it's going to be a *useful* shop.' The name just stuck, and the thing took off in the hardware direction. If I'd known that was going to happen I'd never have dared – I didn't know a screw from a nail. I had no idea that screws in the catalogue took up about six pages and come in twenty different kinds and five hundred different sizes. To me a screw was something with a thread on. Also things called lugbolts, which turn out to be screws, and the like. I'm selling small hand-tools and all sorts of electrical equipment, and all things for repairing inside lavatory systems and underneath sinks, because it's all very old property around here and it gives way all the time. Fuses because the restaurants blow them all the time, padlocks and locks of all descriptions because these old houses are almost impossible to lock up. Brooms and mops and that sort of thing. We make keys, and there are a few tourist items. I suppose I clear about ten thousand dollars a year, which is enough for me to live on.

I do have rather strange customers. I have magicians and street musicians and artists, all of whose requirements we try and fill from things which the maker and God never intended. For example, yesterday I got a girl in who does something quite normal like being a waitress, but she's into punk and the latest punk thing is rubber gaskets as bangles. So I sold her a couple of these which fit in the bottom of the toilet.

How do the locals look upon you – as that odd Englishwoman with the funny voice?

Yes, exactly! That's right. But again, Louisiana is not like New York. In New York they pretend they can't understand me and the only way I can get on is to find a Puerto Rican who speaks Spanish. Here right from the word go everybody has always said, 'Oh we love your accent.'

So you don't feel a left-out lady?

Oh no no, it's very difficult for anyone really to be left out in the Quarter. There's always places you can go and people you can find to talk to.

Could you imagine running a Useful Shop in Ruislip?

Mmm, Ruislip maybe, but not in lots of other places. I'm talking about Ruislip of many years ago, probably not now. But I can imagine running it in Kirkby Lonsdale up in Cumbria, or Pendle or somewhere, but not in London.

Do you feel secure here – you're known to be on your own?

An elderly hardware chap was stabbed and died of it the other day. He was practically retired and just opened the shop as something to do. He was late seventies and hardly doing any business at all – anybody local would have known that. There wouldn't have been more than twenty or thirty dollars there, so it was probably somebody hopped up or somebody not local. He was found very soon after it happened. Somebody wondered why he wasn't sitting outside because it was a hot day, and went inside – and there he was with a knife in his gut.

I have no neighbours here, immediate neighbours, and it's probably just a matter of time 'til something or somebody takes a pot shot at me too. I used to keep a wrench in the cash box, but somebody went off with the cash box – wrench and all! I do have this starter's pistol, which is only to frighten people. I wouldn't dare fire a gun in here even if I could get a permit – and as an alien I probably couldn't – because any shot would be liable to go outside the door and kill somebody passing by.

Most of the crime of which there's so much is blacks killing blacks for family reasons. They live in poor housing, probably without air-conditioning. A lot of the men are out of work and it leads to family fights, and somebody bashes somebody on the head or pulls a knife. Something like seventy-five to eighty per cent of the crime is that, so the other twenty per cent is regular proper crime, and a good deal of it in the Quarter, but I don't feel any unsafer than I do in London these days, where you can't take the tube at night and things like that.

Would you have a go if somebody came in and demanded your money?

I tend to lose my head, and I'd probably get mad and shout at them and make them cross. I never think sensibly in those sort of situations, because the sensible thing to do is to give them the money. Anybody I ever have working odd hours for me I always tell them that: if anybody holds you up, give them anything there is here. But probably myself, being foolish, I wouldn't do it.

How many days a week do you work?

Seven, from nine until quarter to six.

I must say, I find you rather a gallant lady ...

An embarrassing sort of word.

... and I'd like to think you're going to do well here – you've got so much spirit! Now the children are growing up, will it be smooth sailing all the way?

I hope so, unless I get ill. I live in dread of getting ill. One should be carrying a walloping great insurance but I'm not, of course, and having been married to an insurance man I had no intention of carrying *any* sort of insurance at all. Know *far* too much about insurance. There is Charity Hospital which is according to means, so I've *somewhere* to go.

Will you stay and be buried in New Orleans?

I imagine so, because I don't think I'll ever have enough money to go anywhere else. But of course one doesn't get buried in New Orleans – one gets put into these filing-cabinet things. They can't dig holes into the ground because the water level's too low. They're technically known as niches, I think. They're above-ground mausoleums, I suppose. You *can* be cremated, but it's not easy because New Orleans is a very Catholic community.

A niche must be quite an expense?

Well it can be hired for a certain number of years. After that time you're thrown out and somebody else is put in. . . .

THE MARRIAGE DIRECTOR

On Valentine's Day we did 127 . . .

The Little Church of the West is one of the historic buildings of Las Vegas: built on the Strip next to the Hacienda Hotel and Casino, it dates back to 1942. Within the small wooden chapel (use of Church – $45; Minister – donation) stands a showcase refrigerator full of flowers ($10 and up) and cold drinks. Alongside, a display of useful buys: gold-plated nickel wedding rings, garters. . . .

The Las Vegas instant-wedding has become a tradition – certainly with one unsatisfied customer, now seventy-nine, who has been back to the Little Church eleven times. While I was there the romantic atmosphere was somewhat tarnished by a go-kart racing track in full blast next door; this drowned out the recorded music ($8) and sometimes even the organist ($25).

Mrs Mavis Okerlund, a GI bride from Coventry and the marriage director, has been controlling the stream of radiant couples for four years, but her brief ceremonies seemed perfunctory and sometimes rather sad: a young man with a beer-belly hanging over his jeans married a pregnant pink-and-white sixteen-year-old in white net, while outside his hillbilly friends sprayed white fluff and messages over his old car. Next in line, a soberly-dressed Hispanic couple with pretty bridesmaids in long dresses and anxious fluttery parents. Then a pretty girl with thick make-up and an expensive hired wedding dress over scuffed sneakers stood locked in passionate embrace with an amorous groom in slacks and shirt; it seemed the culmination of an unplanned night that had got out of hand. . . .

Many of the waiting groups carried plastic beakers of Bloody Marys; in the resultant confusion one bride was only at the crucial moment saved from marriage to the best man. One groom grew so tired and emotional after the ceremony they had to prop him up for the wedding picture.

Mrs Okerlund handles the complete package, down to glasses of water at the altar and Kleenex for weeping mothers, and takes the money from an endless line awaiting the bizarre ceremony. At night in the lurid glare of the Strip neon, couples patiently queued to change their lives. . . .

I think we've done about twenty-four so far, today, I'm not really sure. On Saturdays in June we'll do eighty-five. On Valentine's Day we did 127. We have an archway where they get married outside, and they're getting married inside at the same time.

You don't often see brides queueing up, I must say....

Well you do here in Las Vegas. Kind of, like, take a number and wait! They all get married, eventually. I mean sometimes they're a little bit late, but sometimes they're a little bit happy.

So I see from all the glasses! But yours is quite a happy job?

A very happy job; I love coming to work because I know nothing is ever the same. Everything's different.

Yet I noticed that last bride, just now, seemed a bit stroppy.... I suppose she'd put all her powers of persuasion into *getting* him here....

That's what I thought; actually getting him through the doors was where it took a lot of energy.

And afterwards, when they came out, I heard her say with great relief, 'Well, it's *legal*.'

Yeah, they seem to like that.

Have these bridegrooms never heard about community property, and all that?

Maybe they don't know about it until afterwards! Today I'll be directing sixty-three – but that's just what we have deposits on. I don't know if you noticed that cab drive up and couple come in with a licence? They just walk in like that and say, 'We want to get married now,' so we'll probably do another ten or fifteen like that.

Impulse marriages! Some people might see Las Vegas as rather a tacky place – how *has* it become the wedding centre of the world?

Because it's convenient, really. Where else can you have all the glamour, see all the shows, get a suntan in the middle of winter? It's only fifteen minutes to get married, so that doesn't take too much of your time.

Yet I don't quite see Las Vegas as a romantic spot – the Strip *is* a bit tawdry?

It's just like apples and pears, isn't it? If we all liked apples, nobody would eat pears. What's romantic for you isn't romantic for somebody else....

You allow them fifteen minutes, but the actual service is seven minutes?

About seven but sometimes we have, like, seventy-five guests to manipulate in and out.

This is not the only chapel in Las Vegas?

I think there're about thirty-five. A lot of celebrities get married here: Robert Goulay, there was Eva Gabor's boyfriend who I understand is a plastic surgeon in California – he brought a couple out here to get married and said that he would definitely bring Eva back. If he's going to do it, he's going to do it here, him and Eva.

Mickey Rooney's been a good customer I believe?

Yeah, I understand from my last boss he liked it real well ... four or five times he's got married in Las Vegas.

You can rely on a lot of repeat business, can you?

Yes we can. A couple came in off the street and he said, 'We want to get married,' and I said, 'Fine, it'll take me thirty minutes to get the minister etc.,' and he said, 'I know all about this, I was married here eight months ago.' And I said, 'Well in that case you won't need a new licence because it's still good, you just want to renew it,' and he says, 'Oh no, I'll have a new licence, *that* one didn't work and this is a new bride. In fact,' he said, 'not even the *pictures* were good.' But we married him, second time. She just stood there like a dummy.

I tell you what else we get: we get a lot of children getting married whose parents got married here. Eighteen is the legal age. Sixteen, with consent. But you're liable to see seventy-nine-year-olds getting married too.

This might seem a little bit like getting married in a post office?

Yes, a lotta people think it's – what do you call that moving sidewalk thing?

An assembly line?

Yes, That's what most of the weddings are viewed as in Las Vegas.

On your list of charges I see for example you've got instant flowers in the fridge for ten dollars and up, and garters for five dollars.

That's an American custom. The bride wears it on her leg, and then after they're married the groom takes it off and throws it to the bachelors in the audience, or what have you. And if there aren't any bachelors, then he wears it on his arm.

I see.

Kind of like a badge.

Another romantic touch?

Yes, a little romantic touch there.

You said this was assembly-line but in fact some of the weddings in Las Vegas are even more romantic, aren't they? People get married under water, in the nude....

Yes, and in a hot tub on the Strip in the back of a limousine – that happened here just two or three weeks ago. The minister sat up and married them in their swimsuits in a hot tub as the car was driving down The Strip.

Other people's ideas of romance ... can be different. You've got six brothers and six sisters in Coventry?

Yes I have. My sisters I don't think are working – they're married. I know two of my brothers-in-law are in computers. One is trying to emigrate to the United States.

You've been married three times?

Never in this church. I was married once in Las Vegas though, but *that* chapel was not very nice.

So you're coming here next time?

I'm not going to do it again. I'm not going to say never, I'm just not planning on it. You don't need someone to put your feet on *every* night. It all depends what you want. It's companionship now, isn't it Alan? I mean, you want to go out to dinner, you can go out to dinner.

So how did an unmarried girl from Coventry get into this racket?

I was looking for a job for my daughter. I called and the lady said, 'Your daughter's too young, she's twenty-three, what are *you* doing?' I've been here four and a half years.

Do you think having an English accent helps?

I think it helps. We have a lot of telephone business, and people would rather listen to someone from London or Coventry than they would from Brooklyn, New York. Helps a little.

Could you see yourself running a little chapel back in Coventry?

I don't really think it'd go in Coventry, do you? I mean, Las Vegas, Reno and Tahoe I think are the only places in the world. . . .

There's a chap in a morning coat! So this is a very plush wedding?

Yes it is. Hats were very big this year, after Princess Di got married in a hat. Hats were big. We do some beautiful weddings – and I'm sure you saw this morning that we had T-shirts and jeans coming in getting married. But that's romance, innit?

After a heavy night at the tables do people suddenly say, 'Come on, let's get married on the way home?'

Yes they do, lots of times. Not at our chapel, because we close at midnight.

At midnight!

But another chapel down the street affiliated with us stays open twenty-four hours. Now they get married at four a.m. . . . but we don't marry drunks and the courthouse will not issue a licence to a couple if the clerk thinks you've been drinking too much. They say, 'You're too drunk – come back tomorrow.'

Anyone else they won't marry?

Well they won't marry people of the same gender.

That seems reasonable. What else?

That's about it. Otherwise we'll marry anything.

All comers?

Yes, all. I had one couple though, he wanted to get married in the nude, him and his bride way up on the mountain at ten-thirty at night. We have gorgeous mountains here, but the minister suggested that maybe it wouldn't be a good idea to do that: it's a little cold on the mountain, with or without clothes.

What was the thinking behind that?

He wanted there to be a *Oneness*, a beginning. They wanted to begin like Adam and Eve did, but without the leaves on.

It all seems to devalue marriage – a bit like a wedding ceremony on a carnival float, or in the foyer of the local Odeon....

Yes, or the Gaumont. You're right. It's not really romantic, but it *is* convenient....

THE KICKER

Sex before a practice gives you weak legs....

Back in St Albans Mick Luckhurst used to turn out as fullback for the Old Verulamians. He went to Balls Park Teacher Training College on a physical education course mainly because they offered him an exchange year in America, at the St Cloud State University in Minnesota. He now has one of the most sought-after and rewarding jobs in sport – the dream of every American boy: kicker for the Atlanta Falcons.

The twenty-eight place-kickers in America's National Football League have the loneliest, most pressurized job in pro football. When any game is on the line it's either a fifty-yard miracle and a tumult of cheers, or misery and thoughts of suicide. For such torment they pick up $200,000 a year, minimum. Professional football in America is the biggest of big business: the Falcons' star player Steve Bartkowski asked double his basic annual salary to renew his contract, bringing him up to a comfortable $900,000 a year.

To every armchair quarterback, kicking field goals looks easy enough, but the successful twenty-eight say because of the weather, distance, stadium, type of field, every kick is different. If a kicker misses a couple in key situations he begins to think about his job, for kicking isn't like other positions: you are first string – or you're at home watching, like everyone else. The Falcons will axe up to half their playing squad at the end of the sixteen-week season, and a player's career lasts on average three years. So far Mick has completed four.

Four or five times a game he rushes off the team bench, kicks, and returns to the sidelines. Every time his team scores a six-point touchdown he has a conversion attempt worth one point; he also has to kick field goals from longer distances worth three points. He must average about seventy kicks a year – which works out at around £2,500 a kick, basic, or rather more than he'd get in rugby converting tries at Twickenham.

Mick lives in a sort of alpine chalet set in seventeen acres of woodland outside Atlanta, drives the white Cadillacs he sponsors on radio, and bought his wife Terri – a professional golfer earning around £30,000 a year – a mink coat to celebrate their first anniversary. An attractive young man with an engaging blend of the ingenuous and the totally confident, he enjoys his celebrity which in Georgia is considerable; it spreads across America and now, by courtesy of television, reaches Britain. . . .

═══

You came to the US for a year eight years ago – why did you decide to stay?

I could see that opportunities were here, maybe for the taking, I was enjoying myself, I was eighteen, it was a fun place to be. I'd qualified as a teacher in England, but America seemed a little more exciting.

In Britain we always feel that in America the competition is so intense, while we're more relaxed, laid back. You were a country boy from St Albans. . . .

I think the combination of my being English and relaxed, but also being very competitive when it comes to sports, helped me tremendously as a kicker in the National Football League. You have to be relaxed, you have to be able to control the situation, control your heart and your stomach when you've *got* to kick that field goal to win a game – and you also have to be very competitive to keep your job. There's only twenty-eight of us in the country and there're twenty-eight thousand who'd like to have the job and are maybe capable of doing it.

You really scorched through once you'd arrived – it didn't take you long to become one of the twenty-eight, out of the two hundred and forty million?

That's right, it was three years. I think it helped because I didn't have the pressure of knowing just how great a feat it *was*, until after it actually happened. It wasn't a lifelong dream that I was fulfilling, it was just something that was allowing me to stay in America. The pressure really wasn't on, a job in the NFL wasn't that precious a thing. It wasn't like everyone was expecting me to be a kicker – no one in England knew what a kicker in the NFL *was*! So it was for fun, and that makes it a lot easier.

What's more, if your basic salary is £85,000 a year and you can double that, we're talking some pretty funny figures?

Yes, having kicked in the NFL for four or five years, I have a beautiful home and a beautiful wife, I have certain luxuries, I have money saved and I could now stop playing and go on maybe to teaching, which is something

I'd love to do. I'd have luxuries that a lot of people who are in teaching couldn't afford.

What do you reckon you'll take home at the end of this year?

Depends how well the team does, how well I do – but it'll be in excess of $200,000, probably. If we're very successful and go on to the Superbowl, there's no *end* to where it would be!

So it's a minimum of $200,000?

Yes.

Well that's about three thousand pounds a week, which is more than you'd get as a physical education instructor in Hertfordshire. . . .

Yes – it's what you'd get in a year! One of the great things, one of the great blessings, is that not only does it pay well, it's very enjoyable to do. To be paid to stay in good physical condition and to compete in something you love to do – what a great thing and what a blessing! My wife plays on the LPGA, a professional golfer, and my off-season is *her* season so not only do I get paid a good salary but I also have six months off and those are the six months my wife works, so the Lord has definitely dictated a very good life for both of us.

You're living the American dream with your pretty young wife, all the money you can handle, a beautiful home. . . . Is there a price to pay?

Being away from my family. We're very close. I don't think there can be a bigger price than being away from the ones you love.

You feel homesick, do you?

Not on a daily basis, but definitely I miss England – I mean, you're brought up with that for eighteen years and those are the years in which the character and the norms of your life are made concrete in your mind.

I get the impression you like St Albans a bit more than your wife does!

Well again, if we were in St Albans she'd be missing *her* family! She has a very close family and they live in this area. We also have sun in Atlanta and it doesn't get quite as cold in the winter as it does in England. When we were back there in January last year it wasn't raining but it was very very cold, so Terri got off on the wrong foot as far as England was concerned.

You got to the top very quickly here, but being America and being football you can come down as fast as you went up, perhaps faster. You might suddenly find yourself without $200,000, minimum. What would happen then?

I don't really know. I've bought a franchise for a magazine. I sell the advertising and in the off-season that brings in money. I'm not worried about that, I feel I have intelligence, I have the capability of working hard.

And you're a known face that people recognize . . .?

Yes, they know the name. Then again I'm not naïve. I know that now I'm hot. When I'm cut, I'm very cold.

'Cut' means fired?

That's it – you're history. You're down the road. People in America don't like someone who's a loser. You're classified as a failure at a very young age.

I still believe that the recognition my name has is going to get me into doors so I can say, 'Look, I'll work hard, I'll do this, I'll do that. . . .' Or maybe, with the money I have, a business will come along that I can buy into. I'm not in the situation where if I lose my job I need another job in the next week. I have enough money where I could live for a couple of years and not have to worry.

But you're going to miss the cheers of the crowd? You've got used to that now.

I'm not sure how much I'll miss it, because it hasn't ever been gone. Since I've had it, I've been *in* it. We have the off-season and that's a very relaxing time – it's nice to get away. You can go out of State and it's more a rarity that I'll be recognized as Mick Luckhurst the field-goal kicker for the Falcons, unless my name is mentioned. There's also that inner pride maybe, or ego, that sort of says, I wish someone would maybe say, 'Hey, there's Mick Luckhurst from the Falcons!' How much I'd miss that I can't tell, but with my spiritual belief I can be very content without that. My life doesn't revolve around other people telling me how good a guy I am or how good a kicker I am, because the praise of men isn't what I'm after.

You've found your religious belief since you've been over here? Has this got something to do with America – would you have found it in St Albans?

I believe that you're chosen to be saved – it's not our choice. I didn't want to come to Atlanta, I wanted to go somewhere else, so I don't think it was coincidence that I ended up here. I believe that was the Lord at work, and I was brought here to meet my wife and to be married, to meet people who showed me there was something more to life than materialism and money.

Will this help you avoid retirement syndrome? You're twenty-six so you're probably a bit over the top now, aren't you?

You never know when it's going to come! Forced retirement, they call it and it's like, 'Cut – you're out of here!' That could happen to me next week. In some other positions it's not quite as quick, but mine's almost week by week. If that happens I'll go on to something else and succeed at that.

You're sure you will?

Well yes, I have a drive within me that's given me the ability to succeed. Whatever I tried I was successful at, and I believe that if you give your heart and your soul to doing something you will be successful. Hopefully your success is measured by Christian success and not man's success, because I don't have to make a lot of money to be successful now. Previously I would have thought my success was measured by monetary terms.

So when you're 'cut', as you say –

Isn't that a horrible word, cut!

Yes, and they're not a very lovable bunch, it seems, in your business?

It's a little bit cut-throat. When you're doing well they're very nice to you but it is a win-at-all-costs business, which is understandable – that's America. You *must* win and when you're gone, you're gone. You know – See you later! They can be very friendly to you but if you're not doing the job, you're out of here and they get someone who *can* do it.

The phone doesn't ring?

They don't call and wish you Happy Birthday. You're gone, and 'cut' is maybe appropriate for that reason 'cause you're actually cut-off, sent to Coventry – or maybe it's Washington, here!

You have to be enormously confident – which it seems you are – and you've got to be determined; have you also got to be as ruthless as they are?

No, definitely not – in fact you have to be loving and caring because if you're not. . . .

In this game!

I'm serious.

Come on – none of them look very loving to me!

Well, I'm not sure about every player . . . but I think you can play hard and not be ruthless. It's a state of mind. You can hit someone as hard as you can to get the ball, or you can hit them as hard as you can to *hurt* them – it depends what way your mind is, whether it's ruthless or just good playing.

Do you think these chaps could go over and play for Manchester and Liverpool and Arsenal and once they'd got the hang of the game, do as well as they're doing here?

No. They're tremendous athletes but they've been trained since the age of five to be *football* players.

Since the age of five!

Here it's phenomenal. They've got things called Pee-Wee Leagues and these are little kids – the helmet is bigger than the kid playing the sport. It's truly amazing to see them at the game at that age, because the coach is still as ruthless – I think that's the word. He'll be shouting at them and you'll see these helmets drop with the head, and it seems like the helmet's hit the ground. . . . Yet they grow into tremendous athletes – I was very surprised when I first saw them. There's no comparison with the size of people in England.

You're a sort of pygmy compared to some of these guys?

Yes, I'm six-foot-two inches and fifteen stone – and I'm petite. It's amazing – I mean these huge men are running a forty-yard dash in 4.8 seconds, which is fast.

And carrying all this armour.

That is correct. They're phenomenal athletes, but the agility involved in football compared to soccer is totally different. I think they could adapt to play rugby, but a rugby player has to run all day. A football player has a different type of stamina. He has that instant hit, take the blow or give the blow and move – whereas in rugby it's continuous motion.

Do you think there are other young rugger players back in England who could come over here and do what you've done and be as good as you are?

It's difficult to say – obviously there must be, I'm not that exceptional. But they *have* tried to do that, the Falcons have gone over to England and Europe and picked up players, brought them back, but they weren't able to make it. The Dallas Cowboys went to Australia just two years ago and picked up a punter and a kicker who were meant to be great amateur players at rugby and great kickers, but they didn't make the grade. There are certain characteristics to kicking an American football that make it a little more difficult than playing rugby.

Like soccer in England, many many people dream the all-American dream of playing NFL football, but very few make it. You see a lot more shattered dreams than you do dreams come true, and that's true in soccer as well. Many kids go through the farm system in England, just as they do here, thinking they're going to make it. That's their dream, their goal and then *bam*, it's taken away. Then there's nothing.

As a kicker, you're lightly armoured compared to the others?

Yes, after the touchdown I kick an extra point and then we have four downs and if after three downs you don't get ten yards, if you're within say fifty yards, you'll kick a field goal, which is like a penalty in rugby. I'll kick that and that's three points. If it's further than, say, fifty or fifty-five yards, someone will throw the ball at the guy and he'll punt it away, he'll kick it away.

You don't get your arms torn off, like the others?

Very rarely.

Sports stars over here are as big as movie stars?

Yes, it's comparable. I can go to other places in America and not be as noticeable – except if the name is used – but in Georgia, yes definitely.

You can handle this, can you?

I try to keep it in perspective. I know, for instance, whatever the papers say about me I'm never as good as they say, never as bad. You can very easily be put on a pedestal and once you're not playing it's pulled away from you very abruptly. Suddenly you're a loser and they don't want to know you. I try to very much play it down. I'm very pleased that I can make people happy by signing my autograph, but I also try to make sure I realize that I'm no more important than they are.

The thing is, you'll go back to England, back to St Albans where despite American football on Channel 4 you're Mick *Who*, aren't you?

No, that's changed. Coming back just last year I was going through the station at Victoria and people were saying, 'Kick 'em straight, Mick!'

Will you be signing photographs in St Albans?

I have! I went to buy Christmas gifts in a toyshop and this fella got my autograph. I was laughing and saying, 'This is *great*!' It was far more meaningful in England than it is here, to me!

In England we tend to say, 'Oh bad luck,' don't we? 'Well tried!' 'Hard luck!'

Very much so.

They tend *not* to say that here – they say, 'Get the bum off!'

That's exactly right. They're either cheering for me or booing me. In fact I was going to change my name to Lou, so whenever the crowd started booing I'd think they were saying 'Lou!' You're as good as your last kick, as good as your last throw, as good as your last catch. It doesn't matter whether you're in business or in sport. You never play a good game and lose – even though it was a great game.

Coming second means nothing. Is that just because of the money? If you're earning hundreds of thousands of dollars and you get cut, your income's disappeared, so you're worrying about losing your livelihood, you're not only worried about your *amour-propre*?

I think that's true of many people. Once the income's gone, then their significance has dwindled. I consciously made an effort to make sure that doesn't happen.

But you'd be pretty sick if you were suddenly back to your old days of bumming lifts and living off five dollars a day?

I don't think so. I didn't feel like a loser then and I wouldn't feel like a loser again. If I wanted to bum around, to hitch-hike, which I'd be doing with my wife, I would do it and enjoy it very much – and again not feel like a bum.

Can you see yourself here for the rest of your life and going to a grave in Atlanta?

It really depends how long I last! I could be run over tomorrow, when it *would* be in Atlanta ... but I would hope not. I've been in Atlanta four years – that's the longest I've been anywhere since I left home at seventeen.

And what about taking out citizenship?

Well I'm a citizen but I'm British, and I'll always remain British. I'd love to go back to England. I would like to have a business that would keep my wife happy and would be something between Atlanta and England. I have a friend who's offered me a job as a distributor of lingerie in England, so what better opportunity! It's a multi-million-dollar business in America and Canada and they're about to extend it to England and he said, 'If you'd be interested ...' so who knows, I might be a door-to-door lingerie salesman!

It seems you have it all here; do you miss anything from England?

People, I think. People there are far more relaxed, far more content with their lot. Everyone doesn't seem to be rushing everywhere, there's time to go to the pub. I drink very little but I would enjoy going to the pub, just relaxing, playing some darts. Here you go to a bar to either pick up a lady or to get some business and hand your card out. There's not the time to relax in America that there is in England. People are still chasing that mighty dollar, and again it doesn't matter if you earn $200,000 or $2,000, you don't have *enough*. I'm sure the fellow that earns $2,000,000 doesn't have enough. That's why this system is so successful.

Sitting here like this you're going to be hard put to convince me you're having an unrelaxed time here. ...

I'm not, not at all. But there again, I'm a workaholic, I'm continually on the phone, constantly looking for new avenues – and that's America, that's not me. I'm trying to fight it all the time, always trying to slow down. My friends say, 'Mick, why push it so much?' And I'll consciously try but something else'll happen and I'll think, God that's a great idea, let's follow that up! Obviously I must have that in me because I wouldn't be where I am without that. All the time there's something churning, turning. . . .

That's more Atlanta than St Albans?

Yes very much so. I don't think those opportunities would be arising so much in England. I think the economy dictates. Again my position as a player in the NFL allows me great opportunities. People come to me with different things and that definitely keeps the old ticker, the heart-rate up and the mind ticking over, which is fine. I enjoy that, I'm not worried about where my next meal's going to come from – except if my wife's out of town and I have to cook it!

In some ways religion seems to play a stronger role here than at home – it's more evident?

Yes, Georgia is known as the Bible Belt. A lot of people believe that's where you come to be saved, or be a Christian. You come to Atlanta and you fail at something and by failing you then turn to your last resort and Jesus Christ. My system is a little different to that, in that I *had* everything. I came here full of life and the spirit of living, had all the money that I ever dream of. . . .

And more. . . .

That's right, and more! The girls, the things you think you'd always wanted as a kid. I definitely wasn't unhappy. I mean if you looked at me you wouldn't say, 'Hey, that guy's suffering. . . .' I was very very happy but I also knew that some nights I'd go home and say, 'Well, I've got everything I ever thought I wanted, but I don't have *everything* – there's a void within me.'

I've now found that the only way that void can be filled is by the spirit of Our Father, of Our Lord, and that's Jesus Christ coming into my life. It's a very very difficult thing to discuss because I know what my reaction would have been four years ago to someone telling me that. I'd have said, 'Sure, on your bike, you're out of here,' and I wouldn't have had much time for them. But again I think the Lord knew how to get to me. What He did was, He allowed me to succeed in everything, every dream I ever had was there, manifest, before my eyes. I didn't need faith, it was put right before me, yet with all that, life wasn't complete.

Did you arrive here with that faith, or did you find it in the Bible Belt?

I think I came out here with it, but it was dormant. And it's like a volcano – when it's ready to erupt, it will erupt. We don't know when that will happen. I think you're born with that and whether you choose to follow that faith or reject that faith is up to the individual person.

The constitution in America was founded on Christian beliefs and by Christians – that's a fact that's pretty well hidden. The South's always been very much stronger religiously than the rest of America. The big difference between England and America that I see is that the point of actually being saved, of being born again, of being a Christian and living a Christian life, is emphasized far more here than in England. In England you have a religious belief, you're either a Catholic or a Protestant, you go to church on Sunday, you've done good, you put your quid in the collecting box and you're all right. You can go and mess around for the rest of the week – and then come back next Sunday.

That's very true in America as well, I'm not saying that's just England, but what I see is that as a Christian you should live the Christian life seven days a week, not just go to church. The going to church isn't very important at all – in fact it is of *no* importance. The importance is in being in fellowship with other Christians and living the Christian life, and there I think is something which is very different from England.

People in England don't so readily talk about their belief or disbeliefs, whereas in America there's very few that actually disbelieve. You can't disbelieve, you've got to believe something, but you don't necessarily practise over here. In England I think there are far more people who actually disbelieve.

If you disbelieve here, it's bad for business?

Yes, you know you've *got* to – even the President! It goes through everyone here. I'm not saying I agree with that but yes, religion is far more evident and it's a plus and that's that. But I also think people are far more conscious of the Christian life and how you *should* be living and that you do need to be born again to be saved and to go on to everlasting life. In England that's a new thing.

What is divine intervention going to do for you in the future, do you believe?

We never know that. We live the life we're told to live, live it to its fullest and give life everything we've got. It doesn't matter what we're doing, whether we be teaching, playing football, interviewing, we give it everything we've got and in that we will be successful and we will reap the benefits, whether they're financial or purely spiritual, and in that we find happiness.

Divine intervention stood back during your last big game because first, you equalled the top scorer in your team, and then you *didn't* get the goal that would have won the game!

Well again, that's divine intervention. I could kick that kick probably eight out of ten times, maybe nine out of ten times. The Lord saw fit that *wasn't* the one I was to make. If I'd made that I would have been the kingpin round here. Maybe He thought it wasn't time to allow Mick Luck-hurst to get too big-headed – he couldn't deal with that yet! I don't know the reasons, I haven't really thought too much about it. You try not to dwell on those misfortunes, but I do know that there was a reason for it and I wasn't depressed about it. Three or four years ago I would have been very very depressed for a very long time. I glorify in what the Lord has given me and I'm very thankful for *that*. We're taught not just to be happy in the good times but to be happy and thankful in the bad times as well.

Sport over here, especially football, is a rather unforgiving business – how do your less religious team-mates react when you miss that vital kick?

Your team obviously has to believe in you and I think they do – I've been here four years now. I think the main thing is management; right now I'm trying to renegotiate my contract.

So that was a bad one to miss, was it?

That's right. They will immediately remind you of that one kick. They forget everything else you've done and how well you have kicked, but they'll mention that *one* kick. That's when it does become difficult. It's very cut-throat, but I just have to sit at the wayside and see what's going to happen.

You have prayers before the game? They look after your spiritual welfare at the club as well as your financial welfare?

It's not really the club that does the prayers, although the coach does, and I think out of forty-nine players, forty-nine pray. In our hour of need we'll go to anything, anything – and we go to the Almighty as Christians. The Christians on the team are very pleased to see that, because you never know when that seed will be planted. Yes, we have very good prayers before the game – and better after, if we win!

There are no atheists in foxholes?

That's it!

They're concerned about your moral wellbeing as well? They don't even let you cohabit with your wife?

I don't know if it's my wellbeing they're worrying about, or whether it's my performance! It's an old wives' tale that sex before a game is bad for you. Sex before a practice gives you weak legs, but I've never found that, so I *think* it's a wives' tale, but that's just the way it's been. We have rules where we go to training camp for six weeks and the wives are not allowed to come to our hotel rooms. We're allowed home once a week. It's very old-fashioned, the rules are very strange, and if you ever ask for an explanation they say, 'This is the way it's always been.' I really don't think it's for our moral wellbeing, though.

On a normal week before a game, do they say you mustn't sleep with your wife?

No, they don't go to that extreme – but we have to go to the hotel on Saturday night for a Sunday game.

They inspect your legs, do they?

No!

But if you have a friend in the hotel it would be against the rules to go into her room, even if you were just going to have a cup of coffee?

Exactly, yes – you're not allowed to go to someone else's room, a female's room, and the female isn't allowed to your room.

And how would you be punished if they found you'd been up there sneaking that quick cup of coffee?

The minimum would be a thousand-dollar fine, but our team is a little different – the fine isn't the main thing. We have rules, we abide by them. If not, if we can't trust you to abide by those rules, we can't trust you to perform – and you're cut. In fact, it's very rare that we'll be checked. We're meant to have a bed-check at eleven o'clock during training camp, and the night before a game when you're meant to be in bed as a curfew.

Does a coach come round, just checking?

They used to! Previous coaches did, and in most other teams they will have a curfew and you *will* be checked that you're in bed.

Alone?

Yes. That isn't done in our team. It's done very much on trust, which is very nice but very unusual. It's a very unusual setting for an Englishman in particular to be an adult and not allowed to see his wife, to have a curfew where you must be in your room by eleven. It's very strange.

But what athlete in England could earn your kind of money – nobody converting tries for the Wasps!

That's right – it's rare in England for someone to earn the income that myself and Terri earn, but again income isn't everything. It's very important when you're striving for it, but when you reach it you realize that happiness doesn't come from your bank balance. In fact you worry about your bank balance and keeping it where it's at, or putting more in it so you can pay your taxes. No, happiness is in many things and it definitely isn't with the fulfilment of a bank account. Fulfilment in yourself and a spiritual belief can come from England or America. I would like to live in England again, but when that would happen I don't know because my wife would have a lot to say about that.

American wives are said to be a little more bossy than English wives – has that been your experience?

Mine is – no, that's not fair, she's not here!

Exactly, so you can tell me the truth quickly before she comes back!

No, she's very understanding, she's a beautiful wife. She's not a women's libber, she believes in what the Bible says – that a wife should do as she's told, basically, in layman's terms.

You *will* go to St Albans!

That's right, and she would do that. She'd be happy doing that, but it would be a struggle at first. My brother in fact came over from England to my wedding and he met a girl from Duluth just down the road here and they were married straight afterwards, so these girls from the South can get us Englishmen – you'd better look out!

Never underestimate the power. . . .

That's it – the peaches from the South will get you, and are they *sweet*!

After eight years in the States, do you feel like an American?

No, definitely not.

You still feel like a boy from St Albans?

No – I'm an inbetweenie! It's one of those strange things because I go home to England and I'm a foreigner, and here I'm a foreigner – they think I'm Australian or English or a New Zealander. In England they're not really sure *what* I am any more.

Does the crowd hold it against you that you're a Limey when you miss a kick, or do they have a soft spot for you?

I think they have a soft spot. Americans generally do have soft spots for the English. It's a great advantage to have an English accent. Sadly mine is, year by year, failing.

It's eroding – but at least you don't have a Georgia accent!

Thankfully! No, they're almost in awe of the English accent! I don't think it's the person, but they just love the accent. People will come up and they'll say, 'I love to hear you talk.' They still do it to me, so it can't be all gone.
There's a thing that I call 'football mentality'. It's in America, but mainly I see it in football. It's where things have been this way for ever, so we're not going to change them. You see it every day. I have to wear my helmet during camp all the time. I'm never hit, all I am is talked to during practice, but they would like me to wear my helmet the whole time. Why? Because everyone else is wearing their helmets.

That's a discipline – I suppose they're trying to save you from yourself because, for example, you must be followed by a lot of groupies? If there are forty strapping eight-foot-six giants, there must be a lot of girls hanging around outside the hotels?

That's true. There *is* a lot of that, and it is for our good, but my argument would be, why not send them home to their wives because there would be a lot less temptation if you were with your wife than if you're on your own in a hotel room, and you're getting lonely. . . .

They want you to live a good clean life because you've got to be vigorous and healthy; they don't want your vitality sapped.

That's true. I'm not sure if they're looking after us morally or if it's just financially, for them. We win, they make more!

It's their double-entry bookkeeping! There's a lot of betting on the games here – it's very big business?

Very much so. In my job you have to set all these things aside. There's billions of dollars a week gambled in the NFL and you can't think about that, but obviously when you're kicking a field goal to win or lose a game there's a whole lot of people who've got thousands of dollars riding on that. You've got the thousands-of-dollars issue, you've got millions of people watching you on television, you've got your own personal statistics, you've got fifty players, you've got management upstairs watching your every move. That's the sort of thing as a kicker I have to deal with.

Do the bookies ever try to nobble you?

Yeah, it's been known. It's never happened to me, thankfully, but definitely people have been called. The NFL is very strong, it has great security and if anyone received those calls they immediately tell the NFL what happened, because not only is it bad for the game but it's very bad for the player. If you let it get out of hand people can get killed.

The other problem today is drugs; do these guys take steroids to build up muscle?

I'm sure that steroids are very prominent in the NFL. On this team I'm sure there *are* a few players taking them. It's not something you announce to everybody, but to get that mass some people do have artificial aids. I think in some teams it's far more prevalent than the Falcons, but I think there's probably some here.

Most of these guys have necks broader than their heads. . . .

That's correct but that's not just steroids, you know. Some players I know who *don't* take steroids are that huge, as well. I mean they work out for four hours a day in the weightroom during the off-season. It's dedication, dedication to their job. They treat this very much as a job – it's not a sport. It's well paid, but you'd better do that running, you'd better do the flexibility, you'd better do everything it takes for you be be best – because there's someone behind you who'll take your job.

Is there someone behind you now, do you think?

Always. I wouldn't be surprised if management was on the phone right *now* calling another kicker, trying to see how he's doing, how he's kicking – just in case something goes wrong with me. I miss three or four kicks and they'll bring someone else in, that's a reality.

Then it's going to be, 'Whatever happened to Mick Luckhurst?'

I won't be remembered. I'll suddenly go from very hot to very cold. There's only one thing that will last for ever and that's your spiritual belief.

One day you're a king and a star – the next day a nobody.

That's exactly right. In the eyes of the other people – in the eyes of man. I wouldn't feel that way if I was suddenly cut. I'd know that I still had great significance to the world.

It seems you've been incredibly lucky – you came out here and bummed around and everything fell into place?

No, it wasn't luck, it was divine intervention. Also a lot of hard work. Now why did I have the know-all to write the letters, to go and see coaches, to make coaches break rules by coming and watching me kick?

Because you're a sharp determined boy from St Albans and you want to get on ...

That's right, so therefore your argument of me being lucky is wrong. It's hard work, not luck.

It's Luckhurst!

THE MODEL

I already have a Pension Fund ...

Models are supposed to be dumb, traditionally. Vanessa Angel, modelling since she was fifteen, arrived in Manhattan alone at the age of seventeen and managed quite well thank you. Now a mature twenty with thick files of glossy covers to validate her position and aided by looks which support her name, she admits green eyes, dark blonde hair and 34–23–34 provide an income of $200,000 a year – though it's probably considerably more. Following the usual New York model's route to Hollywood, she is playing a Russian spy in her first film: 'They've made my army uniform sexier.' Well, naturally.

The night we talked in Albert Watson's studio Comrade Angel had just flown in from Los Angeles, yet after seven hours' travel appeared clear-eyed and chipper and not at all the big-business tycoon who has incorporated herself and whose fat portfolio is stuffed with stocks and bonds. ...

═══

Vanessa, you've really never had it tough, have you? You started modelling at sixteen – and instantly you were doing well?

Yes but that was in London, and I knew London was only a small part of the scene, so. ...

Well, not *so* small ...

Compared to New York it is. I was working about a year in London, I met Eileen Ford and she said, 'Come over,' and she'd already shown my book to a few clients over here. In fact the first person I saw was Albert Watson, literally my first appointment, and he booked me that day for a spread in Italian *Bazaar* and that gave me a boost of confidence. The next day I worked for American *Vogue*, and it went really well from then on. My look was in, at the time. That was when they started to like shorter hair and not quite so stereotyped looks. Very fresh, young – 'cause I *was* very young. They were into fifteen-year-olds, sixteen-year-old schoolgirls, so I was kind of lucky.

What was the difference between being a model in London and being a model in New York?

You don't feel so much pressure in London, it's a much more relaxed atmosphere. Here you have to start working for the magazines straight away because the *money* clients, the big clients, won't pick you up unless you have spreads in the magazines.

Were you very confident? I find New York quite a daunting place and I've been coming here for twenty-five years; you were seventeen!

I loved it. The minute I stepped off the plane I just knew that was *it*! I always knew I could go back if there was a problem. I did have a few problems personally, but businesswise everything really went smoothly.

I'm just an all-round kind of model. I have 'excellent legs' written down on my card so I do quite a lot of stockings, but I'm sure they have a computer and when they bring up your name it has, like on a scale of one to ten, all your bits: eyes, mouth, hands, nails, hair ..., I do a lot of body work, swimming suits. There are those models who really don't have great bodies, so they just do detail. I'm an all-round model, I'd say.

Modelling's not just doing things for English *Vogue*. I'd say seventy-five per cent of the time you have a make-up artist, but not if you're doing something for Macy's and Sak's and Bloomingdale's or mail-order catalogues across the country. It's not considered bad, it's not like Freeman's. I'm getting paid $2,500 a day to do that, and $75 to do *Vogue* – so the reason you do catalogues is to get $2,500 although the work isn't as nice.

I'll make probably $5,000 a day doing TV and then get residuals, so off a TV commercial you can make up to $50,000. They take about two days to shoot one that's just *me*. I did one for Eastern Airlines, of all things, but it was done like a Caribbean special: I was in a bathing suit coming out of the water and then I was walking around the beach. I was there for about half a day. But in a commercial, if you're the whole thirty seconds it takes about two days. I did one for Diet-Pepsi that took a whole week – for every second they took two hours.

My boyfriend is no richer than me, but we have a really nice apartment. He models and he does TV as well, and he's getting into real estate now. He's nearly thirty, so he's fed up with modelling.

The poor old chap's about finished, is he?

Men can go on for a long time – in fact right now it's *in* for men over thirty. I shall probably last another five years, but I think I'll be fed up within five years, anyway. There's girls working at twenty-eight. I'm twenty now and I'll probably be finished when I'm twenty-five, but you can model until you're thirty, thirty-five. Your clients change and you do the more sophisticated stuff, whereas now I can do juniors, I can do young-sophisticated.

I know it seems glamorous and exciting and sometimes it is, but it's also really hard work; I've been doing it for three and a half years and I really feel quite drained from it sometimes.

Many models are ripped off by agents or boyfriends, or into drugs – one hears all sorts of sad stories. . . .

Yes. Well, I'm a pretty smart girl and I was brought up in a way that I'd just never get involved in anything like that. I think it's a lot of girls from the Mid-West who are maybe from broken homes or just, you know, aren't really very cultured. They come to New York and they're not used to a big city. They meet all these people and they're very naïve. I wasn't really like that. I would never get involved with guys that were just after my money – I mean it takes *time* to earn the kind of sums I earn now.

What are you doing with it all?

I'm investing it, saving it. I spend only about a quarter, so I'm really doing good. I already have a Pension Fund, believe it or not, because for tax reasons it gets quite complicated here so I have a special Pension Fund but it's like a short-term one, ten years. So I put eighty per cent of my money at the end of the year into that. It's tax-free until you take it out, but I can invest with that money so it can really build into a big sum. I'm incorporated so that I have expenses I can put against my taxes, so my taxes are really low.

You're Vanessa Angel Inc.?

No, it's worse than that, it's called Langley Models Inc !

I'm sure they don't believe your name really is Angel?

No they don't – everyone always thinks I've made it up. My dad's a stockbroker with S.P. Angel. They were really good, my parents. I think they were a bit worried when I was missing school – they wanted me to go to Oxford and all that, so they were kind of disappointed I never came back and did A-levels or anything.

I know I'm, like, money-crazy; money, money, money. . . . My dad's putting it into bonds and stocks, but I have my money here because I had to set up an American corporation for tax reasons, so I have an account and one of his friends kind of looks over my things here. I'm really lucky I've come from a good background because so many models make so much money and they haven't got a *bit* left when they're in their late thirties.

They get into drugs through boyfriends, and it's just stupidity. Many of them are from broken homes and they just don't have a clue! They come to New York and they start making $200,000 a year and they don't know what to do with it. I'd say that eighty per cent of models are into something or other. It's sad really. There was a model who'd gone through a thousand dollars a week like that.

What do you reckon you make here?

About $200,000. I could never make that doing anything else. People say, 'Oh you should have stayed at school and gone to Oxford. ...' I can always go back and do that. I'll probably make $20,000 from J.C. Penney in one year. They pay good money. This agency is very good about that, because they chase them: also fifteen per cent of $20,000 is worth having, whereas in London it's fifty guineas or whatever you get. In fact the rates have gone up in London, it's not quite so bad, but even then there's just not the volume of work there is here. If you want to take modelling seriously you have to be here. It's amazing, you can *really* make money. I spend probably twenty-five per cent of what I make, but that's due to my dad, because he makes sure that I don't spend any more.

What do you spend that twenty-five per cent on?

Eating, apartment, buying a few clothes and cosmetic things. Everybody says, 'Do you get the outfits you model?' but you don't because they're all samples. You work a season in advance, so right now we're doing next spring. There's a couple of stores I can get discounts at. Clothes are not a big thing of mine anyway. My boyfriend has a Porsche but I don't drive, so. ...

It's mandatory to have a Porsche?

Exactly. We rented a house in Long Island for the summer and thought we needed a car. Actually you don't, because you can get planes and buses and trains, and nobody drives around Manhattan.

Have any other British girls come through since your arrival, and also made it?

Yes, two other girls, Maria Johnson and Joanne Russell. They're with a different agency. There's bound to be other English girls here too, but not quite the same calibre.

What sort of look do they want today?

A sort of fresh look. You don't have to have long hair or be blonde any more. Maria Johnson has this short very dark hair and looks very boyish. You have to have small, neat features. Now there's an agency called Collect which has character models, some girls have noses out *here*, have maybe one strange feature – but they have a wonderful presence. You don't have to have plastic Farah Fawcett Majors looks any more, you can really be any shape or size. The ones that really make the money still have to smile, you know ... but you don't have to be quite so stereotyped today.

You can never just leave London and come here and hope that it's all going to happen. You have to be well connected and organized. A client will say, 'It's $250 an hour, have her in make-up ready,' or 'Clean face, no make-up, green hose, green high heels.' Daily it's $2,500, but if someone just wants to book me from nine to one, then it'll be $250 an hour.

You're doing an ad for Revlon or some shampoo, they'll pay probably $3,000 a day and then you'll get a bonus of $3,000 for six months' usage. It's all kind of complicated. Magazines will only pay about $100 a day but then you get the pictures, hopefully.

But if you're on the cover of *Harper's Bazaar*, it's worth it?

I'd do that for nothing, really. If you do a French *Vogue* cover, which I'm doing next week, then I've got a one-in-five chance because they'll do five covers for one cover, and they'll select – whereas the *Cosmo* editor will pick the girl and he'll really *want* that girl that month, so you don't have any competition. I must have done thirty covers that have never been used. But sometimes you'll do a cover and it'll be on Spanish or Australian *Vogue* – that's if the photographer who does it sells it to the magazine. If it's not accepted a lot of them will sell it to the Germans.

Modelling can be quite bitchy anywhere and I would assume that New York – where the competition is *so* great – must be the worst of all?

Funnily enough it's not, it's the opposite. If you work in New York most of the models are established and they've got nothing to be afraid of. It's when you go out to LA or Paris and there's girls who haven't worked in New York yet, *they* get intimidated. Those are the bitchy ones. In New York ninety-eight per cent of the girls are really nice and maybe the two per cent that are bad have just come in from England or Paris or wherever. ...

How do they react to a Brit suddenly arriving and getting the covers?

When I first came here there was a little bit of jealousy with the American models because there was suddenly an influx of European girls and the all-American look went out, so I think they probably resented it.

But ever since Shrimpton hasn't there always been *one* English model cruising through town and collecting all the good jobs?

There wasn't for a long time in the Seventies. The Sixties had Shrimpton and Twiggy and all those people, but then it wasn't until the early Eighties that there were really good English models. When I came here in '81 there was only one other English model who was doing well. When they saw us succeeding, a few others came over.

You have to work very hard, you have long hours and – apart from being beautiful – you have to be patient, so what about your own life here? Do you have any *fun*, apart from earning a million dollars a year?

You have to be careful – you can't go out and get crazy every night because you *do* have to get up and look beautiful – but yes, I have fun. I have my own life and my boyfriend and a house in the country and all that, but I don't think any more fun than you'd have in England, necessarily. People say, 'Oh you live in New York, must be fabulous going to all the hot restaurants and clubs.' It doesn't work like that. In the beginning I went to all the new places but now I just go home, have dinner and go to bed. It's quite boring, really.

Having made it big here, will you stay for the rest of your life?

That's a tough one. Definitely for the next few years, but you never know what's going to happen. I mean, I might be an actress! In Hollywood if you look right, they want you. You don't have to have any talent. It's crazy! I would only want to act if I thought I could do it well and I'd be good, but here they want you just because of the way you look, and they put you on those silly TV shows. I wouldn't do that – if I was going to be an actress I'd want to be in a really good movie.

And what about your funny accent?

I'd probably have to fix that! They like you to speak either really good British, or American. I do some TV commercials and they like you to soften, because the English can sound very matter-of-fact. When you're saying a little dialogue about a shampoo or something, it's better to have a slightly softened accent. People in middle-America think, 'She's got a funny accent, we can't relate to her.' Instead of saying 'beautiful' I'd say '*beaudiful*'. You just don't say your Ts so well. I don't go around speaking American, but I think my voice has softened anyway, from being here.

I don't want to get married or anything like that. The good thing about what I'm doing is that I'm making my own money so I don't have to live off somebody else.

When you go back to England now as a cover girl from New York, how do your old friends react?

They have a little bit of resentment. A lot of people I don't see any more because their reaction towards me is a little funny. They think I'm a different person.

Well, you *are* a millionairess. . . .

A millionairess! I know, but I don't think I've really changed, I'm still the same person I was when I was at school.

If being a millionairess and a cover girl has distanced you from your English friends, do you make new American friends?

I sometimes find Americans hard to get along with. They seem very overly friendly and enthusiastic and sweet, but underneath they're kind of cold. English people are much more genuine. I think they're just kinder. Americans have a slight falseness about them. They're so materialistic, their values are very different.

The men I've met here, they're money-crazy, particularly the ones in New York. They just don't have the right values really, they don't care about the quality of life, just about how many Porsches they have and how many apartments. They're different, really different. Because we speak more or less the same language they think we're the same, but we're not at all.

I think the men found me fascinating to begin with because a lot of American women are very aggressive; I was only seventeen when I first came and a little shy and kind of sweet, I suppose. They weren't used to that so they liked it, I think! I've possibly hardened up a bit, but I think European women are softer all round. American women have a nasty side to them.

Apart from the money, would you still rather be here than back in Harrow?

I don't know. Sometimes I'll be riding in a cab and I'll suddenly think about London. There are things that I do miss: the people are much more genuine, the cab drivers are so much nicer. . . . The people here just don't care about anybody but themselves. It's so cut-throat, and you really feel alone. I just miss my family – I don't really *have* anybody here.

But how much do you still have in common with the people you've left behind?

That's the trouble. I see my old schoolfriends and I haven't changed but they *think* I have, so they act really strange towards me. It's hard to go back and have people treat you normally. They think because you live in New York, it's a different life. Just because I make more money than they do it doesn't mean that I'm any happier. . . .

My sister is still studying art restoration in Florence – she earns nothing and I earn thousands of dollars in a day. I really don't mean to be grand – I can't help talking in thousands of dollars, but she's a student who hasn't earned any money yet, and I've been earning since I was sixteen. I think she maybe resents that a little bit.

My values are different because I'm earning twenty-five hundred a day, and *more* sometimes. I think three thousand dollars is nothing, whereas that's like *so* much money to her. Even my parents say, 'Calm down, money doesn't grow on trees, it doesn't come easy.' But it *does*, in a sense, you know. It's difficult to keep your values when there's me earning this much money, it's really hard. I earn more than my father's friends. . . .

Who earns at least £200,000 a year in England?

Not that many people. But it doesn't last for ever – there's only a few years you can earn that much money.

You haven't yet reached the stage when you see a seventeen-year-old and start worrying. . . .

No, I don't think so. I think most of the young models are stupid anyway. I remember when I was the youngest model: I came here at seventeen and there really weren't that many young girls around. Now I'm twenty-one next month but it's ridiculous if you start worrying and thinking, God I'm twenty-one!

You're a very well-preserved twenty-one. . . .

But in a way I feel kind of old. . . . I think I've grown older because I've done so many things. I do feel old for my age. . . .

THE PHOTOGRAPHER

She was actually getting paid $40,000
for the day. . . .

Albert Watson took Vanessa Angel's first pictures in New York; he was already a top photographer, but a few years earlier had been a labourer, then the penniless dependant of his wife, an exchange schoolteacher in California. His ascent by way of a happy accident from opportunistic art student to extremely rich photographer with a big studio in Manhattan and an estate in Connecticut, was meteoric – the classic American success story. Small, bearded, intense, he looks older than thirty-eight – which must be what can happen to a chap who spends his *entire* life ordering beautiful women about. . . .

===

David Bailey and I were both staying at the same hotel in Paris. I was working for French *Vogue* and he was working for German *Vogue*, and they'd asked him to do a cover of Catherine Deneuve, who he was married to. The following night I did a cover of her – which is on the wall downstairs – and the morning after I was having breakfast with him and he said, 'How did it go?' I said, 'Terrific.' 'Let me see it.' I showed him the Polaroid and he said, 'Hmmm, it's good.' He'd obviously been thinking about it and as we're saying goodbye he said, 'You're a real shit for doing a better cover on her than I did.' Then he turned away and, typical Bailey, said, 'But I got my leg over, and you didn't!'

People are nervous being photographed – everybody's insecure, even models. You're photographing Catherine Deneuve or Isabelle Adjani or Brooke Shields, there's still an insecurity there, even with the most beautiful women. Sophia Loren is the same way. I did the cover of her book and she's very very nervous. She wanted to do a cover that was totally unretouched, and that book cover *is* truly unretouched. I still have the original.

It's been my conclusion over the years that men actually are better-looking than women, because there are *very* few women you photograph that are truly flawless. It has to be a twelve-year-old child. Brooke Shields, perhaps, when she was younger – but she has a lot of problems now with her face. You don't really see them, but when she was fourteen Brooke Shields was a real, real beauty. I photographed her then: she was *almost* flawless. Sometimes if the mouth is a little too big, that makes it better, you

230

know. Brooke Shields' eyebrows are a little bit bushy for perfection but somehow that doesn't matter, it makes her more beautiful.

But when you think about men, they come in here and sit down and you don't have to make them up or do this or that and there's something in the face that seems to work better. It has to do with men being a bit more confident about being photographed, which they generally are. Men are less self-obsessed than women.

I would not spend my whole life photographing women unless I liked women. Sophia Loren is not *that* beautiful. The impression, the charisma of Sophia is fantastic, but when you really begin to isolate her – put her on a grid and start chalking off the sizes of everything! She *photographs* well. Same thing with Marilyn Monroe. ...

What made you sure that your camera was going to lay the golden egg?

What happened was, my wife and I got married when we were seventeen. ... I was working as a stonemason's labourer, and we virtually eloped. She was in England and I was in Scotland and she came back to visit and suddenly said, 'What school did you go to?' I told her the name of the school and she said, 'I was there too.' It was just a small private school in the middle of Edinburgh. I said, 'Who was your schoolteacher?' 'Mrs MacIntosh' – so we even had the same teacher. That night I went home and pulled out the class photograph of forty-two kids – and we were sitting together, two five-year-olds on the front row! She was very sophisticated, and I was fat and freckled. ... We met again just by chance at a dance in Edinburgh. After we got married she went to teacher-training college when she was twenty and I went to Dundee College of Art for four years and the Royal College of Art in 1966.

I lectured at London University, did talks on Film for seven or eight months. I soon had certain reservations about the way things were going. In my initial thrust to get started, I really felt I was running uphill. I think there was a resistance, then, to people who at least *wanted* to be talented – I wouldn't be presumptuous enough to say talented, but wanted to be good. Then my wife got the chance of a teacher-exchange to Los Angeles and I said, 'We've got to try it!' We had nothing to lose. So she got a teaching job in LA and I went as her dependant. At that time I was not a photographer – I started taking photographs when we got there to try to make some extra money.

I had one person to contact in LA, in an agency which handled Max Factor. I took a few photographs up to him and he said, 'Where are all your photographs of women?' I said, 'Well I've done a few but they're in England.' So he said, 'Look I'll get a girl for you and get some clothes together and if you'll pay for the film I'll pay for the girl for a couple of hours.' I went out and rented a Hasselblad and a tripod.

We had no money at that time. I came to America with two hundred and forty dollars plus my wife's job. We had enough to buy a small car because we'd allowed for that, and we'd got a nice apartment – that was part of the job. I had a cup of coffee with the girl the day before the shooting and said, 'If I do some extra pictures for you, will you stay longer?' So I started photographing this girl at eight o'clock in the morning, just on my own – she did her own hair and make-up – and we went on 'til about seven at night.

I took the pictures up two days later to this guy and he looked at them and said, 'How did you do so many?' I said, 'We did it very quickly' – I didn't say we'd been doing it for twelve hours. I called him next day and he said, 'We're using two of them as ads and I'd like you to come up and get a purchase order.' This is something they give you with billing information on it. So all day I fantasized about how much money I was going to get from these two photographs. I said to my wife, 'You know it *could* be quite a bit of money!' I was figuring on maybe a hundred dollars for the two shots and I thought this was going to be terrific.

So I went up there and he gave me the purchase order in an envelope and said, 'I want to do more things with you.' I rushed into the elevator and ripped open the envelope to see how much money I was going to get – and it was three hundred dollars!

At that point I drove home. I was laughing and I showed it to my wife and said, 'Just come and look at *this*!' We were looking at this piece of paper for twenty-five minutes with those dots and zeros, and it wasn't three hundred but three thousand dollars! In 1971 this was more than my wife's salary for the year.

It seemed an impossibility to make three thousand dollars in a day at that time. Nobody made that, not even the Beatles, so I called the guy and said, 'I think you've made a mistake – you've given me three thousand dollars.' He said, 'Well I'm sorry, that's *all* we pay,' so I said, 'O K, OK, it's fine.' I put down the phone – my hand was shaking – and thought, Well it's not a bad way of making a living. . . .

It looked better than Dundee?

It looked better than living on omelettes in Dundee. So I began bit by bit to learn the business from that point, but it was difficult because I kind of started at the top: that was some of the best advertising you could get. And within six months I had a studio and in a year and a half I had one of the biggest studios in LA, and within three years we had a couple of houses, a couple of cars, the usual American dream-scene: swimming pool, everything, whatever we wanted.

Then bit by bit I realized European *Vogues* had the most creative work, so I based myself in New York with all the advantages, and worked a lot for Europe. The majority of the European *Vogues* are controlled via New York.

English *Vogue* is ninety-five per cent New York photographers, so New York really controls that whole fashion magazine scene.

This is the classic success story – penniless immigrant to the man who has everything?

I've never forgotten that I'm British, because I think that's something one shouldn't forget. A couple of weeks ago I was in Stratford-on-Avon, my favourite place, round about the countryside there. There's nothing quite like it here.

Americans are wonderful because they give you a chance, and that's very good. It's something the British in the beginning of the Seventies were a little bit slow in doing, a little bit hesitant. Here it doesn't matter how old you are or what your background is, there's not such a strong class structure.

The other thing about the Americans is that they tend to specialize *– they're experts?*

They're expert specialists. If you want an ice cream go to Baskin Robbins because there's thirty-one flavours right there and they only do ice cream. In Britain the ice-cream shop also sells sweets and chocolate and does a bit of bread on the side and has bacon in the refrigerator – and *also* sells you an ice cream. Here if you want a hamburger you go to Macdonalds. A Holiday Inn in New York is the same as a Holiday Inn three thousand miles away in Los Angeles – and even London, if it comes to that. That specialization's affecting everybody.

So you specialize in beautiful girls?

Only beautiful girls.

Not a bad subject for concentration!

We do beauty and fashion, and occasionally some still-lifes, but basically I photograph women. If someone just photographs glassware, it's hard for a photographer in LA or London to compete with him because every day of his life he's photographing glassware. *Whicker's World* specializes in its own way. I remember the lady who lost her leg on Norfolk Island. ... I don't need to tell Alan Whicker that *Whicker's World* is successful because everybody remembers *Whicker's World*. It doesn't mean that because you specialize you're automatically better, it doesn't follow, but you stand a better chance if you're concentrating on that one thing.

233

What's the difference between running a photographic factory here, and one at home?

I think it's back to specialization, because of the cost of models and make-up, photographers, studios. ... New York is so expensive, with models being five thousand dollars a day, a hairdresser and make-up about eight to nine hundred dollars a day, so shooting – sometimes with four or five models – can very quickly get up to ten to twelve thousand dollars a day. Actually we've shot with certain models that are a *lot* more than that: I worked for Brooke Shields when she was actually getting paid forty thousand dollars for the day, so therefore things have to be a little bit tighter here because of the money situation than they might be in Europe. The advertising side of New York is quite high-powered and there's not a lot of room for mistakes with that kind of money around.

But then your rewards are also going to be that much greater here?

Being Scottish, you always like to get a few extra pounds if you can manage it! The rewards are greater because there's more work here. Basically the majority of the best photographers in the world are right here in New York. There are several good photographers still in Europe, for sure, but there's something like ten thousand registered photographers in Manhattan – not New York, but in Manhattan – so competition is very aggressive and very highly specialized. There are guys here that just photograph glassware, that just shoot bathing suits, do nudes and so on, so therefore the calibre, the quality of each individual photographer is very high.

To enjoy such rewards you've got to *live* here; is that a pleasure or a penance?

I have a very nice small estate out in Connecticut that is wonderful. Connecticut for me is the closest thing I can get to English countryside – not so much that it looks like it with the architecture and so on, but there's somehow a feeling of calm out there that I associate with the Scottish or English countryside. It's the one place where you can relax: it's about an hour and a half from New York, and part of the American dream. Connecticut is truly one place that if you've never been before, you feel you *have*, through movies, through the image of soapbox houses, white churches, lots of stone walls. ... It has a very calming effect and it's a complete contrast to Manhattan, which is really a bit hectic, a bit of a jungle. New York attracts aggressive people and all kinds of ambitious people. It's not often you actually meet somebody who was born in Manhattan – they were born in Paris or Ohio or San Francisco or South America.

You wouldn't become naturalised?

No, never. I plan to stay British right to the end, there's no question about that, although I'm here in the middle of Manhattan, which John Lennon said was the centre of the universe. I'd never become American. I'm Scottish first, then British after that. I still push being British, I ram it down other people's throats quite a lot. I do my best – I bought a Jaguar! I try whenever possible to make people know a little bit about Britain because Americans have a rather strange view about the British.

Anne Hathaway's cottage?

Absolutely. They have a quaint view. They're just now getting used to the new, the punk, the eccentrics, because the British are probably the greatest eccentrics in the world, but they still have rather an old-fashioned view about everybody British. It's like us looking at Americans and thinking everybody's a cowboy or an Indian! They think if you're Scottish you must wear a kilt and if you're English you must have a bowler hat and a moustache and glasses and sound like Alan Whicker....

THE PROFESSOR

I have the spurious authority of the Man from Mars. . . .

Professor Marcus Falkner Cunliffe founded the American Studies Department at Manchester University, and was from 1965 at the University of Sussex; fifteen years later he became Professor of American History at the George Washington University in Washington DC. Academically white-haired and bearded, he has been married three times – always to Americans – and lists his recreations, quite suitably, as 'the pursuit of happiness'. Life and Liberty, fortunately, may be taken for granted.

Though remaining British in appearance and speech, he has grown judiciously mid-Atlantic: 'My Oxfordish vowels have flattened,' he says, 'and after my first few months here, visiting Englishmen began to strike me as affected and absurd. Their voices, their mannerisms and what I took to be their tedious gamesmanship offended me. . . .'

═══

Did an English academic receive automatic kudos here?

Somewhat! I think one of the nice things is to be in a country where you're a bit overvalued. There are elements of anglophilia in the United States in some parts of the population – though not everywhere. There *are* silly British people who believe that every American adores them and yearns to be back with the Queen, which is not so – but there is within the worlds of universities, publishing and so on a disposition to think that English people are good and write well and have been well-educated, and to overvalue them. So you'll hear people – I'm sure you have – say, 'Oh say that *again*,' when you've just asked, 'How much is that bag of tomatoes...?' They'll also of course ask you how you like it over here, always with the assumption that you're going to stay for ever – that *must* be your main goal in life. So when I originally came here merely as a visitor for a month or a few months and it turned out that I was going back to England, they were slightly puzzled. Almost affronted, in a few cases.

Do you then feel slightly overvalued here?

(Laughs.) Well I mustn't let anyone hear, but yes, I suppose, slightly. But then there's some law of compensation, because I believe that I was under-valued for a large part of my life.

I was at Yale, which is a relatively élite place. Some of the professors are wonderful, some seemed rather poor – but then I wasn't all that enamoured by the Oxford dons I'd seen! Some were lawyers, some were just reading their notes out, many of them weren't good lecturers. The Americans are generally much better at lecturing. I had the feeling that they were anglophiles; *too* anglophile, some of them.

I thought the libraries were absolutely wonderful, and this I was not used to. I'd done a bit of work in the Bodleian which has a terrible catalogue, you couldn't find things. To be in a library with a lot of money and wonderful catalogues and cross-referencing and all the reference books, it's just terrific. Some of the facilities I thought were comical. There's a Yale gymnasium which looks like a cathedral; they have a trophy room in there and the mascot of the university is a stuffed bulldog called Handsome Dan. It *was* a live bulldog, and when it dies they stuff it. By the time I was there they had something like Handsome Dan IX, so all these previous incarnations are around in glass boxes. Somebody said when going into Yale gym you never know whether to take your clothes off, or genuflect.

And they have so many inductions into their secret societies. Each of those has a building on the campus with no name on the outside and no windows and ivy growing over them. There's a ceremony called Tap Day, where everybody who wants to become a member stands round in a big quadrangle and is tapped on the back by runners from these societies and invited to join. Desire Under the Elms, somebody called this.

All that, when I first came, was grotesque, because I hadn't seen anything like it. American football, I half laughed at and half revelled in because it's such a great sport, with all the bands and cheerleaders. Some years back I remember Americans at college in England and the dean of one of these colleges showing me that they had a pub in the building and were encouraging these American students to go and get a glass of beer. He said, 'If only we can get them off drugs and *on* to beer!'

You've just been back to London – what was it like going home?

It was delicious. It's so familiar that I sat in the tube from Heathrow and didn't look out of the window. Then I thought, I'm here, why don't I *look* instead of reading the paper? So I started looking and thinking, What *is* it about England? I noted that half the people in the compartment were non-white, and I suppose that's a change since my days. Obviously since my youth the composition of the population in Britain has changed, but I don't feel bothered by that because of course Washington DC is seventy per cent black and it generally makes for a more interesting world. I noticed, as one does, the quality of life in England is different. The sky seems much *lower*.

I love seeing double-decker buses and pillar boxes, with a real pang of homesickness, hearing voices, accents that are familiar to me. The delight of being in a small, old theatre. Being in a pedestrian city tends to be a rarity in America – there aren't many areas where you can walk around and feel that the thing can be done on foot, without recourse to buses or taxis or a car or whatever. I love antique shops and old bookstores – Americans themselves will tell you that's why they like to go to Europe.

I don't think modern architecture is all that great anywhere in the world, but there is a sort of fun and brilliance about the best of American architecture, and it seems to me the English level of city rebuilding was God-awful, wasn't it? Piccadilly and those areas. . . . I lived in the North Country long enough to remember the rows of streets and be glad to see them go in slum clearance – and then to see what they put up was even worse! At least the old houses had some character.

There is a sort of North-countryness which is not very likeable. There's a joke about somebody going to see his next-door neighbour in Yorkshire: the neighbour's wife has died and is in her coffin. He doesn't know what to say, but says, 'She looks very well, considering.' The bereaved husband says, 'Ay, well she should – she was on holiday in Blackpool last week.' This sort of thing I find endearing as a joke, but if you actually live among it you can find it tiresome.

I'm very fond of Sussex, where I lived and taught for fifteen years, so I didn't leave without some terrible feeling of shaking the dust off my feet, but I had personal domestic reasons why it seemed a good idea to move on.

You were at Manchester University, at Sussex University – how does the intellectual level of those students compare with these at George Washington?

It's generally true that British students write better than Americans, but don't *talk* as well. The students I have at George Washington University are also rather more miscellaneous; some of them work in government jobs. There are more people in this country than in Britain who have taken courses after work, or after retirement. The Open University I know has made a big difference, and Sussex itself used to set great emphasis on so-called mature students, but for example in my class of say thirty people at the moment I have a retired army colonel, a woman who's probably sixty, a teacher in California who's just here for the year . . . and at the other extreme, people of nineteen or twenty. The alumni can take courses, and so you'll sometimes find somebody as old as eighty sitting in the room. They're not always completely relevant in what they say, but there's a sort of awe surrounding them which is very nice, I think, because kids don't see enough of other generations. I remember giving a lecture on early twentieth-century America and some very elderly lady said, 'Yes, I remember that *very* well,' and gave a little lecturette inside the class, which was charming.

Do you ever feel at a disadvantage, being British in such a situation?

Occasionally, when I say something that is wrong – pronunciation or whatever – but not really very much now. I'm used to it. I think I have the spurious authority of the Man from Mars who's been up there and seen it all. . . .

Who also talks strangely. . . .

Who talks a bit funny, yes. But the students here are very mixed – that is to say, some of them have travelled. One boy I remember in my first year came and said, 'Do you mind if I ask you a question? You have a job here in the United States now but you were a professor living in Brighton in England, a lovely town on the South Coast. Why in God's name did you leave and come here? It's not as good a country. . . .'

People *do* seem to regard Britain as the last civilized place . . .

Yes, that's what I've heard a lot. Meaning of course for one thing, you don't get mugged, and for another, people will form lines of queues readily. They're generally polite and more friendly, I think, than they've been told the taciturn Brits *will* be. Also it's nice if your money goes a fair way.

The intellectual level here is lower if one can work out an average, because a larger proportion of people are going to college. It's lower in writing skills, but not in speaking skills. I do believe that a large proportion of the English undergraduates are rather lazy and frivolous. I don't know whether it's a national style – it isn't a working-class style. I think they let too many of the riff-raff in. I think if anything it's a sort of Evelyn Waugh upper-class pose, one's a gentleman, an amateur, and one doesn't *bother* about things. . . .

So they do work harder here? Americans are *supposed* to work harder. . . .

Well, yes. They of course cut corners too, so that teaching does tend to be somewhat mechanical. They're less good than British students at reading things on their own and working out an argument of some complexity, but they *will* work hard. They're much more competent at some basic levels – using a typewriter, putting footnotes in. . . . They spell abominably, but then so do English students in my experience. They may work more superficially but I think they tend to work with more sense of obligation. English students are apt to tell you they didn't feel like doing their work, or invent sometimes quite amusing ingenious excuses, whereas the Americans feel that they *have*

239

to turn it in, that they've got to plead with you, beg you to let them have a little more time.

There's a greater sense of urgency here? They feel they've *got* to learn, whereas in England they can drift off and go to the cinema?

Yes, that's so. They're very well aware what it costs to have an education. Quite a lot of them are working part time. Even if you've well-to-do parents in America and can afford these huge fees at prestigious private universities like Harvard and Yale, it's still going to cost you an awful lot. You'd have to be a millionaire to make no comment to your children about the costs of a four-year BA degree, so I think there *is* a feeling that they've got to get their money's worth – which means among other things that they're going to put their hands up and say, 'What do you mean by *that?*' It's very good for the teacher to have that sort of challenge.

There's also the huge premium in this country on so-called publish or perish: you don't get tenure – a permanent job – until you have published a reasonable amount and performed other good tasks, like sitting on committees and showing you're an efficient teacher. In the British scene – although it's changed I know in the last few years – it used to be quite difficult *not* to get tenure if you were reasonably competent. I think in many places you didn't have to have published very much; it was enough for you to be working on some masterpiece which might or might not appear in the next five or ten years. That can have its absurd side here – there are far too many boring articles published in innumerable scholarly magazines. But the best side is, there's some sense of crackle, of people keeping you up to it.

I've been told many times about the low level of general education among adults in America. The curator of a zoo was telling me their description signs had to be designed for thirteen-year-olds, and an ecologist said 'No, six-year-olds.' Is that a fair comment, or is it cruel?

It's half a fair comment. There is a level of ignorance which is probably the result of the educators not pushing them enough, not *expecting* children to read; the babying of children. Alas, perhaps the very profession that you have helped make glorious may count! I don't know how many hours a week the average American child or teenager spends looking at television, but I think it does have a rather bad effect. There are fewer good bookstalls here per capita than you'll find in Europe – reading as a habit seems to be less widespread....

I accept television's responsibility; it can be abysmal here....

Generally, yes. Awful, awful – apart from the BBC and ITV – and this of course is yet another of these comical ways in which Britain tends to be nicely overvalued. People will sometimes speak to me of *Masterpiece Theatre*, as they call it here, as if I had personally invented it. I suppose Alistair Cooke is also seen as part of the cultural trade that we have.

I find the idea that Alistair Cooke is required to top and tail, to *explain* perfectly understandable BBC drama programmes quite maddening!

I find that, yes. It's a good example of a silly babying of people, of nervous fear that they won't *get* it. Of course this for years and years must have kept out perfectly good British programmes – the notion that they would be incomprehensible. I can remember Americans would see *Monty Python* in the UK and say, 'It couldn't *possibly* go over here!' Now it has a cult following.

Some twenty-eight years of *Whicker's Worlds* have suffered in the same way, I'm sorry to say!

On the visual-display side of it, the positive aspect is that American museums are very well designed at their best to be informative, to be educative. It was something that struck me when I first started coming here, that the layout of such places was excellent. British galleries and museums have vastly improved in the last generation, but in the old days you would wander around some of the less famous museums and wonder what on earth something was – you couldn't find the inscription. It was in tiny typescript somewhere, or there'd be no inscription at all. Here if you go to a very well-designed, a very well laid-out exhibit – and Washington is gloriously full of these – you can get an education just by reading the captions.

On a personal note, Professor, you've formed the habit of marrying American women . . .?

Well I'm in good company of course – Harold Macmillan, Winston Churchill and Tony Benn and all *kinds* of people have had American wives or American mothers. I think it's an Anglo-American tendency. A great number of males in the British Isles have found happiness, variety, with American women. They've found somebody who has a certain boldness and strength of vision, and of course we know when the big wave of American women started coming to England in the late nineteenth century, quite a high proportion of them married into British families – rather more than the other way round.

Americans don't always find British women all that attractive. I remember an American called Henry Adams sitting at a café table somewhere in Europe and characterizing English women: 'There they sit, with their tusks!' I suppose this was a reference to the British teeth of one hundred years ago when they tended to stick out quite a lot, to be very horsey. As we know cartoons in France and Germany also show British women not wearing clothes very well. If there were a wrangle about Anglo-American women I think the Americans would score a fair number of points, as women.

Yet it was Mark Twain who said that anyone who married a Mormon woman had performed an act of Christian charity?

Yes – in Salt Lake City the girls all marry Young! That was one of those polygamous jokes, wasn't it, because their Mormon leader Brigham Young has so many wives.

Do you find yourself enormously in demand by predatory ladies?

Not really. This city is said to have a large number of surplus women, but singles bars and so on are not my role. I'm not really a womanizer – but I suppose if I'd been here twenty years ago when the juices were flowing more vigorously I might have been less discreet!

Is there anything in common among the Brits who come out here and drop anchor, do you detect? What's the psychology of this sort of migration – are you adventurers, are you acquisitive ...?

It's a fair spectrum, obviously, it's people who are able or willing to pull up stakes. They may of course have very good motives for doing this, they may have decidedly dubious ones. They may feel they've made a mess of things in one place and go to another, they may even be criminals, which I think has long been a supply for this country – the people who beat it just one step ahead of the police! It would be nice to think that there is more of an element of *enterprise*, but I think there must be a proportion of people a bit malcontent, going back to Tom Payne at the time of the American revolution. He had a couple of failed businesses and marriages in England, and then he comes over here and writes his blast against the Royal Family and the British connection and so on. Then later in his life of course he's writing blasts against the Americans too. That is a personality type.

There's something about betterment, is there not? You surely have bettered yourself, Professor, by coming here? Your stipend is greater than it was at Sussex....

Yes it is, yes. That was not my prime reason for coming, but I would be a hypocrite if I pretended that it did not count for people. Pay is better here generally. The heart of all immigrants' reasons for coming is to feel that they'll be better off, and better-offness is often material – though it doesn't have to be that entirely. America then becomes to many of them a place where they've made it, so to speak, and that very phrase is interesting. On the make, making it, means just making money, apart from anything else, but it also means *succeeding*, being able to do things you couldn't do in some other place, so the degree of freedom and the degree of income are all mixed together.

That's complicated for me because I also have my savings in the British University Pension Scheme and alas, because of the overstrong dollar, they're losing value a great deal. That's a nice point for all people who come to this country from Britain to think about: where are you going to lay your bones, and what are the motives about it?

As you get older there are conflicting elements: you do become more disinclined to travel, to rack your bones on an aircraft, but you also feel a stronger return to childhood. You wake up and something reminds you of something *way* back, so this can almost be a condition of exile in another country – it sharpens your awareness of where you come from. It can be pleasurable and valuable. I think writers have often noted that when they're living abroad they write better, more vividly and in a way with more anguish, about the place they come from. James Joyce in Trieste thinks about Dublin all the time.

Yes, and Henry James.... When you go back to England, what do you miss from America?

Ah, I miss sunlight. I miss the sense of the variety of people here, a certain polyglot quality. I miss black people in large numbers. I miss places staying open at night a lot – I love going into them at two o'clock in the morning. If you're, let's say, in Edinburgh on a wet Sunday and you want to do something, you're confounded – you wish John Knox hadn't been quite so successful!

I can appreciate the ease of living here – but what's on the debit side?

Violence is a big negative for me. I personally have not suffered anything at all during about four years here, but I do know a number of people who've been mugged, held up. I'd say almost half the people I know would have some personal story of their house being – as they say here – burglarized, or being held up. One woman I know was raped and her house robbed. The police did eventually arrest somebody for that. There's always a little edge of uncertainty.

I also dislike very much the American response to this, which is to have far too many guns around. There's a man I know, a doctor down in Texas who keeps a handgun in the glove compartment of his car. He's driving down a road late at night and sees a couple by their stationary vehicle trying to flag him down. He decides not to stop – but then he remembers the gun and takes it out and thinks: I am after all a doctor, with my Hippocratic oath. He goes back and finds the couple is actually a man with an extremely pregnant wife, and their car's broken down on the way to hospital. He said, 'You see, I wouldn't have stopped unless I'd had my gun.'

You have to be street-conscious. You have to be a little bit aware of what you're doing, where you're going. I go out for a walk in my neighbourhood with the dog every evening to exercise him and I have no fear about that, but I take off my wristwatch and leave my wallet behind and take a stick with me, as a matter of course.

That *is* bothersome, and my own feeling is that it's quite true the remedy lies with people, which is not that everyone walks around with guns but that the more people who use the streets, walk around in them – with or without dogs – the better it is. One reason why I like my own suburban neighbourhood is that people actually *do* that, so at one o'clock in the morning you find one or two couples are out walking, talking.

I've also wondered from time to time about whether I shouldn't open a business and import large ashplants and various forms of stick, because that's what people used to have in the Middle Ages. Of course there's a shop in London where you can buy swordsticks! I'm sure that's against the law here, but it's a lovely idea. If somebody confronted you with a gun, you just draw this sword out as though you're Clint Eastwood, and put on your sinister look. . . .

THE VENDEUSE

You certainly can't afford to die here....

Mrs Pamela Symes runs the Gucci jewellery counter in Worth Avenue, Palm Beach, with daunting English accent and dangling horn-rims. She is extremely thin and elegant in beige and cream with a little black jacket, but confesses the dress cost three dollars at a thrift shop and the top is an old silk shirt; she could have stepped out of St Laurent.

She left England for South Africa in the Fifties – 'I was the second-highest-paid woman in South Africa' – and came to Palm Beach six years ago by way of Cannes and Atlanta. She lives alone with a Siamese cat and had trouble remembering her own phone number – so presumably does not receive too many calls from the savage society world of Palm Beach matrons....

Widowed more than twenty years ago she gradually slid into genteel poverty, but is totally matter-of-fact about her circumstances and not in the least bit sorry for herself. In America's most smart and social resort, only the loneliness gets worse as you grow older: 'It's the sharing. My husband died twenty years ago – but I still want him to see something I've seen, still turn round to share a joke with him....'

Next day, talking to Pam as she crisply controlled her counters, the store was aflutter: it was receiving a visit from Dr Aldo Gucci, founder and creator of it all. He looks a charming sixty-five but, they whispered, he was eighty-six – and very proud of beguiling Luciano Pavarotti into singing 'for nothing' at a charity benefit in aid of Covent Garden. In gratitude Prince Charles had invited him to Buckingham Palace: 'I accept on one condition,' said Dr Gucci, 'that your Mother will be there!'

Would you ever live in England again?

Oh heavens, no! I couldn't stand it – the weather kills me, you work like a slave – which is fine because I work like a slave here – but you only look forward to the three weeks you spend somewhere *warm*. That really is not for me any more. When I left England it was freezing to death and I vowed

245

I would never again pay to keep myself warm, and I haven't. Well last year I must admit it got a little bit chilly for about three nights so I took the cat to bed. (Laughs.) But other than that, there's no way I'm going to spend money keeping myself warm.

But here you've got to spend money keeping yourself cool....

But that's not the same thing, not the same thing at all – and apart from that, I don't. I live in an apartment on the lakeshore, it's on the third floor which means there's always a slight breeze off the lake and I have my french windows open and I find it very pleasant. In fact half the time I sleep out in the summer on my balcony; very comfortable. It really is a joy to be here. Even in the depths of winter it's still beautiful, and people swim.

But you're not a very athletic lady – you're not going to swim....

How *dare* you say so – how do you know I'm not? No you're perfectly right, I'm not ... but I must say I like the idea that if I wanted to, I could.

What would stop you going back to England – apart from the weather?

I've been away too long. I've not actually lived there since 1953/4 and on the occasions that I have been back it's changed. The first time I went back I was appalled because it depressed me so much, everybody looked drear and you'd see three people in a line and everybody just tagged on behind in a queue, not really aware of what they were doing. It just didn't have the spark and sparkle that I remembered. Therefore I'd rather not go back.

All the friends I had in those days have scattered over everywhere. I've lost touch with them, and I think London can be an incredibly lonely place to live in. Furthermore I doubt very much whether I could live as I live here. I mean, I'm a working woman and I live remarkably comfortably. I have a very pleasant apartment, I run a car, I go away on a holiday. If I was doing what I do here in London, I think I'd have to live in the outer wilds of God knows where – some slum in Ealing – and perhaps give myself a treat once every month, go up to town and have a meal out; even then it wouldn't be a terribly good meal because I couldn't afford it.

Can you afford it here?

Oh yes, certainly I can. I mean, all right I don't do anything incredible, but one can go to a very pleasant restaurant. The style of living is quite different, it really is. I have a very good friend whom I first met in the South of France, and she and her husband came back here – I'm in Palm Beach because *they* came here. She has a little house and we get together and it's sort of fun.

Yet you're a single lady without very much money, it would seem, living in a place where every lady's *got* to be very young and very rich....

Oh no, they don't have to be very young at all, they just have to be very *monied*. That is all. I mean, to see a young woman of fashion in the Season in Palm Beach is a miracle. They're mainly widows. It's like the South of France with, what, six women to every man! They're all sixty-plus, you know, and all the men floating around, unless they happen to be husbands, are young men who escort the ladies.

Gigolos?

To all intents and purposes, yes. The women who come down have followed the Season from place to place. They live the same sort of life of bridge parties and dinner parties and charity affairs that are a very big thing here. They have a chance to really go to town and dress to the eyes. Jewellery drips all over them.

You're on the periphery of all this – you're not taking part?

I'm very much on the periphery, very much, because I live here and the fashionable women are here for the Season, and then they have their houses over in Europe or perhaps they go up to Long Island or Maine. Even the theatres here have first-class productions only during the Season when they have all these tremendous charity balls where they spend, you know, $250, $300 for a ticket. They all go, they're jam-packed to the doors and it's almost like a lifestyle of thirty years ago.

It's a remarkably unequal society, needless to say. It's a million-aires' ghetto, and you've been rather excluded, have you not? You're a spectator, you're not taking part?

But I wouldn't *want* to. I'm absolutely a servant of much of the crowd who come here, you know, but one can be incredibly superior on these occasions.

It's a passing parade, isn't it? I don't find Palm Beach has much to do with real life.

Well there are some very serious people making a very serious living in Palm Beach, which is rather nice. Selling things, or services....

Now we're back to your gigolos again!

Well I mean they're not the same people you would find in the South of France who really are, for want of a better word, professional gigolos. I don't think many of them are, but there are still people down here, because of the age group, who think a dinner party *has* to be man, woman, man, woman – and there just aren't the men. So they acquire all these people who're only too delighted to eat out. If you wear pants and you're alone, you can eat every night of your life somewhere, as a guest.

What about the people *you* look after?

Incredibly mixed. During the Season I have people who come back year after year, who are quite delightful. Of course it does become very awkward when they rush in and say, 'Do you remember last year I bought a whatever-it-is ...?' and of course you don't remember them at all because you see too many people.

Do you think being English has helped you in this Establishment?

Definitely – as soon as you open your mouth. It isn't so much that you're English, as that you're different.

I'm told that a lot of your customers are a bit scared of you, and I'm sure you *can* be pretty snooty: those fierce glasses frighten me, for starters.

I wear these because I can't make out a bill – which is the important part of my department – without my glasses, but equally I can't see across the counter with them on, so I normally walk around with them round my neck, because I'm wearing a very nice ... uniform.

Don't you use a bit of disdain as well to keep them in their places, as part of the built-in reception procedure?

It used to be so for some years but it's rather died out now. People would come and say, 'Oh God, I can't stand going into Gucci New York, they're so snooty and toffee-nosed!' We've tried very hard to eliminate that kind of thing, because to a lot of people just walking inside the *door* would be frightening because it looks so damned expensive ... so we have to be pleasant. I mean, we greet everybody who walks through the door – but of course there *are* ways and ways of greeting people! My God, the other day to my absolute horror I happened to run my finger underneath my counter and found a lump of gum!

Perhaps it was yours!

I have an absolute *horror* of gum. I smoke like a chimney but I find gum disgusting, and you get these pleasant-looking well-dressed women bringing teenage daughters in and they talk to you and blow a pink bubble in your face, ugh, no, that is *awful*. The thing I find fascinating is that the mothers don't seem to mind their daughters doing it. I think it's horrible, it's disgusting, it is really awful, awful, awful! However one has to smile and bear it.

Could you be doing what you're doing now in Bond Street?

I don't think so. To start with, as I mentioned before, nothing's going to get me working in England again. That is not living. I mean I don't live with a capital L, but I enjoy what I do.

You're alone in a small flat, with a cat. . . .

Sinatra, Old Blue Eyes – my beautiful Siamese.

Alone in a millionaires' playground where you can't take part in the daily minuets that go on around you. . . .

Right, but then I don't want to, I really don't want to. I mean, I enjoy myself immensely. After I finish my day's work I totter off home, have a glass of milk, which is my favourite, talk to Sinatra. I usually have a chat with a friend of mine – and there's an excellent library. I love books. I'm very fussy about the television I watch, I don't just turn on the box as everybody does. I love old movies so I belong to the cable TV old-movie channel, and it is delightful; I'd rather watch *African Queen* than *Dynasty* or some soap opera. . . .

What will you do on Christmas Day?

Oh last year was appalling! You know that in America there's no Boxing Day, so the next day is a working day. Last year Christmas Day fell on a Sunday and we had to work on Monday, which was a horror. People on the staff and various other people say, 'Do come and join us,' but I don't really like to because I make a series of phone calls to friends and people all over the world on Christmas Day, and then I have my darling little Fortnum and Mason Christmas pud with brandy sauce always, which I find very nice. The other thing that is very important to me, I go home and I undress, climb into a robe and I don't dress again until it's time to come to work the day after. That's a tremendous treat.

249

Back at work, do you have favourite customers?

I sell jewellery, therefore they don't come back every week, or for that matter every month, but from year to year they do come back. Most of the nice ones, it's really quite interesting, are Americans who live for the summer in the New England area, very well-to-do business people. They come down, the wives are dumped for two or three months and the husbands pop down for a couple of weeks here and there. The ones who come down from Detroit and Pittsburgh are fascinating, believe me, they really are fascinating because they are um, monied, Jewish a lot of them, and they love things that are, you know, *splashy*.

But you're not in a splashy business – Gucci is into understatement, isn't it?

Gucci is understatement – but if you wear *enough* Gucci, particularly the handbags with the Gs and so on and so forth.... I have one Texan who comes in, he's fascinating. He's a man of about sixty-five I suppose and he loves gold, as gold, but also gold as a colour. I think he runs a string of hotels somewhere but he wears – do you remember that siren suit that Churchill used to wear? A zip-up gold lamé siren suit!

That's an understatement if *ever* I heard one.

He came in once absolutely fuming and furious. He knows I'm English and as he walked in the door, the first time that year, he started waving his arms around and saying, 'You, do you know I've just been over to England to buy a new Rolls-Royce and they wouldn't supply me with what I wanted? It had to be painted gold with gold fittings.' He was livid, absolutely livid. I was so thrilled that Rolls-Royce had refused. But he came and had one done *here* and had it outside the door, can you imagine! A gold Rolls-Royce!

As a vendeuse, how do you set about selling things to Americans?

Well, it doesn't really matter whether they're Americans or Eskimos from heaven-knows-where, you have to sell *yourself*, to my mind. It's up to me to talk to them and get them interested in something. You see where they're looking and you pick on something and say, 'Isn't that interesting,' or 'So-and-so really *is* very pretty.' The number-one thing about selling anything, particularly jewellery, is that you have to get it *into* their hot little hands. Normally they'll say, 'Oh I rather like that emerald ring, how much is it?' Now you don't make the mistake of saying, 'It's X.'

Because they'd faint?

They would, probably. Equally they might say, 'Oh thank you,' and walk away, so what you have to do is say, 'That's awfully feminine when it's on,' and while you're doing this you're opening the case and whipping it out and so you get it on to their finger or into their hand. I've discovered, particularly with women, once they've got it in their hand and they like it, they're *very* reluctant to return it.

It's those *anxious* little hands. . . .

Anxious little hands, that's very true. The price is incidental to the piece, really incidental.

Perhaps it is in Palm Beach, but it can't be anywhere else, surely?

Peculiarly, Gucci is awfully good as far as price is concerned for jewellery, so they're usually quite pleasantly surprised. I've found that in nine cases out of ten somebody who's looking at jewellery has already priced a whole lot elsewhere on Worth Avenue, so they have some idea. When I say what it is – making sure that first of all they've got very enthused about it – they say, 'Oh really, is that all?' and I mean, the job is done. It's surprising but that's the number one, to get it into and *on* to their hands. Very important, very important.

You have no nostalgia for London?

Yes, for the theatre. There's *nothing* like the London theatre, nothing. I must admit that occasionally I start thinking about gorgeous – oh my God – thinking about wonderful things like Scotch salmon and pork pies and bangers and mash and Young's potted shrimps with brown bread and butter. . . . Marvellous, but all right, they have things here that are also very good.

Like what?

Er . . . I can't think for the moment. You shouldn't have asked me that question, but there *are* some nice things. I hate hamburgers.

Well the fruit's lovely, isn't it? Canteloupe is good, and. . . .

Yes there are all sorts of strange things you and I have never seen before. Er, the vegetables are good. . . .

Can you see yourself ending your days here in the sun, with a cat?

God forbid.

So where do you go?

I don't know. Somewhere warm. I don't think I'll be able to end my days in Palm Beach because I don't think I shall be able to afford it. Comes the moment when I can't work any more, then I really don't have enough money to live on. I shall have whatever it is the Americans dish out because I've been here long enough, but it isn't all *that* much, and Palm Beach is one of the more expensive places in the States. I honestly don't know what I shall do. I avoid the issue, I really do.

Apart from that I smoke, and I smoke heavily. Hopefully I won't live too long. I'm serious, because you can't afford to be ill and you certainly can't afford to *die* here. So what do you do? I don't know, I really don't. It is a problem, and a serious one at that....

Back to London and the Welfare State?

Oh no definitely not – I couldn't afford that either. It's very difficult, very difficult. In addition to which, as you get older, you get lonelier. I have a sister. My husband has been dead for more than twenty years and I haven't found anybody that I particularly think is thrilling and neither have they found me, let's be truthful about it, so I think I face a rather miserable and lonely old age. All my contemporaries have popped off, so I'm sort of – touch wood – hoping that I shall pop off also. I really would very much like it if I could pop off before it gets to the moment when I'm too ancient to work. That would suit me very well....

THE SPOKESMAN

When scepticism becomes cynicism, that's very bad. . . .

John Hughes seemed to me the perfect State Department spokesman: his journalistic credentials were impeccable, and superior to those he addressed; he had done his stint amid the Washington hierarchy, running the *Voice of America*; and he had the unfailing ability to produce rounded eloquent statements that were not dull – surely a heritage from his Welsh ancestors.

I watched him in his panelled State Department office, then handling the press, then at the Maison Blanche (not *that* one – a restaurant nearby) where he recalled his days on a London suburban newsagency, on Reuters and the *Daily Mirror*. Already he was looking forward to leaving Washington and retiring to run his country newspaper which will doubtless not be covering State Department briefings: the *Cape Cod Oracle*.

———

Does anyone ever comment upon the fact that the State Department spokesman has a noticeably British accent?

Yes, I think they do, for not only do we have that daily briefing for the press but those words get piped throughout the building on an intercom system – and to some other buildings in Washington, other government agencies. I think for a while people were a little startled.

And you're on national television too?

Some days if the news is such, and if what you say is meaningful, you're on televison. Occasionally we'll get a letter from someone of Irish extraction saying, 'What *is* this?' They're not quite sure because my accent is a bit muddied up, having lived in various parts of the world. Some of the time they say, 'What is that Australian fellow doing articulating foreign policy for the State Department?' But some Irishmen do have a suspicion that this is an Englishman performing.

Or even a Welshman?

Not very many people get that! My father was Welsh, my mother was Welsh, we were living in London but in the way of many Welsh folk, they decided that the baby ought to be born in Wales – so the baby *was* born in Wales, in Neath in 1930. Then I went to school in England, after World War II. I went to South Africa where I started in newspaper work for a few years, went back to London to be in newspaper work there, then back to South Africa and finally came to the United States in 1954. I worked as a foreign correspondent for the *Christian Science Monitor* in Boston and that took me to Africa for six years and later to the Far East for six years. But basically I've been in and out of the United States since 1954, and been a citizen for twenty years. I had decided to make my life in the United States: I warmed to the society, I married an American girl. Both my children were born here and are Americans, so it seemed to me the logical and proper thing to be a citizen of the country that had been very good to you.

You were the editor of the *Christian Science Monitor*, a most significant paper here, you were director of the *Voice of America*, now you're the spokesman of the State Department. Do you think, had you stayed in Britain, you might have edited the *Daily Telegraph*, run the BBC World Service and been a Foreign Office spokesman?

I suppose the interesting thing is that I've done the equivalents, *not* being a native-born American. That's one of the refreshing things about American society – its tradition has been to embrace people from all parts of the world irrespective of background and race, where they come from, and that of course has contributed to the strength of the United States. There's no prejudice.

Without wishing to be unkind, is it possible that it's easier to climb the ladder here?

It may be. I think this is a society that opens its arms to people from all around the world and rewards industry, effort, talent, achievement.

You never found people saying, 'Here comes this Limey?'

No, I really haven't. I'm sure there *are* prejudices, but if you could produce, you got the job.

I'm deeply impressed and jealous because we were both foreign correspondents – yet I'm still carrying my spear and you're running the nation!

But I suspect you have more fun....

I doubt it; you seem to enjoy this job.

Well I do enjoy it and it is fun, particularly on a good day.

Yet if you put a phrase wrong it's instantly flashed around the world and you have committed the United States to whatever it may be ...?

If you're a spokesman for the foreign policy of a government in the kind of environment in which we're operating here, you're actually talking to several audiences. You're talking to the television cameras at your briefing, and the television networks are looking for ten seconds, fifteen seconds of colourful quote for the evening News: one snappy phrase. You are at the same time talking to what we in the United States call the wire services, the news agencies: Reuters, AP, UPI who are looking for a two-hundred-word short story to move on the wires. You are talking to the *New York Times* and the *Washington Post*, the *Christian Science Monitor* and the *Wall Street Journal* who are going to write longer, more thoughtful pieces about foreign policy. You are also talking to governments.

I shouldn't have been surprised, but that *did* come as something of a surprise to me shortly after I started this job. I was at some reception and the ambassador of a particular country said, 'Ah Mr Hughes, good evening, I want you to know that every day I send back to my government every word you say about my country.' That makes you careful! There are certain key words, there are certain key phrases, and if you get them wrong you could conceivably be shifting foreign policy, or certainly causing problems.

We've got a Secretary of State, George Shultz, who is very direct, very open. When he suggested I come to the State Department I asked him what his philosophy was of dealing with the press, and it's a very straightforward one: his view is that you be as open as you can, be as forthcoming as you can, to a certain point. Obviously you draw a line, and beyond that line you cannot go. If there is some delicate piece of diplomacy going forward, if the President is involved in some delicate negotiation with Prime Minister Thatcher that should not be disclosed, you obviously cannot disclose it for fear of jeopardizing whatever that initiative might be. Beyond that obvious restraint the philosophy of this Secretary of State is that you have a responsibility to be as forthcoming as you can, primarily because however good an administration's foreign policy is, it doesn't get anywhere, it isn't effective, unless it has the support of the majority of the people, so it's important to try to explain that foreign policy in as coherent a way as possible, and gain public support for it.

You've been a poacher, now you're a gamekeeper and you're talking to the world's press every day. How do the press conferences here compare with the briefings at the Foreign Office or the Westminster Lobby people?

At the State Department we have about five hundred correspondents accredited here – some five hundred people who purport to cover foreign policy. You have a kind of hard core inside-group of perhaps forty correspondents who follow foreign policy regularly every day, who are very close in, who know the subjects. Most of them have been foreign correspondents and served abroad in the areas they're writing about, and they're very good. Nobody should think that you can delude those canny correspondents.

You have others. We have a lot of Middle Eastern journalists covering the State Department, both Israeli and Arab countries, and you have a sort of outer fringe of people who really don't cover foreign policy except on an intermittent basis and obviously they're not as informed, but each of those constituencies is reporting to a different kind of audience.

One feels there are big-name correspondents here who have the ear even of the President – while in England very few correspondents have the ear of the Prime Minister – so do you sometimes feel you're being sidetracked, that reporters are going behind your back and getting it straight from the Vice-President's mouth?

I think a good reporter will work every channel he possibly can. Government is large in Washington, there are many agencies, and a good correspondent is all over the place, getting a snippet of information here, testing it against another source, collecting another bit here, and finally putting it all together.

Investigative reporting goes through cycles in the United States. I think it was in its heyday during the Watergate crisis and for several years after; the journalism schools were flooded with young men and women who all wanted to become Woodwards or Bernsteins – they're the reporters on the *Washington Post* who broke the Watergate story. The market was flooded.

Now I think the public and the press have had some second thoughts about investigative reporting. Some interesting publishers, Kate Graham of the *Washington Post* for example, have talked about the problem of the pendulum swinging too far in an overly critical direction. My own feeling is that it is good for the press to be sceptical of government and to test what any official or Cabinet officer tells them. What concerns me is when a reporter or a news organization is totally cynical about government. When scepticism becomes cynicism, that's very bad, that is not a constructive development in our society.

One or two news organizations have got a little burned with investigative reporting, with stories that turned out to be wrong, turned out to be fabrications, and so I think there is a shade more common sense, a shade more responsibility. Don't misunderstand me, I'm not against investigative reporting, but it's a unique craft. A newspaper that goes into investigative reporting has to spend a lot of money, a lot of time on it. You have to be prepared to make that investment and at the end, face up to the fact that you may have a dry hole. It takes a special breed of journalist to do that. The press is very influential in the United States, there's no question of that; some people call it an additional branch of government.

It's always believed that, scepticism and cynicism apart, the press here has more power than it does in England; are individual journalists more powerful?

I think that the role of the political columnist is probably more prestigious than the role of the columnist in Britain. I don't say that in any derogatory way about British journalism, but I think it's fair to say that a major columnist on a reputable newspaper will certainly be read by the President and by the Secretary of State and by other Cabinet ministers. Doesn't mean he necessarily *moves* the President, but his view will certainly be taken note of.

You were saying you thought I might be having more fun – do you ever regret becoming a gamekeeper?

No. I never expected to serve in the government – it came as a surprise and I've enjoyed it. It's fascinating, especially if you've been a journalist, to be at the centre of the foreign policy operation for a while. I don't suggest it's a career for everybody, but to be close to the Secretary of State, to see how he tackles a problem in foreign policy from the beginning and to see it evolve and go through to its conclusion is really a rather rare opportunity.

There's nothing drawing you back to the Valleys, is there?

As President Reagan says, one never says Never. I'd love to go back to Britain but I certainly don't have any plans to live in Britain again. Our heart is in a place called Cape Cod. We own some small newspapers up there and I would expect to grow old gracefully on Cape Cod, running my newspapers and maybe doing some writing.

Back to poaching again?

Back to paradise....

THE DANCERS

Americans are very prudish about topless sunbathing ...

Las Vegas can be one of my less favourite places, but this time the visit was made when I went backstage at the MGM-Grand Hotel to talk to three English dancers – and discovered their company manager was called Fluff Le Coque! You can't ask more than that.

The names of the girls – ex-Bluebells from Paris – were less exotic: Suzanne Lunn, the line captain aged twenty-three from Nottingham; and two twenty-one-year-olds in Vegas for eighteen months: Jill Marshall from Paddington Green and Rachel Davies, a named dancer from Cleethorpes. Known as 'dancing nudes' they are separated by height: Short (five foot eight inches plus) and Tall (from six foot to way up). Suzanne, the most settled, had bought a home in town. Jill went nude because it didn't really make much difference and the tops were uncomfortable: 'But you do have to learn to *run* correctly, when topless.'

MGM's 'Jubilee' Show in the vast theatre was predictably spectacular: it cost $15 million to stage and should run for ten years. Among other things, they sank the *Titanic* and, as the girls were at pains to point out, a few bare breasts amid that dazzling maelstrom were neither here nor there....

===

Where else have you danced, Jill, apart from here?

J: I've been to Paris and Tokyo and Italy and Germany.... I lived in Japan for four months and they supplied us with our own apartment. I was surprised to see Japanese dancers. All the women were little cute dumpy things and I thought, Well there's not going to be anyone really elegant ... but they *were* – they're beautiful! And when the Japanese dance, they really dance!

S: We've got all sorts here in Vegas. We have people who've never been on stage before. People in tutus, poncing around on tippy-toes in *Giselle* and *Swan Lake*. There's Lisa, who was a teacher for fifteen years, she's a singer and she just has so much pep! We've got Sandra, Miss Know-it-all, she just knows everything, she's been to college and she's got degrees up her arm. As line captain I'm in charge of twelve girls and have to make sure they go on stage in their costumes and behave themselves – you know, they smile and do the dance steps correctly.

You're the sergeant-major? How long have you been here giving them hell?

S: Four years.

So you're an old-timer – but you're a dancer, not a showgirl? Showgirls are the nudes?

R: We all get quite insulted when we're called showgirls. A showgirl is someone who wears a backpiece and walks across the stage. They don't need any kind of dance-training at all, just so long as they can walk nicely. You can't be a showgirl in this show – you've got to have a good dance background to be able to cope. It's the only hotel in town you can say that for, all the others have showgirls.
S: We have a joke that a showgirl wears a red shoe on the right foot and a green shoe on the left foot and you have to tell them: 'Put your green shoe forward, *now* put your red shoe forward!' They have no idea....

So you're much more important – but you *do* flash the body about a bit, I'm told?

S: We're versatile. It's done in such a glamorous way there's nothing offensive about it at all.

In the best possible taste?

J: Yes, absolutely.
R: We have so much on anyway, jewels and bracelets.
S: It takes away from not wearing a bra.
R: You don't even notice. You watch the show and you don't even notice.
J: A lot of people have said to me that until Sampson, which is like *way* into the show, they didn't notice that we're topless.
R: If you're not told before you come in, then you can watch the whole show without even realizing, 'cos there's so much going on. You know, it's huge....

OK, let's leave your breasts alone for a bit, let's get back to why you came over here: are you better off today than you would be if you were dancing in Paris or London?

S: Yes, definitely. I earn a lot more than these guys do because I'm line captain. I earned thirty thousand dollars last year. These guys on average get about twenty-five thousand.

R: I'm a lead in the show, so I earn more too.

Thirty thousand dollars, that's well over twenty-five thousand pounds. What would you be earning if you were dancing in Paris or in London?

J: Eighty pounds a week in England, I know that, eighty to eighty-five pounds a week, and that's before tax.

Surely it must be more than that?

J: Not unless you're in London and you're on one of the big shows. I know my girlfriends are only getting eighty pounds a week minimum.

Four thousand pounds a year?

J: I don't know what it works out at – that's why I'm a dancer, not a mathematician!

Quite. Yes. Well ... put your green foot forward and tell me if you like living in Vegas?

J: It's versatile, because you can ski and sunbathe the same day.

S: I love living here, I love the convenience of twenty-four hours, I like to get off work at night about one o'clock and be able to go and do my grocery shopping at a supermarket, do my laundry – go banking if we want.... Anything you want to do, you can do it because there's no night or day here, the city just carries on.

So that's a convenience, an advantage, but is it a reason for living somewhere?

R: The whole living standards are so much more comfortable than in Europe. In Paris you're lucky if you find an apartment with a bathroom. You'll have a toilet but you'll probably wash in the kitchen sink or in a closet. Here if you have a two-bedroom apartment you'll usually have two baths in it, and a dishwater. Dishwashers don't even *exist* in Paris. If you don't have a car here, forget it, it's impossible to get around. There's no public system at all.

So those are all good things: the living conditions, the money.... Any disadvantages?

S: Yes, the heat.

J: There's no culture in this town. You can't see a good play, I mean they just don't exist.

R: You can't go to the ballet.

OK so there's no culture, but that has to be a small thing, I suspect. What other reasons – what's the man situation here?

J: About zero. We're at a disadvantage because of who we are. If we go out in the street in our make-up, which is a thing a lot of people do, we still get stared at because of our height. We're all about six foot. We all still enjoy wearing heels and it's not an easy thing to do, to walk into a discotheque in three-inch heels. That makes us six foot three.

S: Men feel a little intimidated here – they don't feel that in Europe. I've had many boyfriends smaller than me and they love my height, but here men have got this thing about being macho and that they've got to be taller than the woman.

The other thing is, do they not think you're fair game?

S: Yes I think they do, but you put them in their place. You just say *No*, very firmly.

You go all Paddington on them, do you?

S: You just have to be blunt with them.

J: We do meet a lot of really weird men, men in bars. I don't know why but there are some really weird people out at one o'clock in the morning.

S: That's true, that's very true.

But you know how to handle them, do you?

J: You can be very intimidating. I put on my very English accent and I say 'Excuse me – are you talking to *me*?' and they feel very intimidated and they usually sort of disappear.

Suzanne, you've got a house here – are you worried about security and that sort of thing?

S: I live in a very good neighbourhood so that's not something that bothers me.

Yet you're going out at odd hours – but then again I suppose Las Vegas doesn't *have* odd hours. . . .

R: A lot of other people are going out at odd hours too.

S: I feel safer because I have my car. Travelling in Paris and London I go by underground and bus and I'm with strangers and strange men follow me frequently, but here the minute I get in my car I lock the door. I go to where I'm going and I get out and there's people there. If there's a bartender they're never going to let anything happen to their clients' health, you know. I feel safer here than I do in Paris.

Would you stay here if you weren't dancing – would you settle down here?

S: I don't see why not.

R: Absolutely *not*! Can't think of anything worse than to stay in Vegas for the rest of my life. I do love the States and it's very easy to get hooked on living here because, like I was saying about the living standards ... but it's a long way from home. I think I was kind of hooked on Paris when I lived there, so maybe I'd go back to France. In the summer I hate the heat: I'm just not a heat person, I can't stand it. There're no good dance teachers in town. They're sufficient enough to follow but if I was trying to train here I don't think I'd get very far. Some girls, their pay cheque goes into buying leather dresses from Norma Kamali. They don't save at all, and that's not wise.

J: I just go to a place and make the best of it. I came here with nothing and I've got a lot. I just take every day as it comes and enjoy it.

Have your parents been over to see you?

S: Yes, my mum and my sister. There was a union strike going on in the hotel so unfortunately she didn't see the whole show, but she was very impressed with the living standards and my car and all the little things, so she'll be back next April to see the whole show.

How about Americans in general – the people you meet?

S: Very nice, very friendly, very outgoing. Anybody will do anything for you. Get into trouble and there's always somebody you can reach on the telephone: 'Oh don't worry about it, things'll be fine, I'll come and pick you up if your car's broken, don't worry that you live six miles out of my way, I can still pick you up.' You know, this generous.

I suppose it *might* just be because you're young pretty girls...?

J: No, this is friends too, you know, friends in the room, the girls we work with. I mean yesterday I didn't have a ride home and a girl who lives on completely the opposite side of town said she'd give me a lift and didn't think anything of it. They really do help you out.

Jill says you meet some pretty weird people; do you ever go out with a punter?

S: No. I think you find there are strange people in town because there's so many tourists coming through. They're not really people that live here. They come for three days, they get drunk, they go out, cause trouble....
R: It's difficult to have friends *out* of the cast because of the hours we work, unless you socialize with other dancers from other shows. You have to sacrifice so many things when you're fifteen, sixteen and all your school-friends are going out with boys to the disco. You can't do it, you have to go to ballet.

Men aren't really that important?

R: Men aren't important at all.

Well, that's lucky....

R: You have to go home, go to sleep, get up and take a class in the morning. If you don't go to sleep you miss class the next day and you suffer.
J: And anyway, who says men earn more than women? We earn quite a lot.

You'll be able to support some chap in the luxury to which he's not accustomed....

J: That's right, if I chose to – but I wouldn't.

Why is it that English girls are so good at Bluebelling around the world?

R: We're tall. Discipline has a lot to do with it. Even in schools in America, they don't have any discipline.

When you take your eyelashes off and go out into the hot street, is it still a good life or would you rather be back in Cleethorpes?

R: I certainly wouldn't want to be back in Cleethorpes!
S: It's still a good life, it's a good life.
J: I wish we could just package the whole place up, ship it over to London or Paris. That would be ideal, because you've got to *cope* with Vegas a little bit.

S: You see, there's no excitement of the big cities here, it's so small.
R: No art galleries, no real museums.

Come *on* – how often do you go to a museum?

J: There's the Liberace museum....

Er, yes. Anyhow, I'm going to see your show in a minute so I'll know all about the cultural life in Las Vegas when I've seen that.

S: Well, we do sink the *Titanic*!
R: You have to put up with where you're living, and so long as you're dancing, it's your whole life and that's all that matters.

But it helps to earn thirty thousand dollars a year?

R: It does, yes.

When you're not dancing, what are you doing here?

R: Oh God, a million things. Go to class, go to the gym, work out. Very body-conscious people, we have to be.

You don't go sunbathing because you mustn't get tanned?

S: No, we can't come in with bikini lines.
R: There are places where you can sunbathe topless but I think the English have gotten more liberal about topless sunbathing than the Americans have. They're very prudish about it.

Americans in Las Vegas are *prudish*?

J: Yes they are, terribly. I mean G-strings at the pool, they freak out! ...

THE STEEL MAN

Lurking danger is part of the attraction of New York. . . .

After more than twenty years with the giant Consolidated Goldfields company, David Lloyd-Jacob became chairman of its North American arm, the Amcon Group Inc. He was president of the New York City Opera and on the boards of the Washington and Santa Fe operas; the 1983 arts festival 'Britain Salutes New York' was his idea, and his chairmanship of its directors was recognized by a CBE.

Loving his work, his interests, his adopted city, he lived in a large house on East 81st Street with his first wife – who hated the place. They divorced, he remarried and, as he returned from his honeymoon to his palatial Park Avenue office – he was sacked. The days when he flew to London by Concorde each week had ended.

He set about getting up off the American floor – an exercise which included borrowing fifteen million dollars – and creating a new private life. He bought the top of a 29th Street warehouse, a loft he and his wife Caro decorated with rounded doors, pharmacists' shelves, abandoned shopfronts, antique rugs and fabrics. Mrs Lloyd-Jacob, challenging but hesitant, imports English antique lace to sell at considerable profit to Texas wedding-shops for a company she's called The Fabric of Society. Together they contrive to enjoy a tranquil and cvilized life within a dirty and clamorous city.

━━━

I came to live in New York in '74, but I'd been here spiritually for at least four years before that with Consolidated Goldfields. I really came over for two weeks in September 1970 and stayed. They'd bought a company in 1963 and it was a complete and utter disaster, and I was the young man who made himself unpopular by always pointing it out – you know, the court jester. Finally the only thing to do with the court jester was to exile him to go and *deal* with the problem. So they did, and I had a lovely experience of shutting down and selling off and trying to clean up something that was losing thirty thousand dollars a day, which in 1970 was real money. That's what got me to America.

I'd been swanning the world as a market researcher – that's making rather British noises about how straight-up everything is, and advising. Here one couldn't just be rather British and comment acidly from the side-

lines. I had to get some people and they had to understand one's impene-
trable English accent in St Louis and darker parts of Texas, Oklahoma and
Illinois and so on. This was a major point for me because having done that
I said, 'This is where I want to operate.'

Could you run rings around the people you found here?

I don't think run rings round, except verbally. We can dance on the end
of a tape-recorder pretty well, but when it comes to giving ums and ers and
body language to persuade people to do something for you or with you, the
Americans are probably better.

They say we're the experts in class structure, but corporate structure *is*
the American class structure. It's much more fluid of course. Once you're
thrown out of heaven you fall, and you disappear. A week later you are as
nothing. I fell from heaven, but in a more British context. Over the years I'd
got to know New York, got to know America, made a number of mistakes,
got some things right, made one very *large* mistake – and Consolidated
Goldfields and I fell out of love. . . .

In short, you were fired?

In short I was fired – but they gave me a golden handshake which
enabled me to have the down payment on a business: $600,000. A very
nice piece of change.

Was that enough to get off the ground in this sort of economy –
you're talking steel mills, not buying a corner shop.

No, I'm talking about a business which has a lot of borrowing capacity,
so I borrowed a lot of money – *that* was just the down payment.

Ah. How much have you had to borrow?

Just buying the second business, the loan agreement that we've finished
negotiating is for fifteen million dollars, which produces interest payments
somewhere around ten thousand dollars a day. This focuses the mind wonderfully.

And this is why you've stopped flying back to England on Concorde!

That's right – I'm in the back of the bus! Obviously it makes a difference
to your operating style if it's your own money, but not *that* much. I don't
think I've worked any harder in the last year, but I've had a lot more fun
because it's *mine*. I can see directly the impact of something I'm doing and

if it isn't working I have a very strong incentive to get out early next morning and change it.

So all you've got to worry about is ten thousand dollars a day?

So long that I can earn enough to pay ten thousand dollars a day interest, I'm doing OK.

Can you sleep nights?

Well some nights I don't sleep very well, but usually boring self-confidence takes over. Also, what's the worst that can happen? We'll lose it all, and we'll start again. Sorry about that! It wouldn't be *so* awful.

The alternatives are not amusing but the results, if you get it right, are super. If this one I just signed works the way the first one worked within, say, fifteen months from starting with a few hundred thousand, I ought to expect to own a business which is making a profit of a few million a year. That's if I get it right. And if I don't get it right, well, I haven't signed any personal guarantees and therefore they'll not be after our jewellery.

Don't they put you in The Tombs, or whatever the jail's called here? Or Bankruptcy Court?

You may go. I would hope to avoid that, but debtor's prison was abolished in both countries I think some time in the nineteenth century, so we'll probably survive. I'm prepared to risk it.

Are there many Brits doing this kind of thing, with this kind of enterprising, buccaneering spirit?

I haven't met very many British people doing it. A number of people who see what we're doing tend to say, 'This is fascinating, tell me how it's done!'

How *is* it done?

It's done very simply and easily by finding the right kind of business that you can borrow money on, which you can turn round fast enough ... so having bought it as a loser, having bought it for very little, it becomes a reasonable success. Then you've got the assets of that business and the earnings record of that business as something people can look at. And they'll say, 'OK, we'll lend you some more for the next one.' If you can make the next one a good fit with the first, all the clever things you did first go around can be done again. You've now more than two businesses – you've got a record and you're somebody who's *doing* things.

Wasn't that what Jim Slater was about, incidentally?

He got involved in so many things. I'd much rather stay with things I know about and just do more of the same, so long as more of the same is actually more efficient and works better. On the list of the great and the good, I would like to go on building up a very serious business. So we've got a steel business in Pittsburgh, we're just buying one in Atlanta, in Birmingham, in Orlando Florida and Mobile Alabama – that'll be five sites and we're talking about two more at the moment. This all in the last year.

I had my house on East 81st Street, a very nice big house, and my first wife and I split it fifty-fifty. It never occurred to me that one wasn't going to be able to *afford* 29th Street. The question was, given alimony and the need to work quite hard, how to find something fairly quickly that would pay the bills? So Pittsburgh, small business, sales about twenty-two million dollars. I've taken three million dollars out of its labour bill and added one million dollars to its margins by doing various things.

What sort of people have you taken over?

My chief accountant is thirty, my computer guy is in his late thirties, the new treasurer is probably just forty and the president, who was the president before but never really got anything done because there were too many layers of vice-chairmen and stuff, he's the oldest of the team at fifty-four.

Why should these frogs suddenly turn into princes because you've kissed them?

They don't suddenly turn into princes, they're good but limited. You're undoubtedly good but *un*limited and so am I, but we're rare – right? Most people are good but limited. Someone's got to ask you, 'Please go and do so-and-so,' which gives you a chance to do not only that, but something else.

You can get more done for money here. In America you could hire a new workforce – there'd be lots of yelling and screaming, but the job would get done; you'd *pay* people to do it. In a way it's a more innocent country ... mankind never being so innocently employed as when making money.

Have you detected they're saying among themselves, 'This Limey doesn't know his way around?'

I didn't get that. When I bought the thing I did assemble everybody and did the bullhorn-in-hand: 'I'm so-and-so, let me tell you why I'm here.'

Did they understand what you were saying?

S-l-o-w-l-y.... The combination of using one word in a hundred that they don't recognize, talking a little too fast and occasionally clipping off the ends of those words....

Or accentuating differently – they give up don't they? They stop trying to follow you....

You watch the face, you see when it's happening. I use it as a form of interview. Who do I want on my team? I want those who are smart enough to follow what we're talking about. So I end up with most of the young bright guys around who are perfectly adaptable, fairly international and don't have a problem.

There's a tremendous built-in respect for the boss. It's a much more static society than England in the way the dynamics of businesspeople work. If you're the boss, and particularly if you're the boss *and* the owner, it is assumed until proved otherwise – by your going bankrupt – that you're really rather competent, otherwise it all wouldn't have happened. They have to think that, or they wouldn't be happy to work in the business three levels down from this guy.

The first business I bought had far too many people achieving far too little, with almost no direction. It was a family business, fourth generation, sixty-eight related shareholders up to fourth cousins, all fighting – and when they weren't fighting, they were thinking about the things that interested them, rather than the family business. It's always the way – the first generation works terribly hard, the second works pretty hard ... but by the time you get to the fourth generation they'd rather be psychiatrists or dentists – they don't really want to fool with a lot of steel.

A certain proportion of people are going to take you for a ride; it's fascinating! I'm busily trying to borrow money at the moment for a deal I signed yesterday.

When you've got the money, *they* have the problem?

And I've got fourteen pages of legal argy-bargy.... You've got to worry about them because you're not *that* big. If you've borrowed a billion you're in a strong position, and they're not. If you've borrowed ten million and it's a decent-sized bank, they're just about organized to take you apart. If you've borrowed ten thousand, you're out the door! Ten million, that's fine.

About a hundred people go to these banks and talk about a deal, for every one that *does* one, so your first deal is like the touchstone. If you've done it and done what you'd said you'd do, then you're in a very much smaller growth. We're talking about the money men. We're talking about the people who're prepared to bring you a deal, to lend you money, to take you seriously and you only get through the first doorway after you've done something. It's the success thing.

What about publicity – if you're in the *Wall Street Journal*'s gossip column, this is good?

Oh yes, and you have it mounted and send copies to your five thousand close friends. On Monday the main thing I've got to do is write a press release, a kind of useful short article for the lazy journalist.

Have you got a PRO?

Can't afford one yet. Having been around them, I can write this stuff. This was actually the biggest single problem with Britain Salutes New York. In New York you need to have a fairly precise relationship with the public relations community, because it is another world. The Brits hate it – don't understand it, make an effort *not* to understand it.

There *is* a total gap. Putting it in a British context, there is no way of building an Atlantic bridge on the ethnic or the pushy woman or the PR ways of doing things in America. It is a country full of people who've decided to make it, and roughly half of them are female. More than one per cent are mighty successful at it, and much of being successful here is saying, 'Sure thing darling!' on the telephone – and then doing nothing about it.

One British person who was involved with a music programme for Salute said, Could they please have an analysis of all the concert programmes played in New York during the last seven years to see the frequency with which certain works were performed, so they could design their music programme! A lot of the British fine arts community saw us as a cornucopia of money come from left field, or wherever the English for left field is – a quite unexpected bowl of sugar. So the difficulties were entirely from the Brits – ninety-eight per cent of our difficulties and fifteen per cent of our money. Eighty-five per cent of our money and one per cent of our difficulties were from the Americans.

The Brits were not peddling much that the Americans wanted to buy?

A lot of the things that came were very much what they wanted to buy. They tended, unfortunately, to be the safely dead! The Monteverdi choir and orchestra is fairly safe, but if you are a struggling mime show in a city that has mime coming out of its ears, it's awfully tough to get an audience. You certainly can't get an audience by royal command.

At the end of the day was running the Salute a rewarding experience, or a nightmare?

I'm not good at nightmares – you have to be able to turn over and say, 'Let's try the other side of the pillow.' It could have been a nightmare if one had taken it seriously in every aspect, if I'd been worrying about all the criticisms, particularly from the Brits – but we'll forget about that. The man and the boy and the donkey finally got to market, and probably the donkey got sold. The only thing to do was to ignore a fair amount of it and have a lot of fun and do something that seemed to make sense in New York, which is what we were trying to do it for. We were saluting New York, rather than ourselves.

The British have got tremendous strength. I think they went through a perfectly ghastly period during most of the last seventy years, having had their entire leadership class shot in the First World War, and an awful lot's happened in that seventy years. To try and get Britain and New York to understand one another, even a little bit, seemed to be useful. That's really what I was trying to do.

But is the Sadler's Wells helping my Manhattan liftman to understand Britain?

Is it helping the Brits to understand New York? The reason for Sadler's Wells or whatever, it had to be big in New York to make any impact at *all*. It had to be fashionable, it had to be smart, it had to have enough goodies. We weren't able to get any royals, because Prince Charles came back from New York and said, 'None of us should *ever* go there again!' So without the royals to make it big and splashy, anything we could get, practically, that was of high-enough quality not to be put down as second-rate not-up-to-New York. We had the Royal Ballet, which is not bad – even in New York!

At an hour's notice, there was the British Government's contribution: HMS *Hermes*! Mayor Koch and the Admiral went up to Yankee Stadium and did a song and dance together and the Admiral threw the opening ball and got *that* lot on the way. That was done by the US Navy, who said, 'Don't worry about it, we'll do it.' The rest of the time we simply took the Admiral in full fig to all the openings – he looked wonderful, and they loved it.

You were getting married to Caro when you were getting divorced from Consolidated, but it never occurred to you to say: 'Right – back to London, get a little pad down in Reigate and think about buying a steel business in Corby'?

I'd be very bad at it. All of my experiences were in America. The business I took on I knew exactly what to do. I wouldn't know what to do in Corby. It's much tougher there to borrow the money, it's much tougher to buy a business with its own money, which is what I had to do with the first one. I had to find assets in there they weren't doing anything much *with*, and then I had to turn things round rather fast. Here I knew I could, in Corby I guess I wouldn't have been quite sure whether I'd get the collaboration of management or the labour force.

Georgia is a 'Right to Work' state, which means there aren't so many unions, and the unions are not strong?

Yes – but that wouldn't be a problem. Pittsburgh is very highly unionized but I've honestly had no trouble. They're very nice to me because they reckon that with twenty-two men there's a real business there, and the next move is upwards.

The other thing, I suppose, is that an angel coming out of the West bearing money is always welcome?

Not very much money, but just enough to get it done. I can't say to them, 'Why don't we all take a week off from selling steel and paint the tracks?' We don't give goodies away, but slowly they're seeing that if they do a better job, we notice and we pay them more, even though it doesn't say we have to in the union contract.

In England if you have enough money, it's fine. However you define 'enough', it's terrific: you relax and you say, I can now play golf on Mondays and Fridays. Here there are plenty of people who are very adequately well off. You're not competing with them to see who gets to be the richest, you're competing with them to do certain transactions that for some reason rather matter to you – buying control of *Time* magazine, or something. It's not that you need it in order to spend it on non-dandruff jewellery, you need it to spend on the next deal, and somehow the more you have the more conservative you are in financing that next deal, so algebraically you could never have enough because you're always trying to tuck it away somewhere.

Is that a compulsion?

Probably – but America's a very compulsive place, in almost everything. If you're compulsive about making good documentaries or about writing good books, it's all right to be English. That kind of compulsiveness is thoroughly understood, but to be compulsive about *deals*, you get the sort of Clive of India syndrome where the rich nabobs have come home. It's all right to do it overseas. You come back and so long as you buy enough hospitals, you're acceptable. That's so long as it wasn't done at our expense, but was done overseas and you simply took it off the natives, whether the natives were Americans or Indians. It might be seen as deplorable if there was a scandal about it – Warren Hastings. If there wasn't a scandal and you did have a good time, it's perfectly all right in England to have made money *somewhere else*. To make it in England entirely by making left-handed widgets in North Staffordshire is not so appealing, is it?

There's such a different attitude to money here – one of the kindest things you can say about someone in England is that they're terribly wealthy but you'd never *know* it . . .

Yes right – but here you're *meant* to know it. If we came back to England with a nice pile of gold sovereigns, it wasn't quite so socially degrading as actually making money doing something in England. You could return as it were from outer space, with riches.

The East India Company! Indeed I suppose making money out of the Americans is also quite socially acceptable?

Perfectly legitimate. Many of the best early investors in America were British, but almost all of them went home. They built some amusing houses and had a very good time on the profits they'd made from the Colonies.

Are you going back to Box Hill to build a stately home with your ill-gotten gains from Pittsburgh?

I don't think we've got to the planning stage of that yet. Most people *do* go back, eventually.

Including the Lloyd-Jacobs?

Probably not. I would doubt it. We probably won't stay here but I don't think we'll go back there. Somewhere in between – France or somewhere. We feel very *world* people at the moment. Goodness knows how we'll feel in twenty years' time.

In the very long run the British have decided not to be in the economics business. It might work quite well, actually, if you have a very long look. You can argue that the British are very bad at what the world's been doing for the last hundred and thirty years – the era where we all stood next to Nelly and did what we were told. It was a very un-British thing to do. We're good individualists, we're quite good at writing software, so just possibly the century beginning now could again be the British century, as 1760 to 1860 was.

But it's terrifying what's going to happen to the uneducated unemployed. It's the worst aspect of class structure. Watching the ticker-tape of the Healey budget in March '74, it wasn't that I had any money but I had some ambition, and I thought I was quite good at making things work better. What I said to myself at the end of that was, These people don't *want* me! They don't want anyone disruptive. If you've got money you'll pay some-body to get you round all this stuff and buy you a forest or a Jersey corpor-ation, but if you haven't got it and you're trying to make it, you're too disruptive, go away.

That was just the time that Gordon White left, after Healey's 'squeezing-the-rich'?

But he'd *got* some, and I was a hired hand. I still felt it was more fun to be a hired hand in America than there. The quality of life here for people with our income is very high. It's ridiculous in a way that within a year of starting up we can live as well as we do, but that's because I've done a three-million-dollar turnaround on one business which would enable me, if I didn't want to plough that money back, to live extremely well. We're paying money back, but we can still afford to have a flat in London, a funny little house in France, and that ridiculous palace on 29th Street.

It's a savage way of life; not *intolerably* savage in comparison with what it must be like to be an uneducated English union person. My peers in England are merchant bankers who're on boards of directors and saying, 'My God, you've got to go north of Potters Bar for a day and sort that out.' They're chaps who're living in Sevenoaks, having a chauffeur to drive them into the City every day and the wife is playing golf, that sort of thing.

Just like Pittsburgh?

Yes, only they don't have chauffeurs because they have an automatic instead, but it's very similar. A friend of mine at Bethlehem Steel in Pennsylvania says his dream is to die and go to heaven and be told he's allowed to go back to earth again as a housewife belonging to the country club, sitting by the pool eating lunch and putting it on her husband's account.

So you have this penthouse palace on 29th Street, a farmhouse in Burgundy, a small flat in Covent Garden.... You're tolerably well-housed?

Extremely well-housed. Don't get too carried away by this place. This was a manufacturing space when we bought it. It had been a series of factories on each floor and it had no walls inside. We've done everything.

It's what's known in New York as an attic?

A loft, actually.

Beg its pardon – a loft. A *hell* of a loft, is all I can say! It's the in thing, the smart thing to have?

Yes, but they're called lofts all the way down. The first floor is *also* called a loft.

Now you've flummoxed me totally.

This is a loft building – each floor is a separate loft. A loft is just a space with a high ceiling. It can be on the ground floor, but it's still a loft! Linguistically it makes no sense, but remember in America they haven't spoken English for years.

Once you'd worked out the difference between a loft and a loft, what other problems did you have?

I certainly had a continual problem of speaking English in an American context. They really *are* two languages – but having built a house in France without speaking French, I suppose to build a loft in New York is not impossible. A few things had to get rebuilt, because we'd failed to make ourselves totally clear....

On this level you operate as an affable English eccentric – how does Caro operate?

Caro: As the eccentric's apprentice! Everyone told me when we moved here, 'You're used to English people, it will be dreadful when you move into this loft – you'll find American workmen are terrible.' In fact they were *wonderful*. At eight clock every morning twelve of them would come through the freight elevator. One morning we went down at ten to eight and there they all were, waiting on the sidewalk, as they say, waiting for eight o'clock so they could all come up. They banged away and worked and hammered and got the whole thing done in no time at all – they were fabulous. None of them of course was born here – the painters were English, the plumbers were Greek, the plasterer was Italian, the tiler was Spanish. They'd all been here an average of fifteen or twenty years.

Little by little you get it done. Of course everything in New York is on sale. You never buy anything that isn't on sale – it's always fifty per cent off. Starting from fifty per cent off, you then need to get your twenty per cent off your fifty per cent to really feel you're getting anywhere at all. It's a game that you play, it's for getting everything off off *off*.

Sounds like an Arab bazaar?

It *is* an Arab bazaar. New York is full of games. There's a money game, a deal game and there's a living game too; getting things built is a form of life game as well.

You'd rather be in your 29th Street loft than living in the equivalent penthouse in Kensington?

David: I've never been in London living the kind of life that goes with a penthouse in Kensington. I suspect it's not much fun in England trying to build up from essentially nothing, to build a series of businesses by mirrors and reputations and continual borrowing, as I'm doing here.

I'm not quite sure what the fun *is* here, because this is a most relentless place, where they're not very kind to losers.

So long as one has the maturity and the experience to have been a loser *and* a winner, you can cope with it. You recognize other people for what they are: how nice, how helpful, how difficult they will be.

You can bounce back more quickly in America than you could in London?

You can certainly bounce back here if you've got what it takes – and luck. It's easy to be unlucky here, and the place is not very forgiving of bad luck. Bad luck is just another form of failure.

The harder you work the luckier you get, isn't that true everywhere?

Maybe, maybe, but a number of people around New York did seem to work very hard, were very smart – and still somehow something went wrong.... I don't think we should say, 'Well they didn't deserve it.' Some of them just had bad luck.

The key to success in corporate banking is to have everybody's secretary's first name – just be nice and polite. The way I think I managed to get this Atlanta deal done was because the English boss's English secretary – who came over at the same time as him – is a tremendously nice impressionable girl. She always answered the phone and I'd say, 'Jackie I've got another problem and how are we going to deal with it? What does his diary look like?' And she would say, 'If you slip in at four-thirty, as if by mistake, I think we can get it done.'

A friend of mine seems to get on well enough with the Yellow Cab drivers because when he gets in he looks at the licence and name and *uses* it....

I always look at that, but that's for disaster prevention: 'Mr Williams, I've written down your numbers!' One cab had seventeen different notices in it: a sticker said, 'The tip is part of my salary, please be generous.'

What about the compensations for living here? The cab-drivers are horrible, the climate's fierce – much less good than England – and the climate in the streets is also less good?

The climate in the streets is quite tense sometimes, but all of New York is full of energy, I find – particularly coming back from London. You land at the airport, you get in a rather battered-looking cab, the driver's had sixteen important experiences today which he *longs* to tell you about, usually in some impenetrable dialect ... but you get a real burst of energy as you come over the Triborough Bridge. You see it there, almost vibrating!

Yet there's a very high level of snarl here?

A *very* high level of snarl – but I'm not always just a snarlee, sometimes I snarl back!

Can't be easy for you, a well-bred Briton?

It's *perfectly* easy here. Almost everyone else in New York is a foreigner, not necessarily from abroad but from somewhere other than New York City. Most of them are scared half the time. Most of them have had good experiences and bad experiences. They're very human, but on the way into New York there's a filter, so to speak, that catches you and throws you out if you don't have enough energy. It requires great oomph, great strength, to do anything in this place. Once you get to the critical speed that gets you through that filter, then you can achieve things.

There *is* a sense of urgency on the streets down there. Up here in your fortress-loft, you're reasonably secure, though not totally; down in the streets, it's another story?

Down on the streets it is tough. It's particularly tough for the people who go to the Salvation Army rest home for elderly ladies, just down there; the Moravian Coffee Pot, the day-shelter for the homeless, which is a block away. We have so-called bag ladies whose main economic occupation is breaking open garbage bags to get the bottles and cans to sell back for five cents. It's a very rough city for those who haven't made it, and it's made worse by the appalling policy of letting people *out* of facilities designed for those who can't quite cope with themselves – those who are not suicidal or homicidal, but mentally not all *there*. They're thrown back on the streets all the time.

And New York is full of flaky people – a city where people talk to themselves in the streets. . . .

I find myself doing that all the time – I'm walking along negotiating with this goddam bank! Don't *you* do that?

Not yet – just give me another couple of months. . . .

Well, owe ten thousand dollars a day and you will! I don't feel that New York is terribly unsafe. I've lived here for ten years and most of the people I know have had some slightly bothersome experience. There have been one or two really rather nasty ones, but on balance one never quite believes it's going to happen to one.

My younger daughter had her purse stolen by a black boy who was about her size. She very sensibly gave it to him – there was only $1.46 in it. Someone tried to pickpocket Caro on the steps of a concert hall, but he wasn't very good and we told him off. Everybody turned round.... He was a Puerto Rican.

But we do know some horror stories: there was a very bad time when my Number Two at Goldfields in America was shot on Park Avenue at ten-thirty in the evening. He was walking with his wife, there was a hold-up and they ran. He turned round to see if they were following, and was shot in the face. He lost a third of his blood on the pavement and would have died if he hadn't been so close to the hospital. He's nowhere near recovered now, two years later.

I think you should really hand over your wallet. Don't carry too much. Keep your most favourite things somewhere else, because you'll never get them back. It's a form of paying Danegeld.

But this is like being shot in Piccadilly – Park Avenue's the West End of things. . . .

Yes but of course there *is* a sense of lurking danger almost everywhere, and in London there isn't. In London there are certain areas which you might say are known to be unsafe, and outside those you feel comfortable. I feel comfortable in Pittsburgh too; a very friendly non-threatening place, rather like London. New York is just of its own kind. It's rough.

One of the Salute people was murdered in a hotel room. The poor English girl was between apartments so she was staying in an hotel on 57th Street, asleep with her window open, and a naked black man dropped on to her balcony, having had a row with his boyfriend upstairs. He came in, murdered her, stayed the night – and went out in the morning in her clothes.

When I left home this morning I thought, What have I got in my wallet? In fact I've got things in it that it would be ghastly to lose: my driver's licence, Green Card. I think the answer with a Green Card is, never carry it.

Life *has* to be very rewarding, either financially or socially or in some other way to overcome this sense of lurking danger, doesn't it, to make it worthwhile to live here?

I suppose lurking danger is part of the attraction of New York, in a dreadful way. You get a sense of tightening up. You're under more pressure – and that's not always bad. Certainly we could live, probably *should* live, in one of the places where we have some business to do. It's rather frivolous to live in New York without having one's main business occupation here, but we love it, despite – not I think, because – of the danger. But the danger does add to the manner in which people are never here by mistake. People in the city, apart from those who can't afford to get away whom I've described, are here because it's the place that, more than anywhere else in the world, tests you as you try to make it. So you get a very high level of personal involvement. They're all working, trying, inventing, doing things first, doing things harder. With that you get a very exciting society to live in – so if you want to develop a new idea or find out what's wrong with one, you can do that in a day in New York. It might take a week in Pittsburgh; even longer in London.

If there are six people you need to talk to for ten minutes each, you can get to them in New York. They'll say, 'Sure if it's important, I'll make another ten minutes.' If you're part of the network, so to speak, that can get to people quickly, you're also part of a network where they will reach *you*, so your day gets to be fascinating. Not only are you trying to achieve something, you're helping other people who've also had a brilliant idea....

If I can make it here, I'll make it anywhere, the song says....

I think so, and if you *do* make it here you probably have met along the way an enormous number of extremely exciting people. They're super, they're wonderful to do business with and work with. They're also very nice, many of them, to be with. And so I think you can make life-long friends, even if you then move away from New York and go back to London. If you ask people how many good friends they have, they'll say five thousand – because that's actually their Christmas card list!
Caro: They can be much more friendly, on a superficial basis, and helpful in so many ways. If you say suddenly, 'I've decided to open a dance class,' no one's going to jeer. They'll say, 'Terrific, what a wonderful idea!' They'll even say, 'How can I help?'

Have you had to trample over a lot of people to get to your loft?

David: I don't feel that I did. Certainly a corporate person working with other people's money probably has certain corporate tensions, but I don't think they were any worse with us than anywhere else.

'Corporate tension' is a euphemism for what?

Well, maybe your Board of Directors decides they don't want to be in a certain business so would you, the local boy, please get rid of it.

Lay off a thousand people?

Or get us out of the left-handed widget business – just get *rid* of it. That's a tension, but it's a corporate tension. It's something that one as a good soldier was told to go and do.

So the rumour that business is not really very gentlemanly in the United States is true?

There are very very tough aspects of working in America with your own money. If you guarantee a loan and it goes wrong, you can expect to find yourself on the wrong side of what's called the bank Workout Department. They're the heavy brigade. They have broader shoulders than most bankers. They come along and say, 'Right, you've guaranteed this loan, now we need $150,000 from you. You haven't got $150,000? Of course you have – what about your wife's jewellery? What are these rugs worth?' And so on. It's a rough world when it happens.

Do the British banks in America have Workout Departments?

Fortunately I've never had to find out! I rather doubt it. I hope they don't need to develop major ones but my guess is, they may have to. If they haven't, they have problems.

Sounds like Mafia debt collectors. . . .

This is a society where if you get something wrong, they really come down on you like a ton of bricks.

They break a leg?

Right, they break *both* legs. My friend John Samuels, for instance, is a fascinating example of somebody who thought he had made it, when he'd really only got a temporary commodity success. He was in coalmining, and coal did terribly well. He behaved superbly, he spent it wonderfully – but he didn't actually *have it*. He bought a house, the Dupont Mansion in the Hamptons, the Louise Morgan house on the North Shore of Long Island, etc. etc. I once got a ride in a Falcon jet he was wondering whether to buy. He had Marion Tree's house on East 79th Street, he was chairman of the New York City Ballet and all sorts of things, he gave away lots of money – and all of a sudden the price of coal dropped and the whole thing imploded. Now there's a new generation who've made money selling tax shelters, and some guy he knows has made a hundred million or some enormous number of hundred millions, selling tax shelters.

Tax shelters?

If you're a boring American manufacturer of something and you have a computer, he buys it. He then sells your computer in lots of little slivers to people with more money than sense who can then deduct the depreciation on the new value he's put on the computer from their tax bill – except they probably can't but it takes the Revenue three years to catch up with them. In the meantime they pay him a lot of fees for finding a tax-efficient way of wasting their money, and he reports all that as income.

So is this a good place in which to live your life?

It's very good for us now. I don't think it would be much fun to be old and decrepit on 29th Street.

You enjoy it, but your first wife didn't like it at all?

No she didn't and I don't think my two daughters really love it either. They're all in the nicest sense *very* English and found it threatening, a little surprising all the time. It was overstated and they liked being understated. You spend a lot of time here selling yourself and if you're apologetic and disguise the fact that you know about things and say, 'Well I have a *slight* interest ...' you don't get anywhere. It's very difficult for people who don't like selling themselves to adjust to that. Not just difficult for them, they don't want to do it, they feel it's a form of insincerity. So my first family is very happily back in London and I don't think my first wife will ever come back here again. My children come once or twice a year. They say they like it, but they never seem to stay longer than they planned to....

Are you dependent upon the economic state, the climate?

Not really. I do quite well in bad times and quite well in good times and very well in the transition from bad times to good times. I do very badly in the transition from good times to bad, but I carefully miss that stage in the cycle. I'm buying and selling steel but I'm not doing anything *to* it. I'm holding it and cutting it and let's say, I turn it over four times a year. If the price of steel goes down for three months I don't make any money for three months. After three months I'm buying it at a lower price and selling it at a lower price, but the margin's still there. On the way up, I've got steel that I bought cheap and the margin has opened up, so I make more on it.

But if Washington decrees that South Korean steel can come in without duty ... that sort of thing?

My customers will stop saying, 'Make sure it's domestic,' and say, 'I don't mind if it's South Korean, at a price.' So long as I remain reasonably good at forecasting – I'm still a professional forecaster.

Each transaction you're in you meet some new people and yes, the first reaction to somebody from overseas or somebody with a different accent is to play a game with them, to try and see how they do. Certainly when I first arrived as a corporate person I didn't know an awful lot of things, and many many Europeans have come across and set the trend of being the expensive buyers of businesses or apartments or whatever it might be. New Yorkers tend to negotiate harder than Europeans. Now we're New Yorkers by adoption we're getting to negotiate almost as toughly.

Caro, are you a tough negotiatior in the lace business?

C: I have a nice lace business in England, so when I came here it seemed a good idea to bring the lace, and it's worked very well. I now go to England six or eight times a year to buy the lace and bring it back. It sells and gets lots of lovely profit. . . .

Must be enormously expensive, if it's antique lace?

C: The very wonderful really *really* antique lace doesn't come here at all. That tends to go back to Europe, because lace was never made in this country, but eighteenth-century lace tends to go to Texas, where it's put on ten-thousand-dollar wedding dresses. I think in a sense these dresses will keep the lace. The people who own them respect them – they think they're wonderful because they cost so much and they won't get thrown out or given away. Therefore I don't mind at all selling wonderful lace to be cut up and put on those sort of dresses.

How about protection in the lace business? You've never been asked to pay anybody off – no arsenic among your old lace?

C: No no. When I had a shipment held up in the Customs there was no suggestion that this was being done in order to extract money, they just didn't know it was old.

What about living here? David's away buying steel and you're on your own in this echoing place – do you feel secure?

C: If I'm in here for one night I can just about put up with it now. I've got used to it. I bolt all the doors, but I don't put the alarm system on because alarm systems go wrong and I know the chances are it would go off, it would sort of short-circuit – and I'd die of fright! If I wake up in the night I get nervous, but I know I'm fairly safe up here, but one does live in New York with the constant fear of mugging, shooting, raping, whatever. You have to come to terms with that I think. It's always there. I would hate to come back to an empty place – and I wouldn't. Do I feel that in London?

No, I feel very safe. If the plane's late and I get into my flat at two o'clock in the morning I don't feel nervous, but you live with all sorts of things. We live with the fear of cancer or heart attacks or being run over by a bus. This's just one more thing, I suppose, but it is there, yes.

How do you ever come to terms with it, I wonder?

C: These are terms that you *have* come to, but they may not be very satisfactory terms. You buy a dog, you buy six cats, you turn on the radio very loud – all the usual palliatives. I would hate to have a gun because I feel I wouldn't use it very well and then the man would pick it up and shoot me with it.

Here on 29th Street you're in the middle of the Junkie Belt, aren't you?

C: There's a lot of hookers around here, because we have tunnels going to Long Island and to New Jersey and all the truck-drivers cross town at this point, so we have some beautiful girls. One of the reasons I won't leave David alone very often is because the girls here are beautiful – I mean they're all wearing lamé dresses and sort of fishnet stockings and looking fantastic.
D: When I leave to go to Pittsburgh, Caro wonders why I catch the early flight! (Laughs.) But because the girls are here, you have the Mafia going round looking after their interests, and the police going round the blocks to keep the girls moving. There's always *something* going on in the streets down here so the more respectable areas are, in a sense, more dangerous. . . .

THE COWBOY

I thought of putting myself up for Sheriff. . . .

David Harvey, a Metropolitan mounted policeman for eleven years, was on duty outside the Iranian Embassy during the siege. Since then his life has changed noticeably; arriving in the US four years ago on a circus rider's visa, he's now a cowboy on a twenty-thousand-acre ranch up in the Colorado Rockies.

In the glorious scenery of the High Pasture one hundred miles west of Denver he learned to cope with the ten-thousand-foot altitude, to fight cabin-fever during snowbound winters, to be accepted by cowboys in the bars of Fairplay. They in turn needed to adjust to the fact that he only carried a pocket knife, not a .357 Magnum, and that his interest was historical research. He must be the only cowboy expert on the Crimean War and the Charge of the Light Brigade. . . .

In summer he runs an equestrian centre. In winter the isolation means there's no medical help at hand for the cattle – or for the men: in tussles with the herd one cowboy lost a finger, another was castrated. All carry work scars.

To help ranch-hands handle sick cows, David has drawn veterinary cartoon-diagrams and, using coloured dots, prepared a table that records the history, progress and condition of every animal. Many cowboys are illiterate, but they can understand this system and are proud of it.

To keep him company during the long winter in a cabin without television, the hands on his ranch clubbed together and bought him a puppy, but in this macho world were too shy to admit it – so said they'd found the Doberman bitch abandoned by the roadside. . . .

There's a mystique about the Wild West; when you were a copper did you ever yearn to be a cowboy?

Funny thing is, I didn't. I was never into cowboys. This is just a job out here, that's all.

Most kids who don't want to be train-drivers want to be policemen or cowboys – so two out of three's not bad!

284

I'm going to be a train-driver one of these days, but I'd have to join a union – that's what put me off!

There are people in Sevenoaks and Plymouth and Rugby who dress up in cowboy gear and go and play Wild West – that Butch Cassidy thing; so you're living a lot of people's fantasies, but you don't appreciate them....

I don't. I'm a natural-born cynic. The cowboy life *does* exist, exactly as you see it in the movies. The attitudes are very similar. You get these guys coming into town.... They'll spend a few months working at one of the spreads and move on to somewhere else, but the things they do, the branding, everything is done very traditionally. And when they go into town, some of the bar-room scenes here are very similar to what you'd see on the movies.

You don't ever feel like pushing through those swing doors and arresting a few of them?

Depends how much I've had to drink, Alan, to be honest with you! You're very isolated here and this altitude – we're at ten thousand feet – does affect you. This winter we'll have snow on the ground for eight months. The only hobbies people have got are drinking, and that leads to the things that drinking leads to.

I must say I have a slight hangover this morning, *not* having had a single drink last night! At ten thousand feet if you take alcohol it has a considerable effect – like drinking on an aircraft?

That's true. It'll take you three months to get acclimatized up here. If I go back to Britain for a while and come back up here, it takes me three months to get fit.

In the winter this must be a desolate life? Lonely at all seasons – but in the winter you've got far less to do?

This time of year all I can do is help out checking the stock and checking the fences and doing any doctoring on the cows that needs doing. It's so isolated, you see, you can't get a veterinary up here.

Living by yourself, do you get cabin-fever?

Yes, yes – after a few months up here you desperately need to get in town somewhere, anywhere but here! I whoop it up down in Denver – just like the feel of concrete under my feet....

But does the loneliness, the magnificence of the Rockies affect you in any way – have you, as they say, *found* yourself?

I think I found myself real quick! I was getting to know where I was coming from before I came, but I certainly found out when I got here. People can go mad up here, and cabin-fever does exist: we've got some neighbours about ten miles away who've been in maybe two or three months, and the woman can't stand it – they're going back to the city. If I haven't got time to get to Denver, which would take a couple of hours, I go into town and drink in the bars with the guys – generally play around and try not to get into trouble.

With the Law?

With the Law, yes – if you can *call* it Law, up here. Denver's fine, but locally – don't touch 'em! A local Marshal got arrested about two months ago for having an unregistered firearm and selling drugs, but he's still in office – he's the best they can get! I thought of putting myself up for Sheriff, but I don't think it's quite my image any more.

I think it's *exactly* your image – you're a sort of McCloud in reverse ... but if it isn't the life, if you didn't dream of living like this, it must be the money?

That's part of it, yes. I'm sounding very mercenary now, but that's part of it.

On a day like today – this to me is a sort of paradise....

Let me ask *you* a question: what appeals to you up here?

The sky, the air, the snowy mountains, the wide open space – all those things cowboys sing about....

Mm, well I sing about them too, in *town* – but I don't necessarily have to believe what I'm singing about....

As a city boy, you just long to go in to Denver and get jostled on those pavements?

That's it – and have to push through people, that's what I like! It'll probably be about ten to fifteen below, tonight. We can get up to three foot of snow at a time here. The temperatures have dropped down to about forty below. You're probably noticing the wind – that can get up to 130 miles an hour. We don't go out *too* often, but we have to check the stock. They do real well in winter out here. This is what they call High Pasture. Most of the people who have cattle up here will take them down to lower altitude during the winter – it's just too much.

If you were in the Mounted Police for all those years you certainly knew about riding, yet it's a different activity in the Rockies?

I run horse shows up here, and people love to pretend they're riding English. They wear all the English riding gear, they'll walk around in boots and breeches, they'll have the dogs with them – Jack Russells and things – but *this* is very different. These saddles are very practical for what they do up here.

This is a saddle for living in, twelve hours a day?

That's about it. We've got the rope and saddlebags to carry medicines, so if you're out ten miles from a ranch you can treat cows instead of bringing them back all the way down here. A mounted-police saddle is not, funnily enough, much smaller than this, but they'll have whites on the front for keeping your personal radio and the other equipment we carry. I say 'we' – I'm still talking as though I'm a policeman!

You still feel more of a cop than a cowboy?

Yes, I think once you've been in it, it's something you don't lose very easily. I certainly enjoyed my time there and I do, as you say, talk in the present tense as though I'm still a policeman. I'm very upset if anybody knocks the job....

When your friends in the Mounted Police come out and see how you're living, do they envy you?

Yes – but they don't have to live here the year round. They enjoy a couple of months or a couple of weeks – then they get fed up with it too.

If it *is* still the Wild West, as you say, how did they take to a Limey cop riding into town in a funny way, talking in a funny way?

I live in America now – or live in Fairplay, which is not the same as living in America – so I adapt to them. I think they're getting used to my sense of humour, and I try to fit in as best as possible. I don't tell them that English riding's best, because it's not practical out here. It's best to ride Western – that's practical.

Do they think you're a softie? Do they think your Mounted Police friends are effete Englishmen?

They're a little bit wary at first – they were expecting somebody like Roger Moore in the old Saint programmes, which they show out here, or the complete opposite. They're very surprised when they enjoy helping with the branding and doing everything else, and it seems to work good. My friends were worried how people were going to react to *them*, but they're getting used to me, so anybody I turn up with now they just think, Another weird Englishman's arrived in town!

Of course you're a weird Englishman who *doesn't* carry a gun – that sign of Western masculinity?

I carry a pocket knife! I'm wearing a cowboy hat, but I'm not trying to be macho; it's what everybody wears up here. You see guys carrying guns in town, you see the fights going on.... I go and look for some fun when I go in town, I'm not going in to fight anybody.

You're not packin' your truncheon?

No not a truncheon, not any more. I had to hand it in – that reminds me, I haven't got my deposit back....

Any notches on your truncheon?

One or two, one or two....

What most surprised you about life in America when you first arrived?

The openness. I find people very honest here. I'm a very patriotic English-man but these people out here *love* America, they really do, and I find it very touching. These are honest people, they're good workers and I like their attitude about life. They're guys that will work twenty-four hours a day, if you'll let them – those are the people that work for us at the ranch here, that doesn't mean everybody in town. We're real selective.

I always thought that rounding-up was done with Jeeps and trucks today – yet you still use horses?

It's the most practical way of doing it out here. They've tried motorbikes, skimobiles in the winter, but still the horse is king up here. Bud here's the ranch foreman – he looks after the cattle.

So you're the *real* thing, Bud, while this guy is just an ex-cop who's spent his life riding those beautifully manicured horses through Hyde Park – and that's a hell of a long way from the range! What do you make of him?

Bud: Well he's very good at what he does. He's learning me about the English ways, but I'm not too familiar with these aliens. Dave doesn't volunteer anything about England and I'm one that kinda wants to know – I've never been across the Mississippi River. I don't know if you go west from here to England or east!

Dave doesn't, for example, carry a gun – and most people here are into guns?

He was brought up that way – different strokes for different folks. I've been around guns all my life, don't know anything different. I've worked fifty years on ranches: one position was sixteen years, the next was nine years, the next was nine years and I don't intend to move. I don't like moving. If we have a group of cowhands, the first snow that hits up here – they're headed for Arizona where it's warm, but they'll never have nothing, never will. They just live from hand to mouth.

In your truck, is that a .45 under the steering wheel?

That's a .357 Magnum – next to the biggest pistol you can buy.

D: You call him 'Sir', Alan.

Yes, he sits *exactly* where he wants to, doesn't he?

D: He most certainly does. Are you comfortable there, Bud?
Bud: I don't know of anybody that doesn't carry a gun when they go down to town. The gun's in the car, until they need it. I don't know of anybody that wears them inside, unless they're looking for somebody.

It's still lawful if the gun is visible? If you've got a gun on your hip, you could still walk into a bar?

Any place in Colorado. There's different laws in different towns. You don't carry guns across state lines until you know the law, but Colorado is a free-gun state.

Dave was telling me about one sheriff – do you have any respect for the Law here?

Bud: I don't know him, but I doubt I'd have much respect for him.

If people don't take kindly to Law, do you keep it a bit dark that you were a cop?

D: If a lot of people in town knew what I was, I think they might look at me differently. They're very surprised we don't carry firearms in Britain – and there I go, using the royal 'we' again. They're very surprised the police are unarmed, they find that hard to understand.

Most Brits who come to the States come for a more sophisticated life, a more modern life; you in fact have chosen to go *back* a few decades?

America's very much a twentieth-century place, but what we're doing here is all very traditional. We sewed this calf up yesterday and we're just giving it some Teramycin to keep infection away. It had a prolapse, the whole of the rectum came out of her back. It's a parasite they've picked up.

How about the people down in Fairplay – they're a pretty conservative group?

Redneck would be more appropriate. I find them very bigoted, very right-wing. I lean left in politics. There's one black guy works for the county, but the last I heard they were setting up a Ku Klux Klan in Fairplay to deal with him.

To run him out of town?

He's a nice guy and everybody likes him, but they're trying to make the point they don't like anybody not from Park County, not from this area. If you're Mexican, if you're an Indian.... I got into a fight with an Indian in a bar last week – and I'm the only guy that's talking to him and buying him a drink! I'd met him a couple of years back. Everybody says, 'Don't buy him a drink, he's going to get nasty.' After about two or three drinks he did turn very nasty indeed – I'm still suffering! I'm not prejudiced about it but as I say, we don't see many black people in town, or Mexicans.

With all this do you ever wish you were back on a nice shining horse, controlling football crowds?

Windy days, yeah. I enjoyed it for the time I was there, now I'm doing something else. I miss working with the guys there, that's about all.

Do you see yourself finishing up on the lone prair*ee* – or back at Parsons Green?

Parsons Green I would think, but there's a lot still to see out here and enjoy. I'm going to be an old man by the time I get back....

THE GENTLEMAN'S GENTLEMAN

You could be kidnapped and held at ransom....

Peter Neal always wanted to go to America and be a butler. He now works for John Dick, the Canadian-born businessman behind European Ferries and the Denver Technological Center – a vast land development in that mile-high city. Peter achieved his second ambition when he found himself running the Dick mansion on Sunset Drive in Englewood, a select suburb in Denver, along with other palatial homes in Palm Springs, Berkeley Square and Jersey. For a quiet bachelor it was a considerable transformation from life in Cleethorpes....

═══

I found it fascinating, but then I also found it lonely at the beginning because I didn't know anybody other than Madam and Sir, and oft-times I didn't go out. I'm much of a home bird – this is the way of my life. I was under the impression that there was a lot of violence and things like that here, so of course I was a little bit nervous....

You were pitched in at the posh end of Denver, without knowing anyone?

I didn't know a soul, but I'm always kept busy – I'm a bit *like* that, the more I've got to do the better I am, and the more people I've got to look after the better I am. They fight for me to take time off, they do literally! And if I *do* have any time off, it's all appertaining to the house. I don't drink and I don't smoke. Occasionally I go out to dinner, very very rarely.

You were born in Cleethorpes – had you travelled much?

No. Actually it was an ambition – I decided when I was a certain age that I wanted to come to America to be a butler. I was offered a position with Estée Lauder and her husband and two days afterwards he died. I saw her personal assistant, and *talk* about being vetted – she wanted to know how many times I cut my toenails during the month!

If you're being very well paid I suppose it's legitimate that you be investigated to such a degree, but if it's a run-of-the-mill wage it seems an imposition. . . . If someone works for Howard Hughes, has an unnatural life but is paid phenomenally, then OK – it goes with the territory. . . .

It's the same as the Master – he's so generous, and at Christmas time it's unbelievable! I get a bonus, which is a super cheque, and this Christmas they made for me a gorgeous cashmere coat. Even though I'm a servant I'm brought in, I'm not left out. The feeling you get from Mr and Mrs Dick is a unique feeling: they love you, and it *is* a love, it's not just that 'You work for me'. It's something you can't really describe.

He works all the time – his brain never stops. He's a fantastic man – if I had a fraction of his brain I don't think I'd be a butler. I look after him for all his needs, I make sure he's fed and watered and he's taken his insulin and his clothes are kept and if he wants anything, well he'll call me. As far as his business is concerned, I have nothing to do with it whatsoever.

Did America live up to your expectations?

You can't judge Colorado with the rest of America because Colorado people are very polite and courteous and warm and genuine. I've found that. They're delighted to make friends with an English person – but then I have to be very careful in the position I'm in, you see, because this is Mr John Dick and he's the Tech Center, so therefore as Madam says, you can't be too careful. If people think you're attached to Mr Dick – I mean I never thought this way but it's sort of fed to you – you could be kidnapped and held at ransom, or something. We're very very conscious on security. You have to be, even in the posh end of Denver.

Has there been kidnapping around here?

There's been kidnapping and murders, but they're done all over Denver. Actually this is the quietest week so far – usually there's either one or two murders done in Denver.

Apart from that, how does life compare with Cleethorpes?

Life is better in the sense that you can get anything you want at any time. You don't have to think, Oh the shops are going to close at four or four-thirty. You know full well you can go in a grocery shop twenty-four hours a day, seven days a week, fifty-two weeks in the year. If I'm going to run short of something, in a matter of five minutes, I've got it. The only time you can't shop is Thanksgiving and Christmas Day – the rest of the year the stores and everything are open. It's amazing! That's what surprised me when I first came, because I thought they were on par with England at holiday times. The day after Christmas Day the stores are absolutely cram-packed with people – they're just going mad spending money!

Last year was my first Hallowe'en here, and it was hilarious. All these kiddies were coming all dressed up and trick-or-treating and I thought, What the heck? Madam and Sir were away but fortunately I had candy in. I keep it in for the Master because if he has a sugar-reaction, if he eats chocolate very quickly it sort of settles him down. So I'd got candy, but I gave it all away to these trick-or-treaters at the door.

My only friends are a couple who live at Loveland, a doctor and his wife, the most loving couple you would wish to meet with four super children. About two months or so ago I spent the most super day up at Loveland and I thought, How lovely to come across two people so happy, with gorgeous children. On Saturday they were in my thoughts, because I *have* this sort of thing: Madam and I, she can be one end of the house and I'll be in the other and she'll think of something and I'll go and knock on the door and say, 'Madam, would you like so-and-so?' She'd thought that she would like it, you see.

So they were in my thoughts, why I don't know, but something was telling me. I was thinking about them – and then I received such an upsetting phone call. They'd parted. It really did upset me.

Relationships do seem less stable over here....

It's their way of life, it's so fast. That's why I think it's lovely to go back to Jersey, because it's a steady pace. I'd spent a few holidays there, but to live there is something entirely different than going for a holiday. It really is fabulous, super.

So you return to England with pleasure....

Oh with great delight, great joy! At the moment my battery is running low. During the period in which I stay in England, I sort of charge myself up. Actually this is the longest we've stayed here, three months. Normally it's about eight weeks – and we're away.

Yet the whole principle of American life, especially Frontier America, is one of open friendliness and welcome, where nobody goes hungry?

I've no ambitions of seeing any other part of America at all. None what-soever. I know full well when it's my vacation I could go to California, anywhere, but it just does not interest me one bit. Honestly. I'm a very strange person in that respect. Those outside things don't worry me and I've no ambition of going to Disneyland. I live in my own world.

The thing is, I love the sea, and here there's no water. There's perhaps lakes, but in Jersey I can walk to Bonne Nuit or Bouley and to me that's just sheer paradise. I can get in the car and go to the other side of the island and find a quiet little bay and I can take my needlework and sit there and I'm not worried....

THE TRICHOLOGIST

*She left my office so happy that
she didn't have to have sex....*

Philip Kingsley is a quiet elf: small but well formed. He wears neat
suits and a boutonnière and his hair, as you might expect, is *extremely*
healthy and beautifully arranged. Philip is a trichologist.

He has always edged towards success: he grew up in the East End,
where his father was a tailor, left school at fifteen and went to work
in his uncle's barbershop. In 1960 he opened his first clinic off the
Marylebone Road, in '65 moved to Park Street, in '68 to Green Street,
in '78 to New York. He had been diagnosing hair problems and
staring at the scalps of people like Candice Bergen, Norman Mailer,
Mick Jagger, Audrey Hepburn and Lord Olivier for many years before
he was encouraged to chance his arm in the United States – a gamble
which almost came to grief, but which has now made him a multi-
millionaire.

Three-quarters of all American women and a quarter of the men
colour their hair, he says, and eighty per cent have dandruff; this is
no longer merely white speckles on your collar but seems to be
regarded as an indication of chemical abuse or a social disease. It
means personal weakness, lack of self-respect and many unenviable
qualities. It also means Philip's business is brisk....

====

Why did you venture from London, where you were known and had
a sort of protective shell around you, into this New York jungle?

First I didn't want to. I had at the time two or three hundred people
coming to me in London who lived in New York and they used to say,
'There's nobody like you over there.' I didn't really believe there was no
trichology but I came over and looked around, and sure enough nobody
was doing quite what I was doing.

It's extraordinary, because this is the most narcissistic society in
the world ... this is where they live by the toupee, where every
second man you see on television wears a rug. Appearance is everything?

That's right, but they didn't have anything like me, so it was a challenge. I decided to do it and thought I'd be very successful. Not at all – it was really tough. I almost went out of business, because the two or three hundred people only come once a month, or once every three months. I had started off with a large staff and thought I'd be able to fill my clinic. I had to go back to England to get money to pay the salaries. The doctors and the dermatologists looked at me askance and said, 'Who is this guy?'

You were getting in on their act, I suppose?

They didn't believe trichology was worth anything, that there is an Institute of Trichology founded in 1902, that we are trained qualified people. They just thought that I was going to take business away from them.

What sort of money was involved, and how did you get it?

I got a group of investors together. I thought it was going to cost about $160,000, which is now about $700,000. The investors got forty-nine per cent and I got fifty-one per cent, which I thought was fair as I was doing the work. We all nearly went broke! When they saw things weren't going quite as well as everyone expected, they sort of backed down a little bit, and I had to bring the money over from my personal account in London to pay the salaries. We were supposed to be starting in September and as is so often the case, the builders weren't finished on time. When I arrived the *New York Times* wrote this absolutely wonderfully flattering article about me – half a page on me being the first trichologist in New York and pretty well in the United States – and when it came out nobody could get through because my building wasn't ready. There were no telephones. there was nobody here, so the impact from that wonderful piece of publicity was lost.

I finished up owing the bank something like $1.8 million which is just *extraordinary* for me, you know. If the company had gone broke, I'd have gone broke too. I got the money because it was loaned to me by Samuel Montagu, a very well-known merchant bank. There's a friend of mine, Staffen Gadd, who's chairman of the board. He went to another friend of mine, Doug Hayward the tailor in Mount Street, and said, 'We've just done the most amazing deal with Etna Life Insurance in New York and we have so much money we don't know what to do with it.' Doug said, 'I'll tell you what to do with it – a friend of mine is looking around for somebody to invest in his product company in New York.' Staffen said, 'I know Philip, he cured my dandruff ten years ago.' So the bank put up the money. It's very unusual for a conservative merchant bank to put up that sort of money, which finished up at $1.8 million.

I forgot totally that I owed all that money, I always thought I was going to make it. Joan and I were living very well. We have a flat in London and a house in Sussex, a flat in New York and we've just recently bought a house in Long Island.

I couldn't live here and *not* be happy, irrespective of how much money I've made or, hopefully, will make in the future. It's a great city. It's a different way of life than London, and I must say when I go back to England it's almost like having a holiday, because things go a bit slower. New York's a sort of vibrant city, and it's got great restaurants, great places to go, reasonable theatre – theatre's not as good as London, but pretty good – and the friends I've made here take me round and introduce me and I have a nice life. . . .

Now you're successful, do they treat you differently?

Yes, everyone does. It's a great success-oriented society. First of all it never occurred to me that I was going to be successful, and then it never occurred to me that I was going to be *unsuccessful!* I did badly at first, then I did well, then I did better and better and *better* and I got very well known in New York, which prompted me to start the company that's selling my products in stores like Saks Fifth Avenue, Bloomingdale's, Neiman Marcus and fine stores throughout the United States. It was a concept that's unique – prescription hair care based on what I've been doing for twenty-five years in my London clinic.

But *without* making a million?

Without making a million, exactly, without making a million.

You couldn't have gone public at home, as you have over here?

No, I don't think so. Having made it, so to speak, in the United States – which is exceedingly tough – one could come from here and bring a successful product-line to England, but we couldn't have a successful product-line in England and bring it here.

So you've gone from owing $1.8 million to being a multi-millionaire in seven years. A lot of English people would think doing business in New York was a bit fearsome – *are* businessmen here so much more efficient than we are?

Oh absolutely not! It's a myth. They're much *less* efficient than the British are – if we had the resources the Americans have we could knock spots off everybody. They're a very powerful strong country of course, I'm not knocking them, I've made a lot of money here and I adore being here and adore the Americans, but it's a myth that they're more efficient than the British.

They're absolutely not. They're very tough, very intransigent. they dig their heels in.

So what is it they have that we don't?

They start pretty early in the morning and they work late at night. They run harder, but they don't do as much in that running harder. People think that the British are lazy. I work a long day, I work very hard, I've always done so. My friends in London, they all work hard but they don't get up at six in the morning to be in the office at seven, and they don't stay in the office until seven at night, or whatever, yet they get things done equally as well and in fact, often better.

I know when I first came here I used to get on the telephone to order products, and I was kept talking for forty-five minutes – to order some bottles! In England you're on the phone for five minutes. They have long lunches here, three-hour lunches often. The double-martini lunch is usually true. Lots of business is done socially, whereas the British are not quite like that. If you have a business meeting with somebody you go to their office, you don't take them to lunch to persuade them to make a deal by plying them with drink. This has happened to me here.

They were courting you, so they were entertaining you – and then they bought you out for $5½ million; so now you're a target for the banks?

The banks treat me very nicely now, I must say – they take me out *all* the time! When I had two companies after my product-company – one of them was Bristol Myers, the other was Eli Lilly – they were really courting me. When you're having a drink or two you're saying things that often you don't mean, and they may say things that often *they* don't mean. That's not the way that the British do business, not really.

Were you a pushover after a couple of martinis?

Probably – but fortunately I had a great lawyer!

– who doesn't drink!

Who doesn't drink, and he said to me, 'Philip – No!' I said, 'It's fantastic, look what they've offered me.' 'Not good enough, you're worth more than that.' I mean the lawyers here are *really* tough. They earn a fortune and they're worth every penny of it. My lawyer Ron Connochi is just incredible. He's a perfect gentleman and when he says No he says it in the most charming possible way, which I couldn't of course. If I didn't think something was fair I'd have an edge to my voice saying No, but he says, 'Oh no gentlemen,' in his American way.

So now you're laughing all the way to every one of your free lunches?

Well I don't have lunches now because I work too hard! They take me to free dinners and free other things you know, but not free lunches. It's lovely to be in a position where one isn't beholden to anybody. I don't mean to sound pompous or anything like that, but I don't *have* to work as I'm working now. I do it because I love it. They've bought me out for a great deal of money and I have to do a certain number of days per year for them, but they know and I know I'm going to do *many* more days than my contract says, because I enjoy it. I just adore it.

But *living* in New York is an acquired taste is it not, especially after London and Sussex?

It is, and I couldn't get used to it at first. I was mugged here a while ago and that was really rather terrifying – but at the time I *didn't* think it was terrifying. It's extraordinary because this clinic is on the third floor and I was going out at seven o'clock at night, got into the lift, went down to the ground floor, the lift doors opened – and there was a black man. He was very well dressed and I thought, How strange somebody coming in at seven o'clock at night, so I moved to one side to get out, thinking he'd move to the other side. Instead he had his hand in his pocket with a gun, and said, 'Get back in there!'

I was rather taken aback. This was the time of the Falklands crisis and I was furious that the Argentines had invaded one of our islands – I mean I'm a really patriotic British subject and it was a couple of days after the landing and I was really feeling upset about the whole thing. Then this man, this great invasion of my privacy rather than an invasion of our island, pushed me into the lift and said, 'Take off your gloves!' Of course it was the winter and I had gloves on, an overcoat, a briefcase under my arm. He was actually a bit stupid because I took off my right-hand glove where I have no rings. I have these rings that were presents and my watch on this left hand, which was clutched underneath my briefcase. He was so stupid he didn't say, 'Take the other glove off.' He looked at my hand and saw there was nothing on it. Then he said, 'Give me your wallet,' and I said, 'No!'

I was stupid, but I was utterly angry that this man should do this to me after the Falklands, you see. I said, 'No!' and went to push the emergency button. He said, 'If you do that I'll shoot you.' I won't say exactly, but he used four-letter words, so I took my hand away. He said, 'Give me your wallet,' and I said, 'No!' He leaned forward – and *this* was his mistake –

and put his hand in my pocket to see if I had any loose change, and his *gun* hand that was in his pocket brushed against me – and it *wasn't* a gun! It was a pen I could feel. I went crazy. I said, 'You bastard', and I pushed him away and I hit hard at him. He fell away and hit out at me and knocked my glasses off – and ran out of the building. I chased after him, by which time people had heard the shouting and come down.

Afterwards I was really shaking because I realized I'd behaved stupidly. I got home to Joan, my wife, absolutely white-faced and told her, and she said, 'You fool, he could have shot you.' I said, 'But at the time I didn't really *care*. I was absolutely furious with this invasion of my privacy and the invasion of the Falklands and so on.' I don't know whether I'd ever behave like that again, mind you!

For days I was being British and carrying my umbrella around with me. I would recognize that man today and if I saw him, I'd absolutely kill him, you know. That was the first time I got mugged.

The second time, which was not really a mugging, was the day before Thanksgiving. Joan and I were walking home. Joan hailed a taxi and as she got in, a car came up on the inside and knocked her over. She started shouting. I didn't know what was going on, because I was looking for another taxi. Joan got in the taxi and this man got out of his car and started at my wife, making obscene gestures, obscene language. I said, 'How dare you speak to my wife like that!' *Bonk!* I didn't see it coming, he just knocked me out, knocking me into the taxi. I had twelve stitches in my eyebrow because I hit my head on the taxi roof. I was bleeding profusely everywhere. I had the biggest black eye you've ever seen. I was going to Dallas the next day to make a personal appearance promoting the products, the shampoos and things, and I had to go with dark glasses on with this huge black eye. Joan had the presence of mind to take his car number, and we got him and took him to court, but anyway that's another story.

Those two things, violence in the city, makes me a little more wary of not walking in the dark, and of course not walking in Central Park at night. Up until then people had told me they thought how extraordinary we'd never seen anybody mugged, and then suddenly in the course of six months, I got mugged twice. The second one was just an attack, which I don't think would happen in London. They wouldn't get out and hit you without any warning, no warning at all.

In your hair-care book you write all sorts of improbable things, like 'Masturbation is good for your hair.'

I wrote a chapter called 'Sex and Hair', and in it I mentioned something about masturbation, of course. What I said is that any stress is bad for your hair – that is, you can have thinning hair and worse dandruff because of stress. The worst stress is sexual stress, so if you have a good sex-life the chances of your hair being better are greater than if you have a bad sex-life, because of the stresses involved. There's no worse frustration than having a bad sex-life. I mean, masturbation has been going on for centuries and centuries, it's a release, so rather than have the tension, if you want to do anything you like as far as sex is concerned you should *do* it, rather than have yourself frustrated, which eventually can show on your hair.

Gives you thick hair, does it? They used to say it made it fall out!

Doesn't necessarily give you thick hair but it doesn't give you thin hair. Saying sex is good for the hair is only right in the context that it's better to be happy than unhappy. A few months ago a women who'd read my book was sitting in my office and said, 'I hear sex is good for your hair?' and I said exactly what I said to you, went through the whole thing. She said, 'Do you mean I don't *have* to have sex?' I said, 'Well not if you don't want to,' and she said 'Thank goodness for that, because I *hate* it....' So I said, 'If you hate it you're undergoing more stress by doing it than by *not* doing it.'

So for her hair's sake you gave her a chit excusing her sex for a couple of weeks?

She left my office so happy that she didn't have to have sex. Mind you, she had other problems.... Hair is what's termed a secondary sexual characteristic and maybe why I'm so successful here is that you can't flaunt your primary sexual characteristics in public, at least not here nor in London, but you can and do flaunt your secondary sexual characteristics. People think, If my hair looks good, I'm more sensual – so they spend a lot more money on it because they *have* the money. In England they *want* to spend the money but they haven't quite got enough.

It seems to me your waiting client, Mrs Jackie Stewart, is far too young to be listening to this kind of conversation ...

She is. I know Helen has a copy of my book which she hasn't read – but now she's going to rush off and read it!

H.   Jackie and I should go over it tonight....

I'm a psychiatrist to my clients. I have a woman coming to me who's a princess, an obscure French or Italian princess who has a place in Olympic Tower, but when she stays in a hotel she insists that all the carpeting, everything in the hotel, is covered in fresh-laundered towels. Not only that, she takes her own towels. That's a bit of a maniac. She won't step on anything that somebody else may have stepped on. Needless to say, she's got *very* thin hair.

I knew Claus von Bulow twenty-two years ago when he first came to see me, and he was pretty bald then. He used to love having the treatment, with the girls massaging his head. I said, 'Claus I can't grow your hair.' He said, 'Well, how about this transplanting I've heard about in New York?' I had met Philip Lebon, so I supplied his first patient, because I was then chairman of the board of the Institute of Trichologists. Claus was his first patient for transplant. He had a thousand transplants over a period of about a year and a half.

Now Helen's hair is not bad – it's a bit dull-looking and it's a bit split. You haven't been taking the care of it that you usually do! It's got very dry on the ends here. I mean really dry. You had it coloured, which makes it even drier. You should shampoo it every day. You can see at the end of the day how dirty your face gets, and you take your hair to the same places. This is a terrible city for dirt – they're building all over the place. Within five blocks of 53rd Street, where we are, there's about twenty buildings going up, so you walk out in the street and come back absolutely grimy.

This is a city where appearance is very important, so do you find people are more concerned about their looks than in Switzerland or London?

H: Yes, particularly in New York. I dress up more, it's a great social life – everything's an occasion. When you come up 5th Avenue you always feel you should look smart.

Success is rather different here to success in London isn't it, Philip?

Yes, they treat me differently. I've always been treated the same in London, but when I came to New York nobody knew me so I was always seated in Siberia. I didn't know where Siberia *was*, so it didn't matter.

But now you've got almost as much money as Jackie Stewart, you get the best tables? It matters here, doesn't it? It *matters* where you sit.

It actually does. You go into restaurants here and if you're sat in a bad table, your guests look at you rather askance and think Oh . . .

H: I always get a good table because they know Jackie, and why not? It's a club city. Switzerland's rather dull by comparison, but I have a lovely home there and it's very tranquil when I go back. When I arrive at Geneva airport at seven-thirty in the morning, and I'm driving home, it's the most wonderful feeling, it's like arriving in heaven, after being here. Then the other way around, I find it tough the first two or three days until I settle down. I'm frightened to walk out at night. You do have to be careful – I wouldn't just walk anywhere, I always take cabs. It's not as bad as people think, but it *is* tough.

You need a big strapping chap like Philip to take care of you....

What Helen says is true. I was in London a few months ago and we went to the theatre. We had dinner at the St James's and it was one o'clock before we finished and walked home to my flat in Green Street in Mayfair. It would have been a total *impossibility* to have done that in New York, to walk through dark streets. That's one of the main differences. You could walk anywhere in London, or pretty well anywhere, and not be frightened of being mugged....

THE GOSSIP

The wives are just spread out as decoration between the action....

Washington is a town where sounds travel faster than light, helped on its way by Diana McLellan from Norfolk. She is a gossip columnist. Small and blonde, she presides cheerfully over a terraced Fulhamish townhouse on Capitol Hill, where she's lived for twenty years. I was greeted by an elderly dog with long toenails, and a heavy husband, an historian who had just injured himself arm-wrestling.

Mrs McLellan spends her days lying by the Washington Hilton swimming pool while her answerphone collects 'tantalizing tidbits': as soon as President Reagan was elected Nancy's manicurist was flown from California to Washington to teach the staff of Lord and Taylor how to do the First Nails.... When dismissed from the White House a member of President Ford's staff left a legacy for the next team: he tiptoed into the rose garden and planted lots of marijuana seeds....

Washington is a prudish city where when advertised on radio 'The Best Little Whorehouse in Texas' becomes 'The Best Little Bleephouse....' Though the capital is totally committed to the spectator sport of politics, social life is restrained. 'If people stay at a party until eleven-thirty' she says, 'they're having the kind of time that'll go into their memoirs. If they stay until twelve, they're bombed.'

═══

I came here with my father in '56 or '57 – he was the Air Attaché at the British Embassy. I stayed and married a Yank or two, and lingered on.... Became wife, mother, grandmother and gossip columnist, but not in that order.

When I married the second time, to my absolute horror my husband said I had to get a job – he was an academic, a PH.D. teaching history at Johns Hopkins. I finally got a job peddling classified ads on the business counter of *The Star*, and decided that I could write better than anybody there. Eventually moved into promotions, wrote their radio and television commercials. This must have been '63 or '64. I'd become a resident then and I was writing a column every day.

Are you naturalized?

No, and it's really laziness, not galloping patriotism. Of course I love England but I'm only there a couple of weeks a year and I suppose it *would* make more sense, especially as here I'm sitting in the middle of the nest, sniping at everybody. I've just got to get my juices flowing to do it.

Do you find your English accent a help or a hindrance?

I think it might be a little bit helpful but I don't think it's essential at all, because Americans on the whole can't tell the difference between upper-crusty English and cockney.

It's not because I'm English, but you *can* talk to people here. You can talk to, if not the President, his right-hand man, his left-hand man, if you really need to. The head of CIA – you bump into him on somebody's yacht. And remember in Washington the cast changes so often, at least every four years, not to mention the Senators and the Congressmen and so forth. Everybody's using everybody else and if you're perceived as a useful person, or even if you're not and are poking fun at them slightly, you just find yourself caught up in it all.

I've been doing the gossip column now for about nine years. On the *Washington Star*, then it went to the *Post*, then to *The Times*. I do it five days a week now. There's always enough stuff. I write just the day before, I like deadlines, don't you? I do a lot of media gossip, lots of political gossip. When you say gossip you must realize that it's all *true*, more or less – because you have to watch out for libel suits – but you try to make it sound almost as though it's *not*. I gladly embrace the title Gossip.

Washington is the power base of America, the capital of the Western world – yet it's a gossipy villagey sort of place?

It is a terribly small town, kept small by the fact that the permanent residents are hard-core Washingtonians who're really quite a minority. Everybody else swoops through, so just by being in this particular town for a long time you become a fixture, you become as much a part of the landscape as the Capitol.

As a gossip writer, do they see you as the lowest form of journalistic life or the most important?

To some people I'm very important. People who are on the hustle or trying to establish themselves think that getting their name in the gossip column is something that's interesting. They want their friends to know they're important enough to be written about – yet a lot of people spend a lot of energy trying to keep *out* of gossip columns.

Washington is a town that runs on the oil of gossip. Everything is gossip, partially because there are so many different segments of Washingtonians: there are the ones on Capitol Hill, the White House, embassies, and so forth. They really have very little to do with each other and they feel, I think, when they read a gossip column that they're getting something of the other part of Washington they wouldn't be getting in their day-to-day business. I think they tend when they read my column to say, 'Oh boy I've got something that would fit in there!'

I try to keep the tone of the column light enough so that people don't think, Is she going to dump on me, or us, if we do such and such? I try to keep the informational flow going.

You say quite bitchy things in a lighthearted way, is that it?

Yes, the nastier the thing you have to say, the more delicate you have to be about it. That's because of being in Washington for the long haul – you don't want to get a reputation as a complete cow, because *they've* come and gone. Many many Washington Gossips finally bitched themselves out of a job because sooner or later no one will talk to them, except the sort of creepy people who slink up to you at parties, or people with great axes to grind.

Everybody here has something to sell, usually themselves?

Remember, Washington is a city where power and access are the most important products. They mean money, they mean everything – so everybody wants to get *at* something. It's not a sexy town at all. There *is* sex, obviously, but sex isn't nearly as important as power and access. The times when it does rear its charming head are few and far between, believe me, as a topic of gossip.

There couldn't be a *Private Eye* here in America?

They keep giving it a go, you know. Every now and then a little magazine pops up and has a go at it. There's one called *Mole* that's trying to be very amusing, satirical and so forth, but they can't get the money to back it because they've got to get advertisers, they've got to get the big-time corporations to back it – and they're terrified of being satirized.

Malcolm Muggeridge would not be popular here, neither would *Private Eye*. People don't like it, especially on television. They won't forgive cruelty, the sort we take in our stride at home and say, 'Oh they don't really mean it.' Here people get too offended. There are only 600,000 people in the city and I know I can't write like that here – they'd never speak to me again. You have to make people laugh. You can't make people cry.

307

People of course have very different Achilles heels – they're worried about different things, and offended by different things. What causes you most trouble?

There are certain things I just won't cover because they're so slimy and they make the reader feel slimy too. I don't think readers like to leave a gossip column feeling ill, and saying, 'Oh I wish I didn't know that.' I don't want to drag homosexuals out of the closet and that sort of thing. If I did the whole city would be crawling, because the streets are *thick* with them. I don't want to be the first to tell a wife that her husband's messing around. I don't want to send people sobbing into their pillows at night. Just this week we had a little blind item in passing, mentioning the ex-diplomat's wife and the Senator people are talking about. I certainly wouldn't dream of going further than that because them as knows, knows – and them as doesn't, it doesn't matter.

Even British Ambassadors' marriages have been known to come to grief right here?

They certainly have!

Were you the first to reveal the Jay break-up to the world?

I'm afraid I was. I did it in a very peculiar way really – I mean I did it in a very *tasteful* way, I thought. I write very carefully indeed with the twofold aims of showing the reader a good time and communicating when I have to communicate, and I think in that particular case – you are referring, I gather, to Mrs Jay and Mr Bernstein? – I think I just mentioned something about the fact that *he* was going into television and learning the ropes of zooming, booming, you know, the various er....

Technical terms?

Technical terms which I had to turn to my thesaurus for, to imply it as delicately as I could. I wasn't in the bedroom.

A lot of people believe a bad mention is better than being ignored?

Some do, some do. I have one friend – or a former friend who isn't speaking to me at the moment – who is about to appear in a movie and I mentioned that so-and-so has been discovered with a capital D. No darlings, not *that*. He's going to be absolutely livid with me. I don't know what his guilty secret is, but I can only guess.

Do you check your sources or do you avoid confusing a good story with facts?

It depends on the source. If it's anonymous I have to check it from here to Christmas. There are some people in this town who actually call up to plant items about themselves, pretending to be someone else. The one who called yesterday wanted me to know – by the way I don't quite believe it – that she was a very pretty girl who was armpiecing Pierre Trudeau at a restaurant the other day. She also told me she was a lawyer and I found out she wasn't, so I didn't use that. She just wants to be known. People like their moment of fame. Andy Warhol said everybody got it for ten minutes; well in a gossip column you get it for two *seconds*. . . .

Politics is a sort of spectator sport here is it not?

Oh absolutely – the most entrancing spectator sport of all.

And you're helping the man in Lynchburg Virginia to learn what's happening as soon as the people in the Washington street hear about it?

I hope so, yes. I believe in equal gossip for all.

Politicians need journalists the way the Royal Family need them, do they not? They don't like them but they can't exist without them?

Yes, yes, yes.

Journalists are a necessary evil, and gossip writers perhaps more evil than most?

They're more unnecessary, and more evil.

Are journalists popular dinner guests here, despite their table manners?

Very much, yes. If you're inviting a gossip columnist, everyone presumes that you want some publicity. They can also bring gossip to the party itself, enliven it with bits and bobs. . . . You must remember that people don't entertain for a good time here, that isn't the objective at *all*. People entertain to get things *done*. It's a very pragmatic town, so if you have a Washington dinner party you'll be selecting not the people who you think are going to keep everybody in raptures at their wit and so on, you're going to have people who can *do* something for you. You're going to have, probably, a Senator and his wife, a lobbyist and his wife, a diplomat and his wife. You need pay no attention to the wives at all, they're just spread out as decoration between the action. This is where business gets done, in the cocktail hour before dinner.

Who gives the best parties here?

The best ones were probably given by the Shah's old ambassador, Ardishir Zahedi. He was a real party boy. That's where the caviar and champagne flowed and of course there were hints that far more than that went on there too. He was a rather exotic person. Some gossip out of California has just revealed a night of passion with Ardishir which makes him sound far more interesting than anyone thought at the time. He was the one who armpieced Liz Taylor around here for a long time, before she met John Warner.

The White House is very good with the press, I must say. You hear a lot of bellyaching from the White House press corps but they're far more generous to the press than the ones before. For example the Carter people cut off various members of the press who said anything at all they didn't like from their Christmas party lists, whereas the Reagans have expanded it – so everybody gets a little snuffle at the trough!

What about the British Embassy?

Um, well they're nice people. I like the Wrights very much indeed but they don't understand how to deal with the American press. They don't have somebody on the royal beat, and what Americans adore is all the royal tittle-tattle. They love Princess Di, she's on all the magazine covers. They like love and youth and aristocracy and money.... You call up and ask, 'What colour shoes did Princess Di wear' – as you can do at the White House – and they enrage American journalists when the darling boy there says, 'I've no *idea* what colour shoes she wore,' as if it was an outrageous question. I wish the embassy would have someone to deal with the small-time chicken-shit royal questions. They have a very hoity-toity press department and nobody there who can come up with all the nitty-gritty. It really would do an enormous amount of good to the image. It's the best thing they've got to peddle abroad.

Except the Foreign Office doesn't have too much clout at Buckingham Palace....

I suppose not, but it could even just be an English journalist or someone who knew what American journalists were after. It's terribly hard to squeeze anything out of them. I don't even bother any more. I sidle up to somebody at parties and ask them, rather than go through their press office. They should have somebody who doesn't feel it's infra dig to talk about such things – after all, the Royals are one of England's most saleable products and I'm sure must be very useful as publicity for the country generally. It isn't universal of course. There are lots of Americans who say, 'To hell with them....'

They say the only love affair, the only *true* romance in Washington, is a love of power – and also it's a rather prudish town?

Very prudish town. You have to tiptoe around the edge of all sorts of things here. You can understand *why* because a lot of these people are elected from very small towns. You've got people from Oklahoma, the Bible Belt places – and imagine the horror of their constituents when they go back and everyone there knows, because the columnists have indicated, that they sleep in red heart-shaped waterbeds, or that they quietly shucked a couple of wives during the August recess.... This doesn't go over too well with the folks back home.

Power is everything here, but when you lose it the public reaction is instant?

It's a little bit poignant ... a lot of people want to hang around the town and keep going, when they're *out*. Democrats tend not to have as much money as Republican government appointees, and when they were in power this was the best time they'd ever had. The Republicans tend to go home and get even richer!

People get very philosophical about where they are. It isn't like England, it's a very pragmatic class system. What your power is and what you can do, *that* is your standing. It's very much, What can you do for me today?...

Dr Kissinger's not a survivor in the ultimate sense, he's given up his Washington residence now and has a very small role in the Reagan administration – they use him for odds and ends, when they think he's going to impress the internationals, briefing Reagan for the Gromyko talks and so on. I remember about two or three weeks after the change of administration when Reagan came in, Kissinger went to the barbershop he'd been using for years and Milton Pitts, who's barber to the divine – the President and so forth – told him, 'I'm afraid you're going to have to wait, Mr Kissinger – we have a VIP coming in....'

THE OCEANOLOGIST

There was a nasty murder here last night. . . .

The life of Richard Lord is totally devoted to fish, and he is most content. A solemn earnest twenty-six, he is son of the late Cyril and Shirley Lord – who queens it uptown while he works very downtown at the Fulton Fish Market on the East River, below the incongruous high-rises of Wall Street.

Fish buyers arrive at the South Street Seaport at 3 a.m. every day. Richard leaves his shared apartment on 34th Street around 4 a.m. and travels to work on the subway, the only white face on those dark subterranean platforms. 'With the clothes I wear to work,' he says, 'I'm obviously not worth mugging.'

He is the market's spokesman and each dawn offers a free ninety-minute lecture tour among the blood-'n-guts of a wholesale fish market, moving between piles of tuna, snapper, softshell crabs and swordfish: 'Here we have a black sea bass. These fish are hermaphrodites – when they're small they're female but when they grow large they're male. When spawning the male develops a characteristic hump on the head, right here. This is a sheep's head porgie: the reason it has such a good set of dentures is that it eats shellfish. . . .'

Even when not lecturing Richard's conversation rarely strays far from fish. . . .

━━━

This market handles about four per cent of all the seafood in the United States, about 140 million pounds a year, whereas Billingsgate handles 80 million pounds a year. We have many different ethnic types of people in New York and they like seafood from their country of origin, so we try and supply it.

You seem to be a round peg in a nice round fishy hole, because you've studied fishery – and that's not always very marketable knowledge?

I'm very lucky to have found this job. I went to California straight from public school in England and was looking around for a job there unsuccessfully, went back to England, was unsuccessful there as well, came to New York and was fortunate within a year to have found this job.

I knew your father, who was a rich man, so you don't *have* to work?

I do, in New York. It's very expensive to live here, it really is. Especially as the pound isn't as strong as I'd like it to be. I'm still very much in a student environment, sharing a kitchen with other people, you know.

You're sharing a bathroom, I'm told, with a pet eel?

That's right: Rupert. Actually he passed away last night. I had a very traumatic experience. He had migratory urges and he wanted to get to the Sargasso Sea. I had found him on the floor of Fulton Fish Market and took him home and cared for him for a year, and now he's no longer. He tried to leave the aquarium I'd kept him in all this time, jumped out and during the night just lay on the floor and passed away.

Too sad – he was heading for the Sargasso Sea down Bleaker Street and through Greenwich Village?

That's right. He would have had to swim over land quite a way but of course as you know, eels have a great tolerance for staying alive out of water and he could have made a couple of hundred yards, had he not confronted the stairs of my apartment.

So you're living in eel-less squalor. . .?

That's right.

Over a bar?

On 34th Street over a bar and a warehouse. I hear fights commonly outside at about 2 a.m. when the bar closes. I see a lot of interesting activity outside my window: I've seen a policeman on horseback charge into a retail store to arrest a shoplifter, right below and next to the bar. New York's full of surprises and intrigue.

Doesn't happen much in South Ken, does it! Do you have the time for girlfriends and that sort of thing?

I do at the moment – in Canada, but obviously that's a long way away and I only go up there once a month at the most. Social life in New York can be good if you want it to be, but really it's very expensive. You can go to parties every day of the year, to discotheques, comedy shows, theatre, cinema. You can do almost anything – this city's open twenty-four hours a day, but I prefer just to come down to the Fish Market and enjoy the atmosphere.

I'm told there's quite a shortage of eligible young bachelors around?

With my English accent I do have a slight advantage. I think Americans are fascinated by Europeans in general, but specifically because we speak English they tend to like us a great deal as well.

I was up at four this morning, and sometimes I put in an eighteen-hour day and sometimes I take off early. I go on commercial fishing boats when I have the opportunity, try to find out how fish is caught, how it's processed, how it's distributed and finally how it reaches the consumer and the retail stores.

If you were in England now is there work like this you could be doing?

England is a little ahead of the United States in terms of fisheries. They have much larger companies, much better handling conditions. It's more of an industry there, whereas here it's very fragmented and really a small business. I take a lot of ideas from England and hope to implement them here, or at least tell people about them so eventually the American industry can catch up.

What about the future – what do you hope to do?

Eventually I'd like to return to England, that's my home and I think that's where I want to live. I have to say if I left the seafood business, I'd leave New York. Fulton Fish Market with all its vitality and atmosphere is keeping me here.

I suspect a lot of young chaps in your position, with a certain income and no responsibilities, might lie around admiring the view, taking it easy, getting into drugs and that sort of thing. . . .

I shun drugs and alcohol because I don't particularly like them, and for some reason I have this bizarre motivation towards seafood and fish in a marine environment. All my life, as early as I can remember, I was always fishing on the rocks, going out in boats, talking to the fishermen. I just love that, and I think I'll continue to love it.

I must say your interest doesn't often stray far from fish, does it?

The Steelman: David Lloyd-Jacob and his wife Caro

The Cowboy: David Harvey

The Trichologist: Philip Kingsley

The Gossip: Diana McLellan

The Oceanologist: Richard Lord

The Up-market Car Dealer: Anthony Thompson

The Down-market Car Dealer: Ken Crutchlow

The Head of Protocol: Elizabeth Daoust

The Doctor: Paul Buisseret

The Demonstrator: Anise-Yvonne Palladino

The Deposed: Colin and Veronica Draper

The Lancashire Lad: Tony Corbett

No, I'm *very* narrow-minded unfortunately. Sometimes my enthusiasm wanes, but then it only takes a few days down the Fish Market to regain that enthusiasm, to see the variety of fish delivered from all over the world, to see the type of characters that come down and buy here.

What do these characters make of *you*, because they're pretty tough cookies, aren't they?

They are tough, yes, in fact there was a nasty murder here last night – someone was stealing some fish and he was shot to death. That does happen once in a while. Unfortunately the person who stole the fish tried to stab someone and went over to his car to get a handgun and was shot in the process of trying to shoot back, so it *is* rough-and-tumble here, but you live with it. They're very pleasant to me, the people in the market, the actual workers, very friendly, very polite.

Do they regard you as a young English freak?

I don't know, I haven't really talked to them. I try and befriend them. There *are* some people who I don't get on with, but the majority I get on with very well.

You haven't been shot, anyway....

No, no, I've come through unscathed. I've seen some fist fights but it's all in good humour, you know.

This market is totally controlled by the Mafia, is it not?

Certainly a number of years ago there was a sting operation down here. The FBI came down and one of the bosses was put in prison for twelve years.

They exact a toll on every pound of fish that's sold?

That's true, but then again they're in the sanitation business, they're in food business, vegetables, they're not *just* in the fish business, they're in many many businesses.

Everything?

Yes, they really are.

Every pound of fish that's sold here, the Mafia get a dollar fifty – it's still a Marlon Brando waterfront, isn't it?

Yes it still is. Unfortunately we don't think it's going to remain much longer. There's tremendous character in this market: it's very much like the old Billingsgate that moved a few years ago. It's been in existence since the 1820s and retained its identity. The fish is still handled in the same fashion, it's still moved around by porters or journeymen – there's no mechanization whatsoever.

The Syndicate make sure of that?

The union certainly puts a bar on any mechanization, yes.

The thing about Billingsgate of course is that people get shot there rather *less* don't they?

I've been to Billingsgate and I like the people a great deal. I like them here as well but they're definitely different to deal with. Obviously the people from Billingsgate are good old English stock, whereas here you have Italians, Japanese, Koreans, Portuguese, Chinese. . . .

For every box of fish that's delivered a dollar twenty-five is paid to the unloading crew, whether the fish is unloaded by them or not. That's like a tax, and that maybe goes to the Welfare fund or to the union or to the unloaders themselves.

Or to Sicily?

Maybe it helps build another high-rise, who knows. . . .

THE UP-MARKET CAR DEALER

*You can't drive your four-million-dollar house
down Rodeo Drive. . . .*

Anthony Thompson sells the stars their cars. The President and Chief
Executive of Rolls-Royce of Beverly Hills Ltd is indeed a suitably
Hollywood Englishman: large and jolly and booming, with a fruity
turn of English phrase. If I were a film mogul or a footballer with a
suitcase full of Vegas winnings looking for lush wheels, I would hope
to find Tony smiling at me across the silver Spirit of Ecstasy in the
hush of the showroom.

He left Loughborough University to become an officer in REME, and
in 1958 emigrated to the United States to join Jaguar Cars Inc.
Twenty years ago he found his natural home in Beverly Hills and
grew into a sort of civic leader and national monument: Chairman
of the British-American Chamber of Commerce for the Southwest,
Director of the English-Speaking Union and Chairman of the British
Olympic Association – which financed the British team at the 1984
Los Angeles Olympic Games. The culmination of the fund-raising was
a dinner and show for seven hundred West Coast glitterati which
raised half a million pounds. It was attended by the stars and presided
over by Prince Andrew, fresh from paint-spraying the press. . . .

═══

The most exciting thing was that it's the only time in the twenty-seven
years I've lived in America where the British have been rallied to a cause.
Ever. It was interesting, demanding, fun, tear-making. . . .

Our team was very responsive, I gather? Americans in the stands
were saying the British team was very demonstrative, and fun. . .?

That's true. There was a great feeling about the Zola Budd incident, which
was really atrocious because it was a dreadfully unsporting performance –
and she was only a tiny thing. I think they liked the spirit of the British.
We had one enormous team – because I paid all the bills, I know there were
509 people we brought from England!

How many were athletes?

About 325–330. I was offered three Royals, and made the choice that Andrew would be our Best Buy. He kindly agreed to come, and we had to pay for him all the way. They pay *nothing*. We put him in the Beverly Wilshire.

He had all the mandatory bodyguards?

Would you *believe* what we had in there!

And you had to pay for them as well?

Everything. Princess Anne and Prince Philip stayed at the Huntington Sheraton in Pasadena – he wanted to be next to the Equestrian Centre. It wasn't at all convenient for her but he said, 'She'll stay with me,' and she did. I got to know her quite well, with all these comings and goings; I found out all sorts of things about her which were very likeable. Number one, she's enormously human. She's a little *retroussé* to begin with, but she really is a funny lady and she was awfully nice. I had a little chat to her private secretary and he said, 'Well you know, she *has* her moments.' She never had a moment round me. I'll tell you – she was absolutely charming. I've never seen any Royal work as hard as she does, other than the Queen.

The ticket income for our dinner was $527,000, and we raised $325,000 in profit. The expenses of the evening were $200,000. You can do a lot for 700 people for $200,000, when you add it all up. So the first ingredient was to give the event charisma, and of course the significant thing was that Andrew *is* charismatic. He'd never been to Los Angeles before and he was very interested. He's stunning-looking, and also very nice and funny; twenty-one, twenty-two years old – he's a lad, but a good lad.

I recognized very early on that the British were *not* the people who were going to come to this. The Americans were the people. Now Sir Gordon White is a man I'm extremely fond of and I said, Gordon will you underwrite the entertainment? Gordon took his cheque book out and wrote a cheque for forty-five thousand dollars, which touched me very deeply.

We said, 'We've got to put on the best show ever' – so I went to see Michael Caine and he became Chairman of the Entertainment Committee, and Vice-Chairman was Leslie Bricusse. Our answer was to get the best possible entertainment value and give it some really serious publicity. We did that.

Then we decided we had to get a dinner cheque. We thought, We don't want somebody who's so charismatic that he'll in some way impact Andrew. So we got Lew Grade. He's the *funniest* little thing! We thought that would be amusing, and it worked out quite nicely. As a result we drew in some more support from his company – so that was a good choice.

Then we said, 'We've got to have a great orchestra, a great dinner, and a great evening.' We did what was by Beverly Wilshire standards quite an expensive dinner: it ran seventy-seven dollars a head, but my view is this: if you want somebody to pay a thousand dollars a go ... then you have to make it good.

And on top of that – it's tax-deductible?

All but seventy-five dollars; you cannot deduct the price of the dinner. We got the champagne wholesale, and for every two bottles we bought they gave us one, and so on. The LA Police pipe band, which is twenty-one strong, greeted everybody as they came in. We had 390 press here. They weren't allowed to come to the eating part, but they came to the entertainment and the greeting.

The people who did the entertainment were terribly generous – Julie Andrews, Michael Caine, Dudley Moore.... When he first started in the business Dudley worked for Cleo Laine and Johnny Dankworth, so we brought Johnny down from San Francisco and three-quarters of the way through his act he stopped the show and told his pianist, 'You're just dreadful – *out!*' Then he said, 'I've got to find another one,' ... and Dudley Moore saunters out, sits down at the piano and does his thing.

We had *Stop-the-World* Anthony Newley, we had Tom Jones; Engelbert we didn't have. Someone we thought we were going to get but in the end didn't was Paul McCartney: Rod Stewart was travelling, so Paul was going to come. Joan Collins didn't come, to my surprise. We had a gouache given to us by David Hockney which we sold for $45,000 and we had two caricatures – one of all the stars in the production Lew Wasserman paid $10,000 for, so I was very proud of him.

The thing which was most interesting – you know this crowd in Beverly Hills, they wrap up the streets at quarter-past-eleven. *Nobody* stays out later. Do you know what time this emptied? Ten minutes past one – and nobody had left!

Why didn't Joan Collins come?

She said she was very tired. Samantha Eggar came.

But Joan rarely misses a party....

Well, she missed this one. Everybody you can think of who should have been there, was there. And we had all sorts of nice offers: Frank Sinatra said, 'Can I come and sing for you?' and Doris Day said, 'May I do...?' We said, 'Thank you but this is an all-British evening.'

You could have made Sinatra an honorary Brit for the evening, I would have thought?

There's a reason for this. We said, 'Look – the whole thing is British.' And it was – even the orchestra was led by the guy who wrote all the Bond music, John Barry. Everything was done by Brits.

They must have gulped a few times when they turned down Frank Sinatra?

Yes; Bob Hope came but didn't perform. We thought he was a little past it at eighty-seven years old. And I must say the whole thing went with amazing smoothness.

Did all this extra-curricular activity cut a hole in your social life, or enlarge it?

It enlarged it enormously, but it cut a big hole into *business* life, because I was going out speaking somewhere three nights a week for nearly eighteen months, and rallying the troops and getting them organized. The tickets were $1,000, $500 and $250. We sold 400 tickets – thirty-eight tables at $10,000 a table. We sold all but five tables at $500, and then we sold the last five tables at $250.

The thousand-dollar tables got to have drinks with the Prince?

That's right, we did all that. And of course the other thing I learned was the great subtlety of the Palace: you don't pay a thousand dollars to go and shake the Royal mitt, we made that *very* clear. It was just the more generous givers!

It started at six o'clock and it was a very busy few hours. It aged me twenty years. Now when you have a Royal, you get an exit interview if you've had something to do with it – they call you to go and say goodbye. So I marched up and sat down and we talked a bit and Andrew said, 'I've had a wonderful time,' and he really meant it. He said, 'I'm just terribly sorry about that paint thing. I do hope it didn't cause you a lot of embarrassment.' And I said, 'Well there's a precedent with your dad – he's good with a hose!'

He said, 'Do you know what really happened? They were painting the side of a house and said, "Why don't you spray it?" and they gave me this huge paint gun. You realize it's not *too* often we get the opportunity to use a paint gun? I picked it up and sprayed. Then I turned round, as a joke – I'd no idea it would go off like that.'

If you think about this and be really realistic, if you're spraying a car you use about 28 lbs a square inch pressure, because paint-per-pound is about the same consistency as water. If you're spraying a house with heavy paint you use a hundred and twenty-five pounds per square inch in a paint gun, and it almost has a kickback! He was very bothered about this. It was unfortunate, because he was absolutely wonderful – but we got a lot of publicity out of that, what with Margaret and the Irishmen! One of the things that was strange was that they didn't send a press officer out from the Palace.

What are you doing for an encore?

There isn't an encore for me, I'm keeping quiet. If I say I feel I've used up favours, I hope you'll understand the spirit in which I've said it. I used not to owe anybody anything, but I owe a lot of people a lot now!

The British press was very bad, actually, and the American press was fine. I'll tell you about the British press – and I say this with absolutely no reference to your own profession – but I would be called from Britain on average ten times a week. The thrust varied enormously from 'We're proud of what you're doing, tell us about it' to 'I hear it's not going well with the British community.' I found this very troubling. I had four people working on this constantly, and it wasn't always the easiest thing in the world to do. Nobody called without getting a call back. Anybody who wanted an interview got an interview – TV, radio, we dealt with them all.

I had 408 people working free of charge for me around America, and that's a lot of Brits all giving their time and effort and money and gasoline and food and drink and whatever, to support this cause. I'd set up a company for Federal and State tax exemption and established ourselves as a charity, which is very important because what we got was actually net, tax free.

But apart from all that, how did you enjoy the Games?

I went to *one* event, which was the closing. I think the British left a good taste in everybody's mouth, which is nice. It's funny but the whole attitude of the British *in* America towards Britain is a very strange class problem, and I never knew this.

I found the people who are artisans, I mean electricians and bricklayers and so on, see themselves *absolutely* as Americans with regard to most things. They have their own pubs and their British clubs – there's eighty-two British clubs and societies in Southern California and I've been to every one, except six. They all drink beer and throw darts and eat sausage rolls. It's unbelievable. The most esoteric was the Piccadilly Club: that's for people who were born round the Piccadilly area. There's the Lancashire Society down in Gardena, which holds a dance every other Saturday night for four dollars a head, so you can imagine when I told them about our thousand dollars a head! They sulked about that. They thought: Look at him, toffee-nosed son-of-a-bitch. I understood all that.

The class thing I found so interesting was, there was a feeling among this artisan level that, Why were we doing this here when we should be doing it in Britain ... because they're now living here and they're part of *American* society. At the next level up, the professions, they were supportive, and the top level, the rich, they were supportive too.

I have a whole theory about this: we in Britain are not trained to give. In America they're trained to give – they *understand* about giving. Here the Brits' view is more critical: Why are you doing all this, What do you need the money for, How are you spending it – like I'm putting it all in *my* pocket! They were of the impression I was a salaried person and I was taking twenty per cent of the income. Well I would reckon that little exercise cost me personally fifteen thousand dollars over the period.

What's going to happen to your Olympic successors – the British businessman in South Korea?

I should think they can all meet in a phone booth. ...

So with all this excitement you've hardly had time to look over your shoulder and sell a Rolls-Royce?

Rolls-Royce in the past year has made a quantum leap into the 1980s, if not indeed into the twentieth century. In my company of forty-three, forty-four employees the managers are really very good, but there's no fertilizer like the owner's footsteps in a business, believe me! The clients like to talk to you and meet you and shake your hand.

I don't actually close sales, because I'm just not as good at it as my people. Selling a car is a skill, like training a horse, but who goes into Moss Bros, for example, when they say, 'Here's a splendid shirt, Mr Whicker, it's £43,' and you say, 'I'll give you £37 for it', and they say, 'Well let's try £40,' and you eventually buy it for £39. ... There's a tremendous psychological impact with all this, Alan. We deal with the rich and the famous and the powerful. That's our business, and these are people who earn a million dollars a year – *more* than a million in quite a number of cases – and they'll come and sit down for two hours and negotiate $3,000. Up and down, on the phone, walking out the door and being dragged back in again. ...

The impact of the recession on the sort of business I'm in has been considerable; '81 and '82 were very difficult years, interest rates were up at twenty per cent ... yet we sold sixty-four cars that year, or sixty-five. And of those we financed one on HP, we leased one – and sold sixty-three for cash.

In suitcases?

In cheque books, chiefly! We don't do *too* many sales for cash in suitcases! We've done one this year, so far. I remember O.J. Simpson went to Las Vegas and won $225,000 at the fights. As he flew back to Beverly Hills he thought he'd like to take a new car home with him, so he stopped off in a taxi at our door and nipped in with a suitcase full of money and bought the car there and then – and paid for it in ten-dollar bills! It took us four hours to count the money. He overpaid by seven hundred dollars, so we had to deliver back seventy ten-dollar bills.

I've learnt a very interesting lesson and that is: there is nobody who *needs* a new Rolls-Royce, they all do perfectly well with their old ones. Then all of a sudden you find you're facing problems of overproduction, and why I found this so interesting is that they didn't sell any cars in Britain, so they started making them for America. We got cars arriving at a rate which was frightening – at one point I had thirty-one new Rolls-Royces in stock. I couldn't *pay* for them! I don't have $3½ million-worth of new-car floor. I usually have about $1.6 million-worth. So I had half of them floored, and the rest of them sat there. I said, 'You can come and take them, I don't need thirty-one cars in stock, I'm very happy to have fifteen. They said, 'Please take care of them because they're no good to us!' Which was all true. So I took care of them. The insurance alone on that little package is quite considerable.

I order at the rate of about six cars a month, about seventy-five a year. So we sold one in one month and two in the next month, and they kept trotting them out. They were doing about twenty-five a month in Britain and we were the top-selling dealer in America at sixty-five. The next guy behind me was like fifty-nine – that was a guy down in Newport Beach.

The people we sell to, by and large, are no different to the people I sold Rolls to when I started in 1976. They are the people who you know – or you know many of them: successful entrepreneurs, successful businessmen, some of them in the entertainment business.

But the Rolls still has the Clan badge?

It is still absolutely the definitive emblem of success. The theory I've always had is that you can't drive your four-million-dollar house down Rodeo Drive so everybody can look at it, but you *can* leap to the wheel of your car and drive that down. If you go bankrupt, the last thing you dispose of is your Rolls-Royce. I've been to owners' homes without a stick of furniture in them: they're busy with their fourth mortgage and somebody's called that mortgage, so they've sold the contents but they still have the house, because there are certain rules about how you can foreclose, and they still have their Rolls-Royce parked outside the front door.

And I think there's a certain amount of, as Jewish people say, chutzpah involved in all this, but on the other hand it's OK, I understand that. I support that. It's the badge of office, the badge of success. It means that people know they can invite you to their parties.

It may sound very silly but there's no question that Americans at all levels think the British have nice voices and they like to hear us doing our British bit. They relate to the British more than to any other people, although there's an enormously strong Irish and Italian contingent – but did you see the 1980 census? Forty-two million people in the United States said, 'We owe our background to Britain, one way or another,' so we're talking about twenty per cent of the population which says: 'We are British,' or 'We have a British background.'

Another thing they like about us is that we have in Britain a heritage of antiquity, which they don't quite have here. They realize that the British root in America is a very strong root, plus the fact that they adore our monarchy. It's a great selling point for Britain. So when you put all these little bits together you suddenly find you're really quite welcome, not as a star turn but as some sort of intangible endorsement of what's going on. They'll say, 'It's going to be all right because there's this British underpinning.'

I was talking to somebody about this quite recently and they said, 'Why do you think it is that a French person isn't regarded as being a good solid citizen who could be depended upon?' The response is that France has never given *quite* the impression. The last respectable Frenchman was Charles de Gaulle. Nobody recalls anybody since him, very much. If somebody says, 'Quickly, who's the President of France?' they can't remember his name.

We are regarded as being intrinsically honest, properly behaved, well-motivated, properly brought up, speak nicely, know how to do the right thing. And if there's a problem we can even be asked about it, without taking the mickey out of the questioner. I find this totally fascinating, I find it quite humble-making.

The community we're in here probably reacts more favourably to the Britishness of us all, than other areas. I don't think for example that the British are looked upon highly in New York, or in Washington DC. I think they're looked upon more highly maybe in Boston. I think in the Mid-West being British makes you a curiosity. I accept all that – whatever turns them on. We British have a certain ability for pointing the finger of fun at ourselves, and I think that's liked. The other thing is, we're all *expected* to be very stuffy.

I cannot understand why the British manufacturer does not take a more aggressive view towards the potential of the western United States, overall. Those who do, do very well out of it. Now Sir Arthur Bryan is a real merchant – he's the Chairman of Wedgwood. He comes out here and he really hustles, he goes out and explains about Wedgwood, does his lordship thing – which of course we adore over here. But there are so many types of product which are well made in Britain but not marketed over here.

A man comes to see me – I happen to be Chairman of the British Chamber of Commerce – and says, 'I want to sell English soap over here. I work for Floris and we're suppliers to the Royal Household.' He whips out his note-paper, which shows the royal warrant. I said, 'I think that's fantastic – a soap with a coat of arms on it!' I call Michael Gould, the President of J.W. Robinson's. So as of today, all twenty-eight Robinson's carry Floris's soap with the royal wrapper. He sold $55,000 worth of soap through *one* phone call!

The thing I couldn't believe was why people don't come out to this market. They regard LA as further away than Hong Kong. I've talked to dozens of people from Britain and they say, 'It's not worth the trouble,' or 'It's too far.' One man came to see me from Barnsley and said, 'I make pumps which do forty to a hundred gallons a minute, or whatever – and these are very special pumps.' He asked me how many I thought he'd sell. I said, 'You could do $250,000-worth of business a year.' He said, 'Oh it's not worth all the trouble.'

I thought, Jesus, if it's not worth it to do a quarter-of-a-million-dollars'-worth of business, what's he out here for? And of course I discovered the government had paid the bill for the trip, so he's just having a little jolly which is tax-deductible, a market-research trip. The man's not serious about doing business. . . .

THE DOWN-MARKET
CAR DEALER

I'm trying to make good. . . .

Things have not always gone too well for Kenneth Crutchlow. A cheerful cockney chappie, he left Bethnal Green in 1965 at the age of twenty-one to hitch-hike round the world, living on his wits. He reached California in 1969, liked the look of it, and became janitor at a San Francisco hospital. He was made hospital press officer, married an American girl, moved 60 miles north to Santa Rosa in the vineyard country, and started importing old London taxis.

Then he sponsored a man who rowed across the Pacific, and went on to raise ten thousand dollars for the release of Richard Knight, an Englishman jailed by the Vietnamese when caught searching for Captain Kidd's buried gold on the isle of Con Tre Lon. Crutchlow felt some sympathy for the treasure-hunter because in his hitch-hiking days he had twice been mistakenly jailed – in India for murder, and in Japan for spying – but such quixotic financial adventures were to lose Ken most of his money . . . and his wife.

———

I'd often wondered where old London taxis went to die. . . .

This is the place. We bring in the parts from England and we can take a cab like this – looks a bit of a mess – totally rebuild it and get another half a million miles out of it, we really can. These cabs were running around the streets of London for at least half a million miles, easily.

You can't bring into the United States vehicles dated after 1967 without qualifying for the American regulations – and the fact is, London cabs nowhere *near* qualify. Previous to 1967 you can bring 'em in. This is why we have them this old. We've found there's a lot of people over here who kinda like 'em: real-estate men driving people round in the back to show them property, or as toys. There's a lot of people, particularly in Los Angeles, who have them as a fun car just to go and get the shopping on Saturday afternoon. This one here – this wing is orange because it's brand new – this sells for ten thousand dollars.

Come on!

Thing is, the freight cost of bringing everything over is very high. Then we bring over English mechanics. We've tried American mechanics but they just can't master 'em – so we bring them over from London; pint of beer once a week, and they're happy!

For ten thousand dollars you could get an old Cadillac. . . .

Not quite – the Cadillac's about twenty thousand dollars. The price of cars here is now quite high.

You were born in Bethnal Green – what made you think the wide-open spaces might be better?

I was an apprentice printer in London and I tried to join a rowing club on the Thames, but they didn't think I had the right accent. I never really got on with what I perceived to be the class system in London – it seemed the only thing I was destined for was a printer. I'd done my time in the print and the general attitude was, 'That's what you are, that's what you do.' I didn't seem to find the opportunity that would enable me to go up the ladder.

Some of the richest people I know are printers in Fleet Street – they're on the last gravy train!

Well I never caught the train – so I got the train out of England.

But you're not unconfident – I shouldn't have thought the class system would have worried you too much. . . .

It wore me out a little bit because I did always feel on the outside of it, frankly. I never really got on with it. One of the beginnings was my school-leaving report when I was fourteen. The headmaster, Mr Somerville, put on my report, 'Kenneth Crutchlow is a smart alec.' I could have done without *that* on my school-leaving report! I thought, This doesn't seem quite right. . . .
I always used to look at the map at school – this old geography map, and I was the only one in the class who could always point to the cities without having it written on the map. That was the beginning of my wanting to travel round the world. I went to sixty countries, and America was the last one. I did a lot of time going all through Europe and Asia, a lot of time in India, went to Vietnam for a while and then Australia, and came here last. Once I came to California I realized that this wasn't a bad place to be. And

amazingly, the class thing does not exist here. It's like it should be: if you have the ability to do something, you can very easily do it.

What did your parents think when you sailed away to make your fortune?

I was the first one out of the family; I'm the eldest of four, and they didn't really go much for the idea – most parents want to keep their family around them, but they didn't stop me. When I was arrested in India on this murder charge, and then they declared war with Pakistan, Mother sort of wondered, 'What's going *on?*'

I finally did get back and told them I'd decided I'd prefer to live outside of England, and they really worried about it. My Father's still in London. Unfortunately about five years ago my Mother died of a heart attack. She was fifty-nine and as a matter of fact she died in the back of a London cab! Amazingly ironic situation. She'd been down the pub in the East End with her sister and came out and had a heart attack. Amazing. An incredible coincidence that, dying in the back of a cab. You miss your Mother and you always regret that you weren't there, and should have been. What can you do? This is part of life.

You wanted out of England, yet you still think about it?

Oh very much so – in fact when Her Majesty visited America I was honoured by being introduced to her, and that was a highlight for me. I found myself to be a real royalist, and loved the whole thing. When I met the Queen it was wonderful.

So you're jumping on the class bandwagon, after all?

Well, yes. Strange, isn't it? What can you do? I don't necessarily think the Royal Family are in the same category as the snootiness. I mean class itself doesn't worry me, it's the snootiness about it.

But you're a sort of wide-boy – you're pretty sharp; I wouldn't have thought you'd be worried about that sort of thing, when you can look after yourself?

I guess I get intimidated a little bit by it. I don't fight it.

So have you found the classless society here, that Bethnal Green was not?

Well America *does* have its own class structure, of course, but right now I really don't have too much to complain about. I get invited to affairs –

like they recently opened a new hotel up the road and they invited me to the opening. I'm not quite sure why, but I went along and enjoyed it, so the class thing is just not the same as it ever was in England.

Yet I find expatriates around the world among the most class-conscious and snobbish of any British I meet. ... The remaining Brits in India – the remaining Brits in San Francisco for all I know – can be pretty damn snooty! They worry about titles. ...

That's true, and I generally avoid that. There's no point being here saying how wonderful England is and how terrible America is. I find that to be a bit odd. If it's so wonderful, they should go back.

Well *you're* saying how wonderful England is, what are you saying about America?

I like it. It's more direct.

Listen, yesterday at San Francisco airport I had my briefcase stolen with my passport, money, credit cards, driving licence and everything that supports life – and *you* had your car stolen?

That's right.

Yet you still like it here?

I got my car back! (Laughs). They called me at four o'clock this morning and said, 'Sir, we've found your car – it's out of petrol.' I think the people who stole it are a bit miffed it didn't have a full tank! Anyway, it's only down the road. There's crime in America, as there is in England. Six weeks ago I was in London with a chap from the *Daily Mail*; we were at Tottenham Court Road station, he went down to his tube and I went to mine. Next day he called and said he'd been mugged! On Tottenham Court Road station! I was quite amazed.

You feel safer here?

A little bit, yeah.

You married an American girl?

That's right. Met her here and have been very happily married for ten years. I got into some financial difficulties, I really overdid it, ended up with too much money going out and not enough coming in. Classic business thing! I think the stress and strain of it all ... we had some difficulties and basically we're temporarily separated, for now.

She's gone?

She's not gone altogether. I didn't kill her off and put her in a bin. No, we're separated. It was the stress of what I was going through. It was better that I lived in Santa Rosa, and she lived up the road.

She's left you to concentrate on your cabs, and she's earning more money than you are?

That's right.

So you were spending her money, right?

That's, er, a direct way of putting it! (Laughs).

Do you feel, Ken, that you've made it?

I'm *trying* to make good. I don't think I've made it yet because I've lost a lot of money, but I've got the opportunity and I'm going to take advantage of it.

Might you have done better if you'd stayed in Bethnal Green?

Ah, that's always the question! I think the secret is, you've got to go to work for it. The streets are not paved with gold. If you're prepared to put in the hours and work hard, you have the opportunity to be successful, and I think that's the key.

So why haven't you done it?

Well I *have* made the money, once. Two things I've done recently: I got involved with the rowboat to Australia. I've no regrets about it, but I did end up spending a few bob on that. Then even more recently there is a chappie got himself in jail in Vietnam that I helped to get out, and his fine was ten thousand dollars. I took the company money and used it to get him out of jail. Those kinds of expenses from a small business create a bit of a problem, so the lesson I've now learned is that when you're in business with yourself, you mustn't take the money out and use it for unrelated expenses.

So now you're back where you started?

Yes, I suppose I really am. I've still got my house and a few cabs.

But no wife?

Unfortunately she is very much a casualty of it all, and I'm sorry about that, very sorry.

There's no question of your giving in and going back to Bethnal Green?

I think I'll finish what I began. I do have some debts, I mean, there's no question about it, I have some obligations here in California. I don't have any obligations financially in England, so I intend to stand my ground here and see it through. . . .

THE HEAD OF PROTOCOL

Every eye in the room was riveted to his glass. . . .

To hear the well-modulated tones of the Head of Protocol for the House Foreign Affairs Committee you'd think she should be looking after dignitaries at Buckingham Palace – yet she left England in 1948 and has been showing them how to do it up on Capitol Hill for the past nine years. Mrs Elizabeth Daoust, House Speaker Tip O'Neil's right-hand lady, comes from Herefordshire and appears to be the only Brit on The Hill. A handsome divorcee in her fifties, she is formal and discreet; to question her about the procession of world leaders who come wending their way up Capitol Hill with their begging-bowls would have been like expecting a lady-in-waiting to reveal the secrets of the Queen.

Mrs Daoust has three all-American upwardly-mobile children, lives in the fashionable Washington suburb of McLean along with the Kennedys and the CIA, and exudes a smiling but decorous air of formality which makes you suddenly aware of your table manners.

———

Are people surprised to find a quiet and restrained Englishwoman welcoming them to this seat of American power?

They don't think of me as an Englishwoman – I'm an American or I couldn't work here. Everyone on the Committee has to have a Top-Secret clearance. I've been a citizen for twenty years, a taxpayer; it's not a good thing to live in a country and not be part of it. I wanted to vote. The children know that they are Americans and their roots are here – and so why should I be the only foreigner, so to speak? Then when we go abroad I'd go one way and they'd go the other!

How do you think of yourself?

I know where my roots are, or were, but I think of myself as being American and have done for many years. Accents mean nothing in Washington, there's so many of them!

I married a man who came from San Francisco; he was an army officer, so that's the reason I've lived all over the United States at various times, plus four years in Paris and two years in Germany.

How did an English divorcee come to achieve such a position?

Sounds very frightening, calling me that! It happened – *both* things happened – roughly about the same time, which is why I took the job. I'd been married for twenty-eight years and had three children and suddenly there was a divorce, which is a very tremendous step and an emotional time and I, for the first time, had to start thinking about doing things for myself rather than *en famille*.

Could you imagine doing such a job in Westminster?

I've been to the House of Commons two or three times, either officially or on my own. Speaker Thomas showed me around, but I don't know how they operate. Our House is relatively new to this sort of thing; it was usually done by the Senate, but a series of circumstances forced the House Members to do a little more. . . .

Entertaining?

It's not so much entertaining – you see this Committee among other things has a responsibility for the Foreign Assistance Bill. . . .

This is where the money comes from?

Exactly! They legislate money, and the Foreign Assistance Bill is very important and very large. They legislate and then it's sent to the Appropriations Committee, a very powerful committee also, who decide exactly how much money goes where, but the House Foreign Affairs Committee does all the legislation. So you can see why foreigners want to come here and see the Chairman and talk to members ... it's very very important to them. Then also when our members from the whole House of Representatives go overseas, they're always treated very nobly.

The Chairman of the Foreign Affairs Committee is given the responsibility for the reception of all Heads of State and foreign dignitaries. A Head of State, if he's here at the invitation of the President, immediately wants to come up here. In the last few years Third-World countries have finally realized where the money is – it's in the House, not in the Senate! And of course they all want to have as big an exposure as possible and that's why there's a tremendous number of requests. Almost everybody who comes, the first day they see the President or the Secretary of State, the second day they want to come here.

Let's say Margaret Thatcher or Mitterrand or a Head of State or a Prime

Minister comes, the hosts would be the Speaker and the Chairman of Foreign Affairs. All the members of this committee would be invited, plus the Chairman and ranking minority leaders of all the big committees of the House Appropriations, Defense etc. So when we had Sadat and Begin during the Camp David peace conference, we had almost four hundred Members. It just depends.

When did you start your present duties?

Almost nine years ago, and there's never a dull moment; the place is never the same two days running. Now I've worked out a *modus vivendi* it's much easier than it used to be, but you never know who's going to show up at these things. I remember we had Juan Carlos from Spain, and the Speaker's office called me five times. He's coming – no he can't – yes he is – he absolutely *cannot* come – and with that the Speaker walks through the door with the King! So you never know. That's why it's fun to be with the House because they're very flexible and freewheeling, and you just move everybody down one.

Americans are known for their exuberance and friendliness, but perhaps not always for their grasp of protocol. How do they take to you telling them what to do?

I don't tell them what to do, no, not at all. I send out a letter inviting them and then we set up a meeting at a time we think would be best to get the most Members. It's a very difficult thing because people who say Yes they're coming, don't. People who say No they cannot, show up. You never know quite what they're doing: if something comes up on the Floor, they must go to the Floor. We've had many meetings when we've had three votes – when the bells go, you see, they have to leave.

When you return to England do you feel at home, or strange?

It's always lovely. I love England, it's very beautiful, but it's changed so much that sometimes I really don't quite know where things are any more. Where's the Café Royal that I remember? Piccadilly used to be so elegant, and I don't think very much of what they've done to Leicester Square.

When you retire from here – this is the *significant* decision – where will you go?

My brother lives in a lovely little part of Devon, and has an old vicarage. I was there in June and every evening we'd walk up to the pub and the mists would come rolling in from the sea, and it nurtures one because it's so gentle. But America is very exciting and you feel there are worlds to conquer, rightly or wrongly. That's how I feel now, and I'm very glad I feel that way because it took me a long time. But of course children are a great stabilizer.

They decided they were Americans long before you did?

Oh, no question! They all went to a French school, and they've lived in California and so on, but Elizabeth the oldest went to college in California and then to Harvard. Ellie's married to a man in the State Department. Ann went to school here on the East Coast. In other words they go to Europe, but this is where they belong, this is where they *want* to belong. Never has there been any question about that. If they had married an Englishman and wanted to live in Europe, that's something else. They know Europe, they go there all the time; it's very important to know where you come from.

This is an easier place, a more satisfying place for a woman alone?

I must say I've never known such kindness and generosity, and it's still the same way. It was a particularly emotional and difficult time for me.

They came and offered you the job, you with your English accent?

They don't notice it – at least no one's ever mentioned it. Look at the Speaker, no one could be more Irish than him! I don't think he's ever noticed that I have an accent – if he has, he's never said so. Here if you do your job and they like it, it doesn't matter *where* you come from.

But you created the job?

Yes – and it's grown, like Topsy. You can't do it for nine years without all kinds of strange and odd things happening. When we had a Prime Minister of India, Mr Desai, several years ago, a week before he arrived there was lots of publicity and *Time* magazine printed an article saying he didn't smoke or drink, he didn't drink tea or coffee – but he *did* drink a glass of his own urine every day!

So at the lunch I said to the waiter, 'Be sure and put a glass of fruit juice for the Prime Minister.' I suggested orange juice but he came back and said there wasn't any. I said, 'Well just get some juice.' He came back with a glass resplendent on a big silver tray – apple juice! He put it down in front of the Prime Minister and every eye in the room was riveted to his glass. They were thinking: is it or isn't it?

Did he drink it?

No, he didn't touch it – but every eye in the room was on it. ...

THE DOCTOR

*Some sort of great breast the entire population
has to suckle from birth to death. . . .*

Dr Paul Buisseret practised in Norfolk and Ilford, at St Mary's Paddington and Guys, on cruise liners. He now lives at Covington, one
hour's drive from New Orleans across Lake Pontchartrain on the
world's longest highway bridge: 23.8 miles of brackish water. His
wife Jane is a surgeon in a hospital near the Slidell Memorial, where
he has a flourishing practice. Their house on a wooded estate backs
on to the twelfth hole of the Covington Country Club.

Though Dr Buisseret does well in Louisiana he finds, surprisingly,
that people are suspicious of doctors: his neighbours do not return
invitations. He is also unimpressed by the banks and even had difficulty depositing the fourteen thousand dollars he brought with him
in 1979. One bank clerk, hearing he'd emigrated from England, was
most disapproving: 'Don't you think that's very disloyal?'

Though he still sends to Oxford for books and enjoys a glass of
port, Dr Buisseret has so grown into the American lifestyle that he
spends two hundred dollars a month on his psychiatrist: 'Wonderful
man – remembers everything. I love a good cigar but I'd rather give
up my cigars than my shrink.'

====

I was at St Mary's, and I was a ship's doctor back in the Sixties. I had
lunch with the surgeon on the *QE2* and he told me that if I stayed on the
ships another month, I'd never get off – the life was too good! He'd been on
it twenty-seven years. So I blasted myself off the ship with terrible reluctance. They almost had to put me on the baggage conveyor, I could hardly
bear to walk off.

I came here from Guys, where I was a senior registrar, in '79. I wanted
to do chest medicine very badly and there's a tremendous shortage of chest
training jobs and consultant jobs in the UK. The Louisiana State University
in New Orleans happened to be looking for someone who was interested in
chests and also in immunology, which is what I'd been doing up until then.

When I was at Ilford Hospital we had to have a special committee meeting
– that never actually came to any conclusions – to decide if we could afford
a bed that cost about £800. When I came here we needed a new lab that

336

cost about $82,000 and all I had to do was ask, and justify it. It was discussed once and ordered, without any messing.

It really drove it home to me how bad it was, outside the teaching hospitals. At Guys and St Mary's you were, to some extent, coddled, but you get out to the district general hospital and intensive care is the bed nearest Sister's desk! They have no facilities to put patients on mechanical ventilators. If you needed a ventilator you either died, or you were put into an ambulance and driven somewhere else. That was endlessly frustrating, because part of my training was in intensive care.

The reason I left England was political. I disliked being a Government employee. I don't believe the National Health Service is for the likes of me – but that isn't really a full answer; I think restlessness, curiosity, wanderlust. ... I'm earning more than I was earning in Ilford, but that certainly wouldn't be enough to make me leave England, no. Once you earn enough to keep body and soul together, other motives take over.

Do I get the impression you're working less hard than you were at Guys?

Absolutely not, I work phenomenally hard here all the time. There's no such thing as days off or signing-out to someone else. One of the pleasures of working here is that there is endless scope to work as hard as you like. I didn't come here to take it easy.

At Ilford I think they had a monitor, although I can't be sure; I remember being very frustrated because there were no ventilating machines. It was primitive medicine compared with this and yet the hospital here, bed for bed, is about the same size as dear old King George's, Ilford. So the two hospitals are comparable in size, the towns are comparable in size and yet here you're talking about *real* medicine, there you're talking about excellent first aid.

Real medicine – what do we mean by that?

The ability to care for the community without shipping them off to a large centre when they get more than trivial routine work-a-day illnesses. Here we ship very little to large centres. We can cope with most things up to intermediate-level brain surgery – certainly any major cardio-pulmonary disease, orthopaedics, without having to bring people in to do the fancy work or worry because we don't have the equipment. If we don't have the equipment, we *get* the equipment.

I don't think the American public would accept the standard that's been established as the norm in National Health medicine in Britain. They would abandon the hospital if it offered that, and that only. They expect to get the best we can provide, and if we don't provide, they'll go somewhere where they *can* get it. Obviously there's more opportunity to spend money on facilities here, on plant, on equipment, on beds and ancillary things, because it isn't the Government dishing it out. The hospital charges patients for its services, and the money is ploughed back.

We do hear the most frightful stories about American medicine – about ambulancemen going through your pockets at the scene of the accident to make sure you've got a credit card before they'll take you to hospital ... about being charged $5 an aspirin in hospital and people presenting the bill while you're full of tubes in Intensive Care. ...

They are 99.9 per cent propaganda. There are rotten hospitals in the United States, there are rotten hospitals in the United Kingdom. I've never seen anyone asked for money when they were in Intensive Care, and if an ambulanceman frisked them or asked them about their financial status he wouldn't stay in his job for a week. There are bad stories, probably a lot of them put about when the National Health Service began seriously to falter. The so-called 'Envy of the world' suddenly turned out not to be quite as good as all that, so when bad things happen somewhere else, this is broadcast loudly in the UK.

Yet I have to tell you that many of the Brits I talk to here say they put at the top of their list of the things they miss about England, the National Health Service ...

I think they're absolutely right. If I broke my leg in a road accident or developed acute appendicitis I'd just as soon do it in Ilford as I would in Louisiana. However if I want to have my hip replaced or my hernia fixed up, I'd rather have it done here tomorrow, rather than there, three or four years down the line. And if you're talking about poor medical standards, that counts. I mean, most medicine is not major trauma or brain surgery, most medicine is hernias and peptic ulcers and angina, and that just *isn't* catered for in Britain outside of the major teaching institutions, the ivory towers. They surely are superb, but ivory tower medicine is for the few. Most medicine in Britain is not of that standard.

You say patients here wouldn't stand for the calibre of much British medical attention. Are they more demanding, more difficult, more outspoken?

All of the above. As far as technical ability and knowledge is concerned, the well-qualified British doctor is as good as the well-qualified American doctor, and again there are duds in both countries. The whole idea that there's something different about American medicine is wrong. The puddle is really small now, the two countries are very similar – it's just that there's *more* medicine available here, patients are more critical so they're more aware of the possibilities that medicine can offer them. They expect to have that, and they're prepared to pay to get it.

In England there's a sort of stoical attitude that one has to be grateful for every little thing. The fact that you're taxed through the nose to pay for it, you forget about, and you think, Oh we'll grin and bear it, rather like post-war rationing. Health rationing, as it exists in England now, is accepted – mostly because people haven't really known much else. I think if they did. . . .

Your Intensive Care ward looks marvellous to me, yet this is not a modern hospital?

This is quite ordinary – it's a good average district general hospital and certainly not exceptional, not a show place by any means. Yet it's fun and I'm very proud of it. But when I went back to England a couple of years ago and tried to practise as a Consultant chest physician there, I found I couldn't do it.

There's the endless frustration of wanting to provide the standard of care that I've been trained to over here, and not being able to do it simply because it was technically not possible. The equipment I needed was in another hospital miles away, and I had to catch a bus to go and use it. Most of the lab work had to be done in some other building because they couldn't afford to build it in my hospital. . . . I suppose once you've tasted the forbidden fruit of the United States, you can never go back.

Your wife is a doctor in an emergency ward?

In an emergency room, an accident room in another hospital about fifteen miles away.

She's having a more exciting life than you?

I think mine's quite exciting – a different sort of excitement. This town is at the junction of three interstate highways and American drivers are, I'd say, about on a par with the Poles. There's a fair amount of carnage going on half a mile from here, and we get a lot of trauma.

Then there's the violence on the streets, which is at a higher level than Ilford?

It is in the big cities – one thinks of New York and Chicago, and New Orleans too. Neither my wife nor I have been raped yet, although my mother-in-law expects it at any moment. . . . So far she's remained disappointed.

Is there a higher level of health awareness here, are people better educated to look after themselves?

I would say they certainly are. They're more interested in sickness prevention, rather than waiting until illness overtakes them.

My impression is that in English hospitals some patients are too frightened of their doctors to find out what's wrong with them. ...

Really? I've worked on the NHS for eleven years and I don't think people were frightened of me or of the hospital. You surprise me.

Perhaps you're approachable, but surely a lot of doctors prefer to remain remote godlike figures in white?

Makes you wonder why they went into medicine in the first place, if they want to be gods! I could be a god, but I don't suppose I'd have as many friends – or as many patients either.

A smiling god, perhaps. ... America is such an intense place I get the impression people are either screaming with joy or screaming with pain. There's not much quiet resignation here?

Americans tend to live lives of a soap-operatic sort of nature. They watch a lot of soap opera, they expect to react to situations dramatically – they never have discomfort, they're always in *agony*, there are never minor annoyances, they go crazy! Everything is terrific, it's never adequate. This hyperbolic approach to life is the way the average American housewife faces life's little problems. They're always slightly dramatic.

Brits living here all tell me they're frightened of the *cost* of being ill.

I think they're wise to be. If you're not insured when a visitor to this country you're facing the possibility of major expense if you're taken acutely ill. If you come here without adequate medical insurance – as I understand you did – you're a brave man. I wouldn't want to be uninsured – not that I would be allowed to lie bleeding in the gutter if I didn't have insurance.
The way things work, if you're ill in America you're taken to the nearest hospital. Even if you haven't got a plugged nickel, that's all right, they'll look after you, they'll what we call *stabilize* you, as long as you're not actually dying. Then if you're broke and uninsured you'll be transferred to one of the public hospital facilities, which are usually attached to teaching hospitals and which are very good. I've worked in one for nearly six years

and my wife trained in one. It's a bit like MASH, but the calibre of medicine's excellent and people are not allowed to bleed to death – that's a popular myth. In six years I've never seen anyone actually go without essential treatment for lack of money.

And secondly, what would you say about your hernia in Burton-on-Trent which gets repaired a year from now – but tomorrow if you've got money? If *that* isn't suffering for lack of money ...! Or your grannie's hip won't get fixed for two years unless she can cough up twenty-five hundred – in which case, 'When would you like it done? Next week suit you?' So it's a bit of a hypocritical attitude to take. The National Health Service is really a National Illness Service.

Is there any difference in the treatment of black and white patients?

Um no, not in terms of quality. Of course there's more poverty among the black population. They tend to be more commonly under-insured or uninsured, so the public health hospitals have a higher proportion of black patients than the private institutions.

But black or white, they expect doctors to have a cure for everything?

I think people the world over think the answer to everything comes out of a bottle of medicine, which of course it doesn't. Yes, they expect the goods.

I've never been sued, but colleagues of mine who *have* will tell you the most litigious patients are also the patients who haven't got any money. They're often welfare cases and they sue much quicker than the average middle-class person will.

It seems to me that medicine in America is not so much a vocation as a very well-run business?

That's absolutely true. I think you're dead right. If success is measured in terms of dollars, then your remark sums up medicine in the United States to perfection. I can't improve on it. I think that a vocational drive to practise medicine in the United States is as important to the practice of good medicine as it is anywhere else, but it is – you're right – a very well-run, very tightly run business.

I also get the impression that surgery is more common here, that patients go on the operating table and under the knife far more quickly?

You're right, elective surgery is commoner here. The immediate assumption would be that the surgeons have their knives in their breast pockets because that's how they earn money, and the more operations they do, the richer they are. I think to a certain extent that's probably true. But the other side of the coin is the surgeon who says, 'Well Mr Whicker, I'm sorry about your hernia, we can probably do that for you three years down the road – unless of course you can *pay*, in which case we'll get you into the London Clinic tomorrow afternoon if that's convenient.' So that's another side of the coin, equally unacceptable. But you're right, a lot of wombs and gallbladders get done, a horrifying number of babies get delivered by Caesarian section. We ourselves have a baby coming next April and I'm rather anxious that it's born by the normal route. They'll section a patient because it's their weekend off or they have a fishing appointment this afternoon. . . .

I can't *bear* it! One hears of preventive surgery for heart bypass operations when someone says, 'This chap's over sixty and one of these days he might need it – let's do it.'

I've never heard of anything quite as gross as that. Triple bypass surgery is performed much more commonly in the United States than it is in England, and I think more often than it needs to be, but the whole question of the benefits and risks of bypass surgery now is being questioned, and fewer operations are being done on either side of the Atlantic.

My experience with American medicine is that there's almost a superfluity of equipment and an anxiety to leap to the knife, to put you into surgery. If you've got Bell's palsy, say, they'll operate right away without waiting for nature to take its course?

I think your average American specialist is a pretty greedy sort of individual who has his mind more on what your money-generating potential is, than whether he can actually do you any good.

I've done several programmes on plastic surgery in Beverly Hills, where they have assembly-line operations in the doctor's surgery, and I'm told one reason for that is that you don't have many good anaesthetists here?

That's not true. They have to pay for good anaesthetists if they're doing it in their offices, and that would reduce their profits. Slidell is the same size, within five beds, as Ilford. Ilford is a good paradigm, I suppose, for a district general hospital, and Ilford was a very good first-aid centre. If you broke your leg or cut yourself or had to have your appendix out, it was as good

342

as anywhere else. But if you were seriously ill, they couldn't handle it at all. Anything beyond a straightforward uncomplicated stroke or coronary would have to go. It was presided over by an administrator I wouldn't have employed as a cook or a bottle-washer – an ignorant person of no education. They had a strike – I can't remember whether the ambulance-drivers were telling us who we could admit or whether the porters were. It was the sort of thing I'm so glad to have got rid of – when the janitor tells you what he regards as a worthwhile operation. . . .

That's intolerable. We've seen on television senior surgeons going out and pleading with pickets to let cancer patients through in ambulances . . . and picketing porters saying, 'No, we don't regard that as urgent.' There's nothing like that here?

Not at all. I enjoy going to work, look forward to being busy. Some friends of ours came out from London recently and phoned me from Chicago and said they'd phoned several times and I wasn't in. I said, 'I didn't get in until after eleven last night.' 'Oh you poor thing.' I said, 'You don't say that to a busy doctor in America, you say that to one who's *not* busy.' We actually like what we do and get on with our patients and they think we're nice chaps.

In England there's a hospital doctor and then there are other doctors, and you only see hospital doctors if you're in the hospital. Here it's the *same* doctor. They don't see anybody else unless they need something that's outside my field. If they need surgery or a heart test, I'm not a cardiologist so I'll ask a colleague to come and do whatever he has to do. He'll tell me what he's found, and go away again. He doesn't hang about.

Is it a good thing to be English, or do you think they regard you as a Shakespearian figure who's behind the times?

They certainly don't regard me as that. I think they like it. In America whether you're a doctor or a lawyer or an engineer, the fact that you speak English automatically imbues you with some extra avoirdupois – that it must be truer, or much more worth listening to. If you ask a question at the end of a lecture, because it's an English voice they all turn round and look!

The patients are aware that doctors do all right and at first they're a bit wary, although the fact that I'm English is novel. I'm regarded by my colleagues as being terribly conservative. I don't leap about and start doing procedures immediately, though they're very lucrative. I only do them when they're absolutely necessary, and they think that's good. One of the most rapacious doctors in Slidell said to me, 'You know, I *like* that. If you want to do a bronchoscopy on a patient I can reckon that he really needs it, you don't just do it for the box.'

And what percentage of doctors would just do it for the box?

Well I haven't actually carried out a poll but I would say seventy per cent. I don't mean that would be their sole motive. If it was a toss-up whether it was clinically indicated, that would be enough to tip them over.

They'd be easily influenced?

Yes, they're looking for the chance.

Could you see yourself eventually retreating to England – or are you going to be buried in Louisiana?

I'm certainly not going to be buried here – I'll stay here and retire to England when I'm ready, but as to going back and working there, no I can't do that. I've tried. There's no way that I can do that.

Because you think the Health Service is becoming decrepit?

It's already *become* decrepit. It's a sort of mental attitude – and doctors will be fuming that anyone could criticize this great Utopian dream. I think it's important to believe in a health service – you've got to think it's the best way to deliver health care to the British public. But if you don't – and I don't – then you're better off out of it, because you'll never be happy in it. That's why I don't work there.

I really don't believe in an across-the-board state-run health or sickness machine. It doesn't work. It doesn't work in England, it's bankrupting the country. It doesn't work in Canada – and incidentally I was in Canada when it made the transition from wholly private medicine to wholly national health. The same thing's happening, or beginning to happen, in the United States. They've already got, essentially, a national health service for the poor, for the old. If you're over sixty-five treatment is, or very soon will be, completely free, and I think it's only a matter of time before some sort of national health system will operate in the United States.

And you think that's a retrograde step?

Yes, I do, I absolutely do. I think you've got to look after the old and the poor, let me say that immediately, but I think that people don't want to be looked after all the time. People who have jobs and buy their own homes and so on, *expect* to look after themselves. They want the responsibility, they want to choose a doctor, choose a hospital, decide what happens to them, pick their school. This idea that the State has to be some sort of great big breast that the entire population has to suckle from birth to death is repugnant to most ordinary reasonably-educated earning people, I think, not only in America but in Britain as well. People are sick of being told what's good for them. I've got a reasonably good idea and I'd rather follow it up and if I'm wrong, there's only me to blame. That's why I don't want to practise in Britain. I don't want to operate a state-run benefit system that I think is poor and would stand a lot of improving, and yet I can't do anything to improve it.

Is there such a thing as a house call here, any more?

No, I made my last house call in 1968. I used to do rounds on a Saturday, back in the Sixties, on my old ladies, most of whom were a bit decrepit or had blood-pressure problems or swollen ankles and made nice chocolate cake. I had to make a round on a Saturday morning and have coffee and cake with them.

So what happens today to similar decrepit old ladies?

I don't know. That was when I was a general practitioner. I don't know what happens to them.

They expire quietly into their chocolate cakes?

Maybe. . . .

THE DEMONSTRATOR

The women marry a bank account, mainly. . . .

Mrs Anise-Yvonne Palladino picked me up in Neiman-Marcus on Wilshire Boulevard in Beverly Hills. She was in fact accosting customers to demonstrate a rejuvenating cleansing cream in the cosmetic department, and had detected an English accent. Doubtless also a tired skin.

Born in Cheshire, she arrived in Miami with her Italian-born husband and son in 1979, and moved on to California for its better schooling. Her husband opened a restaurant and her sixteen-year-old boy fell into the Californian life with delight. As a freelance demonstrator in Los Angeles department stores Anise-Yvonne probably talks to more strangers than your average attractive blonde. . . .

━━

Miami Beach is a pretty horrible place. I would liken it to landing on the moon, only with a lot of sunshine instead of the dark. It's flat, concrete, boring, uninteresting – and unfortunately the majority of the people tend to be that way. Their mentality is the same.

At one time I believe it was very exclusive, but the influx of immigrants from Haiti and Cuba were attracted to living on the beach areas. The accommodation situation for poor people is a little easier – they could sleep out on the beach, even, in the colder times and and still not suffer. I think this tended to dissuade a lot of the better-class people from frequenting the place.

Many people suggested for my husband's talent he would be better suited for California, and we'd been told that the education standard was a little higher in California, more opportunities, should we intend to make this a permanent thing. The alternative at that time would have been that we would have returned to Europe. We were disenchanted with Miami Beach at that point.

Ideally I would have liked to have gone back to England – not necessarily Cheshire, though my home is there. But there are many things in favour of staying in California. The main thing is the weather – it's perfect all the year round. Even in mid-winter it's equivalent to our summer days in July in England. There are a lot more opportunities. In England unfortunately to rise to the top you have to climb the so-called ladder. . . . Here the ladder,

346

rather than being the traditional ladder where you start at the bottom and work your way up, the ladder here is more horizontal – you can step on at any section, depending on how strong your desire is to succeed.

Your boy would rather stay here than go home?

Fortunately, or unfortunately, he's *quite* convinced this is going to be his main country. He still has attachments in England – my family's there – but for vacation purposes only.

The kind of work you're doing now, you talk to more Americans than the average person does in a day – how do you find them?

The fact that I'm British I feel is a little novelty to them. They still have the feeling of, How quaint! Something like a toy in a toyshop, something to be talked about or shown off to their friends.

Can you imagine doing the work you're doing now in, say, Harrod's?

The English area of approach is a little smaller. The Americans are more open, especially with fragrance promotions. To walk up to somebody and encroach upon their private area is a little more difficult in England.

That man who just came up and helped himself to a great splodge of your cream – an English person wouldn't have done that?

Not at all – they would ask first. They would say, 'May I try it?' or 'Is this for the public to try?' There's a little bit more grab-and-take here. This is the way of life.

They don't seem to have private areas here, do they – they come straight in on you.

That's true, and in one way this is very good. I'm quite a gregarious person, I enjoy speaking to people, I enjoy meeting people. Even if they say No, that doesn't upset me. When I'm working, I'm on stage, I am acting my part. . . .

They can seem rather brusque to me – there's a little more rudeness than in England or Japan?

This is because the culture level is completely different. It's something a British person first coming here can't understand – their ways. It felt alien to me, but maybe I've become accustomed to it. I tolerate the rudeness now,

I tolerate the brusqueness. Fortunately I've never had that directed towards me, I've just seen it around me. I've observed it. Particularly, many of the assistants in the stores do *not* have the patience, they don't have the politeness that you would find in most European stores. An assistant here could be rude to a customer and the customer would still spend a hundred or two hundred dollars, and just accept it, I've seen it.

'Do you want it or *don't* you ...?'

'Don't waste my time if you're not buying today!' But I think this is the way they expect people's approach to be. I've come into contact with people from the East Coast, mainly from New York, who're very abrupt. To the British person they would be very rude. There's a large influence of New York origin in Beverly Hills. It's probably the people who have made their money by the sweat of their brow and they've brought their wealth over to luxuriate in the bosom of Beverly Hills, but they've brought their street mannerisms with them. Unfortunately among the things that money can buy, breeding is *not* one of them, and this is quite evident. The diamonds and the furs and the trappings of wealth are visible on the people, but when they open their mouths the words they say or how they speak or conduct themselves ... also in situations where they're eating ... it is quite obvious they're the *nouveaux riches*.

They can buy their English butlers, they can buy the books to read about the correct way to do things, they can hire their servants to perform in the correct way for entertainment purposes, but their lack of knowledge in these things is evident in the way they conduct themselves.

This is the reason for all these self-help books, how to be this, how to do that, how to improve yourself?

Exactly. Miss Manners says this, Miss Manners says that ... and more often than not Miss Manners doesn't know herself.

Along with the lack of manners goes a certain instinctive friendliness, or do you merely find them self-obsessed?

Very. It's the 'Me' society. Everything is 'Me'. They are superficially friendly. I'm not impressed by people's overfriendliness, I sometimes step back mentally and think, What is it that this person *wants* of me? And usually there is something. It's not genuine. When you first meet people here it's, 'Oh this is lovely, you must come round for a meal, we must do something together.' They offer the world, but you know that if you *did* contact them they'd probably say, 'Oh, what is your name? I can't remember when we met.' A British person would not offer so much but he would genuinely mean it. Here the words trip off the tongue very lightly, but you can never respect the promises that are made.

And yet your son is happier here than he would be at home?

He is happier because he *has* more. . . . There are lots of things to distract young people here. He goes to school with children who are far wealthier than we are, who are connected with the entertainment industry, who've always got something interesting happening. He's invited to their homes, he's included in activities that he would never dream about in England.

All these sixteen-year-olds with Porsches?

There's a lot of affluence around.

Are you worried about drugs? It must be hard for him to avoid peer pressure?

Not with my son! If he hadn't had a strict and proper upbringing in England I probably would worry, but he's been brought up to know that Yes means Yes and No *doesn't* mean Maybe. If he desires to do something he knows that he has to consult his parents first. He's sixteen in January.

In England when you're in your forties, you're virtually getting ready for your old-age pension, you're practically a grandmother. Here you can still be young. Not that you want to be a teenager in mini-skirts on roller skates, but you can still do youthful things and not be thought of as an oddity.

Joan Collins is a fiftytwo-year-old sex symbol!

This is marvellous! If you desire something strongly enough, people encourage you out here. Though they're very 'Me'-oriented, it tends to be an artificial situation. They're thinking of impressing people all the time. They're trying to grasp what they've never had. They love to be associated with people who have been part of their roots. This is delightful for Europeans here, but it is usually for their own reflections. It's like – how many umbrellas do you have? You only need one umbrella to keep the rain off, but you have one to match *every* outfit here. It doesn't matter if it never rains.

Do you find the men different to English men?

They're very open with their appreciation. I'm married, so I haven't had any intimate contact with American men, but viewing the relationship set-up here, the woman is the one who sings the song and plays the tune.

349

The man dances to it. It's a strange situation. They're very appreciative of minor things. They would say to their companion, 'This is delightful food' and it's been bought in from an outside caterer. They would compliment the hostess – not that she had cooked the meal herself – and say, 'You've arranged the evening beautifully and the food is delightful.' They are overly appreciative of women. They don't expect much – they've never been *given* much. Maybe it stems from the pioneer days when women had to do men's jobs and pick up a rifle and shoot the Indians on the horizon.

One notices how much more predatory women are here; they're the ones who ring up and say, 'How about it?'

They have taken on a lot of male dominance. The men are so appreciative of the scraps that are flung to them – it's rather like the dog at the table! It's a sad situation. American men are extremely hardworking, more so than a lot of British men; they not only work at one job, they have two and three jobs. They play very hard, and the women spend their money very hard and do *little*, very hard!

The women marry a bank account, mainly. This happens all over the world but here there's a lot of divorce and the next time they marry I'm sure it's not for affection and genuine love, it's 'How much more can this man give me than the last one I had?' It sounds horribly bitchy, but this is how I view it. . . .

THE DEPOSED

Someone has to keep me in gin and mink. . . .

The American business world is known to be ruthless; Colin Draper from Chiswick, a New York executive for seven years, suffered a startling descent from company President with yacht and limousine to unemployed executive – but the axe that fell so abruptly in 1983 was wielded by an English conglomerate. He and his wife Veronica live on the thirty-fifth floor of a giant forty-nine floor block on Manhattan's East Side, with staggering views; and there they sat to experience all the withdrawal symptoms – and the curious reaction of their friends. . . .

===

You were President of Thomas Tilling in America – what did that entail?

Determining what we should do to invest our funds. We had nothing here in 1977, when I came; at the end of the day we had between $600 and $700 million invested in the United States, which was about a third of the total funds in the group worldwide. In the period until about 1982 we acquired thirty-seven companies in various trades and industries. I had ten people in the head office with me and about ten thousand employees, and we were contributing half of the Tilling Group profits worldwide, so when the axe came it was slightly unexpected, and also rather frightening. The take-over was over £800 million, so it was a shock in a sense that one thought it really unlikely it could ever happen.

You suddenly lost your position – you were out in the cold?

It was a take-over, a completely bitter take-over, and from the outset BTR said if they were successful they would dispose of the senior management of the whole Tilling Group. They were able to tuck the things we had under their existing organization in one way or another, to relieve themselves of those of us they didn't need, and that they did – in my case, in a rather unceremonious fashion!

Sir Owen Green seemed to feel that the right thing for me was to go back to England the next day and be fired on the basis of the old salary I had before I came here. Unfortunately he wasn't prepared to discuss this at all. In his own words, I had to take it or leave it. So on the advice I'd received I didn't take it, and we had to litigate to get a settlement.

David Lloyd-Jacob was telling me he got a golden handshake of $600,000, which he used here to get himself off the ground again....

When threatened with action unless we could get a reasonable settlement, BTR's last word to me was £40,000. It was at that stage we decided we weren't going to get anywhere by talking.

How did people react to you as a suddenly unemployed ex-President?

A general and genuine wave of sympathy went round, but then after a time I think people found it rather embarrassing that I was still here and still unemployed, and it became a little more difficult to maintain some of the relationships. Possibly they felt as one does if somebody in the family has a serious disease and you don't really quite know how to cope with talking to them....

They showed their sympathy by dropping you?

They sympathized at first, and then I think they felt that if they couldn't do anything practical they might be better off just staying clear for a little while. I wouldn't like to put it as ignoring, but there was certainly a period when we saw less of some of the people we knew.

Perhaps they feared some of your bad luck might rub off on them?

I think that's quite possible. They might have thought the disease was contagious! They might even have thought I was going to touch them for money or something like that, which could be even more repulsive!

Veronica: The people in England seemed to be embarrassed about everything and didn't want to come anywhere near me, didn't get in touch or contact me or anything. Somebody did actually say, 'Well it's like there's been a death in the family, we don't know what to *say*.' Whereas over here people were ringing up, meeting for lunch, this that and the other. Maybe Americans are more used to that sort of thing than we are in England. In England it's quite serious, I think, to lose a job.

A job of *that* stature after all those years, I suppose perhaps it is. ... Here you go up quickly, but you come down even faster?

Colin: Absolutely. Quite. We do have a totally different set of friends now than we had eighteen months ago. They get tired of saying, 'How're things going?' and they can't think of anything new to say. I don't know why they can't go back to being their old selves and talk about anything. You begin to think it's *you*, but it's not. They're so tongue-tied they don't know what to say to you.

But even with the sack, you weren't exactly on the breadline? You got rid of your yacht, the company car was whisked away?

That's right! (Laughs). It would have been overnight except for, er, physical resistance. We kept the car for a while, then somebody very foolishly ran into it, so I asked through various routes, 'Do you want this car repaired before you get it back?' They replied, 'We want it back like that, and we want it back *now*.' It's not, I have to say quite honestly, a serious disadvantage in New York. If I want one, I hire and drive it for the day. The cost of keeping a car in New York is astronomical. The parking here in the building on a monthly basis was three hundred dollars a month, which is now two hundred and fifty pounds, just to leave it here. If you leave it while you're in a theatre, that's another ten dollars every time. So if you use the car regularly and keep it in the garage you really do have an enormous outgoing, not talking about wearing out the tyres or anything like that.

So what are you going to do now, Colin?

I'm still struggling hard to acquire a company. I have two or three in my sights. Everything takes a long time, even here.

You're not thinking of putting your money into zero-rated bonds and sitting back and accepting thirteen per cent interest?

Oh no, after a few years in America you get *that* sort of thinking out of your head. I want to try to get on the board of one or two British companies which are operating over here, and try to be helpful to them. I've gone on to the board of Tate and Lyle and another British firm in the management consultancy head-hunting field, and I'm talking to seven or eight other companies at the moment.

One of the disadvantages of the freedoms that there are here is that people borrow to the most alarming extent, and speculate with the borrowed money right up to the hilt. Youngish men who worked for me who had good jobs and their own houses and so on would mortgage and re-mortgage their houses to screw every last dollar out, so they could invest it in some scheme: put it on the stock market, build a condominium which they would let – and then mortgage *that*. They get money very easily, and so they are at greater risk.

One of my chaps who was very very bright, a senior American, once said to me, 'You must realize that the first objective of any successful American executive is to make himself financially independent of his company.' They work at that very determinedly the whole time. It has a good effect on the relationship in a way, because the more independent they become the more likely they are to be polished with you about things you're discussing. De Lorean is the ultimate effect of the disease, I suppose, if it's not checked in time. Americans generally like to borrow money, like to use money, and so therefore are suitably at risk.

In the major sense, business here is pretty honest. There's an awful lot of petty dishonesty but that's much more of a personal nature, and of course there's vast *political* dishonesty, but as far as senior business people are concerned, they're an honest and honourable lot of people to do business with.

Veronica: Most young women, if they're stopped by a policeman, say they always hand in their driving licence with a twenty-dollar bill folded inside it, and the driving licence always comes back minus the twenty-dollar bill, with, 'Have a nice day, sorry I had to stop you.'

Colin: In some of the building construction we did here, changing offices and things like that, it was people like the liftman who had to be bribed to bring stuff up and down. He would say, 'The service elevator is fully booked tonight, no more space.' There had to be negotiation, and money had to pass.

There are certain industries which are labelled as being basically dishonest, with large payments and payoffs being made where it's known that organized crime people have their hands on the distribution chain.

We used to live on Park Avenue, and walking up and down the Avenue never seemed particularly worrying; it's some of the side streets that are inclined to be a little bit murky. We have a friend who ran one of the banks here and lived in the United Nations Plaza flats, very nice apartments which were terribly tight on security. He decided one night he needed some cigarettes and kept walking to find a tobacconist. He didn't find one until he got near the West Side bus terminal, which meant he'd gone across about eight avenues. Then somebody tried to grab his money, and stabbed him. He was in hospital for two or three weeks, having been stabbed in the chest quite close to the heart. These things do happen.

Veronica: I think we just accept it, but the places I wouldn't go here are the places I wouldn't go in London. I mean I wouldn't want to be alone in Soho or in Hyde Park at midnight, and the same here. I have to go through the Bowery, where all the drunks hang out. The first time I took Colin he nearly had a fit! But if you're just friendly with them they won't come anywhere near you, particularly if there's a woman in the car. As long as you know your place, and don't go walking about at night. I *have* done it, but I walk very fast. If you're brisk and you look as though you know what you're doing, nobody comes near you.

A friend of mine was made an awful mess of the other day by two muggers: two black eyes, bruised face. It was two young guys on 28th Street, just off Park Avenue on Saturday afternoon. Nobody else in the street, and they pushed her down to the ground. She had a raincoat on, with five dollars in her pocket, and they wouldn't believe her when she said, 'This is all I've got.' They called her all the nasty names under the sun and kicked and shoved her and it was only when somebody else came along they left her. She was in an awful mess.

Somebody did very well out of me the other day on a Fifth Avenue bus. I'd just been to the bank and I'd two hundred dollars in crisp notes – I hadn't touched any of it. They took my whole wallet out of my handbag. It was my own stupidity: I was strap-hanging and I had a couple of carrier bags and I knew what I was doing but I thought, Well the bus isn't very full. ... Normally I have it underneath my arm. I thought I was alert and watching what was going on. I was *so* cross when I got off that bus. I knew who it was: a young girl.

I think one of the funniest things in the summer is when you go into a supermarket, and I've honestly seen this happen at d'Agostino's: it'll be ninety degrees outside and a woman will put on a big thick angora sweater before she goes in to shop, because it's going to be so cold inside, and I suppose it is. Normally as soon as we've had Labour Day you see the fur coats out immediately, even though it's seventy degrees. Mind you I don't even buy heavy clothes here in Manhattan because in the middle of winter it's so warm in this apartment: the apartment above is so warm, the apartment below is so warm and at either side of us they're pushing so much heat into here. We just keep cold air coming out of our air-conditioning unit.

We actually got stuck in an elevator here the other day; there's a telephone inside, so you're in constant communication. The other elevator tended to answer most of the calls, but when that was busy ours answered them but of course the doors would never open. It was an extraordinary thing, every time it came up as far as the thirty-fifth floor it didn't worry me, but the moment it went past our floor I thought, We're going to shoot out at the top of the building! The top floor is the forty-ninth, and both Colin and I went quite white. We were very worried, because it was territory we didn't know. It seemed so high. We were on our way out to dinner this particular evening and when we got to the restaurant the first thing Colin asked for was brandy!

The rudeness I will never get used to – the filthiness and dirtiness I honestly don't notice. I just don't see it. It upsets so many other people tremendously. But I don't think however long I live here will I *ever* get used to the rudeness. That's something that upset me when I first came here, and for the first six months I loathed it, loathed New York with a passion.

Absolutely hated it. I mean, it was difficult to go out and buy a pound of tomatoes because I'd get the 'Quit the please-and-thank-yous, lady, what do you *want?*'

Colin: I think it's very much a feature of New York. One should never generalize about the United States by pretending it's the same everywhere else. There's more anxiety in New York, there's more fighting and struggling, there are more people who come here because they think this is the great opportunity and they're going to get on the ladder, so there are obviously many more disappointed people who feel disadvantaged, resentful and angry. I think everyone's attitude changes as soon as they cross the bridge. As soon as they get into the hustle-bustle of New York City, it's all go go go: I've got to move as fast as possible, I haven't time to say please or thank you or anything – it's *boomph!* Back home in Connecticut in the evening, they're totally different characters.

Everything extends from this petty attitude everybody has here, which is that you should be allowed to get away with whatever you *can* get away with – that you're not being smart unless you get away with all you can.

Coming back from England the last time, I got into a cab at Kennedy Airport with a very nice man who's an American top civil servant. He'd been the trade negotiator. We waited ages for cabs and finally he said, 'Would you like to share?' We got in together and on the way out of the airport the driver turned round and said, 'I'm gonna charge you two fares.' My companion said, 'You won't do anything of the sort, you're going to take us into the city and we just want two drops.' The driver said, 'Two drops is two fares, I'm not taking you any further.' So this American, a very nice distinguished elderly gentleman, this diplomat sort of chap sitting next to me then stuck his head through the hole to the driver and said, 'Now you listen to me, you fuckin' arsehole, I've lived in this fuckin' city all my life and you'll take us and you'll charge one fare for the two of us or I'll have your fuckin' badge.' Then he sat back and said, 'Now what do you think about the Taiwanese imports situation . . .?'

We got where we were going and we each paid half the fare and that was that. But if it had been you and I together, he'd have got away with it. He would have considered himself smart. If he told the story that he *didn't* get away with it, his pals would think he's rather stupid; but he was bullied into giving in, and he gave in instantly.

It's a city of petty crooks and bullies about everything, whether it's crossing the street or anything else. What can I get away with? It's almost unique to New York. The rest of America tends not to behave like this. In San Francisco they have a traffic-light system which everybody obeys, where all the lights are red at one time so pedestrians can cross diagonally, and the traffic waits. Here they won't even stop when the lights are *red!* They just want to keep going, they can't bear the idea of being told what to do.

It would seem if you've got to be out of a job, your thirtyfifth-floor apartment with this view is not a bad place to be?

Veronica: It's wonderful, isn't it! I keep going from one end of the apartment to the other, looking at the view, in case we have to make a rushed exit back to England – because you can't replace this anywhere.

You'd rather he soldiered on here, with the view *and* the rudeness, or would you like to go back to Chiswick?

I'd rather he soldiered on here. That makes me sound as if I'm going to make him work until he drops! But I think as much as I eventually would like to go back to England, I would find it rather difficult at the moment. I'd probably find it a wee bit slow and maybe just a wee bit boring. I think it'd take a little time to adjust, as it took me time to adjust here. I think I would find that – it's awful to say it, isn't it – I think I'd find the pace a little slow, and *someone* has to keep me in gin and mink . . .!

THE LANCASHIRE LAD

They all think you live in a castle and your ancestors were Vikings. . . .

Tony Corbett arrived in Texas from Bardsley, outside Oldham, at the age of twenty-one; his father was a truck-driver and none of his family had been out of England. Now he's a member of the Houston *jeunesse dorée* earning more than all of them put together – and still can't quite believe his luck!

He has an apartment in an 'adult' development for singles with clubhouse and pool – but no pets or children. As vessel operation supervisor in charge of six geophysical survey ships, he can afford to take flying lessons, dine out four or five times a week and, when home on leave, escape from Oldham to fly his girlfriend to Paris. His money is invested in two properties – in the Lake District, not Texas!

＝＝

I was just turned twenty-one – January '82, and England didn't really offer me what I was looking for, the opportunities and things like that, once I came out of college. I was working in Manchester for a construction company, found it extremely boring. I never thought of coming to America but I saw this opportunity in the local paper, applied myself and took a gamble. They took a gamble on me as well, of course, so I had to prove myself.

What sort of money are you now earning?

In pounds sterling a considerable amount, in excess of £25,000. That's just the basic salary, and then all the rest of it on top of that, you know. You're getting towards £30,000 or more, depending on what you do. If you go out on location you're going to get more money: I'll get living allowance and it just goes on and on and on. I calculate I'm earning far in excess of *all* my family put together!

My father was a truck-driver but he's semi-retired due to illness several years ago. He's now got a much better job – a game warden for the local authority. He's very happy. My brother's married with a family and works at the RAC. My sister got married three weeks ago when I was in the Arctic Circle – I'll never live that one down because I wasn't home! She works for

Boots the chemists in Oldham. So I come from a very basic sort of back-ground.

Did they push you?

No, I did it all myself. I did it for my parents. I thought, It's about time somebody in our family did something different. Now I earn more than *all* my immediate family – mother, father, brother, sister and their wives and husbands all together.

If you'd stayed in Oldham you probably wouldn't be earning £30,000 or more a year at the age of twenty-four?

No way, no way at all. Probably be lucky to be on £8,000, or even less.

Yet for the job you're doing, you're not being overpaid here?

By US standards, probably not. I'm sure for what I do and the hours I put in, which are very very long, I could get a lot more money working for a US company doing the same sort of thing.

You hadn't travelled at all, so when you left Oldham you came in at the deep end – and you took to it?

Like a duck takes to water!

What is there about it that you like?

The opportunity – everybody you meet gives you an opportunity. No matter what you're doing, everybody will give you a chance. People back home don't give you that chance – you're always too young or you haven't got enough experience. Of course if you don't prove yourself here, then you're out the door as fast as you came in but. . . .

Did you have problems?

Tremendous problems. I was the first Brit to come over for the company and we didn't realize the problems we would have setting up: large deposits on an apartment, large deposits on telephones and electricity. Nobody knows you, you're a foreigner, so it takes a lot to set yourself up because you don't have a credit rating.

What about the social scene?

Great, it's a young person's town! If you're young here, it's where it's at. You know, you can really go out and swing – yes you really can.

Do they understand what you're saying?

Half the time, no.

That's a good thing?

That's a good thing, yes. Once you open your mouth you score – well socially, you know. It's a sort of, 'Oh he's British, great. From the Mother country.' They say, 'If he's from the Mother country he's all right.' They all think you've been to university at Oxford or Cambridge and live in a castle and your ancestors were Vikings. They're all into that sort of thing.

But how about your Oldham accent?

Well sometimes they say, '*That* sounds a little strange.' Sometimes it gets me mistaken for an Australian 'cos I don't talk extremely posh like some, you know.

But you can turn it on? That might help.

It does help, yes, quite often. When I'm working I get real Oldham. When I'm talking to the lads it's, tha' knows, y'know, and all that. Then when I'm chatting up a young lady it's, 'Oh I say you're *radiant* this evening' – and away you go!

There's a predominance of women here?

Yes, and they portray themselves very well. I like the Texas women, all glamorous and independent. They all drive cars and have apartments and they've all got money. They're independent, you know. You don't have to go and pick her up every night, she'll meet you somewhere or she'll come and pick you up. She'll call you, you don't have to pay for all the meals, you don't have to pay for all the cinemas – she'll meet you half-way. You can insist on paying, if you wish. Back home if you ask a girl out you have to call for a start, then you have to go and pick her up and take her home and stuff like that. Here you meet them somewhere, they've all got cars and they always have a place of their own to go to.

Sexually it's more relaxed than Oldham, I suspect?

Yes, I would say so! You see some sights, I'll tell you. A bit rowdy on a Saturday night, yeah, you see some sights. Skinny-dipping in the pool, things like that.

You're not thinking of settling down with some Texas Rose?

Not really. If you find a Texas Rose, she only wants to go and stay with you in England, anyway. When you meet a girl here and she finds out you're from England, she wants to go home with you.

They want to get married, do they?

Well I won't say they want to get married but they certainly want to go and see England, and so on and so forth. Basically they want to be on the other side of the pond, and you want to be here.

This bar is where we come to pull the birds every Friday night after work, Happy Hour – get some neck oil and away you go. This is where it all starts. We get a few down, you know, litres of Margaritas half-price, and away you go! The world's your oyster.

You're earning more money, you're meeting more girls – and a better type of girl, you say – are there are disadvantages?

There are a lot of disadvantages. It's still difficult to live and work here because I'm still a foreigner and day-to-day life does get difficult. I still haven't got a credit rating – I couldn't for instance buy a car on credit, I had to buy a car with cash. The banks are very difficult to work with. No matter how long you stay here, you're still an alien.

You only have to get stopped for speeding on a Saturday night and there's no questions asked, they just slap the handcuffs on, whisk you away – and you spend a night in jail. It might only be a speeding offence, but if he doesn't like your face. ... And they intimidate you. They're *supposed* to do that, actually, they try to get you intimidated to see if you've been drinking or not. They don't have a Breathalyzer. If you get stopped by a police officer he will intimidate you into becoming aggressive because they consider if you become aggressive, you've been drinking. So quite often he'll say some very rude things to you, like, 'I don't like your face.'

That's not *very* rude . . .

Well it gets a bit stronger than that. They call you things like 'scum' and all this sort of thing. You've got to keep cool. Don't say anything but 'Yes, sir,' 'No sir,' and you'll be all right.

Have any of your friends been arrested?

We've had a couple of people arrested, yes. They spent the night in jail. We went down there and bailed them out the next day. Paid cash.

Really – no receipts?

One time yes, other time no. Depends who's on duty down there, and that sort of thing. Say no more.

I'm twenty-five in December and I might consider a nice car when I can afford the insurance. My age goes against me here in the States, for what I do. I can't buy insurance for posh cars. People say to me, 'Now wait a minute, you shouldn't be doing this, you're not old enough.'

That's weird – I thought America was a youth-oriented. . . .

For twenty-four years old what I do is quite incredible, even by US standards. People say to me, 'You know there's something wrong here.' My age goes against me all the time.

In Texas a man only feels full-grown if he's got a gun . . .?

Every household has guns of course – three, four, even five guns.

Have you got one?

I've got a shotgun, yes. In fact I've got two shotguns, one's in for repair at the moment, but I only do clay-pigeon shooting and things like that. Of course ninety per cent of the cars would have a gun in the glove compartment or under the seat.

That can make driving rather more dangerous . . .?

It must, because someone will come along and you'll do something he doesn't like and he'll honk his horn, but you musn't shake your fist at him or anything like that because there's a good chance he'll be aggressive and the next thing you know you'll get a bullet through the windshield! Happens all the time, you see it on the news – shoot-outs on the freeways. Quite amazing.

You can just go in any store, you can go in a sporting-goods shop in the shopping mall and as long as you've got a Texas driving licence, you can buy a gun. This is why I get annoyed, because I have such a hard time establishing myself here. I'm a foreign alien but all I need is a Texas driving licence and I can buy a firearm, although I could be a terrorist or something. It's only seven dollars to get one.

Everyone has quite a short fuse here?

They're a fiery sort of nation. You're in a traffic jam at one hundred degrees of heat you know, and tempers flare very rapidly.

One of the worst climates in the world!

I would say so. That's one of the things I find very difficult. I don't think I'll ever really get used to the climate, especially when I'm working outside. You go into air-conditioning and you get cold, then you go outside again; the next thing you know, you've got flu. There's a hell of a lot of flu going round, believe it or not.

Also there's a pretty good chance if you're walking around late at night, there's going to be somebody lurking round the corner maybe looking to rob you. The Houston Police Department put out circulars and information papers and they actually advise you, they can almost *guarantee* that if somebody enters your home with intent to rob you, that they'll also be armed – because he knows *you're* going to be armed and you're going to use it. So it's a confrontation situation – it's a question of who pulls the trigger first.

You're quite a well-built young bloke but you can't take care of yourself against a Saturday Night Special, can you?

No, not at all. Everybody says, 'I'd blow his brains out,' but I mean – would you really do it, *could* you really do it? Maybe if he's got a gun on you, you probably could. I might shoot his kneecaps off, or something like that. I don't think I'd shoot to kill anybody, but they do say if you're going to shoot them you've *got* to kill them because he's going to come back and get you – or sue you anyway.

Sue you for causing him grievous bodily harm!

If he breaks into your property and you shoot his kneecap off, he'll sue you for that! You've got to shoot his head off, and then you're OK. You say, 'Well he was breaking in and he was threatening,' and that's fine – they replace your carpet! So it's a crazy situation.

The other thing is, although there's a lot of giving and taking here, this is quite a lonely place; do *you* every get lonely?

Yes I do, quite often. I do get lonely. If everybody's out of town, quite often there's not much to do. You find yourself on your own a lot. You have a specific area of friends and if they're all busy one night, you just get lonely. I'm lonely a lot of the time. Get homesick, you know.

At Oldham you'd go round to your mum's, right?

Yeah, you go round to your Mother's, like, and watch a bit of TV or stroll down to the local. You don't go to a bar here and sit on your own. There *are* singles bars, if you're into that sort of thing, but it just wouldn't be the same as going to the pub, like at home. If you wanted to go out for a drink on your own you're guaranteed to meet somebody you know in the pub, but here if I went to a bar I would be on my own all night, because you're a bit *strange* going to this bar on your own, unless it is a singles bar.

The other thing about life out here is that since it's close to the Mexican border, there are a lot of drugs around?

You come into contact with drugs daily, you really do. If you go to a social gathering or a party, it's there. It's everywhere. People offer you coke all the time. They say, 'Do you want to buy?' I had a party one time and I found a sludge of cocaine in my bathroom – I couldn't believe it. It was the first time I'd come into contact with it. I was quite amazed. But what do I need drugs for? Beer and my pipe will do me fine!

Can you see yourself staying here for the rest of your life?

In all honesty, no I don't think I could.

So where will you be when you're an aging thirty-one?

Hard to say. I may be in Singapore or on the other hand, I could be back in England.

When you do go home to Oldham these days, what's it like?

You run out of things to do on the *first* day! You walk down the High Street, you go to the bank – and that's about it, really. All the pubs shut, so on and so forth. I normally go home once a year for say three weeks, and by the end of the first week I'm ready to come back again because I've done everything I need to do. I've gone and said Hi to everybody, and I'm looking out for shooting off to Paris for the weekend or something like that – or coming back. It's a bit of a disappointment really. It's a shame.

Trouble is you've grown into such a sophisticated international figure!

Do you think so? I don't know about that – I'm *working* on it, though!

THE FILM STAR

After a while, lotus-land begins to pall. . . .

Christopher Lee was for years the best-known name in Horror. Leaving the RAF, he had made his film debut in '47; tall and articulate with an actor's presence, he soon cornered the macabre market in Frankensteins, Jekylls, Fu Manchus, Rasputins and Draculas – but ten years ago escaped Transylvania for the broad uplands of Hollywood and a modern book-lined apartment on Wilshire Boulevard, with his Danish ex-model wife Gitte.

I first visited him there in '79 as his film career flourished – in two years he had appeared in fourteen films. He was delighted they had emigrated and pleased with the place, if not its social system: 'If your last picture made money, you have a higher social status than if it lost money. If you are working and successful, then some people will think it's all right to be seen talking to you. But the climate speaks for itself – it's gorgeous. You have sunshine for eighty per cent of the year, so in that respect it's good for your health and good for your soul – and if you've got a peculiar back like me, it's marvellous.'

He has grown less enthusiastic – even about the climate. . . .

When life in California seems to be getting better in many ways, why are so many British talking about leaving?

I think they feel that after a while, lotus-land begins to pall. The sun shining nearly every day can become a little monotonous. It's a sort of sameness. This is an artificial city in many respects. It has a great deal of the plastic about it, and these people have decided they've reached the point in their lives – young, middle-aged or old – where the plasticity and the artificiality overrides anything else: material comforts, standards of living. . . . They've said to themselves: My background is European, my roots are European, my familiarity with places, sights, sounds, smells even – the smell of the air – is European. I miss that so much that I would rather go back there with the change of seasons, with weather which is not so good, possibly with higher taxation . . . to be happier, to enjoy a greater feeling of cosiness and tolerance, and be more at my ease.

There's more culture there, certainly. There's more tradition, certainly. It is two separate worlds, and you have to decide which one you want to live in. It's as simple as that. Where will I be happiest? Do I want to lead the life of a lotus-eater because of the endless sunshine, because of the standard of living, because of the fact that some things are much cheaper than they are in Europe?

The material side has never been predominant in my life. I've never been controlled by money and I've never allowed money to control me. Do I want to live that life and become bored with it after a while, or disillusioned, living an artificial existence where everything is controlled by money and nothing seems to matter – when you get right down to it – *but* money, and what money will get? Where everything's in figures and there's practically no judgement? Admittedly that does apply mostly to show business. . . .

You see five years ago you said to me, and you'll remember I used it as the title for a *Whicker's World* on California, 'Nothing is Utopia, but this comes pretty close. . . .'

When I said that, I meant it. But things change, it's as simple as that. Attitudes change, ways of life change. I think it's also the older you get – that would certainly be the case with me.

You don't think you'll find yourself living in Marbella next year, and saying nostalgically, 'Remember that wonderful restaurant on La Cienega. . . .'?

No.

Or, 'I wish I were back playing eighteen holes at the Bel Air Country Club?'

Yes I would say that, wherever I lived. Of course I would, because this is something I'm going to miss a lot. There'll be nowhere that I can live in Europe, as far as I know, where 365 days of the year I could play golf if I wanted to. It's ten minutes from my home. That I'll miss a lot – but I have to tell you, that's just about all I *will* miss.

I'm personally only concerned with where I would be happiest. Where do I want to spend the rest of my life? Where will my wife be happiest? Where will our family be happiest – our daughter's already in Europe and has been for nearly a year. . . . Where do I have most of my friends? Where will I have conversation about things other than grosses and who's getting paid what for doing nothing, virtually? Where will I have the theatre and art galleries and museums and concerts? In other words, material things rapidly lose their charm and appeal and the gilt really does wear off the gingerbread, there's no question about it, for all the people I've talked to – and that includes myself.

So it's a question of your roots, background, tradition. The pull sometimes becomes so strong that you say, 'I would rather go back, make less money, possibly pay more tax, but be happier and have a greater peace of mind.'

There's less tolerance here than there is in Europe. People are very friendly all the time, but it's mostly on the surface. They are not very sympathetic. If somebody becomes very sick or very ill they say, 'Tough.' Friendship here is based on convenience, to a great extent, not on genuine feeling. In Europe when you've got a friend, you've got a friend. God knows a friend is something very rare in life – you have thousands of acquaintances but how many friends, true friends? I know I don't have many.

Everybody here's very kind on the surface and very appreciative, particularly if you're successful and you're well known. That of course is one of the less attractive aspects of show business out here – and there are *many* unattractive aspects of it. Somebody who has gone back to England, a well-known person, told me, 'There are three things I don't like about show business in LA: incompetence, treachery and fear.'

People gravitate here more and there's more money to be made, therefore the greed is greater, therefore the cover-up is greater. Now in show business there are lots of pros and cons in every sense of the word. The problem is, we have more cons than pros! There's no secret about it.

The only thing is, this *is* the capital of show business; wherever else – you'll be on the periphery.

That doesn't matter. I've established myself here. I'm perfectly satisfied that I came here for the right reasons and if I decide to leave I will also do so for the right reasons. And the intervening period of nine or ten years has been of great help to me professionally. That's not going to change, because if people want me to take part in an American film which is financed here and made in another part of the world, I'd get on a plane.

Apart from the golf and the weather here, is there anything else you'll miss?

Perhaps the degree of energy. . . .

The fact that telephone engineers arrive the next day and get it done?

Yes. But that's really about all, because I think that efficiency is a myth anywhere in the world. I don't think any country is super-efficient – except possibly Switzerland, where we used to live.

The image of Britain now is not very inviting: the miners and Scargill's contrived strike, the violence of the massed pickets, the weather, the economic decline. . . .

You won't get an argument on that. I get the British papers here a day late and read them with mounting dismay, as you can imagine. You're quite right, the economic situation is not good, with over three million unemployed, inflation at five per cent with no signs of coming down, the strike's been on for months . . . and the violence on the picket lines is something I never would have believed – even after the violence of the football matches. And the taxpayer's going to pay for all this. I think Macmillan, Lord Stockton at ninety years of age, put his finger on it in his speech. He said, 'What a tragedy that you can find amongst those who beat the Nazis people who will throw ballbearings and Molotov cocktails and petrol bombs and darts at their fellow man. . . .' I don't know what the answer is.

This is a violent country, full of explosive situations and hostilities and weird people – yet it's all happening in law-abiding Britain.

One of the reasons it's not happening here is that it is against the law for a public servant to go on strike.

It's also against the law to be a Communist?

Yes it is. Scargill *calls* himself a Marxist and McGahey says he's a Communist – one wonders where they take their orders from. . . .

Curious how this country seems to manage its labour affairs much better than we do?

I think the reason for this is that there's more money available for the management of these affairs, which thereafter gets you a far greater number of qualified people who've been trained to operate at a civic level. You've also got a far stronger police force. Crime is fought by people who can deal with it in an equally violent way, if necessary. That's not necessarily the answer for us, but I do think the laws in Britain are weak in certain areas. The powers of the judges and the courts are not strong enough and the sentences aren't either. I would have thought that was obvious.

The reason there's more violence here is because there's more money to be stolen. There's more money to support the forces of law and order, to back them – and there's more money to be robbed. It's on both sides of the coin. There's more violence because anybody can have a gun, and also we have a far greater racial mixture in the United States – people come from all kinds of societies, varying from the hyper-civilized down to the primitive and almost barbaric. . . .

THE BATTERED WIFE

*I ran away taking the baby –
and the dog, of course. . . .*

Most of these enterprising Brits who ventured into the New World to make their fortunes arrived in the United States with delight: one wept with joy upon seeing the Statue of Liberty, another heard lutes as she landed in LA. Hilary Brookes, a GI bride from Bedfordshire, reacted rather differently: 'I cried for an entire week.'

She had reached her husband's Louisiana fishing village, back in 1969. By the time their son was three she was divorced. Now he's eighteen and she is established in New Orleans, publishing a newsletter for the two thousand Brits in Louisiana. Despite her experiences and a life that even today is not totally secure, the spirited Hilary now has not the slightest intention of returning to her Bedfordshire village. . . .

I married an American GI in the Air Force. He was stationed not far from where I lived in Shefford, Bedfordshire. It was a small village and it seemed almost inevitable that I'd marry an American.

So he carried you home to the States; what was your first reaction?

Quite horrified. It wasn't at *all* like the movies. I knew he came from a fishing village, and had visions of Whitby or Polperro. . . . *Nothing* like that. It was a place full of filthy bayous, mosquito-infested swamps and rather primitive people, not at all like Shefford. The climate was also a problem because I was used to soft English summers and I was immediately catapulted into ninety-degree temperatures and oh, ninety per cent humidity, very heavy and oppressive. The food was a problem too, very strange, very different, very peppery, lots of strange fish, lots of rice. But that could be overcome, you can put up with that sort of thing and even quite like it, but as soon as we got here my former husband began to treat me as a chattel, as a piece of property. He'd beat me quite frequently and eventually started on our baby. He was probably about one and a half, two years old, somewhere in there, when he started hitting him. It was at that point that, despite the sense of failure, I decided I ought to run away and I did, taking the baby – and the dog, of course. That was a long time ago – fourteen, fifteen years ago.

How did you support yourself?

At first I worked as a waitress, then I worked in a factory, then I worked as a shop assistant and taught myself to type and eventually went into business as a freelance secretary.

Did you get food stamps, Social Security?

I didn't know about things like that. I had no idea they existed, so I just got my forty dollars a week from the waitress job and supported us on that. It was very difficult because you're what they consider a failure. There's no help for you 'cos you're not attractive to have around. There *is* help available but you have to be very very poor and very ignorant to get it.

How did you set about bringing up your boy?

I worked, usually two or three jobs at a time, to make enough money. I sent him to England for a year to my parents when he was five, so he did have that initial year which I think gave him a good start and allowed me to get on my feet.

You never thought of following him back to Bedfordshire?

Yes I did. As a matter of fact the strongest urge I had was to go back home, but of course you have to remember this is fifteen years ago and divorced women in a small town in Bedfordshire are not very popular. There was the social stigma of failure: 'Oh, she's divorced, watch out for that one.' *You* know. . . .

No I don't; some of my best friends are divorced!

Some of mine too, but that was a long time ago in a small provincial area in England, and I think I would have been suffocated a bit as well. My parents would have taken very good care of me and I would never have had the incentive to go out and do things. Here I *had* to do things, and then later on when I got all that out of my system Eric, my son, was already in school. To take him back to England would have meant him being put in a class two years behind because the educational system is so bad here, particularly in this part of the country.

So is Eric now a young Louisianan, or a young Brit?

He likes to say he's *harff* British and *haff* American. He's got the character and personality of a British person, I think, very gentle, likes animals, not violent as most Americans seem to be, very easy-going. I think he's more British than American, and he knows he is. He wants to go back eventually, I think, to join the Royal Navy.

The RN – not the USN?

No, we have British ships in here occasionally and he's talked to a lot of the officers and feels very much at home with them. He realizes that his soul is British, you know. He's seen the difference between the American Navy and the Royal Navy, and he much prefers the British Navy. He spent a lot of time with a bunch of the helicopter pilots from HMS *Fearless* and they're fairly crazy people, those fellas, and realized that he had the same sort of craziness which is very British I think, not American. Americans don't seem to understand our sense of humour. I've told jokes that have English people rolling on the floor and the Americans just go 'Huh?' It's because we're fairly clever with words, *double entendre*, and they're not.

He really has the same sense of humour as a British person and I think that's why he doesn't get along so well with the children in school – they couldn't understand him. It did create some problems but I'm still glad he's the way that he is, very British. I mean, he'll join the Royal Navy eventually, it's just that being in an American school his educational standard is not high enough, I guess, for a commission, so he'll have to go to college here and get some more education before he applies.

He does read a lot, which is something most Americans don't do. I have a lot of books and when people walk in, Americans always say, 'My God, look at all those books!' English people just say, 'How nice to see books.' You get those two reactions.

You were saying it's a violent society yet on a tranquil day like today, that's hard to imagine ...

Ah but at two o'clock in the morning you can get murdered right here. Several people *have* been, it's not unusual – or at least mugged. In the dock area alone there would have to be at least a dozen murders every year. When British ships come in we always advise them not to walk around unless they're in groups of three or four.

Have you been robbed?

A couple of times I've been mugged. We've had a burglary. I've had three very close friends who've been raped, one who's been murdered. Almost everyone I know has been mugged or robbed or had a burglary, but you learn to take care. You never leave your door unlocked and you try to nail your windows shut too. For instance, if I were wearing a pendant I'd drop it inside my blouse so nobody could see it when I was walking around. With a ring, I'd turn it around so that nobody could see the stone. You just learn to do these things, it's automatic. You walk as if you know where you're going and you know what you're doing. That way nobody will mess around with you. Yes, you learn to live with it. It's mostly at night but it can happen during the day – it can happen at lunch-time right in the middle of the central business district where all the offices are! There's no special time for it, but the majority do occur around midnight, probably when people have had too much to drink in the French Quarter.

That sort of thing can happen anywhere in the world, but you think there's a generally higher level of violence here?

There's violence in other ways too. You can feel it when people drive cars, it's, 'I'm not going to let you out there,' or 'You can't get in this line of traffic because I'm bigger than you are.'

That competiveness is one thing Eric does not have, that I do make an effort to avoid in him. I didn't like the 'kill or be killed' atmosphere. A couple of kids at his school committed suicide before final exams because they were afraid they'd fail and their parents would be awful to them. I *know* it's amazing when I'm talking about it now. It seems very odd, but living here it's par for the course.

I don't mean to down America; there are a lot of good things, otherwise I wouldn't be here – but it's like living on a volcano. I now understand why people do live on the slopes of a volcano – you just get used to it, because there are other things that compensate.

The compensations must be pretty damn good, that's all I can say! What are they?

Well, look around: this is a very beautiful city. Lots of things to do. We live in a nice area with a beautiful park and a zoo close by, in a safe area. That's a compensation. I've got a good job here now, I've got several things that I do. Frankly I don't know what I'd do if I went back to England. ...

THE RECTOR

We have two men, two women and one monk. . . .

The Rev. C. Hugh Hildesley, Rector of the Church of Heavenly Rest on New York's 5th Avenue, is a sort of Bulldog Drummond, a gentle giant who played rugger and rowed for Brasenose College before going into Sotheby's: 'I am the only ordained art auctioneer in the world.' His enormous church at 91st Street stands in a rather snooty area just south of Harlem and was completed in 1929: 'They paid for it in cash, just before the Crash.' In a frenzied ecclesiastical world of formidable television clerics and radio hot-gospellers endlessly bullying listeners for money, his church is calm, well-organized and moderately high – 'but no bells and no spells'.

The Rev. Hugh, now forty-three, had thought about the ministry from the age of seventeen but became Peter Wilson's protégé and in 1961 was sent to his Old Masters' Department in New York. After seven years as a part-time priest he was elected rector. He now has four assistants, and looks up to the Bishop of New York. His American wife is a landscape architect and urban planner; their son is at Sherborne.

═══

You came to America as an art auctioneer and stayed to be a clergyman – both rather dramatic and commanding roles?

There are some similarities which wouldn't necessarily be obvious. If you think of the auction rostrum and the pulpit as two opportunities to speak in front of a crowd about different concerns there *is* some similarity, and one's been able to exchange skills from pulpit to rostrum and back again.

You never get confused?

I haven't yet – though I have this nightmare that *one* of these days I'll get up into the pulpit and say, 'Lot 1!'

Your parishioners don't come round after the morning service and ask you to value a plate or a painting?

Only very occasionally, and then I remind them it's Sunday and the office will be open on Monday!

Are you doing any art auctioneering now?

I do some, mainly for charitable events. I'm still an associate with Sotheby's so I work for them on occasion; it usually takes the form of lecturing or talking to clients that I've known for twenty years, so I still have a very small finger in that pie.

Have you always had a sense of vocation, or did it blossom here in the States?

I think it was there all along. I studied Divinity at A-level and went to Oxford and studied Law. I felt I was following in the family tradition in becoming a lawyer, but I never lost my theological interest. Then I got very much involved in working at Sotheby's and a career in the art world. It was only after I'd been over in America for about eight years and life seemed to have a settled pattern to it that this sense came back, so I went to school at night and studied at the Institute of Theology which used professors from both Union and General seminaries. I studied for three years and then took the standard Ordination exam over here. Then there was the terrible problem: I was qualified to be a priest but still thoroughly enjoying working for Sotheby's....

So the decision was made, in consultation with the Bishop, that I would act as a priest when I could, and continue to work full-time at Sotheby's. That meant I was involved in this particular parish on a part-time basis, working here every Sunday and then doing hospital calls and counselling at night and being available on an emergency basis.

I don't see art experts as men of God – they seem to have such a strong sense of double-entry bookkeeping....

I hope and believe that my twenty years in the art world proves that a man of God *could* survive in the art world, and indeed I did and enjoyed it thoroughly. I would also state that the Church has not in its history been devoid of ruthless people as well, and so I think the commercial training has stood me in good stead, working in the corridors of church politics. I think there are good and bad people in both worlds, and in fact I've found a really high degree of similarity in the two efforts that I've made.

You were an assistant clergyman here for a while?

Yes, in this very parish. Then eighteen months ago the previous rector resigned after eight years to pursue other interests, and moved to Charleston, South Carolina. The parish went through a long search process when they looked at many candidates and then to my delight, and certainly to my surprise, came back to me and said, 'Would you be interested?' So I then went to my secular boss and said, '*Now* what do I do?'

He said, 'I think if you want to do it and they want you, then probably it's the right thing to do. We would certainly treasure a continuing relationship with you, realizing that you won't be giving quite as much time as you have in the past.' And that's exactly what happened.

This is a smart church on 5th Avenue – yet you're quite near Harlem.

It's a big church in a smart location, but we're very conscious of our need to reach out beyond this particular community, and we spend a lot of our time worrying about what is happening north of here. We're very engaged in Harlem – particularly East Harlem, the Spanish section. We've made a connection with the local Episcopal church up there, which is small and needs our help, and we're very involved in sheltering the homeless at night and feeding the hungry.

Yet 5th Avenue is the epitome of wealth?

That is exactly right, and I suspect that if I could characterize my dream it is to take what we have as our treasure here and help distribute it to those who need it, so that the community of this parish get used to the wonderful sense you achieve in doing your bit to help those who need the help. We've got a lot of programmes doing *just* that, which keeps the community of this parish honest and whole.

How did your congregation take to a British rugger-playing priest?

I think the initial thought was that I'd be rather stuffy – English and reserved. I don't think they really thought much beyond that. They were somewhat surprised that this rugger-playing Englishman turned up and regarded the best form of training for acolytes was to go on a rollercoaster in New Jersey! They're beginning to get used to the fact that we can have fun, that as a community we take what we need to take seriously, very seriously – but we also are people who enjoy being together. I think they're beginning to realize that some of my crazy ideas make sense, that we're not really very different just because we speak in a different accent.

How does your congregation compare with a similar church in London?

They possibly are richer than your average London congregation because there's an enormous amount of wealth. Our average age in this parish is forty-one, which is lower than a typical New York church and I think probably lower than many English city churches. We have a lot of young families here.

Churches seem to take a more dominant role in life in the States than they do in England, I'm sorry to say. . . .

I have a suspicion that might in part be due to their non-established nature, that it is of course a completely voluntary organization. It has no connection with the state. You have in America – as you have had since the Revolution – a great tradition of pluralism: you can be anything you want to be, and your church affiliation fits where you want to be and is not forced upon you. There is a tremendous tradition in this country of service, of volunteerism, and the Church has over the years been one of the natural avenues through which that is conducted.

I think if this congregation is typical, and I suspect it is, there is a great deal of pride in *belonging*, a real sense of involvement. This of course is partly engendered by the fact that the congregation supports this parish. We have to go out each year and raise the money we're going to spend in our programmes – it doesn't filter down from above. Indeed we raise it and we give some of it to the Diocese and the Diocese gives some of it to the national Church, so the connection that is made between the individual member and the Church is a very real one, because our programmes depend *entirely* on the amount the parish give us to conduct those programmes.

There are I would imagine something over fifty active Episcopal churches right in the immediate vicinity of the city, and because it is a totally free country and not an Established church, you have every other variety and denomination you could possibly want. If you've been through Harlem you'll notice a lot of store-front churches which would have tiny congregations, but they serve the particular needs of those who attend them.

Yet from Washington one hears more of Jerry Falwell and Billy Graham than one does of the orthodox church. . . .

The more evangelical part of the Protestant tradition in this country clearly gets associated with political movements, and is part of the concern for every election. Where does state and religion become separated? To what extent can religious leaders come in and advise their congregation on how to vote, or how not to vote? You get that, at the other end, with the Roman Catholic tradition here, where bishops make very definite statements about how their congregations are to think, politically.

Do you offer any political guidance?

I do not. I believe we are here to preach the gospel from the pulpit. We can certainly raise issues and *do* raise issues, but we're not in the position of prescribing to our congregations how they should think.

In addition to having all churches for all men, there does seem to be in America a desire for *instant* remedies? If someone is sick they go under the surgeon's knife instantly, if somebody has a little domestic problem, they go directly to a shrink. How does the Church handle this desire for life to be solved quickly, with one instant capsule?

We're very much aware that people come to their church in crises. It's almost a sense that we might be able to fix it for them on a rather instant basis, which of course is usually not the case, but they very much engage with the clergy in finding ways to attempt at least to fix the crisis. There is a tremendous openness in this country and an ability to admit that something is wrong, and there's also a wonderful optimism about the possibility of changing and fixing it. If one was to compare that with my own experience at home: in England we tend to take a more stoic view of problems and go down to the pub and moan about them a bit, but then head on back *in* to the problem, assuming that there's no way to fix it and that we're here to suffer regardless. That's a very un-American attitude to a problem. They're much more likely to say, 'Here's the problem, let's deal with it.'

In one of the newspaper advice columns the other day a second wife complained that her husband often used his first wife's name when they were in bed. The columnist replied: 'He needs professional guidance' – so instead of laughing him out of it or slapping his face, she was going to send him to some sort of counsellor – on so trivial a matter!

Sometimes there *is* an over-eagerness to get in to the professional's hands. In dealing with people who have these problems, who're looking for the professional fix-it person to help them, I find that with an hour's sitting down and talking, some standard common sense gets to the problem just as quickly as running to a professional office.

And it's considerably cheaper!

We spend a lot of time preventing people from running to the fix-it professional, and helping them realize they can often fix the situation themselves. A little bit of self-help goes a long way, aided by some common sense.

One of the dramatic differences here, Padre, compared to the Anglican Church in London, is that you ordain women?

The Film Star: Christopher Lee

The Battered Wife: Hilary Brookes

The Rector: The Rev. C. Hugh Hildesley

The President's Man: Dr Geoffrey Kemp

The Maid: Patricia Viveiros

The Actor: Jim Dale

The Maître d': David Cotterill

The Songwriter: Roger Cook

The Hansom Cabby: Brendan Fearon

The Social Worker: Mary Hayes

The Socialite: Jane Ylvisaker

Indeed we do, we've been ordaining women for ten years now and on our clergy staff we have two men, two women and one monk – so that we're well provided! I think having ordained women is absolutely *fantastic* – and I came from England where it was a strange idea. The fact of the matter is that we are talking about ministry to women and men and children. Women are not the same as men, and I hope never will be, and therefore in certain circumstances are able to reach where men cannot.

We share in our ministry in this particular parish as a team and I thank God that we have women on the staff, because they're absolutely fantastic. It means that we're providing a whole sense of ministry for those who come here, and I love the kind of mixture we attain that way and the sense that we are able to cope with every level of life.

Yet at home the Church Commissioners might give you an argument there?

They certainly would – although I believe there has been some significant movement, even in England, towards this. All I can say from my experience of having worked with ordained women from the moment it first happened is that the sooner England catches up, the better. It's really an extraordinarily fulfilling ministry that they have. And in answer to a possible question, as men do we feel threatened by this? Not at all. We feel fulfilled and supported, and we feel that we're sharing properly in the work of the Lord, so it's a wonderful thing.

I think England tends to be a little slow on change, and this is one change that I hope will happen in the near future. They really make an enormous difference to what happens in this church.

You met your American wife in England, I believe?

She was coming to be fine-tuned at Oxford and we met shortly after I'd gone to Sotheby's. We lived in London for three years and I came one night and said, 'I've got *wonderful* news, I'm being posted to New York so I'm taking you home!' New York is her city – and she expressed considerable disappointment! She loved London. She's now living within ten blocks of where she grew up.

I came to New York for two months twenty-two years ago and I've just gone with whatever decisions I've made on the way along. I think really as a family we regard ourselves as mid-Atlantic. We're rather happy in both places.

To me you're the quintessential rugger-playing prelate....

I might well be the only one of those you'll find in New York! We have, in fact, two English clergy on 5th Avenue: John Andrew down at

St Thomas's, also an Englishman – though I think he wouldn't describe himself as rugger-playing!

So you get together and put the fear of God into your American congregations ...?

Oh, we do. We get together and discuss how much more of New York we can take over, in a spiritual way! We have a lot of fun. His parish is a very traditional Anglican parish....

Even smarter than yours, possibly?

Very definitely. But he does a wonderful job – he's a real professional, he's done wonders for that parish, really brought it to life again. I don't think we see ourselves as competitors, but rather as doing similar things in different neighbourhoods. My church was built between 1927 and 1929 – they finished it just before the Crash and it's been rather well described as a mixture of Gothic and Art Deco!

It's not Macy's and Gimbell's – you *do* tell each other?

We talk all the time.

What sort of congregation do you have on a Sunday?

Once we're in full swing we'd be talking somewhere between four and five hundred at the main service on Sunday mornings.

Would you say that the Church plays a larger part in life here than it does in England?

Yes, it does. I think its role in most people's lives is less formal, therefore it isn't just a question of going to church on Sunday morning. We are very much involved with our families throughout their lives, and in spite of the incredible difficulty of getting a group of people together in New York during the week we have a very active weekday constituency. I calculated recently that over two thousand people come through the doors of this church during the week.

Do you see a black face in your congregation?

Yes – not a large number but very definitely, a notable few. Anglicanism in New York amongst the blacks is at its strongest with the West Indian population, but by and large our congregation reflects our geographical location; I would say eighty per cent of people in this parish live within ten blocks of here.

So how do they relate to a rugger-playing rowing beefy prelate?

I think they're getting used to it! They probably enjoy it – I think I exude a certain amount of energy.

You do – *I'm* very proud of you, at least; but don't they think you talk a bit funny?

They rather enjoy that! There is in the bottom of the consciousness of Americans the thought that God was in fact a seventeenth-century English-man, so it kind of sits well with that image....

THE PRESIDENT'S MAN

*It's assumed you have a lineage that goes back
to Henry VIII if not earlier....*

Dr Geoffrey Kemp is the only ex-Briton now a senior member of the
White House staff – Special Assistant to the President, with top-top
clearance. He came from Gravesend and arrived in Washington during the Vietnam War when Americans were burning the Stars and
Stripes in the streets. His impeccable British accent has puzzled many
– including Mrs Thatcher when he accompanied Secretary Schultz to
Chequers. He works among the ten acres of floor space in the vast
granite Executive Office Building, next door to the White House and
almost as difficult to enter.

———

I'm Special Assistant to the President for National Security. I specialize in
the Near East and South Asia – that means anything that has to do with
those very tempestuous parts of the world comes across my desk. I'm a
combination of assistant secretary, protocol officer, desk officer, deal with
the press, foreign governments, intelligence agencies – everybody, Marakesh
to Bangladesh. I've got all the pleasant subjects: Gadhafi, Ayatollah, Assad,
the Punjab, you name it!

Could you have imagined having this role in the Foreign Office,
advising the Prime Minister?

When I lived in England it never occurred to me that I would go into
government. I came in really in typical American fashion, by default. I'd
been working in Academe and writing and lecturing, but I never thought
of a career in government – in fact I still don't. I intend to leave government
at some point in the future.

You're the only senior White House staffer of British origin? How
did it happen, that long journey from Gravesend?

In physical terms I departed the shores of England in the fall of 1967,
and emigrated. I'd been offered a job at MIT in Cambridge Massachusetts
and began to work there on military matters, which had been my speciality

382

while I was in England. After a year or so getting used to the American system I decided I wasn't educated enough – I didn't have the right tickets. I decided to go back and do a PH.D., which I did at MIT, and based on that I got a professor's job at the Fletcher School of Law and Diplomacy, which's also in the Boston area, and began to teach. But you never just teach in this country, particularly on the East Coast, particularly if your field is in international politics. You just *have* to get involved with Washington.

So from a very early date I began to come down to this city and get to know the workings of the American Government. It became very clear that in order to do my job better, it was essential to have close contacts with Washington. In the mid-Seventies I applied for a Counsellor on Foreign Relations International Affairs Fellowship which I was lucky enough to be given, and they wanted me to work in the Pentagon. So I went to the Pentagon in 1974 and '75, and after that period went to work on Capitol Hill on the Senate Foreign Relations Committee with a lot of the people who were advising President Reagan – or Governor Reagan, as he then was. Then when the President won the election I was asked to join the National Security Council Staff, in 1981. Packed my bags and came to Washington!

It's a surprise to find an Englishman at the heart of government here. It would be unthinkable that Mrs Thatcher's closest adviser on the Middle East should be American – let alone an American who first came to London in 1967....

Yes, I think that's right. I can't imagine an American advising the Prime Minister in Italy or the Chancellor in Germany or the President in France or the Prime Minister in Japan. This is a uniquely American phenomenon. This is why America's America.

Have you ever been made to feel an odd man out because of your British origin?

No, never.

How in fact do they look upon the English here?

With a mixture of frustration and admiration and envy.

Frustration would suggest irritation?

Enormous irritation about the talent in Britain, which would seem to be going in the wrong direction. I think for that reason, quite apart from political consideration, Mrs Thatcher is terribly popular in this country – and that cuts across party lines. Again, not for the policies she pursued towards the United States but I think based on a feeling that Britain needed to be shaken and get its act together. It's now beginning to do so, however painful it is.

It's exactly the same thing that's happening in this country, in the Rust Belt. I lived in Massachusetts for thirteen years which went through essentially a revolution of the kind that hopefully Britain's going to go through, of moving from the Rust Age into the Computer Age, and did so very painfully. *Very* painfully – the highest unemployment in the United States for a long period of time, now the lowest. So I think a lot of Americans see enormous hope in what's happening in Britain, but just wish it happened a little more quickly!

Does anyone ever comment on your English accent?

Oh yes, yes. You're more noticeable, I think, in the US Government with a British accent than if you have a strongly gutteral East European accent, like Dr Kissinger. That's considered normal, but there *is* something rather bizarre about an English accent in the Government! But now, as you know, we've got John Hughes as the spokesman for the State Department. He's on television almost every night with a British accent, so people are getting used to it.

If you speak with a very obvious accent it's taken for granted – except English. There's something absolutely normal about a Pole or a German or a Trinidadian with a broad accent in the American Government, but I found for a long time that with an English accent they couldn't *accept* that I was American. There was some snobbery about the fact that, 'How could you possibly be an American if you're English?' That's because Americans still have a very schizophrenic view towards England – on one hand they deify the manner and attitudes of the British in the way that to some extent they mirror in their own behaviour.

This is Thackeray and P.G. Wodehouse and Brideshead?

Brideshead's a good example. The only times when I was made very much aware of my British origins was during the Falklands war. Not that I was involved in it directly, but around here everybody clearly was very supportive of what Mrs Thatcher was doing.

Americans in general tend rather to romanticize Britain, do they not?

Yes, very much so. I don't think they do in Washington, which is a very sophisticated city, but certainly in other parts of the country it's assumed that if you come from England you have a lineage that goes back to Henry VIII, if not earlier. For that reason there's a certain bewilderment on some people's part as to why anyone would want to leave the idyllic romanticized Britain which so many Americans see, or want to see.

Is this a civilized place to live?

Washington is, yes. Extremely.

You're excluding the rest of America?

No, no, no. I think there's such diversity in this country that you can't generalize about the United States. The problems are very obvious – they stand out like warts. But the great thing about the United States is that the problems are addressed openly on the front page of the newspapers. Everyone talks about them. There's no attempt to disguise or hide what's going on.

We're talking about violence, crime, colour – that sort of thing?

All the things that are read about so avidly in Europe!

Yet I suspect in many English hearts there's a feeling that the rainbow ends somewhere in the United States. . . .

Historically the links between the United States and Britain are extraordinarily close. You only have to live in New England, as I did, to become acutely conscious of the heritage, not merely in the names of the towns which are all the same as those you have in England, but also the names of the people and their history and background. In other parts of the country where the historical links are less clear there is nevertheless a very warm emotional feeling towards the British. I think the visit of the Queen to Wyoming highlighted this, because after all Wyoming was opened up by a lot of English lords in the 1880s. This is not a well-known fact, but it's something that needs to be remembered occasionally.

Can, you see yourself here for the rest of your life, or will you be heading back to Kent?

If I came from, let's say, an East European country where there would be no chance of going back, I might have some soul-searching torment about whether I was ever going to see my native land again, but the fact of the matter is, I go to Europe a great deal. I can go to Kent whenever I like. The world is becoming a closer place, not a more distant place. It's never occurred to me that I have to choose between settling in one place or the other. I live here, I work here, I'm an American citizen, but I go back to England whenever I like.

You were at Chequers recently with Secretary Shultz: did you then feel more English than American, or that you were part of the visiting team?

I feel part of the team. Very much so. Nevertheless, I clearly feel at home in England. Relations are so good between Britain and the United States that you don't have the problem of choosing, which I might have if I'd come from another nationality in another country and gone back as part of a team.

Some Englishmen have decided not to become American citizens, though they've been here for years. You had to, because of your position?

In part that. Certainly the position I have I could not hold if I weren't a citizen. But on the other hand, I felt very strongly that having emigrated and having put down my roots here, I *wanted* to participate in the government of America. I did not want taxation without representation. So obviously I took out citizenship – I vote.

This is a nation of immigrants. This is the melting pot. When I was sworn in for citizenship in Boston the judge, who was a first-generation Italian, made an enormous point about how his parents came over on a boat, and that there's no attempt to disguise your background. I think if you were to do a census now of the total population in the States, which is about 240 million, I'm certain well over 100 million Americans are new immigrants or first-generation, and therefore the country has always progressed and evolved by drawing upon its immigrants, even though they've come from different parts of the world at different periods of history. Maybe Australia will be the same way twenty, thirty, forty years from now – certainly not at the moment. But this country is unique in that regard.

From your desk at the White House, is there anything you miss from England?

If I didn't go back there'd be lots of things I'd miss, but whenever I feel nostalgic, I take a trip to London. No, there's not much I miss. The sense of humour, I guess, amongst ordinary people. That's a unique British quality which I think is more and more appreciated over here. Since I've been here I've seen a growing popularity of British humour, and that is very appealing to me. It means I can turn on television any night now and watch Benny Hill or Monty Python – even the *Goon Shows* are occasionally heard on American radio. This wasn't the case fifteen or so years ago, and makes one feel more at home.

There are many traits which *don't* go down well here – for example British self-deprecation. If you're modest over here you get a modest job, don't you?

I think that's true, on the whole – particularly in the business world, but I think in Academe and in government there's not a great deal of difference between the two systems. There is in the way they operate, but in terms of personalities I think you find as many egos in Britain as you do in the United States.

It's not a case of having to sell yourself here, to a greater degree than at home?

Oh yes that's one thing I had to learn to do – but on my return trips to Britain I found that it's becoming more fashionable to sell oneself in the UK as well. Maybe things are picking up, after all!

The Brits stick together here?

There's an undercurrent of understanding. For instance, I get on very well with the people at the Embassy, probably much better than a lot of others would, and talk to them more frankly.

I wonder how they look upon you?

As weird, I would think. . . .

THE MAID

If we were Jewish here, it would certainly help. . . .

Patricia Clover Viveiros is an eager young feminist living for the past three years with Nancy, who worked for the West Palm Beach Police. They share an apartment in one of Florida's vast Jewish retirement communities, with pool and clubhouse; it cost $39,000 freehold and is hung with pictures of the Queen, and Charles and Diana.

Her Father was a British soldier from Birmingham, her Mother German. She came first to the United States with her husband, a US Army sergeant. Things started to go wrong: 'We haven't divorced because we've had no time – we're still good friends. I didn't get any money from him because I don't think that's fair: it's a mutual thing that we separated – so why should I get anything from him just because I'm a woman?'

After working for an electronics firm for five years she got laid off; with her compensation she started the British Maid Service, and on business cards calls herself 'English Pat'. Cheerful, hardworking and ambitious, she and her friend ran into a bitter battleground in their quiet community – and in Florida an aura of hostility does emanate from such colonies of the elderly. The other residents evidently disliked the girls on a number of grounds – but mainly because they were young. . . .

═══

It was relatively easy for me to start this business, but it's a lot of hard work. In America you can't just automatically go on the dole when you feel like it, because there is no dole, you *have* to work. I got laid off, which is made redundant, from a good position I had with Northern Telecom. I went on Unemployment for a while and decided OK, this is not going to last for ever, there's no one to take care of me, to give me any money. So I figure OK, I'm going to have to do it on my own. Basically you've got to get out there and work hard, because nobody's going to help you.

I bought a bucket, a mop, I borrowed a truck and stuck signs on it and went out and called myself British Maid Service. I had some cards made up, I went to every mall in West Palm Beach and worked my butt off the first year and by golly, it paid off! I was very careful that I kept a low rate, because the competition was fifteen to twenty dollars more than me at that time. Now I've raised my prices. It just happened that the Americans loved the fact that it was called the British Maid Service, and that I was with the accent. As the jobs came in I hired girls. I checked them out of course.

How do you do this? You go to the house of a friend of mine here, she doesn't know you but she just gives you the key and goes away – and in you go. She *has* to trust you?

I've thoroughly checked out my girls to the point where, if need be, I'll go out and drink in the local bar where they go, just to see what kind of people they hang around with, to see what kind of person they are. Also I have them checked out with the police. I don't just hire anyone off the street – and my friend Nancy works for the West Palm Beach Police Department.

So you run your prospective girls through the police computer?

Exactly – and find out about any arrests in the past, anything that is discouraging.

The fact that you're British Maid is good for business? People expect you to be domesticated, honest and charming?

Yes, they have that idea about British people – I guess it stems from their butlers and maids, who were usually British.
I've got five girls right now, I'm firing one tomorrow. She's very slow and she's called up sick already twice in two weeks and she's still on a probationary period, so she's going. I'm charging ten dollars an hour and paying the girls five dollars an hour, so I'm getting five dollars a job, plus there are some jobs I charge seventy-five dollars for a one-time deal, if someone's moving out of an apartment and they want a crew to go in and clean up after them. I do that, because that way I make most of the money myself. I usually take one girl with me because I don't like to work too hard! I don't do much cleaning now because I'm too busy just running the business. When I'm convinced that I've trained them, that they clean the British way, then the clients are very happy. I've never had any complaints about sending an American girl or a Japanese girl to a house.

Could you see yourself running a business like this in Birmingham, and calling it the American Maid Service?

I doubt very much whether anything like this would go, over there, because I don't think the money's around. I don't think they can *afford* to have a Maid Service.

What do you enjoy most about being in America?

There's a certain kind of a freedom that women have in America, that I didn't feel when I lived in England. Let me give you an example: I'm a feminist, OK, and if I say I'm a feminist in England it's like I've got three horns sticking out of my head! A guy – this actually happened to me – a guy said, 'Oh really, you're a feminist?' and slammed the door in my face! Open the door for yourself, that type of attitude. But over here you're a feminist, so what? Men still respect you.

I'm a Catholic and we go to church every Sunday, to the Metropolitan Community Church. When I lost my brother I was really low and I was looking for something. I'd just got this feeling that he was lonely and cold. God's the only thing that made me feel better. I say my prayers every night, although I hadn't been to church for God knows how long until the MCC – now I wouldn't miss a Sunday. I love it.

The things that the people there *do* for each other, if you're in need.... There's a woman there whose little daughter has cancer. She started going to the church and wouldn't speak to anyone, very unfriendly, and within two weeks they'd had a collection for her daughter. She stood up last week in church and she was crying and she said, 'I've been unfriendly and haven't even spoken to anyone and here you came to my door with a cheque to help me through the hard times....'

If you've got a job here and you work for a firm, OK, ninety-nine per cent of the firms give you medical insurance free of charge. Working for yourself like I do, I pay fifty dollars a month for medical insurance, it's no problem. Right now the insurance I have does not cover the girls, but they have dental insurance. I recently acquired that because I've just had all my teeth capped, so now if anything happens or, God forbid, I should get in any kind of accident, it's going to be covered. I paid $3,200 to get my teeth capped.

Three thousand dollars' worth of teeth – give me a smile! But when you go home to Birmingham, if you played your cards right you could walk in and have them done for nothing, couldn't you?

I guess I could have, but I just like the way they do things over here.

What are the people like, living on this estate?

To be honest with you, they kind of discourage young people from living here. They do not like the young, especially if you're working for a living, why I don't know. We're in the process of buying a house because I'm not going to let them chase me out of here, I'm going to go in my time. Nancy and I are probably going to buy a house together. This is *not* a young people's community.

Yet America's a young society....

Not in South Florida. That's why my business does well, because in this area it's an older type of person that requires a maid service.

So the other residents here make life difficult? Is that because you're young, because you're British, because you're two girls living together, because you're not Jewish – what's wrong with you?

I don't know if I should say this.... OK, it's because we're young and unfortunately it's because we're not Jewish too. You see, this is a retirement area, they don't like young people living here, and it's not that we have any wild parties Alan, we don't. We basically keep ourselves to ourselves, but the only thing they have to do all day long is to sit over in that clubhouse and watch what we're doing.

Are they watching us right now?

I'm surprised they haven't come over to see what's going on.

How do they make their antipathy known?

Well, um, I hope no one's listening.... First of all they're trying to make the cut-off age to move in here thirty. Right now it's twenty-eight. They're trying to up it a couple of years – it's kind of a discrimination type of thing and I think if we were Jewish it would help. It's a predominantly Jewish community – ex-taxi-drivers from New York who've nothing better to do when they come down here.

That's a pretty irascible testy aggressive group, isn't it?

Very, very much so. If you don't do things their way, then watch out.

So what things are you *not* doing their way? Do they think you're not classy enough?

If you *saw* some of those people – we have the class, they don't. The way they speak, the way they conduct themselves, I have to say that we defin-itely have the class and maybe that's why they don't like us – I mean, the fact that we at our age are able to afford something like this, when they at our age couldn't. They were probably living, like I said, in New York in the Queens area.

But what about being British, that magic word – doesn't that do anything?

They don't care – you're under fifty-five, they don't want to know.

Not even if you flash your little Union Jack – still doesn't help?

Doesn't help. Look at my car with things all over it! The police sympathize with us. If we have any problems they're only too happy to help us out. It's not just my problem, it's a problem in South Florida with this type of community. If you're not retirement age, you just do not fit in. They have an association and their rules are binding within this little community, like if they say they don't want trucks, there's nothing you can do about it. It's amazing the rules and regulations they have. But I sleep at night, they probably don't.

Have you heard of those time-sharing places? I went to look at one – and you have to take your husband! They definitely don't want blacks living in those condominiums. Elliot's got a Porsche, but he's black. We drove up there and we were given a free camera, for going. You have to walk around for hours and watch the show. We drove up and I had my arm in Elliot's and we got the quickest tour around that place that anyone's ever had! They were trying to hide Elliot, because there were other people there too, trying to buy. They're shoving him indoors....! But we got our camera. I don't like to discriminate against a race of people, but I have to say that if we were Jewish here, it would certainly help.

Are you going to stay in Florida for the rest of your life, or will you go back to Birmingham?

I wouldn't go back to England, I may move out of Florida. I've just really grown accustomed to the American way of life. I love it. Not counting the business, it's the opportunities over here that women seem to have. The freedom is just incredible. The only thing I miss about England is my family, and things with Charles and Diana and royalty – but if something happens with William, it's on the news over here.

I've often tried to imagine myself being my age in Birmingham, what would I be doing? I can honestly say that I don't think I'd be living as nice a life as I am here. If I'd stayed in Birmingham I would think: I'm a woman and I'm supposed to get married and have kids. That's the frame of mind I would have, if I'd stayed there. Here you can be anything you want to be, if you've got the guts and the willpower. You have to take risks too – but here the risks don't seem as much as they would seem in England.

But when you go back to Birmingham to see your Mother, don't you feel that's where you really belong?

I don't miss England or Birmingham or anything about it at *all*. I'm not putting it down – I love it, it's in my heart. England will always be England, but I don't miss it at all. For me personally it's a better way of life over here. I have better opportunities. If you love doing what you're doing and you're making money out of it and you like where you are, that *has* to be success.

Yet you're living in this community where they're all making life difficult for you, it's cost you three thousand dollars to get your smile fixed.... There are arguments against it?

First of all, I *had* the three thousand dollars to spend and I thought it was well worth it. OK? It's not like I scrimp and scrape for my pennies, I don't. I'm doing very well, OK?

THE ACTOR

If hillbillies can understand Benny Hill....

Jim Dale, from Rothwell in Northamptonshire, went into show biz at the age of nine and worked his way up to being an apprentice in a Yorkshire shoe factory. That, however, was a mere hiccup: he carried on to become the most luminous star on Broadway, playing Barnum in the evocative circus musical that never stops running. Though a considerable actor and a member of the National Theatre Company at the Old Vic, he had first become quite well known as a pop singer on BBC Television's *6.5 Special* in the late Fifties, but then *very* well known as the good-looking one in that constant giggle of Carry-On films too humorous to mention.

His American second wife Julie sells wearable arts – feather jackets that take a year to make – in the Artisans' Gallery on Madison Avenue, and they live in a small flat three-quarters of the way up a Park Avenue tower, with rooms full of antique furniture and balconies full of foliage and flowers.

He is now fifty but, with his merry tinker's face and disciplined circus-acrobat figure, still looks like the juvenile lead. He is better-known in America than Britain, for the Carry-On films are night-time television fodder: if you can't sleep at 4 a.m. – there he is, among the boobs and bums he'd just as soon forget!

———

I can't explain *how* I felt when we first opened in *Barnum* on Broadway: the audience reacted in a way I've never seen before. They just stood up and they wouldn't leave the theatre. Then next day the top critics – the ones you've been terrified of, the Clive Barnes of this world – were absolutely unanimous in their approval of the whole show and the wonderful cast we had. It was a joy!

You were a pop singer, you were a Carry-Oner who carried on to some effect ... so what brought you over here?

I first came over in 1974 with the Young Vic, with Jane Lapotaire. We did *The Taming of the Shrew* at the Brooklyn Academy of Music, and *French without Tears* and *Scapino*. This little show, *Scapino*, clicked and they invited us to Broadway for a sixteen-week season and we stayed over a year, in Los Angeles and San Francisco.

You were the toast of the town, Broadway was at your feet; but since *Barnum* nothing you've done has ever *quite* reached that point, has it?

No – I don't suppose anything ever will again.

But despite that they haven't started saying Jim Who?

I'll tell you what they *do* say: two women were walking out of my wife's gallery the other day and I opened the door to let them out. One looked at me and as she went out she turned to her friend and said, 'You know the woman who owns this gallery? She's married to Barnum.' Barnum, yes – they don't say Jim Who? It's Barnum!

That's not a bad memory, though, let's face it.

No not bad, but it'd be nice to get rid of Barnum. You can do another venture, hopefully, where they'll probably call you by a different name.

Why did you come to the States in the first place? Were you tired of Carrying On?

Frank Dunlop was the one who asked if I would come over with the Young Vic company. I was doing a *This Is Your Life* at the Palladium and Frank Dunlop, in view of everybody, said, 'I'm inviting Jim Dale now to come to New York. He won't come but please beg him to.' I said, 'Right, I'll come over for the four or five weeks.' That was the beginning of it.

When you've had a success on Broadway it would have been silly not to have accepted the challenge that came along with it. The next challenge was, 'Would you like to star in a Broadway musical about the life of a big American called P.G. Barnum?' I would have been a fool to have said, 'No I'm going to stay in England and work over there.' You have to take that step in your career when it's offered you.

Now you've got a Park Avenue apartment, an American wife – so Carry On is a long way away?

Absolutely, but I have to look back on those Carry Ons with the fondest memory because you learn your trade all through your life in show business. That particular vehicle, the Carry On films, taught me to work with the most wonderful talented people, comedic people, and I'm sure a lot of that rubs off.

When you arrived did you take to New York instantly? If you had such a success, I suppose you did?

No I didn't, because it's a noisy dirty filthy horrible city – but it's a wonderful marvellous lovely place to be as well. It has everything, and I'd rather have the whole gamut of experience here than be in some little town where nothing ever happens.

I've never been mugged. Lots of people have, we know that. There are certain areas I hate, I'll never go in, but this applies to any city. If you're going to walk down East India Dock Road in London, you'll probably get mugged.

There's also something about the rewards here; you must be doing better than you were doing at home?

We don't *expect* to do very well as actors in England, do we? You can't. The reason why is because ticket prices aren't the price they are over here. We would sign on with a repertory company and do it for almost a minimum salary. It seems to be our lot in life as actors that we shouldn't *expect* to earn beyond a certain number of pounds or dollars a year, and a lot of people tend to think we shouldn't. But over here you're given an opportunity; if you can attract people to that theatre and those people are paying forty dollars each, the producers say, 'Right, you've been responsible for this so we'll give you a certain percentage, which is negotiable, of the production.'

Are you saying there's a higher standard here?

I'm saying it's a more expensive theatre, and therefore the salaries are much higher.

And a more critical audience?

Critical yes, because they're having to pay a lot more money: forty dollars, that's thirty-five pounds a ticket. They're very particular and they're very, er, well what's the word I can use?

Demanding?

Yes, demanding in what they see on that stage.

So that was 44th Street and Barnum's Saint James Theater; this is Times Square and Broadway – to which we always give our regards – but today, like Leicester Square, Broadway's become a bit tatty, a bit sleazy?

Absolutely – even more so than Leicester Square. This is the place where you don't stay around after the show – you get a cab if you can and you get *out* of the area! Especially at night – not a nice place at all.

At one time the danger in the streets was affecting the theatres, wasn't it? That seems to have eased a bit....

Yes, I think so. There are more police down here now. There's still those x-rated cinemas, pornography parlours – you name it, it's all here. I suppose it has to be somewhere in any city if you allow it, but they're going to try and clean this place up, especially now there's a magnificent new hotel going up with some new theatres in it.

I'm doing *Joe Egg* off-Broadway – it's like doing it at Greenwich, in London. It's away from the West End area, but I like to work off-Broadway, where taxi-cab drivers can still afford to come and see the show.

As a Brit coming over here, do you find you get instant credit? Do they assume that you're going to speak well, that you're going to be a good actor? Are they fond of us?

Yes, they are – very, *very* fond. If you're a British actor, they do expect more from you, I think, because they expect you've had the experience in repertory, which means a lot more experience than the average young American actor has. You have the chance in England of appearing in three, four, five different plays every year. Over here the young actor will spend this time auditioning a lot, perhaps being in *one* off-Broadway play – and then waiting around for months and months for another job. He doesn't get the experience that our actors get, or the training, and so I notice there's a great deal of respect for all of us over here.

Standing here on Broadway, which you've conquered in the past, what do you miss most from England?

Everything. I really do – I love England with a passion, but I live here, I work here, this is my home, so you try to make it as comfortable as possible. You find the right sort of apartment, you find those friends who are wonderful to have around, and you find places to get away to at the weekends instead of being stuck in a city when the temperatures may be a hundred degrees. But it's always a joy and a pleasure to get back to London.

Of course you *could* be back there permanently. Nobody's holding you here – it's a matter of choice?

It's a matter of choice, but I've decided I would like to be where my wife is, where the work is.

The people who're passing us now, how do they differ from people who'd be passing us in Leicester Square?

Just look around: what *is* an American? It's every nationality on earth. In England, you know, they're Brits, but here every face looks as if it came from a different country than the other one.

In the theatre at one time the English accent would put people off, I was told?

That's right, it put producers off. They'd say, 'Can you do an American accent?' The answer to that now is, 'Why? Get an American if you want an American accent.' We *can* be understood. American audiences, especially the television audiences, have many shows from England that they've tuned their ear to – *Upstairs Downstairs*, *Fawlty Towers*. We've had all the big shows and all the *Armchair Theatres*. And of course in the film world we've had the best English films over here for a long time. So those days when people couldn't understand us are gone.

I've just been down to Mazeville in Kentucky and I've been talking to the hill people, the hillbillies, the mountain people – and they asked me if I knew Benny Hill! Now if *they* can understand Benny Hill I'm sure theatre audiences will understand an English actor. . . .

THE MAÎTRE d'

A little more free and, you know, flowing. . . .

David Cotterill, from Southend, arrived in America in 1974 and worked as a window cleaner; he is now on nodding terms with everyone who matters in Texas – indeed, many seek his acknowledgement. He is assistant Maître d' at The Mansion on Turtle Creek, a stunningly elegant Dallas hotel. Small and plump and pale, a blend of the aloof and the deferential, David ushers an endless parade of guests through his restaurant with a sort of swooping palais-glide. After a major operation he was quickly back in command, gliding watchfully around his domain; he had treated cancer of the stomach with casual indifference, as though it didn't have a reservation.

David won his coveted Green Card – which permitted him to stop cleaning windows and start allocating tables – when he married Kelly, a Texan with two children. They live knee-deep in dogs in a small white house on a few acres of scrubland forty-five minutes out of town, between Highways 175 and 635. Traffic noise is fierce, but they are immensely proud of their battered little home with its new bathroom and pool and plastic Madonna in the garden.

Driving home from the hotel one night David came across a damaged car which had apparently crashed, its driver slumped over the wheel. He stopped to help – and two blacks instantly attacked him with tyre irons: it was a highway hold-up. Another motorist appeared, so he escaped and arrived home covered in blood. His wife was furious at such stupidity: 'In Dallas you don't help *nobody*!' She called the police, excusing his rash behaviour by explaining he was from England where people still did such foolish things. . . .

━━━

A dinner for two with a reasonable bottle of wine could cost how much here?

About one hundred pounds – that's with a moderate wine. Our wines range from twenty-five up to seven hundred pounds a bottle.

I notice that one glass of Dom Perignon is twenty pounds. . . .

A little expensive by the glass, you see. We open up a $160-bottle and if we only serve two glasses, then we're losing the bottle.

And the staff are forced to finish it?

Unfortunately, yes!

Tough.... People from Texas are thought to be the *nouveaux riches* of the world, are they not?

Yes it's new money, though a lot of big families are established and have had money for a long time. You can tell by the suits, the dresses, hats, you can tell elegance when it comes through the door.

What are the giveaways?

Gentlemen spend a lot of money buying suits – then they wear a pair of cowboy boots!

Yes, I did see people arriving here for a party in dinner jackets with brown boots and cowboy hats....

Difficult. We have to ask them to remove their hats. We obviously don't allow denim in the restaurant, and they can get a little mad. You get some people from California, they don't understand – they don't *have* a jacket, you know. Californians are a little casual and The Mansion's a little bit more – how shall we say – stiff collar.

Call you tell a Texan millionaire when he comes in?

Some you can, some you can't. All Texans are wearing boots and cowboy hats. They're all well-travelled now, well-dressed, they all go to London, the ladies go to European schools and they've all got class now, a lot of class. You get the odd one coming in wearing his big boots and he's going to wear his buckle belt, his cowboy hat, then you have a little problem. We do have areas for those people. They don't actually come through into the main dining room, we have a promenade where it's a little less formal for guests who will come down in their shorts and shirts and not *quite* dressed for The Mansion.

How do you deal with them?

Very easily, but with kid-glove hands. You've got to be very careful. 'I'm sorry you're not dressed suitably for The Mansion, we do require a jacket and tie....' So then he's going to get a little upset because he's brought his wife, he wants to come in, but we still have an area where we can please them. It might not be actually what they wanted, but we have our code and our standard. I don't think it's right if you're sitting there in your $700 suit with your wife and she's spent $20,000 on a real fur – and then someone comes in with a pair of jeans and a cowboy hat and sits right down beside you! It's not fair to you and it's not fair to us.

How different are the people here from those you were dealing with in the catering industry in England?

A little more free and, you know, flowing. They're given the friendliness and they're very receptive to this. They want good service, which they get – that's the main thing. It's very difficult to maintain a high standard of service on the tables. A lot of training here, not very many professionals. Most of the waiters you have to train from scratch and that means getting table sense – looking at a table and seeing what's missing, whether it needs water, ashtrays, making sure there's wine filled up, enough rolls and butter, little things like that.

How many staff do you have?

Forty-five, from all over the world: Algerian, French, Iranians, Belgians, Germans, Dutch and one English. Only one piece of class in the hotel – me! The Maître d' is Italian, Jean-Pierre Albernetti. Eleven or twelve different nationalities in waiters. In captains we have eight different nationalities – it's incredible!

I know in an American restaurant where you sit is vitally important, and the best table is usually the table where you're *seen*, so status can depend upon where the Maître d' puts you.

We have preferred areas, we have a Siberia – I think every restaurant has its Siberia. We don't as a rule like to use it – but some Siberias people *like*. Some people don't want to be seen. We've got some little nooks and crannies here, we have the library with eight tables which is completely cut off, and then we have the main dining room which has sixteen tables on the verandah and a small area with four tables. As I say, you can sit some people in the main dining room and they say, 'I would really like to be out on the verandah,' and other people say, 'I want to sit in here with carpet underneath my feet.' Then you get people who just want to *see* people, people-watchers, because there's always someone very important in The Mansion. Recently we had Sophia Loren, we've had Charlton Heston, we had a great time with the late James Mason, he stayed here for nearly four weeks. The Duke and Duchess of Bedford are here for two days. David Brinkley, all the media; during the Republican convention we were on *Good Morning America* three days in a row.

All this *placement* is very good for you, I would have thought, because people must always be dropping you a hundred dollars here, a hundred dollars there...?

You're misleading me! I'm not going to commit myself to that! Yes, you do get side-tipped. The average customer that comes in here is a twenty per cent. Most of the service staff are oriented to fifteen per cent, that's what they more or less look for.

So if you give someone a good table, folding money can change hands?

That's what the maître d' lives and dies by, what he makes on the door.

How does it compare with England?

Quite honestly I believe the service has dropped in England because you've got your set money, you're not going to get anything else. Our worst tippers are the English, I must admit.

Is that because we're mean or because we're poor?

No, because you expect it to already be taken care of, you know, fifteen per cent in England. When I left it was twelve and a half per cent, I'm not sure what it is now, but it was already on the cheque, you just used to pay the bottom figure. Here we don't put gratuity on the cheque, it's completely left. We give a total and then it's up to the customer what they wish to leave. And many times we have some very good English people staying here, they leave five dollars thinking that the gratuity is already added. We can't say anything, really.

But sometimes you've got to be fairly severe with your clients? Like the captain of a ship, you're controlling them?

They come in running late and you can put them in the bar, but you've got to be very careful, very very careful. It takes a lot of qualities, a lot of patience sometimes, like bend this way, bend that way, slow a little bit. You're in the highlight, you're in charge, one wrong move from the Maître d' and that's it, that's the evening spoiled.

So you're dressing the set? You want a smart restaurant with the elegant people where they can be seen by others, to keep up the standard?

You've got to set your room. You want some nice pretty ladies where you come in, you want that area to look nice and busy. You don't put all the men one side, all the women the other side because here we have a very feminine lunch – there's a lot of ladies, more than businessmen. At dinner the ladies want to come with their husbands, so it's mixed.

You're a determined man?

Very aggressive, yes.

I don't find you a bit aggressive, but I think you're a thruster – you're more American than English, it seems to me.

Yes, I've been here now seven years, I've adapted to their ways. When it comes to the restaurant, I'm in charge of the service, it's my responsibility. And I get respect the same way that I give them respect.

When you first came how did you adjust to running an American restaurant?

I found it very difficult, because of the personnel. Seven years ago there was probably only twenty, thirty experienced waiters in the whole of Dallas, and in a five-star restaurant maybe only a handful. Now Dallas is getting on a bit, attracting a few more better-class service people, and most of them we trained ourselves. Most employees have been here two or three years because it's busy, you know you're going to earn money every day, it's constant. Some places you come in Monday or Tuesday, you're doing your fifty people and you're going home. Here we're busy all the week. We pay the rate, but with commission and tips out of it, it's probably a little bit above, more consistent. There's probably restaurants here where you could go and throw hash for more money than what we're getting, but here you've got job satisfaction, you've got a good reference, prestige, good insurance. They're ever so good to you.

Yet American employers are said to be quite ruthless?

Some places yes, here no. Here you come, you do a good job, you work hard – right, you've got your job. If you're willing to give some, they will give some. If you work for them, they'll work for you, and I mean that sincerely. I came from the Café Royal, which is Trusthouse Forte, as a captain hoping to get the assistant Maître d's position as he was leaving. I messed around with the wines a little bit because we had no wine steward, and then I took over the assistant Maître d'.

Last January I suspected there was something wrong with me and went to my doctor and he said, 'We believe it's a tumour.' After a few weeks he said I had a cancerous tumour and it had to be moved. It was in my lower stomach, and they said they needed to operate. I said to our manager, 'I've got a problem, I'll have to have two, three, four weeks off.' Of course I'm in a very important position here so it *was* going to create a few problems.

I went into hospital and they removed the tumour. Then they said some of the cancer cells had escaped and they're going to have to find them. It was in Houston, the Texas University Hospital. It's the biggest cancer centre in the world down there, it's phenomenal! The whole of one area of Houston is just hospitals. I had Dr Anderson, who's supposed to be one of the top guys in the world, for my particular tumour. You go down there and you see all these foreigners and they've obviously paid a lot of money to come to Houston to see him, and this company just picked up the bill. I stayed in The Wellington, our hotel down there, and they paid all my bills, my room, my food, my drink, whatever I wanted. I was looked after very well. At the hospital I ran up an eighteen-thousand-dollar bill and all I paid was the first six hundred dollars.

Now I go down every three months for a check-up. They do a lymph node test on me – that's where they hack into your feet and dye your body a nice blue and look for cells. They gave me radiation treatment for three weeks, which I was taking in the day and working at night. I go every three months, stay in The Wellington down in Houston, the hotel picks up the bill. It's very nice.

Must be good for staff morale, that, when the word goes round?

Especially for a family man with three or four children. If you get hit with an eighteen-thousand-dollar bill, then you're going to be in trouble for the rest of your life. I dropped thirty-five pounds, but I've steadily put it back on.

What sort of hours do you work now?

Long hours. I haven't had a day off for nineteen days, but you've got your commission and your tips, so the more shifts you have the more money you can earn. The tronc system invites laziness. In the individual system, each captain picks up his money and divides it individually, pays a bit to the door, pays a little bit to the bartender and a little bit to the bus boy. Then you've got, 'Let's do more customers, let's do more business!' If you have the tronc system some people will lay back, let somebody else do it, do thirty covers and split the money, what's it matter? Tronc is good if you have a perfect crew. But we've got such a big restaurant, so many corners. We can seat 160, and we'll do 300 tonight.

When you're not running this restaurant, what do you do?

I work on my yard. I'm doing my house up at the moment. Other than that I play ball and drink beer, like a good ole Texan.

Have you got friends?

Yes we have, but I don't socialize with the employees. I only had one person I did that with and he took advantage of me and my position, so I try to keep that down to a minimum. I believe there's only one employee now working in The Mansion that's even been round my house. *This* is why we're here. I've got a big four-acre ranch here.

I must say, it's a bit noisy!

It *is* a little noisy, but if you want to make some value quickly, then you've got to be on the motorways. This is just something for maybe five or six years, to make money on. The whole property was on the market for $68,000, we got in at $58,000 and we put in a swimming pool. We've done it up a little bit and I estimate $93,000 now, that's with the heavy zoning commercially, dollar-fifty a square foot.

That's eighty thousand pounds – and you say the advantage is that you're in a commercial area? A lot of people wanting a home might think that was a *dis*advantage!

It is, in a respect, but my wife's here mainly all the time. I'm not here very much. The traffic quietens down. At six o'clock it's dead.

You're working in considerable luxury, you're meeting elegant people, you're coming away from the tranquillity of the hotel to this quite simple place which is noisy and as hot as an oven....

I love it, give me a beer, give me a swimming pool, I'm happy.

What was your training for the loving all this – where did you come from?

Southend.

It's not *quite* as hot there, is it?

Not as hot – but I was in Libya for a year.

That was good practice!

I went to Southend Technical College. I was there for nearly two years training to be a chef, came outside and realized that I didn't want to wait fifty-eight years to run a kitchen, so I decided to go restaurant-side, did several restaurants in England and then I sort of misbehaved a little bit. My brother-in-law said the best way to settle me down – I had no Father – was to join a service for a little while, to sort me out.

Do you want to tell me how you misbehaved?

Well just got yourself in gambling debts and just didn't care about yourself, just went out and spent the money. Never had no responsibility, never had nothing. I had a car and that was it.

I'd come to Dallas in January '78 because of Immigration. They wanted to see you in the Immigration Office to make sure you're not going to live off the government, not going to live off Welfare. You have to produce how much money you've got. I met Kelly, she took us down there several times, showed that we'd got five hundred dollars at least and our air fare back to England – which we never had, we cheated a little bit there.... We borrowed four hundred dollars from my wife, which then wasn't my wife....
Kelly: It was five hundred dollars.

You see, you still owe her a hundred dollars!

I still owe her five hundred dollars, don't worry!

So how did you set about earning an honest dollar?

We started off doing window cleaning. Ken Bailey, he was a very good pastry chef, came over here with me. We couldn't work anywhere legally so we did some illegal work. Both being from London and being a bit of boys, we knew window cleaning, so we went out and bought a truck, an old pick-up, bought a set of ladders, a couple of buckets, had some cards printed and went round delivering and giving estimates. We got a couple of calls for some jobs, we did 'em, we found we were *way* under! We were charging maybe fifteen, twenty dollars to clean windows inside and out and then we found we should have been charging a hundred and twenty dollars – a hundred pounds! It didn't take us long to adjust our tariff. Then we did the silly thing: we got ourselves a little bit of money together and we thought we'd go and see the gold pavements of California. We stayed there three days – no gold, so we came back to Dallas.

More window cleaning?

No, I married Kelly. Ken went back to England. Unfortunately the pick-up truck we left in Arizona, so we got married in the morning and in the afternoon I was on the bus back up to pick up the truck.

When you were married you became legitimate, and with a Green Card you could get a proper job?

No more cleaning windows! I did one job for charity. Someone quoted seven hundred dollars but I quoted four hundred, so I made four hundred dollars for a day's work – *that* felt very good....

THE SONGWRITERS

I wanted to be disgusting, and rich. . . .

Nashville's biggest industry is the printing of Bibles; second biggest, insurance; third and the only one that's known – music. During the past fifteen years some British musicians have drifted into Tennessee and are narrowing the gap between country and pop and revitalizing the Nashville studio scene.

Roger Cook arrived in 1975; born in Bristol, he started his working career as a plasterer's apprentice and his singing career as a choirboy. Gentle and sad-eyed, he has now written more hits than anyone except Paul McCartney, and his thousand published songs include 'I'd Like to Teach the World to Sing'. He formed 'David and Jonathan' with Roger Greenaway and a promising accompanist called Reginald Dwight (aka Elton John).

His partner now is Ralph Murphy from Saffron Walden, Essex, who wrote or produced more than three hundred records before moving to Tennessee in 1977; with drooping moustache, he resembles a benign bandit. After New York, he says, money doesn't speak with a loud voice in Nashville; people are more impressed if you grow your own tomatoes.

Like all the best pop-men, Michael Snow came from Liverpool and has a growling Scouse accent to prove it. He went briefly to Leeds University and in the Sixties, in the shadow of the Beatles, played with groups like The Barons and The Ferrymen, with the Bee Gees and John Lennon. He married an American girl and was driving across the States to join his producer in LA when he read in a newspaper that the man had embezzled $1\frac{1}{2}$ million and disappeared. Michael stayed on in Nashville and when one day Julie Andrews cut a song he had written his parents finally accepted that, after all those years, he had arrived. . . .

Britain's musical colonists gather to drink and reminisce in a dark and dusty mobile home known as Brown's Diner; they seem to be proving that you don't have to *be* country to play country. . . .

Michael: This area of the country – Nashville, Memphis – has so much to do with the growth of rock and roll, so much of what we listened to when

we were in an impressionable time of life. It came from within fifty, one
hundred miles of here: the Everly Brothers, Elvis, Little Richard, Johnny
Cash and all these guys, so it was never that strange. Obviously the horse
that most people ride in town is still country music, there's no doubt about
that, although that has diversified.

You're said to be the first Brit to arrive in Nashville, a dozen years
ago? One hears stories of people being ripped off; were you able to
take care of yourself, even then?

Oh yes – I've been in it so long, as have most of the other guys around
here. We've gone *through* all of that – but not in America. I really think a
lot less goes on than people think. In all the years I've been here I can only
remember maybe two instances of people who I know for sure were mistreated financially. For most big companies, it's not worth their while to
damage their reputation by trying to rip off an artist, because if they've got
good songwriters they're going to make their money anyway. There's no
percentage in trying to get *more* out of the writer. One thing about Nashville
is this: there's not much opportunity for outsiders to come in just to make
a fast dollar, and head out. Nashville isn't structured that way. You'd be
here two or three years before you're really accepted.

I came here at the end of '72. I'm married to an American girl I met over
there – she was doing her last year at a finishing school type of thing. We've
got a house, with an apartment we rent out. I'm into real estate; we own
a couple of houses in another part of town. After living in London, I couldn't
believe how cheaply you can buy things here! You can buy a house for
$25,000, a good-sized house. So we've got that going, but it's been a
gradual thing. At first it was, 'OK you're an Englishman in Nashville and
it's nice to have you, but we don't really have any *need* for you because
we've got all the country-pickers and the rest of it.' So what do you do? I
had to carve a little niche and create something I could do that they wanted.

Three years ago my partner and I decided to invest very heavily in the
digital synthesizer, which virtually means that you can turn yourself into a
one-man orchestra. We've got over $100,000-worth of equipment in about
four keyboards, a board and the machines. I found that was much better
for me, inasmuch as I could turn out orchestra pieces and whatever in a
much faster time, rather than have to sit down the way I used to, when it
depended if the string player had a headache that morning. . . .

Everybody's doing really well. Roger, for example, was such a hugely
successful writer in England, so he basically just carried on in exactly the
same way as back home. Elton John, when he was Reggie Dwight, he played
for a lot of people. I think the situation with him was that he was regarded
as such an ugly duckling before he became Elton John that nobody would
ever let him come to the front, and sing. He was *so* plain! Eventually when
he got the chance it really was Hans Christian Andersen – like, 'Maybe I'm

still ugly, but I'm going to be grand!' He proceeded to be very grand about it and audiences just loved it. I think they kind of liked the idea of a little fat bald man having the nerve to dress himself up like that.

Do you want to get back to Cheshire?

No. My Mother's from Galway and I'd like to have a pied-à-terre in London and a house in Ireland. That's the dream. You can buy a Georgian manor there for £12,500. I think most émigrés have an idealized view, because time stops when you leave. The last time I went home I hadn't been back for almost five years and I found it kind of depressing, I really did. When you've lived here for a period of time and everything works, the telephones work, if you want a plumber you pick the phone up and he's here within an hour, if there's anything wrong with your TV you don't have to wait for a month, if you move to a new town you get a telephone the day you move in....

If you think London's slow, wait until you get back to Galway!

By the time I get to Galway I'll probably be *looking* for something quaint. But generally I was a little disturbed by what I saw in London. This was in 1981. It was strange to be able to view England as a foreign country and see it with a foreigner's eyes. I saw a lot of stuff that really upset me. One thing about that train in from Gatwick is that it was instant reorientation. By the time we got to Victoria Station I'd got totally back into the run of things.

To try and find out something about England from here is impossible, isn't it? We've got ten thousand miners fighting five thousand police, hundreds arrested, the British way of life crumbling ... but do you read about it here?

Ralph: You find out about the really important things. I was aware of the strikes, but the man in the street in this country is totally occupied with all the problems America's got, at home and abroad. With the vastness of this country, there's a *lot* more going on for the average American to be worried about than miners' strikes in England. To an American it's, So what? A little island over there somewhere....

The problem in this country with a lot of people is cocaine. There's just been a big exposé in the paper – they ran ten or twelve pieces on the drug problem in the country music industry. It's not the LA thing, where there's the mirror on everybody's desk. It's kept much quieter here, but it's around. Part of the problem in LA is the cocaine usage at executive level. It's really had an effect on the quality; some of these movies, they spend $30 million and when you see the picture you say, I know what *those* guys were doing!

Roger: Here, when you get just south of town, it's like the Cotswolds. It's got a small-town mentality, even though it's become a very well-known name as a media centre and it's a State capital and all the rest of it. Within the city limits here there are still operating farms. In an area called Green-hills, which is about four miles south of here, there's this one street with a couple of big high-rise condos – and right next door is this old farm. He doesn't want to sell, so you're right in town and there are cows wandering around eating the grass, and chickens and sheep. It's always been a centre of learning – tended to be less of a bigoted town. There were never as many race problems as in some other places. Any of the English guys you ask, they'll all praise the town to the skies as a place to live. It's like living in Cheltenham, or somewhere like that.

Ralph: I love it here. If you get out of the town about five, six miles, it looks very much like Somerset merging into Devon: gently rolling hills. The hills have not been cleared of timber as much as they have in England. It's very pretty.

Roger: Most of the restaurants do a champagne brunch on Sundays and the one we usually go to is out by the airport. It's called the 101st Airborne and it's a reconstruction of the World War II 101st headquarters in Bel-gium. It's a bombed-out farmhouse right at the airport, and they keep the mood from the minute you arrive. They've built a private road to it, and suddenly you turn this corner and there's a tank facing you! You go over this bridge and they have sentry huts and World War II bombers and jeeps and the actual buildings up on the hill where the planes are coming in. And as soon as you go inside, you go through this sandbag corridor and every-body's in period costume, all the waitresses are in Red Cross uniforms, and all the pictures around are of people who are in the military at the time. And Glenn Miller music playing. When you go in the men's room they have a loop of Winston's speeches. That's one of the things Americans do so well – they do a theme. But it's great fun to be there. At the tables they have earphones that you can put on and listen to the control tower.

You're not eating bullybeef and snoek and Spam?

Oh no, it's very elegant dining.

Michael: Nashville has got old traditional values. They call this place the Buckle of the Bible Belt, it's a very moral, religious type of town, and it rubs off on you because there's a *real* world right here. It's not like Beverly Hills. To see the real LA you've got to drive fifteen miles. You can go across the street here to the store and you've just got those real down-home Southern people who are very no-nonsense, and they won't put up with airs and graces. It's, 'Hey Boy!' Everybody's Boy. I find you can keep your feet on the ground a lot easier.

You'd had what, four dozen hits at home – why come to Nashville?

Roger: When I came originally to America I liked New York better than I liked LA, but still not enough to stay there. I just wanted to get away from the British music scene, because it was getting very stale for me. I'd had almost *too* much success to have any credence there any more. I felt I was being shoved into the Green Room Club of society over there, so I came to a town where nobody really cared a heck who I was, and I kind of hustled for a couple of years.

But you arrived with quite a reputation?

Roger: It was no reputation that mattered a damn here – that's the truth. If you hadn't had a No. 1 country song you didn't really mean much in this town.

And you weren't into country at all?

Roger: Not at that time. I'd had a couple of country hits, but inadvertently – only because pop songs of mine and Roger Greenaway's had been covered. It just so happened that I got introduced to this town and met some wonderful people and found that songwriters are *heroes* here! Hank Williams is more remembered as a songwriter than as a singer and balladeer. They *idolize* songwriters here, and if you're a songwriter that's a very flattering thing. It's nice.

Michael: I always figured making it in England was one thing, but America is the root of rock and roll and if you didn't do something in America, then it didn't really count. And I just loved the Memphis music and all of that.

Ralph, what's your excuse?

Ralph: Virtually the same thing: I was producing a lot of bands for CBS in London that just didn't sell. I was the darling of Fleet Street and I was getting great reviews, but I wasn't earning any money – and the bottom line, commensurate with success, you want money! That's the medium of exchange we have. If you're successful, you make money.

It's how you measure yourself?

Yes – I'm wonderful but I'm poor, and I didn't want to be wonderful and poor any more. I wanted to be disgusting, and rich!

Which is what you are today?

Nope, I'm just disgusting – I've got fifty per cent of my goal!

Apart from that, has it worked out?

Yeah, beautifully. It satisfies the heart, and the pocketbook.

Roger: It's getting recognized for what you do, rather than having to keep up some kind of face for the industry, for the media. You lead a quieter life here, but you get a lot more done in the long run. We've got a catalogue that's grown immensely quickly.

How do you get into country music when you don't even speak the language?

Well, y'awl know that we ca-aan...! The truth is, it takes about two, three years living here before you pick up the fact that you can't get away with the English language – you have to learn the language of country music. And it's a specific language – one word wrong in the song and nobody will cut it. They won't tell you why, but they won't cut it because of that one word, and you gotta find out by keeping your ears open and listening.

So what *is* that word?

That word is ... I can't repeat it here!

You did all right, Michael, from the start?

Michael: Not at first, no. First three years it was like I was from the moon.
Ralph: The ballet lessons didn't help....
Michael: The ballet lessons didn't help. No, but at first I wasn't particularly involved in country, and so consequently the first three years I was here – *nothing.*

Also a Scouse accent can be even thicker than a Bristol accent?

Michael: Depends on what you mean by thick! The accent wasn't the thing, the main thing was that at first there wasn't any *need* for an Englishman because they had so many great players, so I had to kind of carve a niche for myself.
Roger: It's over there, on that wall....
Ralph: I think it's also called digging a grave....

How did the other musicians receive you, the originals – weren't you taking their bread and butter?

Roger: No, we weren't really competing when we came to town. We were more pop-and-rock oriented, originally. We were probably part of the cross-breeding. We came here with ideas from Europe that they needed. I think we've made our little contribution.

Michael: Right now, the people are more accepting of pop sound in country records than they ever were, and a lot of that's got to do with the English. . . .
Ralph: The CMA just did a study on country music in England and it's more popular than any of the other forms. The reason is because we're *all* transplants – everyone here came from Ireland, Wales, Scotland, England and settled in this area. So all we're doing is, complementing what *they* do. And helping to repatriate it, in a way. That's what we're here for.

The folk music here originally came, you're saying, from England?

Ralph: From Ireland, the melodies came. . . . Wales, do we hear Wales? So it's coming home. That's all we did, we came home. I don't think we write country songs, we write songs that country people record. It's a very song-oriented town.

Couldn't you have done all this from Carnaby Street?

Ralph: No!
Michael: Nashville has a great expression: you have to be present to win, and if you really think about it, you *do* have to be present to win. It's a very immediate town. They play by numbers here, they don't play by arrangements. It means you can walk in at a quarter to ten on a ten o'clock session and get the song recorded, because they listen to the demonstration record one time and write it down and play it. The numbers system is unique to here. Instead of using notes, you use numbers. If the key is C then C is 1, and if you go to F which is four spots, that's 4, if you go to G that's 5. So you have 1, 1, 4, 4, 5, 5, which is C, C, F, F, G, G. . . .

But, Roger, you can Teach the World to Sing just as well from Carnaby Street as from Nashville?

Roger: Yes, but not country style. Quite honestly, England developed into a place in the mid-Seventies where records were being made, rather than recordings of songs. The industry then started to leave songwriters behind, and I came here to save myself and my art form, songwriting, and I was allowed to grow and become successful here.
Michael: Even for the guys who come and are not necessarily making a lot of money, it's a pleasant place. If you're gonna be poor – be poor in Nashville, because it's a pleasant place to eke your way out.
Ralph: In someone's house people don't turn on the radio or TV or play records – they sit and take out a guitar and *play* you songs. You see, we all got into rock because that was the one thing we could play. We came out of the Big Band era where no one could play it, so suddenly there was music that was accessible. In Nashville now we have music that's still accessible.

We can actually physically play every hit we hear on the radio with two fingers and sing along and make a reasonable attempt at it. It lures new people into the business and keeps our business going.

Roger: The third-largest industry here is music – it's a billion-dollar-a-year business.

Does Nashville inspire and sustain? I had an office in Carnaby Street in the Seventies and a more dreary uninspiring place I've *never* known!

Ralph: But in Nashville if you go to your dentist and he knows you're in the music business, he's liable to pull his cassette out while he's got you in the chair and make you listen while he's drilling. Or a guy selling you a car. . . .

Roger: You go into the bank here and they smile at you. Not only do they smile at me, Alan, they give me loans and advances. For a musician, that's a rarity!

Ralph: When I leave this bar, I get my boat and I go fishing. It's twenty-five minutes away. There's also seven golf courses here which you can blow into for 250 bucks a year, all within fifteen minutes, and play as much as you want eight months of the year minimum, sometimes longer. . . .

You obviously like it – are you going to be buried here?

Roger: I think so – I think they're trying to already! They'll bury me in the hills of Tennessee.

Ralph: In about three hours. . . .

Michael: I wouldn't mind having the body resting here. That'd be OK.

Roger: We'll return your urn here. This is a good place to put your soul to rest. We're closer to heaven.

You don't want to be buried in Bristol. . . ?

Roger: No – I *was* buried in Bristol. . . .

THE HANSOM CABBY

How much you want for your top hat . . . ?

Brendan Fearon, Bachelor of Arts in American Studies, has been driving a horse-drawn carriage around Central Park for four years. An Irish-Liverpudlian with a small clown's face, dusty black bowler and a fast line of patter, he has Horse-drawn Cab 1050.

The Department of Consumer Affairs licences the sixty-eight carriages that are driven in shifts by some two hundred men and women and, like cabs everywhere in the world, they are extremely profitable; a licence medallion can change hands at forty thousand dollars.

When one sad old nag dropped dead in the Park, Animal Rights campaigners tried to outlaw these tourist delights, but without success. Today there are twenty-five horses in Brendan's Manhattan stable; they and their drivers put in a long day and a longer night. . . .

===

I'm a graduate from Manchester University; in 1979 I got a Bachelor of Arts in American Studies.

You knew you were coming here, did you?

It feels like it was something early, that it wasn't a plan – something like I got a postcard when I was eight or ten and I ended up being here.

Do you think you're using your years of study well?

I think I really am. My study of the actual institutions of the United States, the way the whole party works – I feel I have a greater knowledge of the framework than most Americans. I find them generally pretty ignorant of their country.

Do you think Manchester University would regard you as a successful graduate?

An interesting question! I guess so. In a lot of ways I think they would. They'd say, 'Well the guy's doing something, he's not pushing pens in DHSS.'

When you arrived here four years ago, did you go straight into driving a carriage – or did you have to work up to it?

I had to work up to it. I spent a lot of time with the money I already had. It's a city where you go: Oh *yeah*, everything's new, it's a party, it looks like it was novel, it's somewhere different ... but then after a while you realize you can't live on fresh air for ever.

Except that you now get more fresh air than about ninety-nine per cent of the people in this city!

I certainly do – that's the main attraction of the job, working within the park, yet at night the majority of people insist on rides in the *street*. I try to persuade them into the park. I don't like the cars and the buses and the trucks unless it's twelve, one in the morning, when it's quite beautiful.

Central Park to me has some of the best and the worst of Manhattan....

That's why it works – it's a people's park. That was the phrase that the architect used in the 1860s just after the Civil War when he set out the park. In Latin, *rus in urbe*, you know – countryside within the city, and the park was designed in such a way at that time that you could not see any of the buildings outside the park, so you have to imagine that coming into this was like coming into fairyland for most New Yorkers.

You're slipping into your spiel – I get the feeling you've said that before?

Have I said that bit, that particular phrase? Hard to tell which is spiel and which is me, you know.

You operate at night when this is a dangerous place; have you ever had any trouble?

I've taken four thousand rides through the park and I've had one incident. I also have a whip and a *fast* animal!

The notorious muggers of Central Park, they know you've got cash and you scalp all the customers – they never bother you?

I'd be a fool to say incidents haven't happened, I'd be lying to say that. Maybe I've heard of eight incidents in four years, you know, and most of the time they're unsuccessful, most of the time they're petty – they're not very efficient muggers, as muggers go.

But you're dealing with street people; they may be tourists and they may be rich, but here they *are* street people. You've also got a lot of flaky people hanging around the park, so you're handling outsiders all the time?

You go through the whole spectrum. One moment you're walking past someone wearing ten thousand dollars worth of jewellery and the next person's carrying a bag of a hundred cans that are worth five cents each.

I see you're overtaken by joggers – in fact you're overtaken by walkers!

Yeah, joggers and joggettes. When I get into a car I think it's going too fast, I'm so used to five or ten miles an hour – or in this case, *two* miles an hour.

I would have assumed that the only people who hire you are courting, or want to be alone for a romantic moment?

You get a cross-section. During the day it tends to be families of tourists, Mum, Dad, three kids. Then you get the gaggles of women from Connecticut who pile off the buses. They come in their fours and have to do their various things that are on the itinerary. Then you have the couples, you have your drunks, then you have both single men and single women. There's a lot of well-off women who come into the city by themselves and they pick a handsome driver – they don't usually go with the older men – and they go for the prettier carriages.

You get a little romance yourself, do you?

I certainly do. I'm primarily here to enjoy myself, I wouldn't do it if I didn't.

A lot of these horses seem sad and old to me, do you get into trouble with the animal protection people?

The people I work for have undoubtedly the best health record in the city – they never have any problems with the twenty-five horses that come out of my stable. Some of the other stables, well there is a lot of criticism about the animals. I feel that a lot could be improved in this industry just by cleaning the horse every morning, just making him a bath once a week, just by simple basics. There are people within the industry, it's sad to say, who do not do that.

And the poor old things live on carbon monoxide, don't they?

If they're in the park it's not as bad – but you and I live on carbon monoxide too, when we live in Manhattan.

That's so – maybe that's why *we* look so sad.... Anyhow the animal protection people come waving their fists at you, do they?

Oh they come along with routine checks, how many hours you've worked in harness, check underneath the harness to see if there are marks on the animal. Rub their hands underneath to see if there is any break in the flesh. Each horse has got a hoof number on his bottom left and a bridle number on his bridle, on his chin strap, and they co-ordinate those with their records.

Incidentally, can you see this going in Hyde Park?

In all honesty I don't know the geography of Hyde Park. What it requires is a density of affluent people within a small catchment area. You see you get a lot of passer-by trade. However if you were starting in Hyde Park you'd be able to advertise.

What do you charge? Everyone tells me, 'They're real scalpers, these guys.'

Well it varies. In all honesty when we're working through Central Park here we're charging fifteen dollars during the day for a ride which is around the twenty-five minute mark, and I feel that's fair. In a lot of ways, it's underpriced. But then you get people coming up and saying, 'I want to go to a theatre.' Now I'm not a fool, you know, it takes me twice as long to go there and back as it does to do *one* ride in the park, so to me that's worth twice the amount of money, it has to be. But the way the rate is structured it doesn't say that, so in some ways when one reads the law they can say, Yes you are scalping, but to me that's the way of earning a living.

So that's fifteen dollars for twenty-five minutes basic. Then you want a tip, over that – so what do you get on a good day?

On Tuesday night I took twenty-two dollars for a ride that went through the city just over half an hour, and the guy turned round and gave me forty dollars. I didn't say a word to the people before or after the ride. I didn't ask for forty dollars, that's what they gave me. It does happen that people will give you pictures of various presidents, larger and larger, for no apparent reason at all – apart from the fact that they want to give a hundred-dollar bill to somebody. I've known someone just go a block and give you a hundred dollars, because they want to distribute the wealth or something, I dunno what it is.

They don't do it to taxi-drivers – or at least, I don't do it to taxi-drivers!

No, no. (Laughs). My policy around taxi-drivers is that they get ten per cent. I tend to overtip, it's a tipping industry and I feel that what I give is what I receive. On the other hand I won't tip just because I *have* to tip, y'know. I mean some taxi-drivers are appalling. I've got out of cabs in New York City, I've stopped the cab and said, 'Sorry I can't deal with you.'

So what kind of people are paying you this kind of money?

Anybody. Ninety per cent of the people riding this year were Americans, due to the strength of the dollar, from just about every State.

Do they want you to talk or do they want you to shut up while they enjoy the romance of it all?

Some people want you to shut up. You gather that after the third grunt, that's why you don't go into the bit about the aesthetics of the park, right? (Laughs.) But then there are the other people who like rattle questions from the moment you're into the carriage till the moment they're out. And sometimes they'll ask questions before they get the answer.

But the courting couples don't want a running commentary, I presume?

Depends how long they've known each other. You find the married couples usually want to talk a lot more, and relate a lot more, whereas people in their romance or their engagement want to be with each other as opposed to being with you.

You're a sort of gondolier, in a way....

Yeah it's funny, on the rainy nights I *will* say 'Gondola rides!' to people as they're going past and you'll be surprised who'll get in, y'know. It's as wet as a gondola in New York sometimes, it really is. Interesting simile, interesting similarity....

How about English people? Can they afford this kind of transport?

I took some English people the very first ride of this morning. They are living in Australia, working in California but they are definitely from Leeds, and they still talk 'liiike thut, tha' knows'. . . .

Although you're making out financially can you see yourself doing this for the rest of your life, until your bowler hat turns grey?

Oh no no no no, I'm afraid not. I can see myself *owning* an industry like this maybe, but I could not see myself actually sitting and giving the spiel, so to speak, as we pass the various points of interest. I'll give it a year.

Another year – so you'll have had four years on the trot; then what?

I'll move into something leisure-oriented. I like working with my hands, I'd love to do restoration. I think in Europe there's a lot of these old old carriages which can be restored and exported to the States with no problem.

Will I eventually go back to live in Liverpool? I don't think so. Much as I love the city where I grew up, it's not somewhere I want to live any more. I don't think it serves me to do that. I want to prosper in my life and I just feel that North America's the place, north-west England is *not* the place.

There are not many hundred-dollar bills being given away in Liverpool these days, unfortunately.

There certainly are not. You have to work a good sixty hours at Fords or somewhere before someone'll give you that amount of money. I'm going to pull to a halt because we have to get across this traffic.

Do they give way to you, does sail have preference over steam?

When they first drew up laws for combustion engines anywhere in the world they gave preference to the animals, but as you might know, there are more combustion engines than there are animals at this point – Get up, Scott! The majority of car drivers are pretty courteous. Technically speaking I have right of way; practically speaking, it's whatever goes.

I'd been doing the job about three or four weeks and I'm still a little naïve to the aspects of the job and America in general. I was passing the Essex House on my way home and five typical Texans with the hats and everything get out of a car. You can tell from their walk they're from Texas, no problem. They say, 'Hey, we wanna ride, we wanna ride.' I pull over and they yell, 'We'll check in and we'll be right out,' and I said, 'If you give me money I'll sit and wait.' So I sat and waited and out they come. They're like the most boisterous, y'know, as loud as loud can be be 'cos they're from Texas and they're in New York. We're about half-way through the ride and

421

I'm wearing this scruffy top hat which has been through the horse dung and under the wheels and bounced down the street and you name it.... It does not look its best. It really does not look Saks of Fifth Avenue at all. And this guy says, 'How much you want for your top hat?' He says, 'I'm from Texas and I can buy anything.'

Once I heard that (laugh) the dollar signs began to roll, y'know. So I said to him, 'Well, I turned down seventy-five dollars last week, and he says, 'How does a hundred and twenty-five sound?' And I said, 'Yeah, OK.' 'There you are,' he says, 'I can buy anything,' and he shoved it on his head. He practically broke it as he put it on. It probably lasted about another fifteen minutes, I think. Probably ended up in a bar somewhere on Central Park South. But hats are very useful. I went out and bought another one the following day.

Had any offers for it?

I haven't had for this one, maybe it should get a little shabbier. I think they go for the shabby-genteel, you know?

Yes, a touch of the Paul Newmans: 'Raindrops keep falling on my hat ...!' But that was a bicycle; these horses are not the happiest animals I've ever seen, I have to tell you.

I really feel that horses do three things: they work, they run and they eat. They're happiest when they're eating, but they also like to work and run, and as long as they're well fed that's what the nature of the beast is. He likes to pull. He pulled the stones for all these buildings a hundred years ago and today he just pulls a very light carriage. *I* could pull this with people in it.

I can see he knows the way home better than you do; he doesn't need you, does he?

If the horse could make change, I'd be out of a job....

THE SOCIAL WORKER

*I can be a positive role model for black women
in Liverpool....*

Mary Hayes is small, smiling, gentle and determined; she wears bright
clothes and lots of rings. In Liverpool, where she was born, she hardly
realized she was black, but after marrying an American and coming
to Detroit in 1959 had to adjust to the pecking order among the
blacks in the US.

She divorced, remarried, divorced again – and now has three
grown children and two granddaughters. She studied social work
and works for the Mid-Peninsula Support Network, a group dealing
mainly with violence in the family: battered wives, assaulted children,
drug addicts.

I went with her to the jail at Martinez, in the Californian canyon
country behind Berkeley, where she interviewed two women prisoners. The prison was lightly controlled, inmates sleeping in separate
cells and using the coffee percolators and soft-drink machines in the
recreation area. We returned to the residential centre of her New Day
drug treatment programme at Palo Alto, south of San Francisco,
where former addicts disciplined themselves: a few who had offended
some Centre rule sat silently on chairs staring at the wall, as though
class dunces.

Of all the Brits I met Mary was one of the most Americanized – yet
the only one anxious to return home; after a quarter of a century in
the States, she wants to go back to Liverpool.

———

This is a splendid jail – I've been in worse hotels!

Absolutely, I'm sure you have! It's one of the nicest jails I go to. Some of
them are quite gloomy and very jail-like. I remember my very first experience was the San Francisco Jail and it met my every expectation. When I
came here I thought this was wonderful, it's like a country club.

What were you doing with those two women prisoners?

I was interviewing them and making an assessment as to whether I felt they were potential clients for the New Day drug programme.

You call them 'clients'?

I don't like to refer to them as patients or criminals – to me they're human beings.

It's up to them to convince you that they'd be better in your residential treatment programme than in jail, so they're going to be on their best behaviour?

Well yes they are, but some of them come across as being far more motivated than others, so I have to make that determination. I usually ask them some intimate personal questions to get a sense of where they are in life, where they're coming from. Some people I interview I feel flatly that they're not going to be appropriate.

One of those girls said she'd had twenty-three convictions!

I know – but they may all be petty. The nature of their problem, that incredible habit they have, means committing a crime is not to them committing a crime, it's merely a means of fulfilling their own needs.

I get the impression some of these girls are doing a life sentence, six months at a time?

That's quite possible. Maybe some of them are. Hopefully they'll come into a programme that'll alter that lifestyle.

Mary, you left Liverpool twenty-five years ago – could you see yourself ending up in jail?

No I couldn't! I was left with three children and raised my children by myself. My husband wanted to be an entertainer and he left, and I had to struggle by myself. I probably would not have been above shoplifting some groceries to feed my children. I didn't *have* to do that but I probably could have, and if I had, the chances are I might have got caught and could have been here.

Did you manage to keep your children away from drugs?

Oh God yes.

Without problems?

No, can't say without problems. I kept my children in private schools, and I like to think that private schools are less tainted than the public schools, because they're small. My oldest daughter told me that Tony had been smoking pot in our recreation room. I remember coming home and she said, 'Mummy what are you going to *do* to him? Talk to him, he's violated our home.' I wasn't quite sure what to do. I didn't really consider it *that* serious, but my daughter kept putting pressure on me so I felt I had to be a very serious parent. Tony was about fourteen, and essentially I said to him, 'I've raised all three of you to be relatively independent individuals, to basically make your own choice in life, so if you choose to use drugs, to smoke marijuana, that's perfectly all right because I've given you the freedom to do that, and if your marijuana leads to cocaine or heroin and you kill yourself, that's perfectly all right because it's your life – but I want you to know that you'll break your mother's heart.' And he just boo-hooed at the table and he's never touched anything since then.

Now he's in the army – so he cleaned up his act?

He's a Ranger in the Paratroops; and my girls don't even smoke.

After all this, would you like to go back to Liverpool?

Yes, I feel as though I want to go home, I want to work with my people. I've been working with American men and women for the past fifteen years and I think I have a lot of skills and knowledge. I also feel I can be a positive role model for black women in Liverpool.

How do you feel being a black woman in Liverpool might compare with being black in the environs of San Francisco?

I've travelled around the world, I feel very proud of who I am. I'll be just as proud of being a black Englishwoman in England as I am of being a black Englishwoman in America.

Do you imagine the reaction will be different?

No I really don't, in fact it may be easier. I've spoken to some people in my career field and they seem to feel that doors might be readily opened for me, because there aren't an awful lot of black female professionals in the field of social work in Liverpool.

When you came over in '59, how did you find being black in America, after living in Liverpool?

I knew I was black, but there just seemed to be varying degrees of black-
ness in the United States that I was never really aware existed in England. . . .

At the Agency

When the probation officers or the judges, when the courts call the office
here and say they have someone in jail whose crime is drug-related and
that they really want to change their ways, they *want* to come into a drug
programme . . . I go out to a jail, I interview the individual, make an assessment, determine whether I feel they are appropriate for the Agency, and
then the courts make arrangements for them to come into the programme.
When we're full to capacity there are twenty-four men and twelve women.
It's a residential treatment, and we like to think that people will stay for
nine months. I do some counselling here but there's no drug treatment,
absolutely no drug treatment whatsoever – in fact we don't accept anyone
who's on drugs of any type. They have to be drug-free, they have to have
gone through their withdrawals before they come here.

It's like an open prison – they can walk out any time they want
to?

Absolutely. The idea is to instil trust and to allow them the sense of
freedom. Of course if they do leave, we don't go after them, we don't police
them. We contact the court and they put out a bench warrant, and then
the courts go after the individuals.

So it's their choice – they can be in here or in the slammer?

Exactly. However, there are many individuals who come here of their
own free will because they realize that on the street they can't stop. Many
have been in jail for two and three years and have stopped using drugs, but
when they come out on to the street and get right into drugs again they
say, 'I've got to do something,' and they come into a programme like this.

What's the class and racial breakdown of the people here?

Because this is basically a black community, East Palo Alto, there's
usually more black people here. It runs between about forty per cent white,
sixty per cent combination of black and Latin.

Why do you believe they get on to drugs? Is it peer pressure?

Basically if they've started young it *is* peer pressure. With those who have started older, say in their thirties, it's been the pressure of their profession, the job pressures, having to meet deadlines. This whole area, not just East Palo Alto but the whole Silicon Valley, is actually running rampant with coke abusers.

What counselling do you do? I've just been reading your New Day Philosophy which seems to be in 'Americaspeak', from a calendar.... Is that the kind of thing you're telling them?

A lot of encounter-therapy goes on. That is where the facilitator will not allow an individual to lie or to minimize or to deny what's going on. Not only that, but other people in the group will say, 'This is what *really* happened to you,' and 'Goddammit, you'd better tell me.' There's that sort of encounter, so the person is almost stripped. They can't lie. It really is a cleansing process.

They're all representatives of a lost generation?

That's pretty harsh, I think. If I believed that I would not be doing the job I'm doing. I have a basic belief in humanity and I believe that if everyone is given a fair chance, the chances are they can make something of their life. I've seen it happen with some of the people I brought in. I interviewed them, felt very good about them, and I've seen them make incredible strides. One young man has gone on to a four-year college, another man who was a chronic alcoholic, an incredible nervous wreck, has written a play about alcohol abuse and we're hoping to produce this play as a fund-raising means for our Agency.

Can you counsel people out of the habit?

Out of the habit, no. I think what happens is one habit is usually replaced by another. Very often it's replaced by chronic cigarette smoking or religion or overeating or work.

I've seen that Jesus does work – it seems religion can solve the problem instantly?

Some people hide behind Jesus, too. They feel, Well because I'm religious, therefore I can't do anything wrong. It does work, but I also think like everything else Jesus can be used as a shield to hide behind. . . .

427

THE BUTLER

It is so easy to intimidate them, without trying. . . .

There were thirty thousand butlers in Britain before the war; today there are said to be ninety-nine. Part of that wastage must have been caused as English butlers homed-in on their promised land: Texas.

Stuart Heasman, brought up in Tunbridge Wells, was a butler in Illinois before reaching the haven of Texas – where he approved of the climate if not his employers. Like some young Sergeant Bilko with careful English enunciation, balding and outspoken, he takes a lofty view of most of them: 'I spent seven years in Chicago with a delightful employer; unfortunately one cold winter, she died. Socially Texas is impossible: *nouveaux riches*, or to use a local expression, white niggers. Some even have an education. Most of them are only used to illiterate black servants. Dallas is too small to be healthy: they all go to the same Baptist churches, same schools, same university, vote Republican and worship football. If you are not a demonstratively practising Christian you are obviously a Communist.'

━━━

I was in the hotel business in those days eleven years ago, and dumb. The chain I was working for sent me as part of a course to Switzerland, and one of the problems with working such fine hotels is that their standards were so very high: they had umpteen members of staff – the staff-to-guest ratio was incredible. That in a way really spoiled me for the reality of America.

When did you face the reality of America?

Does *anybody* face the reality of America? I came over in 1973, and probably by '77 I'd realized that my career in the hotel business was going nowhere, absolutely nowhere. Sure I could have stayed on as head receptionist or something, scraped together a living and all the rest of it, but why should you leave the relative comforts of Britain to scrape a living in the United States? That to me does not make any sense whatever.

So why did you?

Good question – I've still not really figured it out. Obviously I was young, I was pretty bloody stupid, unfortunately had a few stars in my eyes. I think I saw America as the land of milk and honey.

I suppose everybody does, who comes here. . . .

Well yes, and people who don't want to see the other side of America will *only* see that – because as you know there is a great deal of milk and honey in this country.

Head porters are men of power and influence who get large tips anywhere in the world – and you were at The Mansion on Turtle Creek, a Dallas hotel of significance, so in Texas you should have pocketed even *more*. . . . Where did you go wrong?

I certainly did not make oodles of money. I probably was not there long enough to establish a reputation, but I certainly enjoyed dealing with the guests. They were very pleasant. It was nice to have Larry Hagman call one day and ask for a favour, even though he wasn't staying in the hotel. I met some very charming people and I would have been very happy to have stayed on.

So in that case, why did you stop head portering?

I was fired.

That's a good reason.

The excuse was they didn't think I was quite their material, whatever that meant. It all started when Linda Gray, who stars in *Dallas*, spent the summer with us at the hotel. She's a very charming lady and she would normally kiss me as she went out the door. Well of course as luck would have it, the rooms manager happened to be in the lobby at the time and he thought that was pretty unprofessional conduct on my part.

You should have stopped her kissing you?

That's what he would have liked me to have done.

I suppose it must have been an unusual relationship – I don't see *many* people kissing hall porters, around the world. . . .

Well perhaps not, but Linda Gray is a very warm and friendly lady. You couldn't find an easier lady to talk to. In fact the over-riding impression I got about Linda was she was very odd; I thought somebody in her position would not have behaved in that fashion.

So anyhow, you were kissed-off from your hotel job?

Yes – in more ways than one, folks! Then I became a butler again, though my duties weren't really the traditional duties of a butler. My employer was an Italian gentleman – I mean a genuine immigrant, he wasn't of Italian–American stock, he had a home in Beverly Hills and he maintained this ten-thousand-square-feet mansion in Dallas mainly as a place he could stay in comfort when he had business in town. At the time he had several real-estate ventures in Dallas so it was convenient for him to stay there – and of course like everybody else he hoped to make a nice profit when he sold the property.

I thought the ambition of every rich Texan was to have a butler – that once you had a butler, you'd arrived?

No I think the average wealthy American, wealthy Texan – and let's face it, we *are* talking of the *nouveaux riches* – they live a very subdued quiet lifestyle. For example in the TV series *Dallas*, as you know, you have all these members of the family married and living under one roof. That's not really *that* much of an exaggeration amongst certain very very wealthy Texans. I know of several multi-millionaire oil men in Texas who still live in a caravan, and they're very happy because they can move the caravan on site, so they're always there at the well. I don't know if they're there for security purposes, but I was intrigued to read recently that the amount of theft of well-head equipment in this State is of monumental proportions, so maybe they're acting as their own security guards.

I've often wondered when they get tired of me on television, whether the next-best life might be as a butler in an enormous Dallas mansion....

You would do it very well.

Thank you, thank you.

You'd intimidate the hell out of them, but the trouble is – it *is* so easy to intimidate them, without trying. That's the problem. They're intimidated, in my opinion, by anybody who can string two sentences together which are reasonably grammatical. I mean God knows, I don't speak the King's English – but compared with some of them, yes I do.

But isn't that what they're paying for – intimidation? It's like these creepy Maître d's who you bribe to permit you to have a table in some awful New York restaurant. . . .

Not just New York – you have to bribe them everywhere.

But employers want butlers to be daunting, don't they? They like you to frighten their friends?

They want you to be daunting, perhaps, but they don't want you to be able to think for yourself. They want you to Do as I bid you. . . .

It must be quite hard living up to a butler in England, let alone Texas. You have to change your entire lifestyle, with this ominous black figure emerging and overawing everyone. . . .

I honestly don't think I'm that different a person as a butler, as when I'm *not* a butler. Most people in Texas of course would be totally intimidated by the black striped trousers and the morning coat.

And the fact that you may know the name of a wine. . . .

Well yes, I can just about pronouce the silly thing – but that always intimidates them. Just the other day I was driving with my boss and we passed the St Mark's Prep School, so I just said in polite conversation, 'Tell me Mr So-and-So is this St Mark's affiliated with *the* St Mark's?' He said, 'I didn't know there *was* another St Mark's.' Here's a man who's worth nine figures, he'd never heard of St Mark's! This is what I don't understand about them, they seem to live in a cocoon.

But isn't it your job to evangelize?

Perhaps it is – but I'm not a very good evangelizer.

They want you to dress the set?

Yes, provided of course, I keep my mouth shut.

Well can't you go along with that, if they're paying you heavily?

I am very sorry, they are *not* paying heavily. If they were paying heavily, that would be a different story. We all have our price!

What sort of money are we talking about, may I ask?

I wouldn't get out of bed for less that two thousand dollars a month. Of course it's the kind of money you wouldn't get in England, but with all due respect to my countrymen, they *do* earn a pittance compared with Americans. I don't think the British realize that in this country any Tom, Dick or Harry can make forty grand a year, and even on $40,000 a year in Dallas you would not qualify for a mortgage! That the average doctor starts at $200,000 a year, and that a good anaesthetist after about three or four years in the workplace would command $400,000 a year, and that if you are a decent dentist – and of course many of them *are*, here – you have a licence to print money.

But of course I never was in that bracket. People asked me what I was earning and I used to tell them because of course the natural instinct is to convert from dollars into pounds sterling, and people go, '*Umm!*' They forget, where does that go in Dallas, where does that go in a *safe* white neighbourhood? You're talking of a minimum of $900,000, in fact a million dollars and up, for the standard three-bedroomed house.

Safe white neighbourhood?

Yes safe, this is the big point isn't it? There are many white neighbourhoods all over the United States, but how many of them are safe and in how many of those neighbourhoods could you walk alone at night? The answer is, very few. Of course I realize that probably in Britain there are now areas where you would think twice about walking alone at night, but I know there are *very* few such neighbourhoods in America. To me it's an absolute basic in life. If you don't feel safe, surely something is wrong?

Have any of your various houses been burgled?

No we've never had that problem, I think because the local police department is about a hundred and fifty yards away from us. Of course we have the mandatory security system inside the house. I don't own a gun. Most people have advised me to have one, but knowing my luck either it would jam when I went to fire it or worse, I'd miss. People advise you to buy a shotgun because that way you can't really miss, can you? But we have to make sure if we shoot the intruder that he's absolutely inside the house, because if you shoot him as he's coming through the window and the blast of the gun shoves him *outside* the window, then you can be had up for murder! If he falls inside the house that's fine, that's self-defence.

And if he gets away, he'll sue you....

Oh God yes – I chuckled when I lived in Chicago because a black bus driver had been held up twice in his career and on each occasion he pulled out his .45 and shot the guy dead, and there was no court case – just self-defence, and let off. In Britain there would be some kind of accountability at least, but not over here.

I always believed butlers would be thick on the ground in Texas, that they'd arrive like the swallows and be living in marvellous grace-and-favour cottages on the family estate, driving the owner's Cadillac, drinking the owner's wine....

No. I had my own cottage and I would not have accepted the position had it been any other way – I mean I certainly would not live in my employer's principal house. It wouldn't have worked for them, it wouldn't have worked for me. Both sides have to have their privacy. No, down here the problem is, I think, that most Texans have great difficulty in forgetting that slavery was abolished 110, 112 years ago. They still look upon anybody who acts in a service position as, of course, somebody menial. They don't understand that you can have pride in what you do....

You're supposed to overawe them – yet they've overawed you?

I suppose I let them, yes I think that probably was my mistake.... And yet I don't know, at times it was obvious that I *did* overawe them – but you see that did not make me feel more self-confident, that made me feel *less* self-confident because I couldn't understand how anybody could allow themselves to be intimidated by *me*....

That's Catch 22! So how did you find Americans treat their hired help?

With something not much more than contempt – it's extraordinary, down here. For example, I had two maids working with me, two maids is the *minimum* when you're talking of ten thousand square feet of home, plus laundry for five people. The maids of course were wetbacks, as most of them are. Delightful ladies, hardworking as you can imagine and of course the hard facts of economics are that if you're a wetback, if you have a child but you have no husband, you don't have much choice in America, or anywhere else for that matter. You damn well *have* to work, and they did just that – they worked their tails off. But there was always that attitude from my employers: "Oh well there's nothing else they can do, they should be thanking us for working for us.'

Did they not regard you at least as some sort of status symbol?

They didn't.

How *did* they regard you?

A thorn in their flesh, I think.

You gave them a hard time?

At first I didn't go out of my way to give them a hard time – I just think my *personality* gave them a hard time. . . . The problem is that it's not difficult to give these people a hard time. At Christmas my employer gave his part-ners a rather handsome crystal ice-bucket and glass set. It wasn't just any old crystal, this was Lalique. OK, the ice bucket takes two hands to carry and cost about six hundred bucks and the glasses similar quality, similar price. He couldn't find a silver tray that would accommodate the ice-bucket plus the glasses so he went to Gumps, the US equivalent of Mappin and Webb, to commission special silver trays for the occasion. He wanted me to deliver them in person at night in my tux – and this of course was the week before Christmas when the temperature was right down to nine degrees. It wasn't, 'Would you mind, Stuart?' or 'I have a great favour to ask you,' it was just, 'I *want* you to do this, this and this.' I just literally lost my cool and said, 'If you want a performing seal why don't you go down to the zoo!' Well of course that totally threw him, and he shut up after that. I don't believe that function properly falls within the job description of a butler. At least not in my book.

Sounds as though you *were* asserting yourself.

I didn't assert myself enough, frankly. I don't like to have to put people in their place.

But butlers have been doing that for ages – that's what butlers are *for*.

Maybe, but I don't enjoy telling people what they should know. There are many many people in America who would be, perhaps not overjoyed to employ me, but nonetheless would I'm sure be quite happy to have someone like myself.

In your eleven years in America have you ever felt at home, or have you always found yourself a stranger?

I think I've always felt myself a stranger. Every time you walk into a store and ask for something and heads turn, I realize I'm just tired of sticking out like that. I want to be able to merge, to blend in with the background. But of course with an accent like mine it's impossible. People said to me in the beginning, 'You really ought to lose your English accent.'

I thought it was a selling point – people are supposed to say they just love your accent!

Some people do, provided they're not intimidated by it, but I found with the professional people in particular – doctors, lawyers – the back would arch. They were very threatened by it.

Why?

It's insecurity. It's everywhere, don't you think so? I see Americans as the insecure on God's earth. What it stems from, I think, is partly they know they're a young country and they are of course mad with jealousy because we have a Royal Family that, with a few exceptions, does not put a foot wrong. I think they would give anything to have Her Majesty always here, always with the right word, the right gesture – you wouldn't be ashamed to be seen out with her. . . .

You mean, you can take her almost anywhere?

I would hope *everywhere*! But of course as you know, America has never had this. Poor Nancy, she can't help it but she's been lifted so many times you're wondering when the belly-button is going to show . . .

With the Royal Family of course, there's also a sense of continuity.

That's precisely it. They may not particularly like being the Royal Family, and I certainly don't envy their job, but I think on the whole they do it marvellously well. Americans are very jealous of that fact.

Do you think after your experience with Texans, that if you were a butler in Palm Beach or Bel Air, in New England or Long Island, you might be happier?

There's a good chance, yes. Certainly if you take the north-east you're talking about old money, and that's quite different. They are used to having people in my capacity around them all the time. They want service and they're prepared to pay for it.

They won't expect you to deliver their Christmas gifts. . . .

It's like everything else – if they scratch my back I'll scratch theirs. Obviously if I hadn't felt the antipathy from my last employer. . . .

Do Americans see domestic service as demeaning?

Yes of course.

Do you?

No. Well, it depends. Working for my last employers they certainly made me feel that it was demeaning, but my Italian gentleman, good heavens, he was always totally correct. There was always a 'Please', a 'Thank you', 'I wonder Stuart would you mind', or 'Could you do this....' It was never, 'We *need* you to do this.' Let's face it, there is a way of asking for everything and when somebody says to me, 'We need you to do this,' I'm sorry – that grates on me.

It's curious because Americans are generally polite, are they not – that Have-a-nice-day syndrome?

What does that mean – excuse me, what does that mean?

It's just a pleasant little genuflection that oils the wheels of day-to-day social intercourse like, How do you do?

I would put it this way: I would rather someone said to me with a genuine smile, 'Have a nice day,' than ignore me. True, I would rather have that, but it brings us to the whole frankly bullshine thing that in America, everything is wonderful, life is a bowl of cherries, there are no problems, we are just sort of coasting along, isn't life wonderful, have a nice day. That grates on me after a while, but I think it's perhaps preferable to some of the people I have bumped into in Britain who look as though life ain't worth living. Have you never come across that in Britain? Have you gone into businesses and the people who are supposed to be there to help you really look as though the world's just caved in and that helping you is such a big deal?

Do you think you would have had a happier eleven years if you'd stayed in England?

Oh no I would never have been bitten by the United States. I think all Europeans are bitten by America. We talk very often, very negatively about America, and many of us talk about going – as I *am* going home – but there is no question in my mind that I will come back one day. I have several European friends who've now gone back and are trying to readjust to Europe again, because of course there *is* a tremendous adjustment to be made when you move from one society to another.

What was your major adjustment when you came to the States?

There were quite a few: we have here, conservatively, thirty-three million people living below the poverty line. This is something about America I will never understand. Of course I realize that feeding the poor and housing the homeless doesn't win votes, but I just think there is something fundamentally wrong with any society that would ignore those thirty-three million. I know we have poverty in Britain, but I think we're more aware of the fact, we don't ignore it. Americans ignore it: it's tasteless.

The brashness and the vulgarity I find very hard to take, even to this day. Their gratuitous use of four-letter words – though down here in the Bible Belt of course you rarely hear a four-letter word. There are so many cultural differences. I mean on a very minor level, the fact that the average American, even the average so-called educated wealthy American, doesn't know how to hold a cup and saucer! They've never *owned* a cup and saucer – they drink out of mugs, right? We drink out of cups and saucers and they think that's very prim. Small things like that are confusing. I don't pretend to understand America, don't think I ever shall. . . .

THE HOLLYWOOD WIFE

I married the World Champion Bulldogger....

Lee married Vincent Minelli, ex-husband of Judy Garland; small and slight and blonde and very English, she lives in an old house on Sunset Boulevard in Beverly Hills with her invalid husband, worrying about his health and that of his daughter Liza – who had just gone into hospital with all sorts of problems. On a clear day on her patio, we had tea and cucumber sandwiches....

━━━

I was engaged to Eugene in England – he invented the permanent wave, which was quite a thing. We had a very nice yacht here because he bought the yacht club on Lake Champlain, but when the Germans went into Paris they confiscated all his factories and everything. We went down to Jamaica on our honeymoon and it was wonderful there because I ran into the Governor of Jamaica at the time, and Eugene and I stayed with them at Shaw Park in Montego Bay. Then we came back to America and we married, but things didn't go too well so I got a divorce.

I went out to visit some friends in Nevada – this was during the war – and met the cattle rancher who had just won the world championship at the Madison Square Rodeo for bulldogging. He was very handsome and attractive, and so I married him. I almost didn't marry him, then I did. I said I'd meet him in Wyoming – and then I changed my mind and I didn't.

He called up and said he'd been waiting for me at the airport and I just didn't show. He said, 'What is this, the brush?' Of course I didn't understand those American expressions, so I said, 'No it wasn't that.' Then a strange thing happened: a girlfriend of mine who was at the ranch fell madly in love with his partner and she said, 'I'm going up to see him in Montana,' so I said, I'll come with you. We got a driver and drove up from Nevada to Montana and when we arrived there a big rodeo was on; nobody could get into a hotel, it was jammed. So I changed into my western clothes, and we were married the next day.

He had a beautiful ranch. I lived there for about five years, I suppose, but he just drank too much. He had a quarter of a bottle of Scotch before he got up in the morning, and you can't live with that and ride and work hard like he did. It was a wonderful life for him, but not much for me. We didn't have any children.

The funny thing was, I came to Beverly Hills and there was a girl who'd been at school with me in England. She'd married and had a home down the road, so I came out to visit her because by then her husband had been drafted into the army. While I was staying with her a friend of mine was going to a party at the Romanoffs' and asked, Would we like to come? We said Yes, and among the movie people there was Louella Parsons. I saw this very attractive man sitting in the corner and I said to Miss Parsons, 'Who is that man?' She said, 'Oh he's married,' and I said, 'Well forget it!' But I said, 'Who is it?' and she said, 'It's Vincent Minelli, the Academy Award-winning director.'

Then I met Vincent's wife Denise and she was very charming and we got along and she asked me to parties. If she gave a dinner party here she always invited me and said, 'Vincent always wants you to sit next to him,' so I said, 'Well that's fine,' and we got along beautifully. Then when Denise fell in love with this millionaire from San Francisco – the Hale company, they own all those stores – and Vincent was in Brighton making *On a Clear Day* with Barbra Streisand, there was a big romance. Everybody knew it except Vincent.

When he came back she said she wanted a divorce, and moved up to San Francisco. It was a terrible blow because he had no idea what was going on. She called me and said, 'If you're entertaining or anything, please ask Vincent because he enjoys being with you.' So I did.

So you got married and lived happily ever after! You still keep your English friends, though – I hear the Rothermeres are moving away from Beverly Hills?

Pat has this beautiful house, is she selling that? What a mistake – I *begged* her not to buy that house. I'll tell you why: it's terribly out of town – it's way up and off the beaten track and it takes forty-five minutes to get down to Beverly Hills, so can you imagine on a rainy night.... When we went to London I said, 'You can't buy that house, the man was murdered there.'

The chap who owned it, a choreographer, he had a butler in the house and a housekeeper-cleaning woman who came in every day. One morning she couldn't find him and she went to his bedroom and there was blood everywhere. He was cut to ribbons. He was gay. But Pat bought it because she loved the view. Also she then thought she was divorcing him and wanted some property here....

We went back to England about three years ago. The British Film Institute did a retrospective of Vincent's Academy Award-winning pictures, and they did it beautifully. We stayed at the Dorchester and there was a very elderly gentleman who cleaned the shoes and he remembered my father, and that was amazing. But I lost all my family during the war – I was buried in a building myself. I was born in Scotland. I'm Scots-Irish, I went to Roedean but I went to a church school first, a beautiful old convent.

Strange you haven't lost your accent?

I haven't? Oh I'm glad. Everything happens for the best you know. Liza had a mole on her neck she wanted removed and that's a minor thing – you're back in the show that night. But her reaction to the medication was so bad the doctor said, 'Something's very wrong,' and he took blood tests and he said, 'Miss Minelli, you'll have to come into hospital right away....'

THE SOCIALITE

*It never occurred to me I was taking on
four almost-grown children. . . .*

An English deb twenty years ago, Jane Ylvisaker is now a society
lady in Barrington, an elegant white-fence residential area in rolling
countryside forty-five miles outside Chicago. She had found herself,
at the age of twenty-five, with a ready-made family: 'I was up to *here*
in it!' Now she rides and does charity work, while thirty minutes up
the road her sixty-year-old husband, a prescient but impatient chairman with an English mother, runs the massive Gould Electronics Inc.
On the side, as polo player and property developer, he welcomed
Prince Charles to his grounds outside Palm Beach in Florida.

Jane, slim and pretty, lives a picture-book life with lots of dogs,
homes, stepchildren, stables, twenty horses – and a ten-year-old son
she is keen should become a tennis champion. Their Barrington
house could have been transported stone-by-stone from her native
Cotswolds – indeed on the surface her life seems little different from
that she might have enjoyed had she married a Birmingham indus-
trialist with a home in Gloucestershire – though one of her four
American stepchildren died from an overdose of cocaine. . . .

People tease me and say I only moved here because it made me feel at
home. Actually it was Bill who loved the house and its seven fireplaces. It's
very large – there are thirteen bathrooms and eleven bedrooms, and the
apartment over the garage. Nowadays you can't find anybody to build a
house like this, the woodwork and stonework – but it's the same in England
I suppose.

A friend of mine over here was moving house and she'd seen one she
liked but was concerned because it was *so* old. I asked how old it was,
expecting her to say a couple of hundred years – and she said, 'Eight.' She
was already worried about the roof and the plumbing. To us it's incomprehensible. Eight years old – that's horribly modern!

When you arrived as a former deb, did you fit in to America right
away?

I was wonderfully naïve and it never occurred to me they wouldn't take to me. Bill had only recently been divorced and his 'ex' was still living in Barrington, but everybody thought I was quite nice. It never occurred to me I was taking on children, four almost grown children! It's not easy.

One girl was my age, down to Amy who was nine or ten then – but every year it becomes easier, and we're all close friends. The hardest thing is that we are brought up in a totally different way to them.... It was hard for me and it was hard for them.

You've come through unscathed?

Oh I think so, and I'm now a step-grandmother. I put the emphasis on *step*! I was twenty-five when we were married and far too naïve. It's a whole different way – just as when you have a child of your own, your whole life changes.

Was it difficult, bringing up four stroppy American kids?

They're just different. This is a most wonderful country to be young in – everything is geared to children and their activities. In the country club here they have wonderful programmes, tennis and swimming teams, endless facilities. They have wonderful freedom, I rather envy them – I wish I'd been brought up like that. *We* were always brought up so strictly.

One of your stepchildren died recently of a drug overdose – it must be worrying, bringing up your own child in such an atmosphere?

I think every parent worries all over the world, just as much in England as over here.

How do you cope with that, what can you tell him, how can you protect him?

Give him love and support and one's own standards, that's the only thing.

You never think: I *wish* we were all in Gloucestershire?

Not really. I miss the hills, and the family. America is very warm and friendly and welcoming, it's easy to move in American circles. Chicago is delightful, it's a small town and a small society. I think it's beautiful. I wish more people would come and see it for what it *is* rather than thinking of Al Capone. I love the Symphony and the Art Institute, and I work very hard for the Chicago Boys' Club. The big problem in the cities of America is what they call the ghetto areas and the underprivileged children of every ethnic background. In Chicago they have eighteen centres and there are about

442

thirty-five thousand boys and girls who benefit from programmes or coun-selling. Life is pretty basic in the ghettos, a lot of them are single-parent families and they grow up angry and anti-society. If you can help them and turn them around they can be an asset to society rather than a parasite.

You're patently a very considerable Have in an area where there are a lot of Have-Nots, so are you worried about security?

Just as in England, there's always chance of burglary. It's something I don't care to think about too much. We have a huge fence around here but that's just as much to keep the horses and the dogs in, as anybody else out.

I don't think these pretty *polite* fences will do much; you've got dogs, but they're nice friendly dogs. . . .

They say as long as you have dogs that bark. . . . We have wonderful security systems that send off alarms, usually when there's an electric storm – so the police come rushing out and it's not a robber at all.

I've been concerned about the schools over here, but they seem to be doing things well in advance of what I was doing at that age, and of course they have such facilities over here. My son John's ten and he's going to win a tennis tournament this weekend.

You're pushing him, like an American mother!

I'm rather worried about that! No, I'm not a pusher. (Laughs). He doesn't really like to play with me very much, but probably all children don't like to play with Mums, they'd much rather play with Dad. He beat me last week. I *let* him beat me, I like to say. I told him I'd beat him this week. Tennis has helped him at school because he has a very hard time sitting still and keeping quiet. He has enormous energy and the tennis has helped him concentrate and really zero-in on work.

Does he feel his British blood?

My greatest boost has been the emergence of all the very popular British pop groups – so thank goodness for them. Now I'm OK – being English before wasn't so good, but now it's very good to be English because of all the pop groups. The drummer from Police came to have dinner with us in Florida – *that* was pretty good! And with fashion too there's a strong wave of English energy – Jasper Conran and all of those. Zandra Rhodes has been over here for a long time and that was Punk and still is, but she almost belongs to the Sixties.

443

You met your husband on a plane to Paris and he pursued you around the world – sounds like a Barbara Cartland romance?

Yes I'm afraid so, very *Woman's Own*. It was amazing how we met, a series of coincidences. We bumped into each other five times in Paris (laughs) just totally by chance. Then he managed to find out where I was in England. I spent four years wandering around the world. The first two years I was with a girlfriend doing secretarial, selling door-to-door, modelling, living very cheap. That was the time when you were only allowed fifty pounds. We were pretty desperate so we were even thinking of gun-running! Then I got into India and all my American friends were sending back hashish and things like that. I felt I should try something like that but I wasn't really cut out for it.

There was gold smuggling at that time...?

Yes, but that's awfully heavy. We decided we didn't weigh enough to wear a belt of gold around us. We were asked to do that, but were rather nervous. You're talking of the Muslim countries, India and Afghanistan, and it's rather scary if you're going to get caught. I was in Iran and my brother was getting married so I came home and bumped into Bill in Paris and really thought nothing about it. Then I took off around the world again, starting in India, and just by chance we sort of kept bumping into each other around the world. (Laughs.)

Your husband was on the national list of the ten toughest businessmen in the land, but now he's off it. Is that demotion?

That first time they interviewed a lot of people who we'd let go from our business, so naturally you were going to have a lot of sour grapes.

'Toughest' I read, may be equated with 'abrasive, ruthless, ill-mannered and egomaniacal'. If he's not on the list any longer, does that mean he's less egomaniacal these days?

Probably all successful men do have a certain amount of ego but Bill certainly is never ill-mannered. He's one of the most thoughtful, kind and generous people you would ever imagine, and extraordinarily creative. I don't know how he does it. When he's working flat out, he still manages to have vision that goes far beyond what I could cope with, and obviously other businessmen too. Whenever you have success, sadly you have a lot of envious people and it's always easier to put down somebody than to build them up.

Fifteen years ago Gould had to become either bankrupt or totally change its management, and they found Bill and he's turned it around. Their sales

444

were $110 million, I think, and now they're over a billion. He gets things done and of course when you get things done not everybody can go along with that. We all tend to reject, to resist change, we all like our routine and this world's changing frighteningly.

You've got a home here, a home in Florida, a home in New York, a home in London. . . .

Some of those belong to the company and we're fortunate enough to use them. We've just acquired a farm in Hudson which is absolutely gorgeous, up in Upper State New York, for breeding racehorses. Bill's put together several syndicates for breeding thoroughbreds and selling yearlings, so we go up there quite often and that's fun.

When you get back to Gloucestershire do you find us all rather dozy and dull?

I love going back, but it is a quieter pace and one tends to do only *one* thing a day rather than doing ten things. . . .

AFTER THOUGHT

One of the penalties democracies pay for freedom is that international television and Press will observe and sometimes spotlight any national defect. Most stories coming out of the United States zoom-in on crime or riot, drugs or sex scandals – any extreme is noteworthy, and sometimes interesting. Like all free lands, Britain suffers: killings in Ulster, football hooligans, race riots, demonstrations, picket-line violence, vandalism; no distressing situation of which we are ashamed remains hidden. We know life's not *all* like that – though viewers of Moscow television do not.

The Police States of Eastern Europe offer no such random freedom to observe and record to their nationals, let alone to foreigners. A television team fresh from revealing drug-running in Florida, sex-change in San Francisco, urban decay in the South Bronx will receive no facilities for similar coverage in Smolensk, Novgorod or Tomsk – they wouldn't even get off the aircraft.

In Russia a crime-wave or a demonstration against nuclear missiles by peasants existing in squalor one family to a room is as unthinkable as a trade union strike. A major aircrash will be ignored as something that could not happen. Even to comment upon such events may prove an offence against the State, offering the possibility of prison or, if repeated, some therapeutic injections in a guarded hospital in the Gulag Archipelago. When all media are controlled straightforward honest reporting is impossible, and unknown.

As I wrote in my autobiography: 'It is hard to visualise a *Whicker's World* filmed around some Siberian labour camp, in a nuclear submarine of the Red Fleet on patrol, or illustrating a couple of weeks of crowded life inside Moscow Centre police station – though these are merely the equivalents of our familiar Strangeways, Nautilus and West End Central. . . .'

To worry an old phrase, a happy marriage is not news. Any reporter, including this one, will chase the unusual, the sensational, the bizarre. Every critic knows it is more entertaining to attack than to approve; reviewers make their names by being the pugnacious Butcher of Broadway, the Fearless Voice of outspoken criticism – not by reporting pleasure, by being delighted.

If that's true of a documentary, a film, a book – it is even more true of a country. Forgive me, but though I know it's obvious I thought I should mention that – and perhaps apologise for any carping on my part about our host nation.

America is a land so free and confident, but so honest and self-critical that its people expect you to join them in grumbling about what's wrong: violence in the streets, avaricious hospitals, inadequate schools.... So we do. It's as though we never left home, where our own family is seen as fair game for instant criticism while we hesitate to be candid to an acquaintance.

The bottom line must be that of all the British I met this time around who have settled in the US – that's more than sixty couples or individuals – only two had even considered leaving.

That would seem to say *everything* about life in these magnificent United States....

ACKNOWLEDGEMENTS

My thanks to all these amiable and candid Brits who received me into their homes and lives and provided sixty-four revealing attitudes about their new homeland. Many were already friends, or friends of friends; most of them Valerie and I met again – or were happy to discover – during our recce around America.

Later, when to my great pleasure BBC Television decided to join in this expedition, my Producer, Jonathan Stedall, reinforced our research by unleashing four young women in our footsteps across the continent. My thanks to him for his agreeable companionship during the subsequent filming, and to Joanna Head, Deborah Isaacs, Sue Crowther and Fiona Murphy for between them running to ground twenty-four of our favoured sixty-four! My gratitude of course to the BBC – particularly to Alan Hart and John Shearer who originally decided to support my exploration with a film crew led by Mike Fox, and to Michael Grade for his final view from the summit.

The photographs were all taken by Valerie Kleeman, while I pointed out there was a far better position over *there*.

The fun and frolic of meeting people on location was followed by stern months of writing and editing this new style of Whickerwork with the tireless Laureen Fraser at the white-hot typewriter; my thanks again to her.

When as usual we ended up with far more illuminating chapters than this book could handle, Weidenfeld's Editorial Director, David Roberts, helped ease the pain of that cruel moment – for me, if not for those friends who sadly are still confined to my files and awaiting the next book.

Indeed relief may be at hand for I *so* much enjoyed everyone here that – let me warn you right now – I can already sense *Whicker's World* is about to take another spin. . . .

INDEX